ARCHAEOLOGICAL RESEARCH IN THE VALLEY OF THE KINGS AND ANCIENT THEBES

Papers Presented in Honor of Richard H. Wilkinson

Edited by Pearce Paul Creasman

University of Arizona Egyptian Expedition
Wilkinson Egyptology Series
Volume I
2013

Wilkinson Egyptology Series, volume I

Series logo modified from *JSesh*: "a free, open source, editor for ancient Egyptian hieroglyphic texts."

The Series logo is an abbreviated writing of the word *rḥw*, meaning "companions, comrades, fellows," an appropriate reminder that these works are offered in the spirit of advancing our collective knowledge (see A. H. Gardiner, *Egyptian Grammar* [Third edition revised, Oxford: Griffith Institute, 1957], 578).

ARCHAEOLOGICAL RESEARCH IN THE VALLEY OF THE KINGS AND ANCIENT THEBES:
Papers Presented in Honor of Richard H. Wilkinson
Edited by Pearce Paul Creasman

ISBN-10: 0964995816
ISBN-13: 978-0-9649958-1-9

1. Valley of the Kings (Egypt). 2. Excavations (Archaeology) – Egypt. 3. Ancient Thebes (Egypt).

1. Creasman, Pearce Paul, 1981-

University of Arizona Egyptian Expedition

Wilkinson Egyptology Series

Honorary Chairman: Richard H. Wilkinson
Series Editor: Pearce Paul Creasman

CONTENTS

PART III: ORIGINAL RESEARCH CONTRIBUTIONS . . . (CONTINUED)

Dedication

This volume celebrates the extraordinary career of one of America's foremost Egyptologists, Richard H. Wilkinson, known to the educated general public as a writer of fascinating, readable books such as *Reading Egyptian Art: A Hieroglyphic Guide to Ancient Egyptian Painting and Sculpture, Symbol and Magic in Egyptian Art, Valley of the Sun-Kings: New Explorations in the Tombs of the Pharaohs, The Complete Valley of the Kings: Tombs and Treasures of Egypt's Greatest Pharaohs, The Complete Temples of Ancient Egypt: Eternal Symbols in Stone, The Complete Gods and Goddesses of Ancient Egypt, Egyptian Scarabs*, and *Egyptology Today*. One can find translations of these books into Swedish, Dutch, Hungarian, Japanese, Spanish, French, German, Italian, and Arabic. For students of Egyptian archaeology, art, and culture, he has become a household word.

However, this is but one side of the man. His scholarly publications and archaeological investigations have also been of the highest quality, and his longtime excavation of the Temple of Tausret (*The Temple of Tausret: The University of Arizona Egyptian Expedition Tausret Temple Project, 2004–2011*) has drawn international focus onto this little-known but important female pharaoh, leading to his invited Oxford University Press book *Tausret: Forgotten Queen and Pharaoh of Egypt*.

Dr. Wilkinson's national and international honors are many. He was named a University of Arizona Regents' Professor, the highest position possible at his university. He became the first honorary American member of the Institute of Eastern Mediterranean Studies in Archaeology (IEMSA) of the University of Athens and the National Archaeological Museum of Greece. He was twice elected to the national Board of Directors of the American Research Center in Egypt (for which he founded their Arizona Chapter and served as its first president). He has been invited to serve on many important editorial boards in his field, and his award-winning book on hieroglyphic symbolism was the first thematic guide to the subject ever published.

The volume before you commemorates his retirement from the University of Arizona, but not his withdrawal from academic life. In fact, without the burden of university daily responsibilities, one can expect his output to increase as he puts his remarkable focus and energy into his research even more intensely.

His remarkable output of scholarly and popular articles and books is a matter of record, but as Dr. Wilkinson's longtime friend and colleague, I would like to offer a few words here about his private side which he never talks about unless one asks him pointed questions. Many will be surprised to know that Richard was originally

English, born in 1951 and raised in a twelfth–to–fourteenth century castle, Hellifield Peel, near Skipton in North Yorkshire. According to the current estate owners, "The Peel" was the last Knights Templar castle built, finished in 1306 to assist invasion into Scotland. His mother came from a distinguished British family but was happily married to a working class gardener she met at a friend's estate. Dr. Wilkinson attended high school in the spa town of Harrowgate and went on to study at the University of Leeds in Yorkshire.

After deciding to come to America to seek his fortune, he attended a small private college in Pasadena where he met his wife, Anna. Both were attending the same college but only met when they were playing hooky from their studies at the same time on the beach in Malibu. After, he received an M.A. and Ph.D. in Egyptology and Near Eastern Studies from the University of Minnesota's Center for Ancient Studies and was promptly thereafter selected as a Scholar in Residence at UCLA. I had the pleasure of hiring him to teach at the University of Arizona, where he has spent his academic career.

Dr. Wilkinson has often been described on campus by his peers as "one of the best-kept secrets of the University of Arizona." Modest and self-effacing in the extreme, one would never know he has been a powerful force in the field of ancient Egyptian studies for more than thirty years. Despite having to teach as many as four classes per semester initially, Dr. Wilkinson nonetheless managed to publish constantly, both articles and books, and to excavate in the Valley of the Kings, with the result that he became renowned in the field of Egyptology, as well as one of the University of Arizona's most respected and loved teachers.

Having founded the University of Arizona Egyptian Expedition in 1988, Dr. Wilkinson conducted research and excavation at a number of sites in and around the Valley of the Kings. Between 2004 and 2012 he re-excavated the temple of the female pharaoh Tausret, one of the few women to ever rule Egypt. His reconstruction of the temple complex and his analysis of the reign of this complex woman add essential new pieces of information regarding this female ruler of ancient Egypt.

For many interested in the field of Egyptology, Dr. Wilkinson's books form their introduction to the field and provide a detailed assessment of many aspects of Egyptian culture. His books are sold throughout the world, particularly in Egypt, in venues such as the Cairo Museum. His many books have been written by himself or with distinguished collaborators. His over one hundred published articles and reviews and the international conferences he has planned and organized, as well as two Egyptological exhibitions, have also done a great deal to put Arizona on the map in his field, as has his creation of a major Egyptian studies periodical: the *Journal of Ancient Egyptian Interconnections (JAEI).*

Dr. Wilkinson is currently already well along on two more major book projects: *Egyptian Cylinder Seals* and the *Oxford Handbook of the Valley of the Kings,* which he is coediting with Egyptologist Kent R. Weeks. However, he will also have the time to travel more now, especially to his beloved Hawaii and to other exotic ports of call frequented by adventurers such as Captain James Cook, the eighteenth century explorer and cartographer so dear to him. Close friends also know that if he wants to go snorkeling or diving, one must remember the rule often applied in dealing with hippopotamuses: one must not get between Dr. Wilkinson and the water, for snorkeling is the one thing he insists on doing when he has the chance to do it.

Dr. Wilkinson continues to live in Tucson with his wife of thirty-eight years, Anna, who is the only individual in our academic community known for being even nicer than he is. Typically, when Dr. Wilkinson retired from the university, he did not want a farewell reception or recognition of his myriad accomplishments. He and Anna have always been known for their lack of ego and their concern for others, but those fortunate enough to have come to know them realize fully the beautiful people that they are. Richard has shown by his publications, research and personal life that he is an acknowledged local, national and international treasure.

David Soren, PhD
Regents' Professor of Anthropology and Classics
University of Arizona

Foreword

In recent years, the number of books published on ancient Egypt has grown enormously. Some are highly technical treatises on specialized subjects; others, broad overviews intended for a popular audience. Often the former are (to be kind) nearly unreadable; the latter (to be generous), replete with errors. Keeping up with the best Egyptological scholarship means choosing one's reading material carefully, exploring works in French and German as well as English, searching for publications found only in a few major university libraries. For a serious student, a young scholar, or an interested layperson, accessing readable, accurate, up-to-date Egyptological information is a formidable task.

That is why Richard Wilkinson's many books have been welcomed by a wide audience and consistently rewarded with excellent reviews and enviable sales. Of course, Richard's c.v. is full of specialized articles that demonstrate his command of Egyptological detail. And his fieldwork at the temple of Tausret at Thebes attests to his skills as an archaeologist and analyst of ancient Egypt's material culture. But it is his books that have had the greatest impact. Both young students and senior scholars turn to them for accurate and comprehensive syntheses of modern scholarship. His *Reading Egyptian Art* (1992) and *Symbol and Magic in Egyptian Art* (1994) clearly introduce Egyptian art in instructive and imaginative formats. His *The Complete Temples of Ancient Egypt* (2000) and *The Complete Gods and Goddesses of Ancient Egypt* (2003) review the complexities of Egyptian religion and its architectural expression in concise yet highly instructive essays. *The Complete Valley of the Kings* (1996, with Nicholas Reeves) was the first proper survey of the complicated history of the valley's development and its excavation.

There have been few Egyptologists who are solid scholars and have the ability to make the complexities of ancient Egyptian culture accessible to students. Fewer still have been able to transfer those rare talents to the printed page. One must applaud the syntheses and reviews with which Richard has informed a generation of Egyptophiles. It's a legacy to be proud of, and one hopes that he will continue to educate his students and colleagues alike for decades to come.

Kent R. Weeks, PhD
Professor of Egyptology
American University in Cairo

Preface

Professor Richard H. Wilkinson, PhD, has served the field of Egyptology, especially in the areas of art and archaeology, with dedication and distinction for nearly three decades, to date. His contributions have been so exemplary that it is likely impossible to honor him appropriately, but the participants in this book (and numerous other colleagues and friends who wanted to contribute) hope that this work in some small way relays our gratitude to Richard. We are grateful for not only his scholarly contributions but his personal ones as well.

The present volume is divided into three parts, with additional front and back matter. Internationally renowned scholars David Soren and Kent R. Weeks welcome the reader with a dedication and foreword, respectively. These sections contain a wealth of knowledge about Richard that could only be compiled through life-long friendships. Part I follows and details the published and presented works of and honors and awards amassed by Dr. Wilkinson during an enviable career. Part II reviews institutions founded and built by Richard and places their inextricably linked histories in context with their contributions to academe. This section also includes manuscripts that summarize the major fieldwork initiatives Richard directed. Part III comprises original research material, offered in honor of Richard by friends, colleagues, and former students. More than two dozen scholars from all corners of the globe have contributed to mark Professor Wilkinson's formal retirement from University life, providing more time for his research.

In hopes of further honoring him, this tome serves as the inaugural volume in the Wilkinson Egyptology Series, published by the University of Arizona Egyptian Expedition. The peer-reviewed series is open to all scholars for publication of monographs, comprehensive site reports, conference proceedings, and other edited works. The goal of the Wilkinson Egyptology Series is to help scholars to bring high-quality work to print quickly, through a scholarly review process akin to those of most major journals. After a period of not more than five years, each volume will be made available online, free of charge. The series is designed to reflect Richard's prolific academic career: producing only the highest quality work in a timely manner.

It has been an honor to prepare this work, establish this series in his name, and tend Richard's legacy at the UAEE. Since the day we were introduced, Richard has been unfailingly kind and supportive, as everyone who knows him can independently confirm. As his successor at the Expedition (there can be no *replacement*), a constant and concerted effort has been required to perform the tasks that Richard has done with apparent ease for his entire career. It is with the greatest pleasure and fortune that I count Richard H. Wilkinson as a friend and mentor.

Pearce Paul Creasman, PhD
Director, Egyptian Expedition
University of Arizona

Acknowledgments

The production of this volume would not have been possible without the support of many organizations and individuals. The following are owed deep gratitude for ensuring that *Archaeological Research in the Valley of the Kings and Ancient Thebes* came to press:

- American Research Center in Egypt (via a grant from the Antiquities Endowment Fund)
- American Research Center in Egypt, Arizona Chapter
- Institute of Maritime Research and Discovery, Ltd.
- Laboratory of Tree-Ring Research, University of Arizona
- School of Anthropology, University of Arizona
- The University of Arizona Foundation

The following individuals made generous contributions in direct support of this publication and in honor of their friend, Richard H. Wilkinson:

- Stephanie Denkowicz, J.D., Special Counsel, Manatt, Phelps & Phillips, LLP (New York, New York)
- Donald R. Kunz, J.D., Founding Partner, Kunz Plitt Hyland & Demlong P.C. (Phoenix, Arizona)
- John W. Olsen, Ph.D., Regents' Professor of Anthropology, University of Arizona

The editor is personally grateful for the assistance of several manuscript reviewers, but *especially* to Noreen Doyle and Stephanie Denkowicz for extensive reviews and innumerable ideas for improvements to this volume. Further, Theresa Musacchio assisted with the Series design.

The editor and authors also acknowledge Egypt's Supreme Council for Antiquities & Ministry of State for Antiquities, including the directors, committee members, inspectors, administrators, archaeologists and other affiliates who have made the excavation and study of much of the material in this volume possible.

And, of course, we thank Richard H. Wilkinson for an exceptional career (with much more to come!) and the occasion to compile the present work.

Pearce Paul Creasman
Tucson, Arizona & Luxor, Egypt

Abbreviations

AcOr	Acta Orientalia; Societates Orientales Danica, Norregia, Svecica
Antiquity	*Antiquity: Quarterly Journal of Archaeological Research*
ASAE	*Annales du Service des Antiquités de l'Égypte*
BARCE	*Bulletin of the American Research Center in Egypt*
BIFAO	*Bulletin de l'Institut français d'archéologie orientale*
BiOr	*Bibliotheca Orientalis*
BMMA	*Bulletin of the Metropolitan Museum of Art*
BMSAES	*British Museum Studies in Ancient Egypt and Sudan*
CdÉ	*Chronique d'Égypte*
CdK	*Les Cahiers de Karnak. Centre franco-égyptien d'étude des temples de Karnak*
CRIPEL	*Cahier de Recherches de l'Institut de Papyrologie et d'Égyptologie de Lille*
Description de l'Égypte	*Description de l'Égypte ou Recueil des observations et des recherché qui ont été faites en Egypte pendant l'expédition de l'armée française* (Paris, 1809–1829)
DÖAWW	Denkschrift der Österreichischen Akademie der Wissenschaften in Wien
FIFAO	Fouilles de l'Institute français d'archéologie orientale du Caire
GM	*Göttinger Miszellen*
IJNA	*International Journal of Nautical Archaeology*
JAEI	*Journal of Ancient Egyptian Interconnections*
JARCE	*Journal of the American Research Center in Egypt*
JEA	*Journal of Egyptian Archaeology*
JEH	*Journal of Egyptian History*
JHS	*Journal of Hellenic Studies*
JNES	*Journal of Near Eastern Studies*
JSSEA	*Journal of the Society of the Study of Egyptian Antiquities*
Kmt	*Kmt: A Modern Journal of Ancient Egypt*
K*RI*	K. A. Kitchen, *Ramesside Inscriptions, Historical and Biographical* (Oxford: Blackwell, 1969–1990)
LÄ	W. Helck, E. Otto, W. Westendorf (eds.), *Lexikon der Ägyptologie* I–VII (Wiesbaden: O. Harrassowitz 1972–1992)

L*D*	K. R. Lepsius, *Denkmäler aus Ägypten und Äthiopien* I–VI (Berlin, 1849–1859)
MDAIK	*Mitteilungen des Deutschen Archäologischen Instituts, Abteilung Kairo*
MIFAO	Mémoires publiés par les membres de l'Institut français d'archéologie Orientale du Cairo
MVEOL	*Mededelingen en Verhandelingen Ex Oriente Lux*
NARCE	*Newsletter of the American Research Center in Egypt*
OIP	Oriental Institute Publications
OLA	Orientalia Lovaniensia Analecta
OMRO	*Oudheidkundige Mededelingen uit het Rijksmuseum van Oudheden*
OrAnt	*Oriens Antiquus*
Orientalia	*Orientalia. Commentarii periodici Pontificii instituti biblici, Nova Series*
PM I^2:1	Bertha Porter and Rosalind Moss, *Topographical Bibliography of Ancient Egyptian Hieroglyphic Texts, Reliefs, and Paintings I: The Theban Necropolis, part I. Private Tombs,* second edition (Oxford: Griffith Institute, 1960; reprint, 1985)
PM I^2:2	Bertha Porter and Rosalind Moss, *Topographical Bibliography of Ancient Egyptian Hieroglyphic Texts, Reliefs, and Paintings I: The Theban Necropolis, part II. Royal Tombs and Smaller Cemeteries,* second edition (Oxford: Griffith Institute, 1964; reprint, 1990)
PM II^1	Bertha Porter and Rosalind Moss, *Topographical Bibliography of Ancient Egyptian Hieroglyphic Texts, Reliefs, and Paintings II: Theban Temples,* first edition (Oxford: Clarendon Press, 1929)
PM II^2	Bertha Porter and Rosalind Moss, *Topographical Bibliography of Ancient Egyptian Hieroglyphic Texts, Reliefs, and Paintings II: Theban Temples,* second edition, revised and augmented (Oxford: Griffith Institute, 1972)
PM V	Bertha Porter and Rosalind Moss, *Topographical Bibliography of Ancient Egyptian Hieroglyphic Texts, Reliefs, and Paintings V: Upper Egypt: Sites (Deir Rîfa to Aswân, Excluding Thebes and the Temples of Abydos, Dendera, Esna, Edfu, Kôm Ombo and Philae)* (Oxford: Griffith Institute, 1937)

PM VI	Bertha Porter and Rosalind Moss, *Topographical Bibliography of Ancient Egyptian Hieroglyphic Texts, Reliefs, and Paintings VI: Upper Egypt: Chief Temples (excluding Thebes): Abydos, Dendera, Esna, Edfu, Kôm Ombo, and Philae* (Oxford: Griffith Institute, 1937)
PMMA	Publications of the Metropolitan Museum of Art (Egyptian Expedition)
RdÉ	*Révue d'Égyptologie*
RT	*Recueil de traveaux relatifs à la philologie et à l'archéologie égyptiennes et assyriennes*
SAK	*Studien zur Altägyptischen Kultur*
SAOC	Studies in Ancient Oriental Civilization
SASAE	*Supplément aux Annales du Service des Antiquités de l'Égypte*
StudAeg	Studia Aegyptiaca
Urk.	K. Sethe, H. W. Helck, H. Schäfer, H. Grapow, and O. Firchow (eds.), *Urkunden des ägyptischen Altertums* I–VIII (Berlin/Leipzig, 1903–1957)
Wb	A. Erman and W. Grapow, *Wörterbuch der ägyptische Sprache* I–VII (Berlin, 1926–1931)
Wb Belegstellen	A. Erman and W. Grapow, *Wörterbuch der aegyptischen Sprache: im Auftrage der deutschen Akademien: die Belegstellen* I–V (Berlin: Akademie, 1982)

Egyptian Chronology

Despite being the focus of nearly two hundred years of research, the chronology of ancient Egypt remains imprecise, especially in the assignment of calendrical dates (that is, years BCE). Therefore, the Wilkinson Egyptology Series generally avoids the use of specific dates for the events, processes, or reigns discussed in these pages. Because the Series strives for accuracy in all aspects, it will present only those calendrical dates that are crucial to an author's core argument or that are scientifically demonstrable. The Wilkinson Egyptology Series does, however, employ the use of relative chronological categories when appropriate, including dynasties and kingdoms.

At present, accurate calendrical dating in Egyptology extends only back to the transition from the Twenty-Fifth to the Twenty-Sixth Dynasty: 664 BCE.[1] While several scholars present strong arguments for the certainty of dates of earlier events, there does not appear to be general agreement at this time.[2] As chronological certainty is pushed further back in time, the Series will update its guidelines accordingly.

Predynastic Period
- Neolithic Period
- Dynasty "0"

Early Dynastic Period
- First Dynasty
- Second Dynasty

Old Kingdom
- Third Dynasty
- Fourth Dynasty
- Fifth Dynasty
- Sixth Dynasty

First Intermediate Period
- Seventh and Eighth Dynasties
- Ninth and Tenth Dynasties (Herakleopolitan)
- Eleventh Dynasty (Theban)

Period	Dates
Middle Kingdom	
Eleventh Dynasty (Unified)	
Twelfth Dynasty	
Thirteenth Dynasty	
Second Intermediate Period	
Fourteenth Dynasty	
Fifteenth Dynasty (Hyksos)	
Early Sixteenth Dynasty (Hyksos)	
Late Sixteenth Dynasty (Theban)	
Seventeenth Dynasty	
New Kingdom	
Eighteenth Dynasty	
Nineteenth Dynasty (Ramesside)	
Twentieth Dynasty (Ramesside)	
Third Intermediate Period	
Twenty-First Dynasty (Tanite)	
Twenty-Second Dynasty (Bubastite/Libyan)	
Twenty-Third Dynasty (Tanite/Libyan)	
Twenty-Fourth Dynasty	
Twenty-Fifth Dynasty (Kushite)	
Late Period	664–332 BCE
Twenty-Sixth Dynasty (Saite)	664–525 BCE
Twenty-Seventh Dynasty (First Persian Period)	525–405 BCE
Twenty-Eighth Dynasty	404–399 BCE
Twenty-Ninth Dynasty	399–380 BCE
Thirtieth Dynasty	380–343 BCE
Thirty-First Dynasty (Second Persian Period)	343–332 BCE
Graeco-Roman Period	
Macedonian Dynasty	332–305 BCE
Ptolemaic Period	305–31 BCE
Roman Era	30 BCE–337 CE

1 For a thorough review of this question see Thomas Schneider, "Contributions to the Chronology of the New Kingdom and the Third Intermediate Period," *Egypt and the Levant* 20 (2010): 373–403; Schneider, "Le casse-tête de la chronologie égyptienne," *Pour la science* 413 (2012): 28–33.

2 For example, Kenneth Kitchen states that "good Egyptian dates" extend only to 690 BCE (K. A. Kitchen, "Establishing Chronology in Pharaonic Egypt and the Ancient Near East: Interlocking Textural Sources Relating to *c.* 1600–664 BC," in A. J. Shortland and C. Bronk Ramsey (eds.), *Radiocarbon and the Chronologies of Ancient Egypt* (Oxford: Oxbow Books, 2013), 1.

Part I

The Works of Richard H. Wilkinson

Bibliography of Richard H. Wilkinson

Books, Monographs, and Theses

The Horus Names, the Serekh, and the "Circuit of the Walls" in Ancient Egyptian Kingship Ideology. MA thesis, University of Minnesota. 1984.

Mesopotamian Coronation and Accession Rites in the Neo-Sumerian and Early Old-Babylonian Periods. PhD dissertation, University of Minnesota. University Microfilms International, 1986.

Reading Egyptian Art: A Hieroglyphic Guide to Ancient Egyptian Painting and Sculpture. London: Thames and Hudson, 1992.

Swedish translation:
Hieroglyfernas varld: nyckeln till egyptisk konst och kultur. Stockholm: Forum, 1993.

Danish translation
Hieroglyffernes verden: Nøglen til ægyptisk kunst og kultur. København: Politikens Forlag, 1994.

Spanish translation
Cómo leer el arte egipcio: guía de jeroglíficos del antiguo Egipto. Barcelona: Crítica, 1995.

Japanese translation
図解古代エジプトシンボル事典 (*Zukai kodai ejiputo shinboru jiten*). Tokyo: Harashobo, 2000.

Arabic translation
Selected by Egyptian Ministry of Culture to be translated into Arabic for use by all Egyptian Antiquities Department (SCA) Inspectors (Cairo, 2011).

Symbol and Magic in Egyptian Art. London: Thames and Hudson, 1994.

Spanish translation:
Magia y símbolo en el arte egipcio. Madrid: Alianza Editorial, 2003.

The Complete Valley of the Kings. Coauthored with C. Nicholas Reeves. London and New York: Thames and Hudson, 1996.

German translation
Das Tal der Könige: Geheimnisvolles Totenreich der Pharaonen. Düsseldorf: Econ, 1997.

Spanish translation
Todo Sobre el Valle de los Reyes: Tumbas y tesoros de los principales faraones de Egipto. Barcelona: Destino, 1998.

Japanese translation
図説　王家の谷百科—ファラオたちの栄華と墓と財宝　(*Ouke no Tani Hyakka*). Tokyo: Mori, 1999.

Dutch translation
Dal der Koningen: Graftomben en Schatten van de grootste Faraos. Baarn: Bosch & Keuning, 2000).

The Complete Temples of Ancient Egypt: Eternal Symbols in Stone. New York: Thames & Hudson, 2000.

Spanish translation
Los Templos del antiguo Egipto. London: Thames & Hudson, 2000.
Dutch translation
Tempels van het oude Egypte: ontwikkeling, bouw, functie, riten, symboliek. Baarn: Bosch & Keuning, 2001.
Spanish translation
Los templos del Antiguo Egipto. Barcelona: Ediciones Destino, 2002.
German translations
1: *Die Welt der Tempel im alten Agypten*. Stuttgart: Konrad Theiss, 2005.
2: *Die Welt der Tempel im alten Agypten*. Darmstadt: Wissenschaffliche Bruchgesellschaft, 2005.
Hungarian translation
Az okori Egyiptom templomai. Kiadja: Alexandra, 2006.
Italian translation
Templi dell'antico Egitto. Roma: Istituto poligrafico dello Stato, 2007.

The Complete Gods and Goddesses of Ancient Egypt. New York: Thames & Hudson, 2003.

German translations
1: *Die Welt der Götter im alten Agypten: Glaube, Macht, Mythologie*. Stuttgart: Konrad Theiss, 2003.
2: *Die Welt der Götter im alten Ägypten: Glaube, Macht, Mythologie*. Darmstadt: Wissenschaffliche Bruchgesellschaft, 2003.
Spanish translation:
Todos los dioses del Antiguo Egipto. Madrid: Oberón, 2003.
Japanese translation:
古代エジプト神々大百科 (*Kodai ejiputo kamigami daihyakka*). Tokyo: Toyo Shorin, 2004
French translation:
Dictionnaire illustré des dieux et déesses de l'Égypte ancienne. Gollion: Infolio, 2006.

Egyptian Scarabs. Shire Egyptology 30. Oxford: Shire Publications, 2008.

Books Edited

Valley of the Sun Kings: New Explorations in the Tombs of the Pharaohs: Papers from the University of Arizona International Conference on the Valley of the Kings. Tucson: University of Arizona Egyptian Expedition, 1995.

Contributors: Edwin Brock, Lyla Brock, Garniss Curtis, Earl Ertman, Erik Hornung, Jiro Kondo, Daniel Polz, Catharine Roehrig, John Rutherford, Donald Ryan, Claude Vandersleyen, Kent R. Weeks, Richard H. Wilkinson.

Egyptology Today. Cambridge; New York: Cambridge University Press, 2008.

Contributors: James Allen, Rosalie David, Peter Dorman, Ann Foster, John Foster, Rita Freed, Suzanne Gänsicke, Michael Jones, Arielle

Kozloff, Ronald Leprohon, Sarah Parcak, Donald Redford, Kent R. Weeks.

The Temple of Tausret: The University of Arizona Egyptian Expedition Tausret Temple Project, 2004–2011. Tucson: University of Arizona Egyptian Expedition, 2011.

Contributors: Aaryn S. Brewer, Adam Cirzan, Pearce Paul Creasman, Robert J. Demarée, Stephanie Denkowicz, Ashleigh D. Goodwin, Damian H. Greenwell, Richard S. Harwood, Rexine Hummel, Karin P. Kroenke, Teresa Moore, Danielle O. Phelps, Gonzolo Sanchez, Douglas S. Sassen, Richard H. Wilkinson.

Tausret: Forgotten Queen and Pharaoh of Egypt. Oxford: Oxford University Press, 2012.

Contributors: Hartwig Altenmüller, Gae Callender, Catharine Roehrig, Joyce Tyldesley, Richard H. Wilkinson.

The Oxford Handbook of the Valley of the Kings. Edited with Kent R. Weeks. Oxford. Oxford University Press, In press.

Contributors: Hartwig Altenmüller, Susanne Bickel, Edwin Brock, J.M. Bunbury, Filip Coppens, Steven Cross, Rosalie David, Robert J. Demarée, Aidan Dodson, Andreas Dorn, Ogden Goelet, Michael Jones, Adam Lowe, Heather McCarthy, Ryan Metcalfe, Sarah Parcak, Lyla Pinch-Brock, Campbell Price, Stephen Rickerby, Joshua Roberson, Catharine Roehrig, John Taylor, Joyce Tyldesley, Martina Ullmann, Kees Van der Spek, Carola Vogel, Alexandra von Lieven, Kent R. Weeks, Richard H. Wilkinson, Lorinda Wong.

Articles

"The Coronational Circuit of the Wall, the Circuit of the *Ḥnw* Barque and the Heb-Sed 'race' in Egyptian Kingship Ideology." *Journal of the Society for the Study of Egyptian Antiquities* 15.1 (1985): 46–51.

"The Horus Name and the Form and Significance of the Serekh in the Royal Egyptian Titulary." *Journal of the Society for the Study of Egyptian Antiquities* 15.3 [1985] (1987): 98–104.

"The ΣΤΥΛΟΣ of Revelation 3:12 and Ancient Coronation Rites." *Journal of Biblical Literature* 107.3 (1988): 498–501.

"The Representation of the Bow in the Art of Ancient Egypt and the Near East." *Journal of the Ancient Near Eastern Society* 20 (1988): 83–100.

"The Turned Bow in Egyptian Iconography." *Varia Aegyptiaca* 4.2 (1988), 181–187.

"The Origin and Development of a Greco-Persian Numismatic Motif." *Numismatist* 102.6 (1989): 887–889, 969–970.

"A Possible Origin for the 'Shoulder Ornaments' in Egyptian Representations of Lions." *Varia Aegyptiaca* 5.1 (1989): 59–71.

"New Kingdom Astronomical Paintings and Methods of Finding and Extending Direction." *Journal of the American Research Center in Egypt* 28 (1991): 149–154.

"The Turned Bow as a Gesture of Surrender in Egyptian Art." *Journal of the Society for the Study of Egyptian Antiquities* 17.3 (1991): 128–133.

"Ancient Near Eastern Raised-Arm Figures and the Iconography of the Egyptian God Min." *Bulletin of the Egyptological Seminar* 11 (1994): 109–118.

"Symbolic Location and Alignment in New Kingdom Royal Tombs and Their Decoration." *Journal of the American Research Center in Egypt* 31 (1994): 79–86.

"Introduction." In *Valley of the Sun Kings*, ed. R. H. Wilkinson, 5. Tucson: University of Arizona Egyptian Expedition, 1995.

"Symbolic Orientation and Alignment in New Kingdom Royal Tombs." In *Valley of the Sun Kings*, ed. R. H. Wilkinson, 74–81. Tucson: University of Arizona Egyptian Expedition, 1995.

"The Motif of the Path of the Sun in Ramesside Royal Tombs: An Outline of Recent Research." *Journal of the Society for the Study of Egyptian Antiquities* 25 (1995) [1999]: 78–84, pl. VIII–X.

"Gesture." In *The Oxford Encyclopedia of Ancient Egypt*, ed. D. B. Redford, vol. 2, 20–24. Oxford: Oxford University Press, 2001.

"Symbols." In *The Oxford Encyclopedia of Ancient Egypt*, ed. D. B. Redford, vol. 3, 329–335. Oxford: Oxford University Press, 2001.

Reprinted in *The Ancient Gods Speak: A Guide to Egyptian Religion*, ed. D. Redford, 339–347. Oxford: Oxford University Press, 2002.

Reprinted in *The Oxford Essential Guide to Egyptian Mythology*, ed. D. Redford, 339–347. Oxford: Oxford University Press, 2003.

"The Identity of the Amarna-Age Tomb WV 25 in the Western Valley of the Kings." *Journal of the Egyptian Study Society* 13.1 (2002): 13–16.

"Finding What Belzoni Didn't Take." *Bulletin of the American Research Center in Egypt* 181 (2002): 16–18.

"Amarna Age Tomb WV25." *The Akhetaten Sun* 6.2 (November 2002): 15–18.

"Egypt and Monotheism." *The Akhetaten Sun* 7.1 (May 2003): 18–19.

"Even The Gods Will Die: Divine Mortality in Ancient Egypt." *Journal of the Egyptian Study Society* 14.2 (Summer 2003): 10–12.

"University of Arizona Egyptian Expedition: Western Valley of the Kings Project (2001–2002) Final Report." *Annales du Service des antiquités de l'Égypte* 78 (2004): 199–204.

"The Tausert Temple Project: 2004 and 2005 Seasons." *The Ostracon: Journal of the Egyptian Study Society* 16.2 (2005): 7–12.

"The Tausert Temple Project: An Additional Feature Discovered in the 2005 Season." *The Ostracon: Journal of the Egyptian Study Society* 17.1 (2006): 9–10.

"The Tausert Temple Project: 2006 Season." *The Ostracon: Journal of the Egyptian Study Society* 17.2 (2006): 9–12.

"Excavation in the time of V. S. Golenischev: W. M. F. Petrie's work at the Tausert Memorial Temple." In *Memorial Volume for V. S. Golenischev*, ed. V. V. Solkin, 160–165, pls. 69–73. Moscow: Association of Ancient Egypt Studies, 2006.

"The Persistence of Amarna Era Ceramic Motifs: A Late 19th Dynasty Example." *The Akhetaten Sun* 12.2 (Fall 2006): 12–14.

"The Tausert Temple Project: 2007 Season." *The Ostracon: Journal of the Egyptian Study Society* 18.1 (2007): 3–10.

"Sobre el Templo Memorial de Tausert en Luxor." *Apuntes de Egiptología* 2 (2007), http://www.ceae.unlugar.com/wilkinson.htm.

"Afterword: The Past in the Future: Egyptology Tomorrow." In *Egyptology Today*, ed. R. H. Wilkinson, 248–249. Cambridge: Cambridge University Press, 2008.

"Introduction: The Past in the Present: Egyptology Today." In *Egyptology Today*, ed. R. H. Wilkinson, 1–4. Cambridge: Cambridge University Press, 2008.

"Anthropomorphic Deities." In *UCLA Encyclopedia of Egyptology*. Los Angeles: University of California, 2008, http://www.escholarship.org/uc/item/5s54w4tc.

"The Tausert Temple Project: 2008 Season." *The Ostracon: Journal of the Egyptian Study Society* 19.1 (2008): 3–8.

"Tausert Temple Project Report for the 2007 Season." *Annales du Service des antiquités de l'Égypte* 83 (2009): 417–424.

"The Tausert Temple Project: 2009 Season." *The Ostracon: Journal of the Egyptian Study Society* 20.1 (2009): 3–13.

"The Tausert Temple Project: Report for the 2009–10 Season." *The Ostracon: Journal of the Egyptian Study Society* 21.1 (2009): 3–12.

"Six Seasons at Thebes: The University of Arizona Tausert Temple Project." In *Thebes and Beyond: Studies in Honor of Kent R. Weeks. Supplément aux Annales du Service des antiquités de l'Égypte* 41, eds. Z. Hawass and S. Ikram, 219–237. Cairo: Supreme Council of Antiquities, 2010.

"The Memorial Temple of Tausert: Was It Ever Completed?" In *Les temples de millions d'années et le pouvoir royal à Thèbes au Nouvel Empire. Sciences et nouvelles technologies appliquées à l'archéologie*, ed. Christian Leblanc, 159–169. *Memnonia*, Cahier Suppl. 2. Cairo: Dar el-Kutub, 2010.

"University of Arizona Egyptian Expedition: Tausert Temple Project. Report for the 2008 Season." *Annales du Service des antiquités de l'Égypte* 84 (2010): 421–428.

"Controlled Damage: The Mechanics and Micro-History of the *Damnatio Memoriae* Carried Out in KV-23, the Tomb of Ay." *Journal of Egyptian History* 4.1 (2011): 129–147.

"The Tausert Temple Project: 2010–11 Season." *The Ostracon: Journal of the Egyptian Study Society* 22.1 (2011): 9–19.

"Gods, Egyptian." In *The Encyclopedia of Ancient History*, eds. R. Bagnall et. al., 2947–2949. West Sussex: Wiley-Blackwell, 2012.

"Tausret." In *The Encyclopedia of Ancient History*, eds. R. Bagnall et. al., 6543–6545. West Sussex: Wiley-Blackwell, 2012.

"Temples, Pharaonic Egypt." In *The Encyclopedia of Ancient History*, eds. R. Bagnall et. al., 6597–6600. West Sussex: Wiley-Blackwell, 2012.

"Introduction: The Queen Who Would Be King." In *Tausret: Forgotten Queen and Pharaoh of Egypt*, ed. R. H. Wilkinson, 1–4. Oxford: Oxford University Press, 2012.

"The 'Temple of Millions of Years' of Tausret." In *Tausret: Forgotten Queen and Pharaoh of Egypt*, ed. R. H. Wilkinson, 92–105. Oxford: Oxford University Press, 2012.

"Afterword" (with Catharine H. Roehrig). In *Tausret: Forgotten Queen and Pharaoh of Egypt*, ed. R. H. Wilkinson, 106–108. Oxford: Oxford University Press, 2012.

"Symbolism and Religious Iconography." In *The Oxford Handbook of Egyptology*, eds. Ian Shaw and James P. Allen. Oxford: Oxford University Press, in press.

Book Reviews

Edna Russman, *Egyptian Sculpture: Cairo and Luxor*. *Varia Aegyptiaca* 6.1 (1990): 96–97.

Emily Teeter, *Egyptian Art in the Collection of the Seattle Art Museum*. *Varia Aegyptiaca* 6.1 (1990): 97.

Eric Hornung, *The Valley of the Kings*. *Kmt* 1.3 (1990): 69.

Gerry D. Scott III, *Temple, Tomb and Dwelling: Egyptian Antiquities from the Harer Family Trust Collection*. *Kmt* 3.1 (1992): 71.

Hans Wolfgang Müller, *Der "Armreif" des Königs Ahmose und der Handgelenkschutz des Bogenschutzen im Alten Ägypten und Vorderasien*. *Bibliotheca Orientalis* 48.3/4 (1992): 502–504.

Janice L. Crowley, *The Aegean and the East: An Investigation into the Transference of Artistic Motifs between the Aegean,*

Egypt, and the Near East in the Bronze Age. Journal of the Society for the Study of Egyptian Antiquities 18 (1988 [1992]): 117–118.

Erik Hornung, *Idea Into Image: Essays on Ancient Egyptian Thought. Kmt* 4.1 (1993), 75.

Donald Redford, *Egypt, Canaan, and Israel in Ancient Times. The American Historical Review* 98.3 (1993): 841–842.

Kent Weeks, *KV 5: A Preliminary Report. Journal of the American Research Center in Egypt* 39 (2002 [2004]): 251–252.

John Rose, *Tomb KV39 in the Valley of the Kings. Bibliotheca Orientalis* 59 (2002): 299–301.

Sakuji Yoshimura and Jiro Kondo, eds., *Conservation of the Wall Paintings in the Tomb of Amenophis III: First and Second Phases Report. PalArch* (October 2005): 1–3.

Dennis C. Forbes, *Imperial Lives: Biographies of Significant New Kingdom Egyptians. Apuntes de Egiptología* 2 (2007), http://www.ceae.unlugar.com /revista.htm.

Jacqueline Phillips, *Aegyptiaca on the Island of Crete in Their Chronological Context. Journal of Ancient Egyptian Interconnections* 2.2 (2008): 27–28.

B. J. J. Haring and O.E. Kaper (eds.) with the assistance of C.H. van Zoest, *Pictograms or Pseudo Script? Non-Textual Identity Marks in Practical Use in Ancient Egypt and Elsewhere. Journal of Ancient Egyptian Interconnections* 2.2 (2008): 25–26.

D. Michaelides, V. Kassianidou, and R. S. Merrillees (eds.), *Egypt and Cyprus in Antiquity: Proceedings of the International Conference, Nicosia 2003. Journal of Ancient Egyptian Interconnections* 2.3 (2008): 50–51.

K. Tazawa, *Syro-Palestinian Deities in New Kingdom Egypt. Journal of Ancient Egyptian Interconnections* 3.1 (2009): 7–8.

C. Greenlaw, *The Representation of Monkeys in the Art and Thought of Mediterranean Cultures. Journal of Ancient Egyptian Interconnections* 3.2 (2009): 28–30.

S. Bar, D. Kahn and J.J. Shirley (eds.), *Egypt, Canaan and Israel: History, Imperialism, Ideology and Literature Egypt, Canaan and Israel. Journal of Ancient Egyptian Interconnections* 4.2 (2012): 60–61.

Popular Articles

"Reality: Is it Necessary for Research?" *Ancient Studies Newsletter* 3.1 (1984): 13ff.

"Reconstructing the Mesopotamian Coronation and Accession Program of the Neo-Sumerian through Old Babylonian Periods." *Ancient Studies Newsletter* 5.2 (1986): 4ff.

"The Hanging Gardens of Babylon." *Minnesota Horticulturist* 114.2 (1986): 36ff.

"The Egyptian Private Garden." *Minnesota Horticulturist* 114.3 (1986): 72ff.

"The Persian Royal Gardens." *Minnesota Horticulturist* 114.4 (1986): 106ff.

"The Roman Villa Garden." *Minnesota Horticulturist* 114:5 (1986): 132ff.

"Royal Gardens of Ancient China." *Minnesota Horticulturist* 115.8 (1987), 204ff.

"Egyptian Temple Design." *American Research Center in Egypt Arizona Chapter Newsletter* (July: 1989), 1–4.

"A Standing Enigma: The Obelisks of Ancient Egypt." *American Research Center in Egypt Arizona Chapter Newsletter* (November: 1989), 1–4.

"The Other Valley of the Kings: Exploring the Western Branch of the Theban Royal Necropolis." *Kmt* 2.3 (1991): 46–52.

Foreword. In *Egyptian Echoes: Contemporary Art Inspired by Ancient Monuments,* Yolanda Muhammad. Exhibition catalog, 3–4. Sun City, Arizona: Sun Cities Art Museum, 1993.

"The Paths of Re: Symbolism in the Royal Tombs of Wadi Biban El Moluk." *Kmt* 4.3 (1993): 10–20.

"Report on the University of Arizona International Conference on the Valley of the Kings." *Newsletter of the American Research Center in Egypt* 166 (1995): 22–23.

"The University of Arizona in the Valley of the Kings." *Glyph* 1.10 (September 1997): 8–9.

"Finding What Belzoni Didn't Take: Foundation Pits in the Western Valley of the Kings." *Bulletin of the American Research Center in Egypt* 181 (Fall–Winter 2001–2002): 16–18.

"The Tausret Temple Project and AEF Training Grant." *Bulletin of the American Research Center in Egypt* 190 (Fall 2006): 5–8.

"The Temple of Tausret: Forgotten Monument of a Queen/Pharaoh." *Kmt* 23.3 (2012): 34–43.

Journals and Directories

Editor, *Journal of Ancient Egyptian Interconnections* (2009–Present)

Editor (1990–2012; with Pearce Paul Creasman, 2012–present), The Directory of North American Egyptologists

Representative Conference Papers, Invited Lectures, etc.

"The Representation of the Bow in Ancient Egypt and the Near East." Delivered paper, Center for Ancient Studies and AIA, Minneapolis, Minnesota, December 1985.

Participant, "Formation of Regional Chapters" discussion group. American Research Center in Egypt meetings, Philadelphia, Pennsylvania, April 1989.

"The Origins of the Pyramids." American Research Center in Egypt Arizona Chapter, Tucson, Arizona, April 1989.

"Conventions in Egyptian Representations of the Bow." Delivered paper, American Research Center in Egypt annual meeting, Berkeley, California, April, 1990.

"The Significance of Trefoil Ear Markings in Egyptian Representations of Lions." Delivered paper, American Research Center in Egypt annual meeting, Boston, Massachusetts, April 1991.

"Nefertiti: The Queen as King." American Research Center in Egypt Arizona Chapter, Tucson, Arizona, November 1991.

"Gesture Symbolism in the Iconography of Ancient Egypt and the Near East." Delivered paper, American Research Center in Egypt Annual Meeting, Seattle, Washington, April 1992.

Panelist, "Egyptian Symbolism." "Egyptian Echoes" exhibition opening. Sun Cities Art Museum, Sun City, Arizona, January 1993.

"Iconography and Symbolism in the Tomb of King Ay." Delivered paper, American Research Center in Egypt annual meeting, Baltimore, Maryland, April 1993.

"New Excavations in the Tomb of Amenmesse KV-10." Invited lecture, University of Arizona Museum of Art, Tucson, Arizona, October 1993.

"New Excavations in the Valley of the Kings." Delivered paper, Egyptian Studies Association, Denver Museum of Natural History, Denver, Colorado, October 1993.

"Symbolic Alignment in New Kingdom Royal Tombs." Delivered paper, American Research Center in Egypt annual meeting, Toronto, Ontario, April 1994.

"Symbolism in New Kingdom Royal Tombs." University of Arizona International Conference of the Valley of the Kings, Tucson, Arizona, October 1994.

"Effects of the Recent Flooding in the Valley of the Kings." Delivered paper, American Research Center in Egypt annual meeting, Atlanta, Georgia, April 1995.

"Understanding Egyptian Art: Reality and Symbol in the Ancient Egyptian Mind." Invited lecture, American Research Center in Egypt North Texas Chapter, Dallas, Texas, October 1996.

"Archaeological and Iconographic aspects of WV23: The Tomb of King Ay." Invited lecture, American University in Cairo, Cairo, Egypt, May 1998.

"Understanding Egyptian Art." Invited lecture in conjunction with "Splendors of Ancient Egypt" Exhibition, Phoenix Art Museum, Phoenix, Arizona, July 1998.

"Symbolism in Egyptian Art." Invited lecture in conjunction with "Splendors of Ancient Egypt" exhibition, Phoenix Art Museum, Phoenix, Arizona, August 1998.

"The Work of The University of Arizona Egyptian Expedition." Invited lecture in conjunction with "Splendors of Ancient Egypt" exhibition, Phoenix Art Museum, Phoenix, Arizona, October 1998.

"Word and Image: Hieroglyphic Writing and Art in Ancient Egypt." Invited lecture, Metropolitan Museum of Art (C. K. Wilkinson Lecture Series), New York, New York, October 1998.

"A Life in Ruins: Excavating in the Valley of the Kings." University of Arizona Speaker Series, Tucson, Arizona, March 1999.

"Perceptions of Ancient Egypt." Invited lecture in conjunction with

"Splendors of Ancient Egypt" Exhibition, Phoenix Museum of Art, Phoenix, Arizona, March 1999.

"Even Tombs Can Die: Saving the Royal Tombs of the Valley of the Kings." Invited lecture, Egyptian Studies Association, Denver, Colorado, September 1999.

"Valley of the Sun Kings: Excavating Royal Tombs of Egypt's Amarna Age." Invited lecture, American Institute of Archaeology, Northern Arizona University, Flagstaff, Arizona, September 2001.

"The University of Arizona Egyptian Expedition in the Western Valley of the Kings." Invited lecture, American Institute of Archaeology, University of Arizona, Tucson, Arizona, November 2001.

"New Excavations in Tausret's Memorial Temple—A Forgotten Queen's Quest for Immortality." Invited lecture, Egyptian Studies Society, Denver, Colorado, October 2004.

"Rediscovering a Forgotten Queen Who Ruled as Pharaoh." Invited lecture, American Institute of Archaeology, Arizona State University, Tempe, Arizona, March 2005.

"The Temple of Tausret: The Queen Who Ruled as King." Invited lecture, American Research Center in Egypt Arizona Chapter, Tucson, Arizona, April 2005.

Session chair, "New Kingdom History." "Evolving Egypt" International Conference, Oahu, Hawaii, February 2006.

"New Excavations in the Temple of Tausret: The Third Season." Invited Lecture, New Mexico State Museum of Natural History, Albuquerque, New Mexico, October, 2006.

"Strange Creature in a Strange Land: The Griffin in Egypt." Invited paper for conference "Griffins and Royal Symbolism in Crete, Egypt, and the Near East," University of Illinois, Chicago, Illinois, March 2008.

"The Symbolic Use of Egyptian Hieroglyphic Script." Invited lecture, University of Istanbul, Istanbul, Turkey, March 2009.

"The Work of the University of Arizona Egyptian Expedition." Invited lecture, University of Istanbul, Istanbul, Turkey, March 2009.

"Excavations in the Valley of the Kings." Invited lecture, Archaeological Institute of America, Honolulu Academy of Arts, Honolulu, Hawaii, May 2009.

"The Memorial Temple of Tausret: A Re-evaluation of Sir William Flinders Petrie's Excavation." Invited lecture, "International Conference on the Temples of Millions of Years: Science and New Technology Applied to Archaeology," organized by the Egyptian Supreme Council of Antiquities, Luxor, Egypt, January 2010.

"The University of Arizona Excavation of the Temple of Tausret." (With Pearce Paul Creasman.) Delivered Paper, American Research Center in Egypt annual meeting, Providence, Rhode Island, April 2012.

Awards and Honors of Richard H. Wilkinson

1972	Summer Study Scholarship, Düsseldorf, West Germany
1973	Summer Study Scholarship, Bad Öhenhausen, West Germany
1974	Scholarship for archaeological excavation, Jerusalem, Israel
1983	Goldenberg Memorial Prize for Research in Near Eastern Studies
1984	Center for Ancient Studies Award, University of Minnesota
1989	Steinfeld Faculty Research Grant, University of Arizona
1990	Heath Literary Award, American Numismatic Association
1991	Nominated, University of Arizona Five-Star Faculty Award
1991	National Endowment for the Humanities/Arizona Humanities Council Grant for Public Lecture Series
1992	Nominated, University of Arizona Distinguished Lecturer Award
1993	*Reading Egyptian Art* chosen Archaeology Book of the Quarter by *Antiquity*
1994	Awarded Research Semester (Fall 1994), University of Arizona
1994–Present	Appointed to Editorial Board of *Kmt: A Modern Journal of Ancient Egypt*
1994–1997	Elected, National Board of Directors, American Research Center in Egypt
1994–Present	Listed in *Contemporary Authors*
1994	Provost Award for Excellence in Teaching, as member of Humanities Program, University of Arizona
1995–Present	Listed in *The Writers Directory*
1995–Present	Listed in *International Authors and Writers Who's Who*
1996	Nominated for El Paso Foundation Faculty Achievement Award

1996	Elected to Board of Trustees, The Amarna Foundation
1997–2001	Reelected, National Board of Directors, American Research Center in Egypt
1997–Present	Listed in *Who's Who in America*
2000	Tenure dossier selected for presentation to Arizona Board of Regents by the Provost of the University of Arizona in defense of the university's tenure system
2000	Nominated for Burlington Teaching Award, University of Arizona
2000	Featured speaker with President Peter Likins for the University of Arizona Capital Campaign, "Excavating the Sun Kings," Los Angeles, California (March 2000)
2000	Included in *2000 Outstanding Scholars of the 20th Century* (Cambridge International Biographical Center)
2000	Featured speaker with President Peter Likins for University of Arizona Capital Campaign, "New Research in the Valley of the Kings," New York, New York (October 2000)
2000–Present	Amarna Research Foundation Grants: 2000, 2001, 2002, 2003, 2004, 2006, 2007, 2008
2002	Nominated, Provost's Teaching Award, University of Arizona
2003	Invited to host ARCE National Egyptological Conference, Spring 2004
2004–Present	Included in online biographical summary of thirty leading Egyptologists, past and present, worldwide: www.touregypt.net
2005	Excavation Grant, Petty Foundation
2006	American Research Center in Egypt Grant for Student Training
2007	Nominated, International Affairs Excellence in International Service Award
2008	Named Regents' Professor, University of Arizona

2011	Invited to be first honorary US member of the Institute of Eastern Mediterranean Studies in Archaeology (IEMSA) of the University of Athens and the National Archaeological Museum of Greece
2013	Honorary Chairman, Wilkinson Egyptology Series, University of Arizona Egyptian Expedition

PART II

THE SIGNIFICANCE OF RICHARD H. WILKINSON'S LEADERSHIP AND RESEARCH

University of Arizona Egyptian Expedition

Pearce Paul Creasman
University of Arizona

Richard H. Wilkinson founded the University of Arizona Egyptian Expedition (UAEE) in the fall of 1988 as a nonprofit scholarly entity and conducted its first season of archaeological fieldwork in 1989. With only a single exception, the UAEE has conducted fieldwork in Egypt every year since. After twenty-four years at the helm (1988–2012), he now advises the UAEE in his new capacity as Founding Director.

The UAEE is committed to ongoing excavation, research, and conservation work in Egyptian archaeology. The expedition's focal area of research has traditionally but not exclusively been the Valley of the Kings and ancient Thebes, in the area of modern Luxor. While most of its fieldwork has been concentrated in this region, the UAEE has cooperated with, supported, and assisted a great many other missions and scholars. Over the past quarter century, scholars affiliated with more than one hundred institutions have formally participated in the work of the UAEE. Furthermore, the UAEE has placed at leading graduate institutions in the field many of its own students, several of whom are now professors in their own right. It is a great credit to Richard that so many colleagues, in the United States, Egypt, and virtually everywhere else, count him—and, by extension, the UAEE—as a friend, mentor, and pillar of the field.

UAEE Fieldwork
Western Valley of the Kings Project
(1989 to 2002)

The first archaeological projects undertaken by the UAEE in the Valley of the Kings involved excavation and research in and around tombs WV 23, WV 24, and WV 25. These projects and their importance are discussed in detail by Richard Harwood elsewhere in this volume.

Amenmesse Project
(1992 to 1993)

The Amenmesse Project, involving excavation and conservation of KV 10—the tomb of the Nineteenth Dynasty pharaoh Amenmesse—was initiated under the auspices of the UAEE. After an exploratory survey, the project was transferred to the University of Memphis. The project is still ongoing under the purview of Egypt's archaeological authority, the Supreme Council of Antiquities (SCA)/Ministry of State for Antiquities (MSA).

Motif Alignment Project
(1993 to 2003)

The Motif Alignment Project (MAP) was instituted in 1993 for study of the location and alignment of reliefs and inscriptions in the royal tombs of the Valley of the Kings. While it is known that as early as the Eighteenth Dynasty the ancient Egyptians considered the entrance to the royal tomb to be symbolically located in the south regardless of its true cardinal direction, evidence for the Nineteenth Dynasty indicates the use of another symbolic orientation, in which the royal tomb was considered to lie on an east-west axis that dictated the location and alignment of a number of texts and representations placed on the walls of the royal tombs. Initial conclusions regarding this symbolic orientation were reached during the course of archaeological work in the Valley of the Kings from 1989 to 1993. After 1993, the Permanent Committee of the Supreme Council of Antiquities of Egypt kindly granted permission for the specific photographing and recording of important scenes and inscriptions in a number of Ramesside tombs. Karin Kroenke describes the MAP in greater detail later in this volume.

TAUSRET TEMPLE PROJECT (2004 TO PRESENT)

The UAEE's current archaeological project is the excavation, conservation, and publication of the remains of the Theban temple of Tausret, the Nineteenth Dynasty queen who ruled as a king ca. 1200 BCE. The temple site was briefly examined by W. M. Flinders Petrie in 1896, but the UAEE excavations have demonstrated that Petrie's work at the site was extremely limited. Numerous artifacts and inscriptions have been recovered from unexcavated areas, and new evidence indicates that the temple was nearly completed, which has significant implications for the duration of Tausret's reign. This project and its importance are discussed in greater detail by Danielle Phelps and Pearce Paul Creasman within the current volume.

UAEE PUBLICATIONS AND THE WILKINSON EGYPTOLOGY SERIES

The UAEE and its fieldwork have produced or supported the publication of more than five hundred articles, books, reports, professional presentations, theses, and research content in a variety of other media. These items have been offered for both the scientific community and the public at large.

Notably, the UAEE has published three edited volumes, including the present one. Its first, edited by Richard Wilkinson, was *Valley of the Sun Kings: New Explorations in the Tombs of the Pharaohs* (1995), proceedings of the International Conference on the Valley of the Kings conducted by the UAEE in Tucson, Arizona, the previous year. The UAEE's second volume, also edited by Richard Wilkinson, was *Temple of Tausret: The University of Arizona Egyptian Expedition Tausret Temple Project, 2004–2011* (2011). This presented the interim site report and included papers by numerous scholars on a wide variety of material from and interpretations of the queen's "temple of millions of years" in Thebes. This publication includes a CD with all images in color, enabling greater resolution and closer inspection.

While the goal of the current edited volume, *Archaeological Research in the Valley of the Kings and Ancient Thebes: Papers Presented in Honor of Richard H. Wilkinson* (2013) is to honor Richard Wilkinson, it also represents a new step for the UAEE: the Wilkinson Egyptology Series. The peer-reviewed series is open to all scholars for publication of monographs, comprehensive site reports, conference proceedings, and other edited works. The goal of the Wilkinson Egyptology Series is to help scholars bring high-quality work to print promptly, through a scholarly review process akin to those of most major journals. After a period of not more than five years, each volume will be made available online, free of charge. The series is designed to reflect Dr. Wilkinson's prolific academic career: producing only the highest quality work without delay.

Directory of North American Egyptologists

Since 1988, and in cooperation with the University of Chicago since 1996, the UAEE has published the online Directory of North American Egyptologists. This provides the names and contact data for professional Egyptologists and current doctoral students in North America, as well as current and recent doctoral dissertations in Egyptology. The directory is updated monthly and now co-edited by Richard H. Wilkinson and Pearce Paul Creasman.

Journal of Ancient Egyptian Interconnections

The *Journal of Ancient Egyptian Interconnections* (*JAEI*), founded and edited by Richard H. Wilkinson, is a quarterly peer-reviewed wholly online scholarly publication integrating Egyptology with Mediterranean, Near Eastern, and African studies, to provide a venue for this growing field of interdisciplinary and inter-area research. The *JAEI* is published and hosted by the University of Arizona and is an independent sister-entity of the Egyptian Expedition. Readers of this volume will likely find the content of *JAEI* of great interest. The home page may be found at https://journals.uair.arizona.edu/index.php/jaei.

Journal of Ancient Egyptian Interconnections

Noreen Doyle
University of Arizona Egyptian Expedition

The *Journal of Ancient Egyptian Interconnections* (*JAEI*), a peer-reviewed quarterly publication, was founded in 2009 by Richard H. Wilkinson, who continues to serve as editor. Hosted by the University of Arizona, it is a wholly online scholarly journal integrating Egyptian archaeology with Mediterranean, Near Eastern, and African studies, providing a new venue for this growing field of interdisciplinary and inter-area research. This brings together the knowledge and analytical approaches of history, archaeology, artifact analysis, and language to explore and better understand the diverse ways in which Egypt interfaced with its foreign contemporaries in ancient times.

Appropriate to the goal of the journal, its editorial board and body of editorial liaisons comprise prominent researchers with wide-ranging expertise from many different institutions in the United States, Europe, and the Middle East. Contributions from authors representing more than twenty nationalities have been published thus far. As an online publication, *JAEI* provides its authors with prompt publication and a worldwide readership. While most items are full research articles, brief papers such as field reports and research updates are also accepted. Reviews of published works, as well as reports and announcements of relevant conferences, symposia, and other scholarly events, likewise appear. Each has been peer-reviewed in a blind screening process by an Egyptologist and a specialist from the outside area of interaction, and all ensure a continuation of lively scholarly discussion of the contact between Egypt and its neighbors.

Temporally, the subjects within the journal have spanned a broad swath of history, from the Epipaleolithic through Roman times. Scholars have presented analyses of language (from individual words to complete texts), of artifacts (from materials and technology to iconography and style), and of politics and economies to explore the many levels and means of cross-cultural interactions in antiquity. The *JAEI* has arranged several thematic fascicles, for which selected authors—both established and early-career—are specifically solicited to contribute. To date, these topics have been: maritime interconnections (2.3); interconnections between Egypt and the Aegean (3.2); a two-fascicle set examining contacts between Egypt and the cultures of the ancient Levant (4.2 and 4.3); and seafaring (5.1).

A new development in the format of the *JAEI* arrived in 4.4: the annual research reports issue, to be published as the final fascicle of each volume. Updates regarding recent, in-progress, and planned work provide researchers an opportunity to deliver "current news." Such sharing in a formal, vetted venue provides the opportunity for additional communication between researchers, for greater dissemination of data, and, ultimately, for increased collaboration between those working on related projects.

American Research Center in Egypt, Arizona Chapter

Pearce Paul Creasman
University of Arizona

In early 1989, Terry Walz from the American Research Center in Egypt national office invited its Arizona members to organize as a chapter of ARCE. As a nonprofit organization comprising hundreds of scholars, institutions, and others with an interest in the study of Egyptian history and culture, ARCE encourages the formation of local chapters: these benefit their regional communities by hosting lectures by international experts, as well as organizing educational seminars and other events. Knowing the importance of such outreach efforts, Richard H. Wilkinson and Penny Clifford Mazer founded ARCE Arizona, with Richard serving as its president from 1989 until 2000. As one of the five original chapters (and now one of fourteen such groups), ARCE Arizona has thrived for nearly twenty-five years. Originally established as an independent but cooperating entity of ARCE, it was subsequently awarded its own status as a nonprofit organization by the US Internal Revenue Service.

ARCE Arizona is based at the University of Arizona Egyptian Expedition. Throughout their joint history, the two organizations have worked together in support of research and education. Since 1989, the chapter has sponsored approximately one hundred lectures and activities across the state. In addition, in 2004 the Arizona Chapter hosted ARCE's sixty-fourth annual meeting in Tucson.

ARCE Arizona had a printed newsletter for many years, produced by Richard Wilkinson. In May of 1989, first chapter newsletter—with an introduction by Richard Wilkinson, an article by "Chuck" Van Siclen about a miniature obelisk of Thutmose III, and an announcement for the forty-first annual meeting of ARCE—

was mailed out to members. Today members receive news by e-mail and from the chapter's web page.

The Arizona Chapter is rooted in the activities of the University of Arizona, especially as these relate to the University's Egyptian Expedition and other academic units on campus, including the School of Anthropology, Department of Classics, Middle Eastern and North African Studies, Art History, History, and, more recently, the School of Consumer and Family Studies, the Department of Geosciences, and the Laboratory of Tree-Ring Research.

The Motif Alignment Project

Karin R. Kroenke
University of California, Berkeley

Richard H. Wilkinson directed the Motif Alignment Project (MAP) for seven seasons, between 1993 to 2003, under the auspices of the University of Arizona Egyptian Expedition (UAEE).[1] The goal of the project was to investigate the role of orientation and alignment in the symbolism of the royal tombs in the Valley of the Kings.[2] The hypothesis was that religious changes taking place in Egypt during the New Kingdom were conveyed by royal tomb structure and decoration. Specifically, a survey of motifs would illustrate the development of post-Amarna solar images and their increased importance throughout the Ramesside Period, as deduced by their prominent and recurring placements in the tombs.

The MAP reached its initial findings during the course of the UAEE's archaeological work in the Valley of the Kings from 1993 to 1995. During this phase the expedition team investigated the majority of the royal tombs. They confirmed (and, in some cases, corrected) the cardinal alignments, and then photographed and recorded the relevant scenes. In its conclusions, the MAP proposed several patterns of relative placement. While identifying some configurations in the orientation of architectural elements and sarcophagi with respect to cardinal directions (external alignment) and to each other (internal alignment), most significantly the project documented two models of internal symbolic orientation articulated by the arrangement of key texts and images on the tomb walls: a south-north axial alignment in the Eighteenth Dynasty (alpha orientation type) and an east-west alignment in the Nineteenth and Twentieth Dynasties (beta orientation type). The MAP also noted specific motifs that indicated a more fully developed theological program in the late Ramesside Period.

The second phase of the MAP lasted from 1996 to 1999, when the Permanent Committee of the Supreme Council of Antiquities of Egypt granted permission for additional work in several Ramesside tombs. During this period the project, discovering additional evidence that reinforced the symbolic east-west axes of Ramesside tombs and distinguished Nineteenth and Twentieth Dynasties, modified its earlier conclusions. The MAP's final results appeared in several publications.[3]

In its investigation the MAP incorporated various studies on the chronological development of the structural design and decorative program of the royal tombs in the Valley of the Kings. One significant contribution was the examination of the evolutionary sequence in axial alignment (bent, jogged, and straight) and the repetition of architectural elements (corridors and halls) that created a two-part, upper-and-lower tomb division.[4] Other pertinent research dealt with the expansion of tomb decoration and the corresponding complex theological development of the royal funerary books that were carved and/or painted on the walls and ceilings.[5] The designations of architectural elements from Ramesside Period ostraca and papyri provided information about their symbolic (as well as functional) purposes.[6] The combined evidence illustrates that, despite variations of how it was manifested, throughout the New Kingdom the symbolism of the royal tomb identified it with the path of the sun. Architecture, image, and text worked together to ensure the successful completion of the sun god's nightly voyage and subsequent regeneration and, by association, the king's safe journey to rebirth each morning.[7]

The choice of architectural features in these tombs likely was influenced by the topography of the netherworld,[8] as envisioned in the royal funerary books, or by the concept of the solar cycle itself.[9] In turn, the specific placements of the decoration on the walls, pillars, and ceilings enhanced the information communicated by the images and texts.[10] In some cases, the wall scenes were even aligned with ideal directions specified in the funerary books.[11] Thus, this body of information served as the foundation for the MAP's dual symbolic alignment patterns that identified the Theban royal tombs with the path of the sun: the alpha and beta orientation types.

With the alpha orientation type, the main axes of the royal tombs are symbolically aligned with the tomb entrance in the ideal south and the burial chamber in the ideal north. Correspondingly, the sides of the tomb represent the east (right) and west (left). Ramesside Period papyri and ostraca provide the names of architectural features that evoke the south-north axial alignment. The fifth underground corridor was called *the first (god's passage) of (the) zenith*, referring to the peak of the sun's nightly journey in the northern sky (the realm of the circumpolar stars).[12] This concept was reinforced visually with the stars painted on the ceilings of Eighteenth Dynasty burial chambers and the vaulted astronomical ceilings of Nineteenth Dynasty sarcophagus halls, of which Sety I's (KV 17; Figure 1) is the best preserved.[13] The complementary east-west orientation of the right and left sides of the tombs is illustrated in Ramesside Period ostraca that name *the sanctuaries in which [the gods] of the east/west repose,* referring to niches that were cut into the upper walls of the third corridor.[14] These niches first appeared in the tomb of Thutmose III (KV 34), suggesting the alpha orientation type had begun in the Eighteenth Dynasty. However, an iconographic program never developed fully in accordance with this theoretical configuration. Deities with directional associations are not arranged into expected patterns. For example, in the burial chamber of Amenhotep III (KV 22) Hathor is depicted on the (actual) south pillar faces as "Mistress of the West and the Western Desert" and on the (actual) north pillar faces as "Lady of Dendera," and is consequently associated with the realm of the dead (symbolic west) and the land of the living (symbolic east), respectively.[15] However, if the orientation of these two forms of Hathor is considered within a symbolic

Figure 1: KV 17, tomb of Sety I (UAEE Archives)

south-north axial framework, the images are reversed. Instead, the beta orientation type, established at the beginning of the Ramesside Period, prevailed through the end of the New Kingdom.

The beta orientation type is characterized by the symbolic reorientation of the tombs' main axes to replicate the east-west voyage of the sun (and its west-east return). Thus, the tomb entrance and the burial chamber lie in the ideal east and west, respectively. The evidence for this alignment pattern derives in part from texts and architectural features, but chiefly from tomb decoration. The tomb plan of Ramesses IV (KV 2) names the right-hand room before the burial chamber (viewed from the back of the tomb) as *the one south of it also* and *the place of the south on the right*.[16] This room would be oriented correctly according to a symbolic east-west alignment of the tomb's main axis. The symmetry of Ramesside tombs and the straightened and more uniformly sloping tomb axes—firmly established with Merenptah (KV 8; Figure 2)—likely developed to conform to the symbolic east-west reorientation that was expressed initially in the decorative program.[17] While some elements of the beta orientation type first appeared in the tombs of Ramesses I (KV 16) and Sety I (KV 17), most were in place by Ramesses II (KV 7). The fully developed symbolic east-west axial alignment occurred with Merenptah (KV 8) and continued to the end of the New Kingdom.[18] There are two main aspects of the beta orientation type: 1) images that demarcate the directional path of the sun and 2) images that reveal the state of the sun god along his cyclical journey.

With the expansion of tomb decoration at the beginning of the Nineteenth Dynasty, traditional underworld texts and vignettes were repositioned from the burial chambers to the entrance passages and halls. Solar-related images taken directly from these funerary books and independent iconographic elements were placed in prominent locations to mark the descent of the sun into the netherworld. The representations comprise the yellow sun disk containing Khepri and Atum above the tomb entrances, winged red solar disks on interior lintels, yellow ceiling and wall bands, and inward-flying vultures set against starred backgrounds on corridor ceilings. Additionally, the inscriptions on both side walls of the tomb are oriented outward, so that they read into the tomb.[19] The side walls also received other symbols that reinforced the theoretical east-west axial alignment. Heraldic devices were paired to represent Lower and Upper Egypt on opposite right (north) and left (south) walls, door jambs, door thicknesses, and (occasionally) ceilings throughout the tomb.[20] The most commonly opposed motifs were either Nephthys and Isis (who also flank the tripartite sun disk on the entrance lintel) or two figures

Figure 2: KV 8, tomb of Merenptah (UAEE Archives)

of Maat, each kneeling on a *nb* basket that was supported by the appropriate heraldic plant (papyrus or lily), although other deities were paired occasionally.[21]

Royal tomb decoration in the Ramesside Period also illustrates the transformation of the sun god as he travels through the netherworld. In general, Re's relationship with Osiris is exhibited by the location of their images in different areas of the tomb. Architecturally, Ramesside tombs are separated into two sections at the first pillared hall. The wall decoration correspondingly marks a symbolic division into front (east) and back (west) portions, with the appearance of the "Osiris shrine" over the exit doorway of this chamber.[22] The supremacy of the sun god in the front half of the tomb is heralded by the Litany of Re—prefaced by the image the king standing before Re-Horakhty—inside the tomb entrance. The lower portion of the tomb is dominated by images of Osiris, thereby associating this area with the depths of the netherworld. While Osiris first appeared in the burial halls of Eighteenth Dynasty tombs (beginning with KV 35), this netherworld imagery was developed fully in the Nineteenth Dynasty with the addition of decorated

Osiris niches opening off the burial chambers and images of Osiris carved on royal sarcophagi from Ramesses I (KV 16) on. Within the two main divisions of the tomb, variations in scale and gestures reinforce the distinct statuses of the two deities at various points along the sun god's journey.[23] The cyclical aspect of the solar route is made explicit in the decorative program of Nineteenth Dynasty burial chambers, exemplified in opposed vignettes from the Book of Caverns on the side walls of Tausret's burial chamber (KV 14) that depict the fusion of Osiris and Re on the left and the rebirth of the sun god on the right.[24]

Although the beta orientation type was retained in the Twentieth Dynasty, further theological developments are demonstrated by the introduction of new solar-related motifs and the modification of existing iconographic elements. First, the deceased king was identified more closely with the sun god, illustrated by the addition of the royal cartouches on the corridor ceilings of Ramesses IV's tomb (KV 2)—following the path of the sun—and the orientation of the sarcophagus along the main (east-west) tomb axis from Ramesses III (KV 11) on.[25] With this change the king's head was to the symbolic west, allowing the mummy to look back toward the tomb entrance and the eastern rising sun. Second, the sun god was now preeminent in both the heavens and the netherworld. Royal funerary books appear in specific locations in the lower parts of the tomb, including Books of Heavens on the ceilings and the Book of the Earth and the Book of the Underworld on the burial chamber walls.

As in the earlier Eighteenth and Nineteenth Dynasties, the burial chamber functioned somewhat as an independent microcosm, with the decoration of this room reflecting the sun's dual diurnal and nocturnal journeys.[26] However, in the later Ramesside Period these scenes also could be positioned according to the symbolic east-west alignment of the main axes. For example, in the tomb of Ramesses VI (KV 9) the image of Nut from the Book of Day is situated toward the chamber entrance (symbolic east), while the corresponding image of Nut from the Book of Night lies at the back of the tomb (symbolic west).[27] Furthermore, the centrally repositioned morning and evening solar barques along the main axes in the tombs of Ramesses VI (KV 9) and Ramesses IX (KV 6) and the addition of the solar birth scene in the rear niche of Ramesses VI's burial chamber—analogous to the earlier Ramesside Osiris niches—clearly delineate the sun god's route.[28] The return of the regenerated deity from the netherworld and, by association, the king's resurrection is emphasized visually by the now outward-facing vultures and stars on the corridor ceilings and royal image on the right corridor walls (viewed from the entrance). The right wall inscriptions also were reoriented to face inward, thereby meant to be read out of the tomb.[29] Therefore, by the late Ramesside Period the royal tomb embodied the complete solar cycle, demonstrated not only by the choice of royal funerary texts and vignettes and independent iconographic elements but also by their deliberate and precise locations.

The significance of the MAP was the synthesis of previous knowledge and new insights on the symbolism of royal tombs in the Valley of the Kings. The MAP utilized established evolutionary trends in tomb structure and decoration from the Eighteenth through the Twentieth Dynasty. Building on the premise that these royal monuments represented the path of the sun (Figure 3), the MAP considered the interrelationship of architecture, text, and image, specifically investigating the role of orientation and alignment in the implementation of this solar symbolism. The MAP identified two new patterns of internal symbolic alignment reflected in the layout of inscriptions and motifs within the tombs: the alpha orientation type in the Eighteenth Dynasty and the beta orientation type in the Nineteenth and Twentieth Dynasties. As tomb decoration expanded from the burial chambers to

Figure 3: Path of the Sun in KV 9, tomb of Ramesses V/VI (UAEE archives)

the entrance passages and halls at the beginning of the Ramesside Period, the repositioning of standard texts and vignettes and the appearance of new motifs with directional associations in specific areas was linked to the symbolic reorientation of the royal monument along an east-west axis. The further importance of the MAP was in refining an understanding of theological differences between the Nineteenth and Twentieth Dynasties that were expressed in tomb symbolism. The work of project demonstrated that the orientation and alignment of texts and images was modified throughout the Ramesside Period as the entire tomb evolved to represent a model of the cosmos, including the east-west descent of the sun god into the netherworld along the tomb passageways, Re's rebirth in the burial chamber, and his west-east return journey back through the corridors and halls.

NOTES

1 The other staff members of the MAP included Richard Harwood, Donald Kunz, Suzanne Onstine, Rita Ellsworth, Anne Lopez, and the present author. I was involved in phase one of the project, assisting Richard Wilkinson in his initial study of the wall scenes in 1993 and 1995. In 1996, the team expanded to include Dick Harwood (team photographer), Don Kunz (assistant photographer), Suzanne Onstine (epigrapher), and Rita Ellsworth and (later) Anne Lopez (graphic designers). The last two women were responsible for a (planned) CD-ROM and website that would allow 3D virtual tours of the royal tombs.

2 The UAEE intended to extend its examination of locational symbolism to tombs in the Valley of the Queens, but when the MAP ended the expedition moved on to new projects.

3 Suzanne Onstine, "The Relationship between Osiris and Re in the Book of Caverns," *JSSEA* 25 (1995 [1998]): 66–77; Nicholas Reeves and Richard H. Wilkinson, *The Complete Valley of the Kings* (New York: Thames and Hudson, 1996), passim; Richard H. Wilkinson, "The Motif of the Path of the Sun in Ramesside Royal Tombs: An Outline of Recent Research," *JSSEA* 25 (1995 [1998]): 78–84 and pls. VIII–X; Wilkinson, "The Paths of Re: Symbolism in the Royal Tombs of Wadi Biban El Moluk," *Kmt* 4.3 (1993): 42–51; Wilkinson, *Symbol and Magic in Egyptian Art* (New York: Thames and Hudson, 1994), esp. 69–82; Wilkinson, "Symbolic Location and Alignment in New Kingdom Royal Tombs and Their Decoration," *JARCE* 31 (1994): 79–86; Wilkinson, "Symbolic Orientation and Alignment in New Kingdom Royal Tombs," in Richard H. Wilkinson (ed.), *Valley of the Sun Kings: New Explorations in the Tombs of the Pharaohs* (Tucson: University of Arizona Egyptian Expedition, 1995); and Wilkinson, "The University of Arizona Egyptian Expedition Motif Alignment Project," *NARCE* 178 (1999): 6.

[4] Friedrich Abitz, "Die Entwicklung der Grabachsen in den Königsgräbern im Tal der Könige," *MDAIK* 45 (1989): 1–25.

[5] For just a few examples of Erik Hornung's prolific research on the netherworld books, see *Ägyptische Unterweltsbücher* (Zurich and Munich: Artemis-Verlag, 1989); *The Valley of the Kings: Horizon of Eternity*, translated by David Warburton (New York: Timken, 1990); and, more recently, *The Ancient Egyptian Books of the Afterlife*, translated by David Lorton (Ithaca and London: Cornell University Press, 1999). See also Friedrich Abitz, *Pharao als Gott in den Unterweltsbuchern des Neuen Reiches* (Freiburg/Göttingen: Universitätsverlag, 1995).

[6] Jaroslav Černý, *The Valley of the Kings* (Cairo: Institut français d'archéologie orientale, 1973), 23–34.

[7] One early study was Hermann Grapow, "Studien zu den thebanischen Königsgräbern," *ZÄS* 72 (1936): 12–39. Two recent examinations of the interconnection of architecture and texts and representations from the Amduat in Eighteenth Dynasty royal tombs are Catharine H. Roehrig, "The Building Activities of Thutmose III in the Valley of the Kings," in Eric H. Cline and David O'Connor (eds.), *Thutmose III: A New Biography* (Ann Arbor: University of Michigan Press, 2006), 238–259 and Barbara A. Richter, "The Amduat and Its Relationship to the Architecture of Early 18th Dynasty Royal Burial Chambers," *JARCE* 44 (2008): 73–104.

[8] For example, the well shaft, oval burial chambers, and bent axes of Eighteenth Dynasty tombs may suggest caverns, the curvature of the underworld, and twisting paths encountered during the sun god's journey, as depicted in the Amduat. For the symbolic association of the well with the tomb of Sokar, see Friedrich Abitz, *Die religiöse Bedeutung der sogenannten Grabräuberschächte in den ägyptischen Königsgräbern der 18. bis 20. Dynastie* (Wiesbaden: Otto Harrassowitz, 1974). For a connection between the cartouche-shaped burial chamber and the curved edging of the netherworld in the twelfth hour of the Amduat, see Erik Hornung, "Struktur und Entwicklung der Gräber im Tal der Könige," *ZÄS* 105 (1978), 59-66, and Hornung, *Valley of the Kings*, 75. Roehrig, "Building Activities," 242 and 246, n. 49, reinterpreted the burial chamber as an oval, related to the cave of Sokar in the fifth hour of the Amduat. A link between the corridor staircases in KV 34 (Thutmose III) and KV 22 (Amenhotep III) and the zigzag route of the fourth hour of the Amduat depicted around the entrances to these burial chambers was suggested by Roehrig, "Building Activities," 244, and Richter, "Amduat," 82–83, fig. 6, and 100.

[9] The bent axis and oval burial chambers also may represent the cyclical route of the sun, suggested by Dieter Arnold, "Architektur des mittleren Reiches," *Propyläen Kunstgeschichte* 15 (1975): 150–170, esp. 163; Winfried Barta, "Zur Stundenanordnung des Amduat in den ramessidischen Königsgräbern," *BiOr* 31 (1974): 197–201; and Richter, "Amduat," 79 and 80, figs. 3–4, who noted that this imagery is reinforced by the layout of the hours of the Amduat on the burial chamber walls of KV 34.

[10] Exemplified by the strategic placement of scenes in the room off the east side of Sety I's (KV 17) burial chamber with a combined message of solar and royal rebirth: the sixth and seventh hours of the sun's journey in the Amduat on the side walls and the king running with a rudder on one pillar face oriented out toward the sunken crypt, as discussed in Erik Hornung, *The Tomb of Pharaoh Seti I* (Zurich: Artemis Verlag, 1991), 25 and 242 (pl. 178, decoration now lost), 244–246 (pls. 180–182) and 250–252 (pls. 186–188); and Erik Hornung, "Studies on the Decoration of the Tomb of Seti I," in Richard H. Wilkinson (ed.), *Valley of the Sun Kings: New Explorations in the Tombs of the Pharaohs* (Tucson: University of Arizona Egyptian Expedition, 1995), 71. Note also the placement of the fourth hour of the Amduat at the entrance to the burial chambers in KV 34 and KV 22 cited above in note 8. Richter, "Amduat," 94 and 96, fig. 19, also observed a connection between the placement of the seventh hour of the Amduat above the entrance of the burial chamber in KV 35 (Amenhotep II) and scenes of smiting enemies on the exterior pylons of New Kingdom temples, both types of imagery protecting the sacred spaces within from chaos.

[11] For the placement of the hours of the Amduat according to ideal directions, see Hornung, *Ägyptische Unterweltsbücher*, passim. The directional notations on the burial chamber walls in Horemheb's tomb (KV 57) also determined the layout for the hours in the Book of Gates (Hornung, *Valley of the Kings*, 41 and 44, illustration). Hornung recognized that the throne of Osiris in the sixth hour was meant to be located on the ideal north wall of the burial chamber. In KV 57 the scene is placed on the back wall of the burial chamber, which, in this case, also is oriented toward cardinal north.

[12] For *p3 sṯ3-nṯr tpy n t3 wpt* see Černý, *Valley of the Kings*, 31–32. The text is O. Cairo 25269 (KV 9). The shorter versions *tpy n wpt* and *t3 wpt* appears in P. Turin 1923, verso (KV 9) and O. Demarée (KV 8 or 15), respectively. For O. Demarée, see R. J. Demarée, "Royal Riddles," in Robert J. Demarée, and Arthur Egberts (eds.), *Village Voices: Proceedings of the Symposium "Texts from Deir el-Medina and Their Interpretation," Leiden, May 31-June 1, 1991* (Leiden: Centre of Non-Western Studies, Leiden University, 1992), 15 and fig. 2.

[13] Hornung, *Tomb of Pharaoh Seti I*, 25 and 236–241 (pls. 172–177); and Hornung, *Valley of the Kings*, 78.

[14] For *n3 ẖmyw nty ḥtpw n3 nṯrw imntt im.w*, see Černý, *Valley of the Kings* (1973, 28). The referenced text is O. Cairo CG 25184 (KV 6). For the shortened version, *n3 ẖmyw*, see O. Cairo CG 25288 (unknown).

[15] Alexandre Piankoff and Erik Hornung, "Das Grab Amenophis III im Westtal der Könige," *MDAIK* 17 (1961): 124–125; and Richter, "Amduat," 101 and 103, fig. 27.

[16] For *t3 rsy im.f m r-ʿ* and *t3 st rsy ḥr wnmy*, see Černý, *Valley of the Kings*, 31. The referenced text is P. Turin 1885, recto.

[17] Wilkinson, "Paths of Re," 47.

[18] Wilkinson, "Symbolic Location," 85.

[19] Wilkinson, "Motif of the Path," 79–81, pl. 8a–b; Wilkinson, "Paths of Re," 48; Wilkinson, "Symbolic Location," 76, 83.

[20] Wilkinson, "Paths of Re", 48–49; Wilkinson, "Symbolic Location," 83–84; and Wilkinson, "Symbolic Orientation," 76–77, pl. I.

[21] Images of Nekhbet and Wadjet are juxtaposed on the door thicknesses of Sety I (KV 17), the corridor walls of Ramesses III (KV 11), and (possibly) on the burial chamber ceiling of Ramesses IV (KV 2). The "souls" of Nekhen and Pe also are contrasted on pillars in Sety I's burial chamber.

[22] Wilkinson "Paths of Re", 45, 48; Wilkinson, "Symbolic Location," 83, 84; and Wilkinson, "Symbolic Orientation," 78–79, pl. II.

[23] Onstine, "Relationship," 66–77, esp. 71–72; and Wilkinson, "Motif of the Path," 81–82, pl. IXa–b.

[24] Wilkinson, "Motif of the Path," 82–83, pl. Xa.

[25] Wilkinson, "Motif of the Path," 80, pl. VIIIb; Wilkinson, "Paths of Re," 48, 51; Wilkinson, "Symbolic Location," 85, 86; and Wilkinson, "Symbolic Orientation," 79–80.

[26] Wilkinson, "Paths of Re," 50, 51.

[27] Wilkinson, "Symbolic Location," 85; and Wilkinson, "Symbolic Orientation," 79.

[28] Wilkinson, "Motif of the Path," 83, Pl. Xb; Wilkinson, "Symbolic Location," 85, and Wilkinson, "Symbolic Orientation," 78–79, pl. III. For KV 6, see also Friedrich Abitz, "The Structure and Decoration in the Tomb of Ramesses IX," in Nicholas Reeves (ed.), *After Tutankhamun: Research and Excavations in the Royal Necropolis at Thebes* (London: Kegan Paul, 1992), 165–185, esp. 173, 175.

[29] Wilkinson, "Motif of the Path," 79; and Wilkinson, "Symbolic Orientation," 80.

The Western Valley of the Kings Project

Richard S. Harwood
University of Arizona Egyptian Expedition

Few living archaeologists are as familiar with the Western Valley of the Kings as Dr. Richard H. Wilkinson. Since 1989, the University of Arizona Egyptian Expedition has worked in and around the Valley of the Kings, and much of that work has been done in the western branch of that New Kingdom necropolis.

The ancient Egyptians associated the west with the setting sun and, by extension, with death and the afterlife. The west bank across the Nile from Thebes was ideal for a royal necropolis. The wide, flat plain stretching westward from the Nile provided excellent ground on which to build temples. The plain ends at the base of a long chain of mountains through which numerous ravines slice towering cliffs of limestone and provided secluded and seemingly safe areas to build tombs.

Geologically, the Theban hills are actually not mountains but rather the edge of the desert plateau, a line of steep cliffs formed some six million years ago when a river much larger and more powerful than the present Nile gouged out a vast canyon.[1] Frequent torrential cloudbursts sent floodwaters surging though cracks and over the cliff faces of the plateau with such force that they eventually cut through the limestone and carved out the giant valleys, ravines, and wadis seen today. The wadis are dry riverbeds through which floodwaters once flowed down to the Nile, the floor of the Valley of the Kings being one of the largest and certainly the most famous of them.

The great, long wadi of the Valley of the Kings cuts into the northern end of the Theban massif at the edge of the ancient Nile floodplain and runs northwest for about 3 km before bending to the south and southwest into the two branches of the Valley of the Kings, known in Arabic as *el-Wadyein,* "the Two Valleys." The eastern and more visited branch is known today as the *Wadi Biban el-Moluk,* the "Valley of the Doors of the Kings," because the gaping entrances to several of the tombs have stood open for many centuries. The western branch is known locally as the *Wadi el-Garud,* the "Valley of the Monkeys," named for the scene on the north wall of the tomb of Ay (WV 23) depicting the twelve baboon deities that protected the entrance to the underworld,[2] a scene famously found also in KV 62, the tomb of Tutankhamun.

The Western Valley, twice the size of the Eastern Valley, is by far the more impressive of the two wadis (Figure 1). Sheer rugged cliffs, pierced by hundreds of secluded clefts, tower above the narrow valley floor. The deep blue sky is achingly clear, with only an occasional raven soaring overhead. No sounds penetrate the desolation of the valley, and the solitude is almost overwhelming. The ancient goddess Meretseger presided over all of the Valley of the Kings, but nowhere is her name, "She Who Loves Silence,"[3] more appropriate than in the barren remoteness of the Western Valley. It is easy to imagine what the entire Valley of the Kings must have been like during the 3,000 years between the last royal burial and the onslaught of tourists in the early 1900s.

Figure 1: Entrance to the Western Valley of the Kings, with Richard Wilkinson on the path (Author)

The Western Valley itself has two separate branches. Shortly beyond the entrance to that valley, the smaller branch sweeps northwest, while the main branch continues southwest between the towering cliffs, becoming ever narrower until it ends in a natural amphitheater of sheer cliffs where once a waterfall cascaded over the plateau to the valley floor below. No tombs have yet been discovered in the northern spur of the Western Valley.

The size and remoteness of the *Wadi el-Garud* would certainly have made the area attractive as a royal necropolis, but those same attributes would also have made the valley very hard to guard and patrol. It may be for that reason that the Western Valley was utilized very sparingly by the ancient Egyptians. There are only three royal tombs and two non-royal tombs known to have been built in the Western Valley, and only two of those five were apparently ever used for original burials.

That is not to say that there was never any other activity in the Western Valley. There are a few pits and probable tomb-beginnings that have not yet been fully excavated,[4] and a number of ancient guard huts placed at strategic locations, as well as what appear to be living, administrative, and storage structures for the workmen who built the Western Valley tombs.[5] Roman pottery has been found in several of the tombs, indicating that the Western Valley was certainly visited and perhaps even inhabited during Roman and early Christian times.[6] However, there is no evidence of significant visitation after the early Christian period until two members of Napoleon Bonaparte's expedition explored the wadi in 1799.

The tomb of Amenhotep III (now designated WV 22 [also KV 22]) is the first royal tomb known to have been built in the Western Valley (Figure 2). Located about 2 km from the entrance into the Western Valley, the tomb was first recorded in August 1799 by Prosper Jollois and Edouard de Villiers du Terrage, two engineers who were members of Napoleon's Egyptian Expedition.[7] They explored the tomb superficially and prepared a plan that was subsequently included in the *Description de l'Égypte* in the early 1800s.

Over a century later, in February 1915, Howard Carter discovered five intact foundation deposits placed around the entrance of the tomb. Based on the inscribed cartouche plaques found in the foundation pits, Carter determined that the tomb had actually been started for Thutmose IV,[8] Amenhotep III's father, before Thutmose built and was buried in KV 43 in the eastern branch of the valley. Amenhotep III, who was no more than an early teenager when his father died,[9] completed and decorated the barely begun tomb and used it for his own burial some forty years later.

WV 22 is unusual in that the tomb has three separate burial chambers, two of which apparently were added later, deviating from the original design. Based on a number of items recovered in the tomb, the first additional burial chamber seems to have been built for Amenhotep III's chief wife, Queen Tiye. The second burial chamber presumably was intended for his daughter, Sitamun, who had been made a great royal wife at least by year 30 of her father's reign.[10]

Figure 2: Richard Wilkinson and guard in the Western Valley. The tomb of Amenhotep III (WV 22) is in the lower center (Author)

It is almost certain that Amenhotep III was buried in WV 22, although his mummy was found in KV 35 in 1898 as part of the second royal mummy cache, probably having been moved there when most of the royal burials in the Valley of the Kings were dismantled at the end of the New Kingdom. There is more uncertainty, however, whether either Queen Tiye or Sitamun were buried in WV 22. Based on some shabtis found in the tomb, Carter believed that Tiye had been buried in WV 22.[11] However, Queen Tiye survived Amenhotep III by at least eight years, and it is unlikely that the sanctity of her husband's sealed tomb would have been violated for her later burial.[12] Fragments of a red granite sarcophagus bearing Tiye's name were found in the royal tomb at el-Amarna, leading some Egyptologists to conclude that her original burial was there.[13] Edward Aryton, working for Theodore Davis in 1907, found in the unassigned tomb KV 55 a large, gilded, wooden shrine that had been made by Akhenaten for his mother, leading others to conclude that Tiye's original burial had been in that Theban tomb.[14] Wherever her original interment, Tiye's mummy was identified in 2010 as the "Elder Lady" from the royal mummy cache in KV 35,[15] confirming that Queen Tiye and Amenhotep III had been reunited since at least the end of the New Kingdom.[16] No evidence has yet been found with regard to the fate of Sitamun, who seems to have disappeared from the historical record after the death of her father.

The tomb of Amenhotep III was, in fact, entered and resealed several times in antiquity. When Carter examined the tomb in 1915, he found the remains of at least two intrusive burials from the Third Intermediate Period.[17] Having been open for at least the last two centuries of the current era, the tomb and its contents suffered substantial damage both from flooding and from visitors. Since 1989, a thorough clearance of WV 22 and the surrounding area has been conducted by Waseda University under the direction of Sakuji Yoshimura and Jiro Kondo.[18]

Part of the surrounding area cleared by the team from Waseda during the winters of 1993–1994 and 1994–1995 was a rough-cut rock tomb dug into the base of a cliff about 60 m south of Amenhotep III's tomb. Discovered by Carl Richard Lepsius in 1845, the tomb (now designated WV A) has a steep set of steps leading down to a single roughly cartouche-shaped chamber, rectangular on one end and rounded at the other. Long thought to have been the tomb of a high-ranking contemporary of Amenhotep III, it is now recognized to have been a magazine (storeroom) for some of the funerary equipment of that king.[19] The "tomb" was robbed in antiquity, but, interestingly, the thieves tore down only a portion of the unplastered stone wall that sealed the chamber from the steps leading down to it.

WV A is perhaps the only tomb in the entire Valley of the Kings that has most of its original sealing still intact.

The tomb of Amenhotep III (and the associated WV A) lies about two-thirds of the way down the southwestern branch of the Western Valley from the wadi's entrance. All of the other known tombs in the Western Valley are clustered near the far end of that branch, and little attention seems to have been paid to them until the summer of 1972 when Otto J. Schaden began the clearance of the tomb of Ay on behalf of the University of Minnesota.

Giovanni Belzoni had stumbled upon Ay's tomb (WV 23) quite by chance during his first exploration of the Western Valley in the winter of 1816.[20] The tomb lies at the very end of the Western Valley, about a kilometer from the tomb of Amenhotep III. There is no question that the tomb was decorated for Ay, but there is much more uncertainty about for whom the tomb was originally begun. One of Schaden's primary goals during his clearance of the tomb in 1972 was to locate foundation deposits at the entrance to the tomb that would answer that question, but no such deposits were found.[21]

Ay was unquestionably an important personage in the court of Akhenaten, and the tomb started for him at el-Amarna was to have been one of the largest in that city. Ay may have been a brother of Amenhotep III's great royal wife, Queen Tiye, and perhaps even the father of Nefertiti, making him both a great-uncle and collateral grandfather of Tutankhamun.[22] When Tutankhamun succeeded Akhenaten (perhaps after a short intervening reign by the mysterious Smenkhkare) and the royal court abandoned el-Amarna to return to Thebes, it is possible that a tomb (WV 23) was started for the young king in the Western Valley, where he would be interred in the remote area first selected by his grandfather.

If that scenario is correct, Tutankhamun's premature death occurred before much work had been done on his tomb, and the elderly Ay, as Tutankhamun's successor, had him buried instead in a nearly completed and hastily adapted nobleman's tomb (KV 62) in the eastern branch of Valley of the Kings. Ay himself ruled for only four years. Whether or not Ay continued to work on the tomb previously begun for his predecessor or actually began the construction of his own tomb is unknown. In either case, WV 23 was unfinished at the time of Ay's death.

During his cursory examination of the tomb in 1816, Belzoni found a badly damaged and lidless red granite sarcophagus in the burial chamber. In the late nineteenth century, the sarcophagus was taken to the Egyptian Museum in Cairo for restoration and display. During his clearance of the tomb in the summer of 1972,

Schaden found the intact lid of Ay's battered sarcophagus buried under a mound of debris in the burial chamber.[23] The lid and the sarcophagus box have now been reunited and can be seen in WV 23, the only tomb currently open to the public in the Western Valley.

Shortly after Ay's interment in WV 23, the tomb was entered with the objective of thorough desecration and, especially, of destroying the names and representations of the king. With the exceptions of one painting of Ay's *ka* on the west wall of the burial chamber and both of the king's cartouches on the top of the sarcophagus lid (which was found top-down on the floor of the burial chamber and seems to have resulted in the cartouches escaping notice), all depictions and cartouches of Ay on the walls, sarcophagus box, and funerary goods were totally defaced in an attempt to obliterate his memory (Figure 3).[24] Similar destruction was done systematically to the monuments of others intimately associated with the heretic king, Akhenaten. It is probable that this *damnatio memoriae* was conducted during the reign of, and on the orders of, Horemheb, Ay's successor.[25] Ay's mummy, if indeed it survived the *damnatio memoriae* and ancient tomb robberies, has not been identified.

The summer of 1972 was a busy field season for the University of Minnesota expedition. In addition to clearing the tomb of Ay, the team also cleared WV 25, one of the most enigmatic tombs in the entire Valley of the Kings. Located about 100 m east of Ay's tomb, WV 25 is an unfinished, undecorated tomb that consists only of a flight of rock-cut steps leading to two roughly hewn corridors beneath a sloping cliff on the south side of the Western Valley. Its design and proportions clearly indicate that it was intended as a royal tomb and dates to the later part of the Eighteenth Dynasty.[26] Yet, for some reason, the tomb was abandoned shortly after construction began and was never completed.

The tomb was discovered by Belzoni (Figure 4) in 1817, and his "battering ram" entry into the tomb has become legendary in the annals of Egyptology:

> Accordingly I set the men to work near a hundred yards from the tomb [of Ay] which I discovered the year before.... The next day we resumed our labour and in a few hours came to a well-built wall of stones of various sizes. The following day I caused a large pole to be brought and by means of another small piece of palm tree laid across the entrance, I made a machine not

unlike a battering ram. The walls resisted the blows of the Arabs for some time ... but they contrived to make a breach at last and in the same way the opening was enlarged.[27]

Figure 3: Painting of Ay from the west wall of his burial chamber, showing the *damnatio memoriae* done to his representation and the cartouche above his head (Author)

Figure 4: Giovanni Belzoni (1778–1823) discovered the tomb of King Ay (WV 23) and the enigmatic tomb WV 25 in the Western Valley (from G. Belzoni, *Narrative of the Operations and Recent Discoveries Within the Pyramids, Temples, Tombs and Excavations in Egypt and Nubia* [London: John Murray, 1820], frontispiece)

While the description of his entry may have been exaggerated to impress his readers, when Belzoni did enter the tomb he found eight mummies in painted coffins. These mummies and coffins have since been destroyed or lost, but based on Belzoni's detailed descriptions they were almost certainly intrusive burials from the Third Intermediate Period,[28] some 300 or more years after the construction of the tomb was abandoned. Neither Belzoni nor Schaden found any indication of the tomb's original owner.

Today WV 25 is presumed to have been started by Amenhotep IV, the son and successor of Amenhotep III, before he changed his name to Akhenaten in year 5 of his reign and moved his capital to the newly founded city of Akhetaten (modern Tell el-Amarna). The construction of the king's tomb in the Western Valley would have stopped abruptly when he moved to Akhetaten and began building a new royal family tomb there in which he was eventually interred.[29]

But without inscriptions or other tangible evidence, the attribution of WV 25 to Akhenaten could not be verified with certainty. In 1972, Schaden had "dug some holes around the entrance of WV 25 in a fruitless search for foundation deposits."[30] Since foundation deposits had been found in front of the tomb Amenhotep III, and WV 25 presumably had been started for that king's son, it seemed probable that foundation deposits had also been placed near the entrance to the latter tomb when its construction had begun. In the summers of 2000 and 2001, Richard Wilkinson conducted a more thorough search for those deposits.

Wilkinson had been a student of Otto Schaden at the University of Minnesota, where he received a master's degree in 1984 and a PhD in 1986 before joining the University of Arizona. After Schaden left Minnesota to join Wilkinson's recently established University of Arizona Egyptian Expedition in 1989, he and Wilkinson served as co-directors of the University of Arizona Egyptian Expedition's fieldwork. As sole director of the Expedition's work after 1995, Wilkinson conducted annual field seasons in and around the Valley of the Kings. Part of that work was a new project designed to search previously unexcavated areas with the goal of understanding nineteenth century archaeological endeavors in the area, as well as searching for tomb foundation deposits in areas that had not been previously dug, such as the slopes to the sides of the entrance to WV 25 (Figure 5).

Wilkinson found that the areas surrounding WV 25 had been badly disturbed by Belzoni when he searched for the tomb in 1817.[31] Despite Egyptology's indebtedness to Belzoni for his many discoveries and his industrious recording of what he found, the circus-strongman-turned-archaeologist from Padua, Italy, was

Figure 5: Richard Wilkinson in the entrance to tomb WV 25 (Author)

a man of his time. As such, Belzoni sought major discoveries and artifacts of intrinsic value rather than scientific and historical information that often come only from architectural features and seemingly mundane objects. In his quest for the former, Belzoni sometimes inadvertently destroyed the latter. Such proved to be the case with at least one foundation deposit at WV 25.

During the summer of 2000, Wilkinson's expedition excavated on the west side of the entrance and found only churned evidence of Belzoni's attempt to find the tomb.[32] The 2001 season, however, proved more productive. The area on the east side of the tomb was much less disturbed, and the remains of a foundation pit were located "in exactly the area one would expect a pit to have been dug."[33] Unfortunately, although relatively intact and still lined with fine, clean river sand, the foundation pit had been emptied of its contents.

The deposits—probably similar to those found by Carter at the tomb of Amenhotep III, consisting of calves' heads, miniature pottery vessels, model tools, and small faience cartouche plaques with the name of the king for whom the tomb had been started[34]—would have seemed worthless to Belzoni. It is likely that he gave the trinkets to his workmen or simply pitched them down the slope, where they may still be buried somewhere under mounds of debris accumulated from 3,000 years of flooding and more recent excavations. Nevertheless, the discovery of the foundation deposit pit has added to archaeologists' knowledge of such features and has helped date WV 25 to the later part of the Eighteenth Dynasty.

It is possible that additional foundation pits may still be discovered at WV 25. In front of that tomb and the neighboring WV 24 is a large area covered by the remains of workmen's stone huts (Figure 6). Although these huts have recently been excavated, additional work in the surrounding areas may reveal another foundation pit or other information that can shed more light on the original owner of WV 25.[35]

The other tomb to the immediate south of the workmen's huts and just 12 m west of WV 25 is an uninscribed and undecorated shaft tomb, the purpose of which can only be presumed. Open since sometime before the 1830s, WV 24 was essentially ignored until the summers of 1991 and 1992, when Schaden and Wilkinson cleared it for the University of Arizona Egyptian Expedition.

The tomb consists of a well-cut, rectangular shaft, at the bottom of which a large doorway leads into a single, unfinished chamber. Based on the extent of the work done on WV 24 and its neighboring WV 25, it appears that both tombs may have been started and abandoned at the same time. Both WV 24 and WV 25 date to the

Figure 6: The University of Arizona Egyptian Expedition's work at WV 25 in 2000. The tomb is in the lower right and the remains of the workmen's huts can be seen in front of the excavation area (Author)

Eighteenth Dynasty, and there is no evidence that either tomb was used for an original burial. These similarities have led Wilkinson and Schaden to suggest that WV 24 was intended either as a tomb for an important courtier of the owner of WV 25 (presumably Akhenaten) or as an ancillary storage chamber for WV 25, with the same relationship that WV A bears to Amenhotep III's tomb.[36]

As with WV 25 and the tomb of Amenhotep III, WV 24 was used after its abandonment for intrusive burials. Excavations have revealed a substantial amount of mummy wrappings and the human remains of at least five individuals, including one infant, all tentatively dated to the Third Intermediate Period.[37]

Wilkinson's University of Arizona Egyptian Expedition, now under the able direction of Pearce Paul Creasman since 2012, has not worked in the Western Valley of the Kings since completing its search for WV 25's foundation deposits. It is hoped that the Expedition will return at some time in the future to continue its work in that visually spectacular and historically relevant area of western Thebes.

NOTES

1. Bonnie M. Sampsell, *A Traveler's Guide to the Geology of Egypt* (Cairo: The American University in Cairo Press, 2003), 28–30
2. Richard H. Wilkinson, "The *Other* Valley of the Kings: Exploring the Western Branch of the Theban Royal Necropolis," *Kmt* 2.3 (1991): 51.
3. Richard H. Wilkinson, *The Complete Gods and Goddesses of Ancient Egypt* (London: Thames & Hudson, 2003), 224.
4. Three such features are found near the end of the southwestern branch of the Western Valley and are sometimes designated on maps as WV–I, –J, and –K.
5. Wilkinson, "*Other* Valley of the Kings," (1991), 52.
6. Wilkinson, "*Other* Valley of the Kings," 48.
7. Nicholas Reeves and Richard H. Wilkinson, *The Complete Valley of the Kings: Tombs and Treasures of Egypt's Greatest Pharaohs* (London: Thames and Hudson, 1996), 110; Jiro Kondo, "The Re-clearance of Tombs WV 22 and WV A in the Western Valley of the Kings," in Richard H. Wilkinson (ed.), *Valley of the Sun Kings: New Explorations in the Tombs of the Pharaohs* (Tucson: The University of Arizona Egyptian Expedition, 1995), 25.
8. Howard Carter and A.C. Mace, *The Discovery of the Tomb of Tutankhamen* (reprint, New York: Dover Publications, 1977), 79.
9. Aiden Dodson, *Monarchs of the Nile* (Cairo: The American University in Cairo Press, 1995), 89; Lawrence M. Berman, "Amenhotep and His Times," in Ariell P. Kozloff and Betsy M. Bryan (eds.), *Egypt's Dazzling Sun: Amenhotep III and His World* (Cleveland: Cleveland Museum of Art, 1992), 37.
10. Kondo, "Re-clearance," 30. Another daughter, Isis, was also given the title of great royal wife, but not until near the end of Amenhotep III's thirty-eight-year reign.
11. Carter and Mace, *Discovery*, 79.
12. Reeves and Wilkinson, *Complete Valley of the Kings*, 110. [But see Nozomu Kawai's contribution to this volume.—Ed.]
13. See, e.g., Reeves and Wilkinson, *Complete Valley of the Kings*, 110, 118.
14. See, e.g., Berman, "Amenhotep," 61.
15. Zahi Hawass et al., "Ancestry and Pathology in King Tutankhamun's Family," *Journal of the American Medical Association* 307.7 (2010): 638–647.
16. [See also Nozomu Kawai's contribution to this volume.—Ed.]
17. Wilkinson, "*Other* Valley of the Kings," 49.
18. [See also Nozomu Kawai's contribution to this volume.—Ed.]
19. Kondo, "Re-clearance," 30–31.
20. Giovanni Belzoni, *Narrative of the Operations and Recent Discoveries within the Pyramids, Temples Tombs, and Excavations, in Egypt and Nubia* (London: John

Murray, 1820), 124.

[21] Otto J. Schaden, "Clearance of the Tomb of King Ay (WV-23)," *JARCE* 21 (1984): 40, 43.

[22] Dodson, *Monarchs*, 112.

[23] Schaden, "Clearance," 48.

[24] Richard H. Wilkinson, "Controlled Damage: The Mechanics and Micro-History of the *Damnatio Memoriae* Carried Out in KV-23, the Tomb of Ay," *JEH* 4 (2011): 129–147.

[25] Schaden, "Clearance," 60–62.

[26] Reeves and Wilkinson, *Complete Valley of the Kings*, 116.

[27] Belzoni, *Narrative*, 124.

[28] Reeves and Wilkinson, *Complete Valley of the Kings*, 116–117; John Romer, *Valley of the Kings* (New York: Henry Holt and Company, 1981), 58.

[29] Donald B. Redford, *Akhenaten: The Heretic King* (Princeton: Princeton University Press, 1984), 193.

[30] Otto J. Schaden, "Preliminary Report on Clearance of WV24 in an Effort to Determine Its Relationship to Royal Tombs 23 and 25," *Kmt* 2.3 (1991): 56.

[31] Richard H. Wilkinson, "Finding What Belzoni Didn't Take," *BARCE* 181 (2001–2002): 16.

[32] Wilkinson, "Finding," 17.

[33] Richard H. Wilkinson, "The Identity of the Amarna-Age Tomb WV 25 in the Western Valley of the Kings," *The Ostracon: The Journal of the Egyptian Study Society* 13.1 (2002): 15.

[34] Kondo, "Re-clearance," 25.

[35] At time of press, publication (by Zahi Hawass) of an excavation of the huts was reported to be forthcoming in 2013.

[36] Reeves and Wilkinson, *Complete Valley of the Kings*, 182.

[37] Schaden, "Preliminary Report," 57.

The Tausret Temple Project

Danielle Phelps and Pearce Paul Creasman
University of Arizona

The current archaeological project of the University of Arizona Egyptian Expedition (UAEE) is the excavation, conservation and publication of the remains of the royal temple complex of Tausret, the last ruler of the Nineteenth Dynasty (Figure 1). Flinders Petrie briefly excavated portions of the temple in 1896; excavations by the UAEE have demonstrated that Petrie's work at the site was severely limited. In the past ten field seasons, numerous artifacts and inscriptions that indicate that the temple was much more complete than previously believed and, consequently, that Tausret reigned far longer than previously thought have been found. Re-excavation of the site has helped to understand aspects of Petrie's investigation and the successive occupations at the site, beginning in the New Kingdom.

Tausret[1] was the last ruler of the Egyptian empire in the Nineteenth Dynasty. Significantly, as a woman, she must have been quite powerful. Indeed, she was one of a very few women who ruled ancient Egypt independently. Initially, Tausret was the principal wife of Sety II, who was possibly the eldest son of Merenptah and therefore a grandson of Ramesses the Great. Tausret, whose parentage is not known

Figure 1: Tausret's Temple in 2012, composite image viewed from the northwest corner (P.P. Creasman)

with certainty, was most likely also a descendant of Ramesses II.[2] After Sety II's death, Tausret became regent for Sety II's young son, Siptah. Nearly completing the sixth year of his reign, the young pharaoh Siptah died and Tausret became the sole ruler of Egypt.[3]

Tausret reigned for at least eight years (including Siptah's six) and likely into a ninth or tenth year. She built a variety of monuments throughout Egypt, few of which have survived. Even before she became king, Tausret's tomb had been started in the Valley of the Kings—an exceedingly rare honor for a royal wife.[4] She was only the second female monarch to be buried there, the first being Hatshepsut, the great female pharaoh of the Eighteenth Dynasty. There is evidence of other monuments built by Tausret,[5] but her most substantial building project was her royal temple in western Thebes.

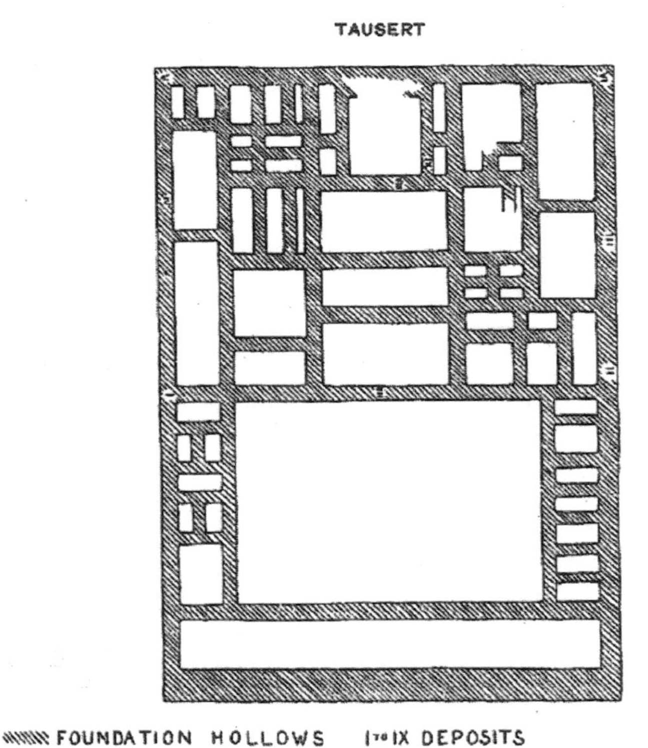

Figure 2: Petrie's original plan for the temple of Tausret; from Petrie, *Six Temples at Thebes. 1896* (London: Bernard Quaritch, 1897), pl. xxvi

Flinders Petrie, the British archaeologist, was one of the first to excavate in Egypt using an early version of the scientific method. Modern archaeologists owe much to Petrie's accomplishments, but his work was sometimes hurried and at times flawed. A prime example of such an excavation was his investigation into the temple of Tausret. He excavated at the site in 1896 and published a plan of the temple (Figure 2).[6] The foundation trenches and the presence of a few stone foundation blocks at the rear of the temple were all that Petrie identified as significant remains.[7]

Over a century later, in 2004, the University of Arizona Egyptian Expedition (UAEE), led by Richard H. Wilkinson (until 2012) and Pearce Paul Creasman (2012 to present), reexamined Tausret's "temple of millions of years" with new technologies and more extensive fieldwork. Thus far, the results indicate that Petrie's excavation were not as extensive as they have long been assumed. In their haste to find objects with intrinsic value, Petrie's workmen overlooked several key areas. Consequently, the map of the site published by Petrie did not accurately depict the remains of the temple but was more a supposition. Wilkinson initiated the Tausret Temple Project to develop a greater understanding of the history of not only the temple but also the reign of this queen.[8]

THE TEMPLE OF TAUSRET

On the western banks of the Nile near modern Luxor are at least twelve royal temples erected by and for individual pharaohs during the New Kingdom. Counterparts of tombs in the nearby hills, these structures on the west bank lie on the edge of the cultivation area and served a multitude of purposes, the most important of which was the worship of the king.[9] Egyptologists have previously considered these structures to be "mortuary temples,"[10] but the term is no longer deemed appropriate, as it does not fit their functions. The ancient Egyptians referred to the temples as "mansions of millions of years,"[11] a name that did not belong to any specific temple but emphasized the intended permanence of all such buildings.

The royal temple of Tausret is one of these "mansions of millions of years," also often termed "temples of millions of years." Tausret built it north of predecessor Merenptah's temple and, to construct the surrounding magazines (storehouses), often used mud bricks from that site and from the temple of Thutmose IV, found to the north of Tausret's site. It appears that Tausret used the inner temple structures of the Ramesseum as a template for the construction of her own temple.[12] While no temple walls or superstructures seem to have survived at the temple of Tausret, foundation trenches remain cut deep into the bedrock to support the massive foundation blocks, a few of which are in situ, especially in the northwest section of the temple.[13] As a result of Petrie's work and the paucity of visible remains, scholarly discussions of similar structures have seldom mentioned Tausret's temple, which is instead treated as a footnote to the better-preserved examples.[14]

PREVIOUS EXCAVATION AT THE TEMPLE OF TAUSRET

Prior to Petrie's excavation in 1896, the temple was little known historically.[15] Petrie dedicated less than three full pages to it in *Six Temples at Thebes*, published the following year. His single season of fieldwork, probably only a few weeks, revealed several remaining foundation stones and the foundation trenches. The trenches were cut into the gravel and marl strata and filled with clean alluvial sand.[16] Petrie concluded that the eight or nine foundation deposits (consisting of model tools, "glazed objects" [e.g., scarabs, plaques], and animal bones) "were the most valuable result attained here."[17] After his publication, the Egyptological community generally regarded the temple as a site with extremely limited, if any, further usefulness.[18] The site became known only as the remains of an unfinished temple nestled among the great royal "mansions of millions of years" on the west bank of Thebes.[19]

THE UNIVERSITY OF ARIZONA EGYPTIAN EXPEDITION EXCAVATION AT THE TEMPLE OF TAUSRET

In 2004, Egypt's Supreme Council of Antiquities granted the University of Arizona Egyptian Expedition permission to reexamine the site of Tausret's temple in order to clean, record, and publish any remains of its construction.[20] Richard Wilkinson chose the site as a result of a study of the historical data, publication of the previous excavation, and satellite imagery. The last indicated that the temple remains were more extensive than had been previously thought. The Tausret Temple Project thus formulated two objectives: to determine the extent of the previous excavation in 1896 and to uncover the full history and nature of the temple.[21]

The Tausret Temple Project began with the objective of verifying the original plan that Petrie published in 1897. In its first field season, the UAEE found that Petrie's plan did not match the archaeological evidence. Much of the area that Petrie had claimed to have excavated was in fact undisturbed.[22] Many of the foundation trenches and their adjoining surface areas (the floors of the temple rooms) showed no evidence of any archaeological investigation.[23] Over the course of ten field seasons to date, the UAEE has systematically reexamined and excavated the temple. The results indicate that Petrie's workmen had not thoroughly excavated many of the foundation trenches and a variety of artifacts and structural elements had been neglected in the publication of the site (Figure 3), but this was not atypical

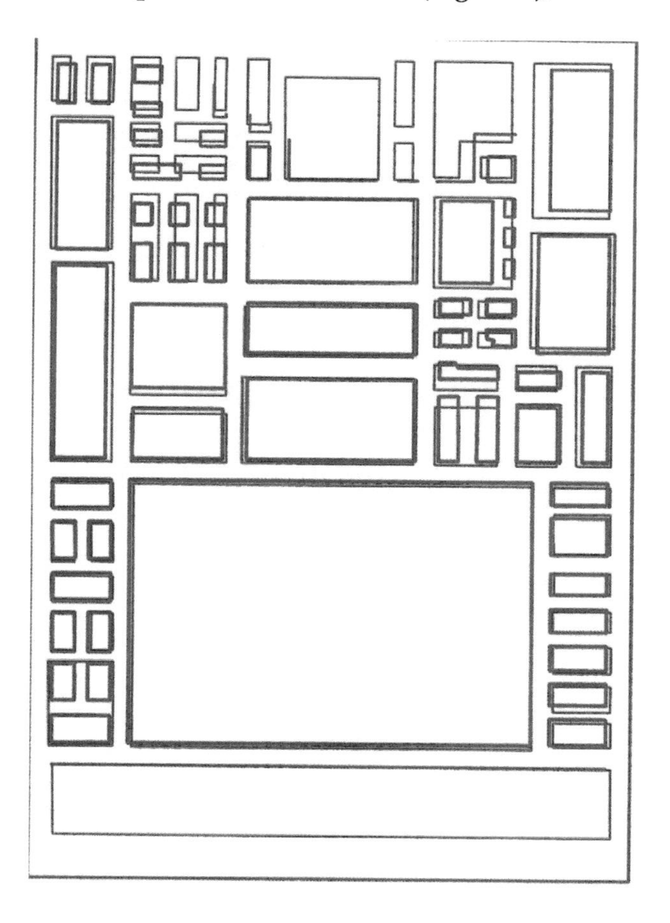

Figure 3: Overlay of plans of the temple of Tausret. The plan in red is Petrie's original. The one in blue is the map created by the UAEE. The right side of the plan faces north (R.H. Wilkinson and UAEE)

for the time and conditions in which they worked. It was, however, a much less thorough investigation than that given to other monuments excavated in the same era.

Artifacts

Within the unexcavated trenches, the UAEE found numerous small artifacts such as amulets, shabtis, ring fragments, decorated pottery sherds, pieces of statues, etc.[24] Typically, these artifacts were found in the vicinity of the larger foundation deposits. However, the priests had placed between the major foundation deposits small clusters of artifacts that Petrie did not record (Figure 4).[25] The clusters, which usually "consisted of a shabti, an ostracon or decorated shard, and a small fragment of a stela, cartonnage, or even linen,"[26] were located in the eastern section of the temple. The inner left quadrant of royal Theban temples has been identified as the "Osiris Suite" or the "Suite of the Royal Ancestors."[27] These clusters may have been viewed as either providing a symbolic connection with the cult of Osiris or as an offering to the ruler's ancestors.

The area with the highest distribution of artifacts was in the northwest section of the temple. These artifacts are unrelated to the New Kingdom use of the site and are most likely part of a plundered Late Period burial. (Petrie's summary publication notes several later intrusive burials at the site, dated to the Twenty-Third Dynasty to Twenty-Sixth Dynasty, appropriate for the UAEE finds.)[28] The artifacts ranged from disarticulated mummified human remains to small faience beads. All are from a funerary assemblage that would have accompanied a burial during the stated period. In total, over 3,000 artifacts have been recovered during the UAEE's excavations.

In addition to the small artifacts, several complete foundation stones were recovered, as noted above. Petrie indicated that "only a few stones of the foundation remained, between the deposits marked II and VIII" on his plan of the temple.[29] West of the area where Petrie found the blocks, the UAEE excavation uncovered additional large foundation stones with hieratic inscriptions.[30] These inscriptions in situ are among the project's most important discoveries to date. Two of the inscriptions date the construction of the foundation trenches to the eighth year of Tausret's reign (which consisted of six as co-regent with Siptah, and then two of her own). This date is significant because it provides evidence that Tausret ruled for a longer period of time than traditionally ascribed. Furthermore, since

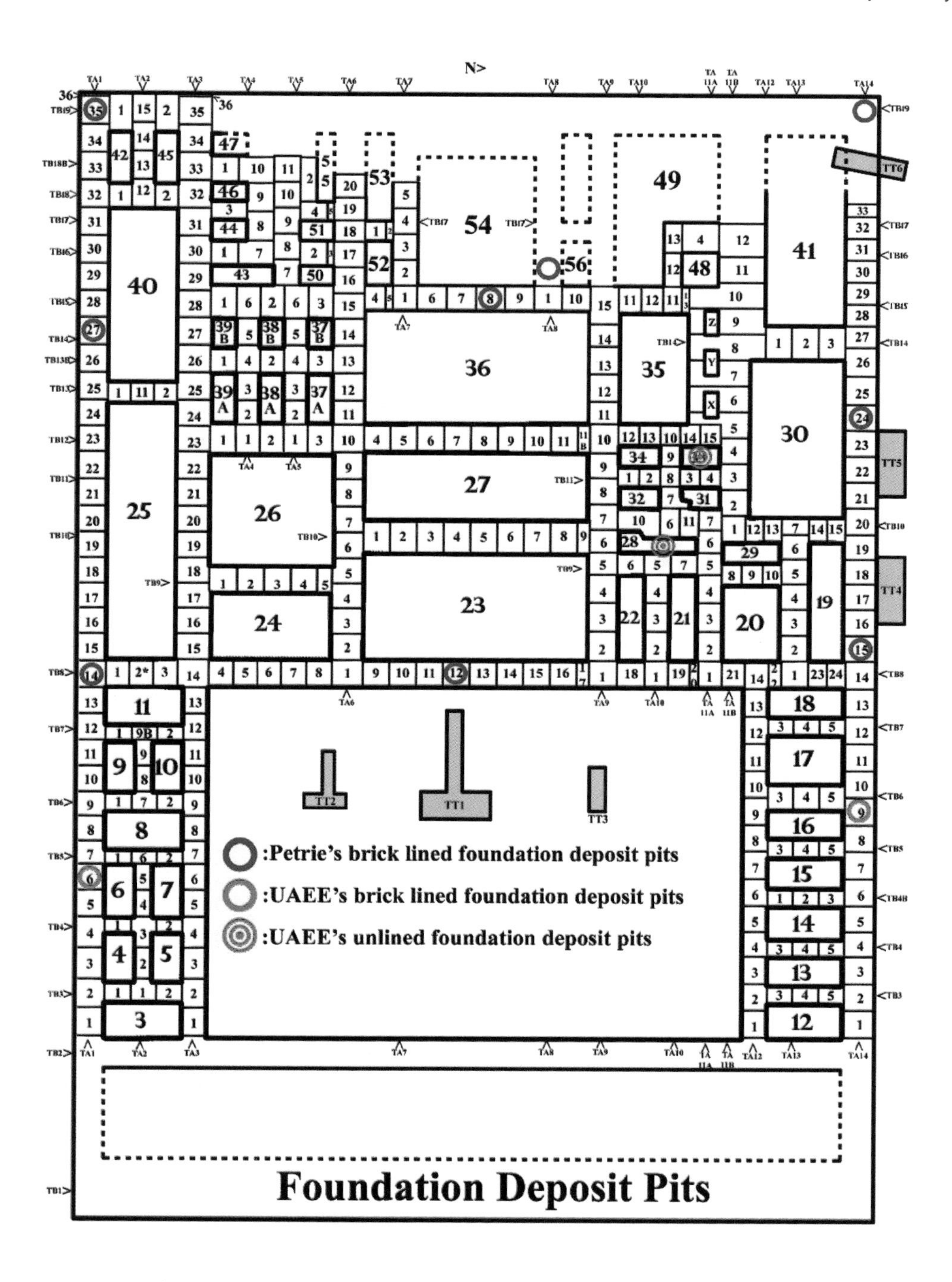

Figure 4: Foundation offering deposits pits found by Petrie (in blue) and by the UAEE excavation (in red) (R.H. Wilkinson and UAEE)

these were found in the foundation and the temple was likely near completion, it can extend Tausret's reign to a total of nine or perhaps even ten years to accommodate the time to complete construction.[31]

The foundation trenches contained two strata. Stratum I held pottery from the Late Period to the late Roman–Byzantine era. Imported pottery from Syria-Palestine was also found in Stratum I.[32] Stratum II, which became sealed during the construction of the temple during the late Nineteenth Dynasty, contained New Kingdom pottery and a few fragments of Mycenaean stirrup jars. Found throughout the site in both sealed and disturbed levels were fragments of blue-painted pottery (so-called Amarna ware).[33] The use of blue-painted pottery ranges in date from the time of Amenhotep II to the end of the Twentieth Dynasty. This type of pottery was utilized as part of the ritual offerings during the construction of the temple but does not seem to relate directly to the main foundation deposits.

Later Burials

Petrie noted the presence of some "later" tombs cut into the escarpment along the western edge of the temple, three of which he recorded. Petrie claimed to have found a few amulets and a set of canopic jars, which he dated to the Twenty-Third Dynasty, and other objects that could date as late as the late Twenty-Sixth.[34] The UAEE excavation revealed evidence of one such burial that probably dates to the Late Period (ca. Twenty-Sixth Dynasty) and is the current focus of excavation.[35] In the northwestern section of the temple, especially in the area surrounding UAEE's surface unit 41, excavation exposed a mud-brick wall and enclosure.[36] It was determined that the mud-brick wall, built over the destroyed New Kingdom surfaces but not in alignment with the temple, belonged to the outer court of a Late Period funerary chapel. In the fill surrounding this wall were the disarticulated and mummified remains of at least ten individuals. Assorted items from the funerary assemblage were also recovered. Wilkinson hypothesized that the burials had been robbed in antiquity. The robbers had brought the bodies out of the burial chamber, hacked them to pieces to retrieve jewelry and other adornments, and discarded the rest of the material in the sand and fill. The ceramics and other discernable fragments from the burial assemblage indicate that the tomb was occupied hundreds of years after the temple had been constructed and subsequently demolished.[37]

A ground-penetrating radar (GPR) survey was implemented in the summer of

2011 to map the western wall of the site in order to "define the size and extent of any archaeological features in the section," such as the presence of more Late Period burials.[38] The GPR results indicated the possibility of three separate subterranean features that correspond with piles of rock chips found on the surface in front of these features. Prior to its discovery, the Late Period burial found in the northwestern corner of the temple had a similar limestone-chip rock mound in front of it.[39]

History of a Temple

The UAEE's work has produced a more cohesive understanding of the stages of construction and the history of the temple and surrounding site. The Tausret Temple Project has revealed a more definitive view of the construction processes that the Egyptians used to found their stone temples, as few other such structures are in this state. It has long been assumed that Tausret had initially a small mud-brick structure built for herself.[40] Perhaps this reserved the space for her temple. Given that she had a tomb in the Valley of the Kings, its corresponding temple is expected. Not later than the eighth year of her reign, Tausret began construction of a grand temple. The small mud-brick structure, of which no clear direct evidence has been recovered, was probably enlarged and incorporated into the complex constructed of stone, or perhaps entirely replaced.

More evidence of the near completion of the temple was discovered by the UAEE when the temple floors were excavated. Here was discovered a mud and gypsum coating, known in Egyptian Arabic as *dekka*, used to smooth rough surfaces in the floor. It was applied after the initial construction and prior to the painted decoration that would have adorned the walls.[41] The presence of the *dekka*, part of the finishing process of the floor surface, may suggest that the walls and roof were already in place and the phases of heavy construction had been completed. The excavation also recovered numerous chips of building stone with the remains of white gypsum plaster remains, though only a few were decorated.[42] This further evidence that decoration of the plastered wall had begun, at least in sections of the temple, may suggest that the temple roof had also been put into place. At this stage, work ceased. The decoration was never completed and seems to have been limited to whitewash in preparation (Figure 5).

Later builders reused the temple's materials for their own projects. Evidence of the removal of the foundation stones was found along the damaged bedrock edges of the foundation trench, where stones had been pried out.[43] The general lack of decoration of Tausret's temple means that its foundation stones and building blocks are nearly impossible to identify among the those reused in later temples. It is not clear who began the demolition of Tausret's temple, but a reasonable case can be made for reuse by her immediate successor, Sethnakht. It would have been logical for him, as the founder of the new (Twentieth) dynasty, to try to discredit his predecessor and remove her monuments in an attempt to establish or confirm his own legitimacy. It is also possible that his son, Ramesses III, a prolific builder nearby, used the site for source material for his own monuments.

The Tausret Temple Project has achieved a greatly improved understanding of the history of the temple and, by extension, of the reign of Tausret. Re-excavation has also helped to better comprehend aspects of the earlier investigation of the site and its inevitable shortcomings, which were products of their time. Many of the

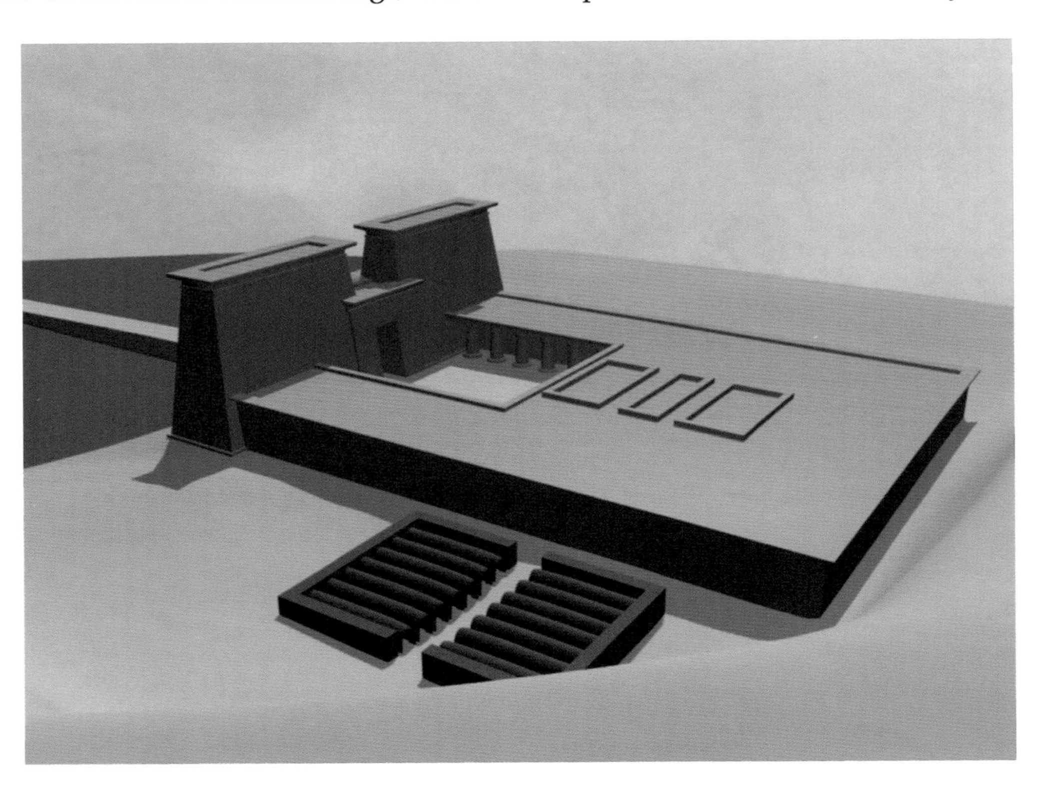

Figure 5: Plausible virtual rendering of Tausret's Temple viewed from northwest corner (A.S. Brewer and UAEE)

conclusions about Tausret and her reign, drawn from Petrie's observations of the site, require additional scrutiny. Tausret's royal temple was more advanced in its construction, most likely a stage in which decoration was being applied. The experience and results of the Tausret Temple Project thus underscore the need to re-examine past excavations.

Through its re-excavation, Tausret Temple Project has rewritten history by bringing back to light a forgotten queen who ruled as pharaoh. No longer only a shadowy figure who was mistaken for a king in the *Iliad*,[44] Tausret is now known to have been a female pharaoh who prospered and ruled for far longer than scholars have previously been able to document.

The history of Tausret's temple did not end with its demolition. Its later reuse as a burial site demonstrates that the ancient inhabitants of Egypt continued to consider the area to be of significance hundreds of years later. Through the hard and dedicated work of the University of Arizona Egyptian Expedition and the Tausret Temple Project, and thanks to the insight and leadership of Richard H. Wilkinson, her temple and the queen herself live again in the historical record.

NOTES

1. See Alan H. Gardiner, "The Tomb of Queen Twosre," *JEA* 40 (1954): 40–44 for more information about the alternate form of spelling of Tausret's name. Several transcriptions of the name have been used, including Tausret, Tawosret, and even Twosre.
2. Gae Callender, "Female Horus: The Life and Reign of Tausret," in Richard H. Wilkinson (ed.), *Tausret: Forgotten Queen and Pharaoh of Egypt* (Oxford: Oxford University Press, 2012), 28.
3. Callender, "Female Horus," 30, 35–36.
4. During the Nineteenth Dynasty, the majority of royal wives and daughters were buried in their own valley cemetery south of the Valley of the Kings. The construction of Tausret's tomb in the Valley of the Kings is unusual. For a more comprehensive look at Tausret's tomb, see Hartwig Altenmüller, "A Queen in a Valley of Kings: The Tomb of Tausret," in Richard H. Wilkinson (ed.), *Tausret: Forgotten Queen and Pharaoh of Egypt* (Oxford: Oxford University Press, 2012), 67–91.
5. A single limestone block found in Giza contained the remains of her name and an offering formula. Two monuments are known from the Delta area. A single block with Tausret's cartouche is known from the area around Tell el-Dab'a. From Qantir a gateway with inscription naming Tausret as the queen of Sety II has been recovered. See Callender, "Female Horus," 39–40.

6 W. M. F. Petrie, *Six Temples at Thebes. 1896* (London: Bernard Quaritch, 1897), 13–16, pls. xxii–xxiii, xxvi.

7 Petrie, *Six Temples*, 13.

8 Richard H. Wilkinson, "Introduction," in Richard H. Wilkinson (ed.), *The Temple of Tausret: The University of Arizona Egyptian Expedition Tausret Temple Project, 2004–2011* (Tucson: University of Arizona Egyptian Expedition, 2011), 1–2.

9 Nigel Strudwick and Helen Strudwick, *Thebes in Egypt* (London: British Museum Press, 1997), 72.

10 See Amelia Edwards, *A Thousand Miles Up the Nile* (2nd ed., London: Routledge and Sons, 1890 [1982]); Adolf Erman, *Die Welt am Nil: Bilder aus dem alten Ägypten* (Leipzig: J.C. Hinrichs, 1936); Gerhard Haeny, "New Kingdom 'Mortuary Temples' and 'Mansions of Millions of Years,'" in Bryon E. Shafter (ed.), *Temples of Ancient Egypt* (Ithaca, N.Y.: Cornell University Press, 1997), 88–126; Anne Macy Roth, "Hatshepsut's Mortuary temple at Deir el-Bahri," in Catherine H. Roehrig (ed.), *Hatshepsut: From Queen to Pharaoh* (New York: Metropolitan Museum of Art, 2005), 147–157.

11 Similar titular components are found in each west bank temple's name, such as the type of building, the king whom it represented, the temple identified as a part of the estate of Amun, and the location; see Harold H. Nelson, "The Identity of Amon-Re of United-with-Eternity," *JNES* 1 (1942): 127–155.

12 Petrie noticed similarities between Tausret's temple and Merenptah's (*Six Temples*, 13–14). University of Arizona Egyptian Expedition excavations have revealed that Tausret emulated the inner sanctuary not of this predecessor but rather of her grandfather and more illustrious ancestor, Ramesses the Great; see Richard H. Wilkinson, "The Temple of Tausret: Forgotten Monument of a Queen Who Ruled as Pharaoh," *Kmt* 23.3 (2012): 34–43.

13 Petrie, *Six Temples*, 13.

14 See Earl B. Smith, *Egyptian Architecture as Cultural Expression* (New York: American Life Foundation, 1938); Strudwick and Strudwick, *Thebes in Egypt*, 89.

15 Petrie, *Six Temples*, 13.

16 Teresa Moore, "Petrie's Excavation," in Richard H. Wilkinson (ed.), *The Temple of Tausret: The University of Arizona Egyptian Expedition Tausret Temple Project, 2004–2011* (Tucson: University of Arizona Egyptian Expedition, 2011), 8.

17 Petrie, *Six Temples*, 14.

18 Richard H. Wilkinson, "The 'Temple of Millions of Years' of Tausret," in Richard H. Wilkinson (ed.), *Tausret: Forgotten Queen and Pharaoh of Egypt*, (Oxford: Oxford University Press, 2012), 128 n. 4. PM II[1], 159 states only that Tausret's temple was destroyed.

19 As of late May, 2013, the Digital Egypt for Universities web page for the temple, http://www.digitalegypt.ucl.ac.uk/thebes/tausret/index.html, still says, "It can be assumed that the building was never finished and already stopped at an early state of construction." Cf. Wilkinson, "'Temple of Millions of Years,'" 128 n. 4.

[20] Wilkinson (ed.) *Temple of Tausret: The University of Arizona Egyptian Expedition Tausret Temple Project, 2004-2011* (Tucson: University of Arizona Egyptian Expedition, 2011).

[21] Wilkinson, "Temple of Tausret," 33.

[22] Petrie, *Six Temples*, 13, stated unequivocally that all of the temple's foundations had been cleared by his workers.

[23] Wilkinson, "Temple of Tausret," 36.

[24] Danielle O. Phelps, "Artifact Distribution," in Richard H. Wilkinson (ed.), *The Temple of Tausret: The University of Arizona Egyptian Expedition Tausret Temple Project, 2004–2011* (Tucson: University of Arizona Egyptian Expedition, 2011), 53–71.

[25] Richard H. Wilkinson, "The UAEE Expedition," in Richard H. Wilkinson (ed.), *The Temple of Tausret: The University of Arizona Egyptian Expedition Tausret Temple Project, 2004–2011* (Tucson: University of Arizona Egyptian Expedition, 2011), 46–47.

[26] Wilkinson, "UAEE Expedition," 47.

[27] Wilkinson, "UAEE Expedition," 46–47.

[28] Petrie, *Six Temples*, 18.

[29] Petrie, *Six Temples*, 13.

[30] See Robert J. Denmarée, "Hieratic Texts," in Richard H. Wilkinson (ed.), *The Temple of Tausret: The University of Arizona Egyptian Expedition Tausret Temple Project, 2004–2011* (Tucson: University of Arizona Egyptian Expedition, 2011), 121–130 for a thorough discussion of the hieratic inscriptions found on not only the foundation stones but also some of the ostraca recovered.

[31] Pearce Paul Creasman, "Excavations at Pharaoh-Queen Tausret's Temple of Millions of Years: 2012 Season," *JSSEA* (in press).

[32] See Rexine Hummel, "Pottery," in Richard H. Wilkinson (ed.), *The Temple of Tausret: The University of Arizona Egyptian Expedition Tausret Temple Project, 2004–2011* (Tucson: University of Arizona Egyptian Expedition, 2011), 72–120. Of importance is a Nubian bowl, which has no known parallel. Much of the imported pottery was found in the northwest quadrant and was most likely part of the funerary assemblage from the intrusive Late Period burials.

[33] Hummel, "Pottery," 94–100.

[34] Petrie, *Six Temples*, 18.

[35] Pearce Paul Creasman and Douglas Sassen, "Remote Sensing," in Richard H. Wilkinson (ed.), *The Temple of Tausret: The University of Arizona Egyptian Expedition Tausret Temple Project, 2004–2011* (Tucson: University of Arizona Egyptian Expedition, 2011), 153; excavations in 2013 have found clear evidence of additional burials at and around the site.

[36] Richard H. Wilkinson, "Tausret Temple Project: 2010-11 Season," *The Ostracon* 22 (2011): 7.

[37] Wilkinson, "'Temple of Millions of Years,'" 104.

[38] Creasman and Sassen, "Remote Sensing," 150.

[39] Wilkinson, "Temple of Tausret," 42–43.

40 Wilkinson, "'Temple of Millions of Years,'" 98–99.
41 Wilkinson, "'Temple of Millions of Years,'" 101.
42 Phelps, "Artifact Distribution," 66, map 5.
43 Wilkinson, "'Temple of Millions of Years,'" 103.
44 Wilkinson, "Temple of Tausret," 32.

Part III

Original Research Contributions in Honor of Richard H. Wilkinson

The Headless Statue of Queen Tausret from Madinet Nasr

Hussein Bassir
Grand Egyptian Museum, Giza, Egypt

A statue of Queen Tausret enthroned and its texts are for the first time published in full.

This photographic essay and catalog is dedicated to my great colleague, Richard H. Wilkinson. In addition to being supportive of what must have been hundreds of Egyptian students and scholars during his career, he has been personally supportive of my own work, for which I am thankful. Richard has been a pillar of the field for decades and I can think of no more appropriate place to publish the first complete recording with full set of color images of the "lost" statue of Tausret, the pharaoh he has academically resurrected (Figure 1).

PROVENANCE	Madinet Nasr (Nasr City), to the east of modern Cairo, in Area 7 (Seventh District), Al-Zohour Division (Division of Flowers).
DISCOVERY	The statue was discovered in 1971 by the late Egyptian Egyptologist Mr. Motawaa Belboush.
DATE	Nineteenth Dynasty, New Kingdom.
OWNER	Queen Tausret.

BIBLIOGRAPHY

Bakry, Hassan S. K. "The Discovery of a Statue of Queen Twosre (1202–1194? B.C.) at Madīnet Naṣr, Cairo." *Rivista degli Studi Orientali* 46 (1971): 17–26, pls. I–VIII.

Roehrig, Catharine H. "Forgotten Treasures: Tausret as Seen in Her Monuments." In Richard H. Wilkinson (ed.), *Tausret: Forgotten Queen and Pharaoh of Egypt*, 38 (fig. 2.3), 55–59, 56 (fig. 3.1), 121 n. 22–31 (Oxford: Oxford University Press, 2012).

Figure 1: Statue of Queen Tausret from Madinet Nasr, three-quarter view, left side (all figures courtesy Grand Egyptian Museum)

STATUE NUMBER Heliopolis (Matariyah and Ain Shams) number 346 in register book 1.

MATERIAL

Probably limestone, very close in form to marble. Bakry states that it is made of local sandstone,[1] while he mentions that the Red Mountain (*ḏw ḏšr*)/Al-Jebel Al-Ahmar area in which the statue was found was very famous for its red-brown quartzite sandstone (*biꜣt*).[2] Meanwhile, Roehrig assumes that it is made of quartzite.[3] However, it is not known exactly whether the statue was sculpted from local stone of the area or not.

MEASUREMENTS

a. Statue: Height, 133 cm; width, 95 cm.
b. Base: Length, 95 cm; width, 38 cm at the front and 46.5 cm at the back.

CURRENT LOCATION

After its discovery, the statue was first stored in the Matariyah and Ain Shams storeroom at the inspectorate location and then was moved to the storeroom of the Giza Pyramids area (Al-Haram storeroom) in 2011 after the January 25 Revolution to keep it in a safe location because of the lack of security and stability at that time. The statue is now located at the entrance of the Giza storeroom to the left-hand side of the visitor. In 2013 the statue was chosen by the Archaeological Selection Unit (ASU) of the Grand Egyptian Museum (GEM) at Giza for display there. It will be soon transported to the Grand Egyptian Museum magazines, to be exhibited at the GEM when it opens. It will probably be displayed in the New Kingdom Gallery or in the Kings and Queens Gallery, according to the exhibition GEM scenario and storyline.

BRIEF DESCRIPTION

This life-size statue (the seated figure of the queen is about 110 cm high) represents the late Nineteenth Dynasty queen Tausret sitting on a block throne

Figure 2: Statue of Queen Tausret from Madinet Nasr, front

Figure 3: Statue of Queen Tausret from Madinet Nasr, left side

Figure 4: Statue of Queen Tausret from Madinet Nasr, back

with a back pillar and wearing a long, heavily pleated garment (Figures 1–4), a typical feature of Nineteenth Dynasty sculpture, which abnormally does not reveal the outline the queen's legs at the sides and in the front. The head of the statue is lost, and there is damage at the upper right-hand side of the statue, the right thigh, top right angle of the block throne, and left side and back of the lower base. There is a severe cutting into the middle of the lower part of the statue. The calves of the queen are visible from the sides through the pleats, although there is a triangle panel at the front of her garment with heavy thick front folds of cloth and a strip hanging down from her belt over her knees; its fringe has approximately six uraeus-cobras, each with a sun disk on its head, hiding the queen's knees and lower legs from the front, a male characteristic in sculpture of the Nineteenth Dynasty.

Due to the absence of the head, the facial features of the queen remain unknown. The queen was probably wearing a *nemes* headcloth, because its lappets are easily seen on her shoulders, which are 36 cm wide. The youthful queen wears a 9-cm-wide broad collar around her neck (which measures 7.5 cm wide). She furthermore has sandals on her long, well-sculpted feet. There two deep holes in her right foot.

Her clothing hardly reveals the feminine beauty of the queen, so she is depicted with small breasts, clearly visible sunken navel, and slim hips. The sculptor probably represented Tausret wearing masculine attire as a king capable of ruling Egypt, not as a queen wearing feminine attire. The elegant queen leaves her ankles, left hand, and right forearm uncovered. She holds firmly the damaged *ḥḳꜣ* and *nḫꜣḫꜣ* scepters in her right hand and directs them toward her right shoulder, while putting her left hand on her left thigh (which measures 61 cm in length).

The statue has a base inscribed horizontally in sunken hieroglyphs on four sides. Moreover, there is a hieroglyphic line inscribed on the back pillar of the statue. The two sides and back of the block throne are covered by 2–3 vertical lines of hieroglyphs. The name of the queen is inscribed horizontally on her belt. There is a vertical hieroglyphic line inscribed on her skirt in the middle between her stomach and knees. A *smꜣ-tꜣwy* representation is portrayed on the two sides of the block throne of the queen to confirm the legitimization of Tausret as the powerful king of Egypt and the unifier of the Two Lands, especially in that time of political unrest. The inscriptions always address Tausret as a king in the masculine form, except for her *niswt-bity* names, which call her *sꜣt-rꜥ-mry-imn* and *tꜣ-wsrt-stp-n-mwt,* respectively.The statue was probably placed within a shrine of the goddess Hathor.

Figure 5: Inscription on the queen's belt (text A)

Figure 6: Inscription on the queen's garment (text B)

Figure 7: Inscription on the front of the base (texts C–D)

Figure 8: Inscriptions on the right side of the statue base (text C) and throne (text E)

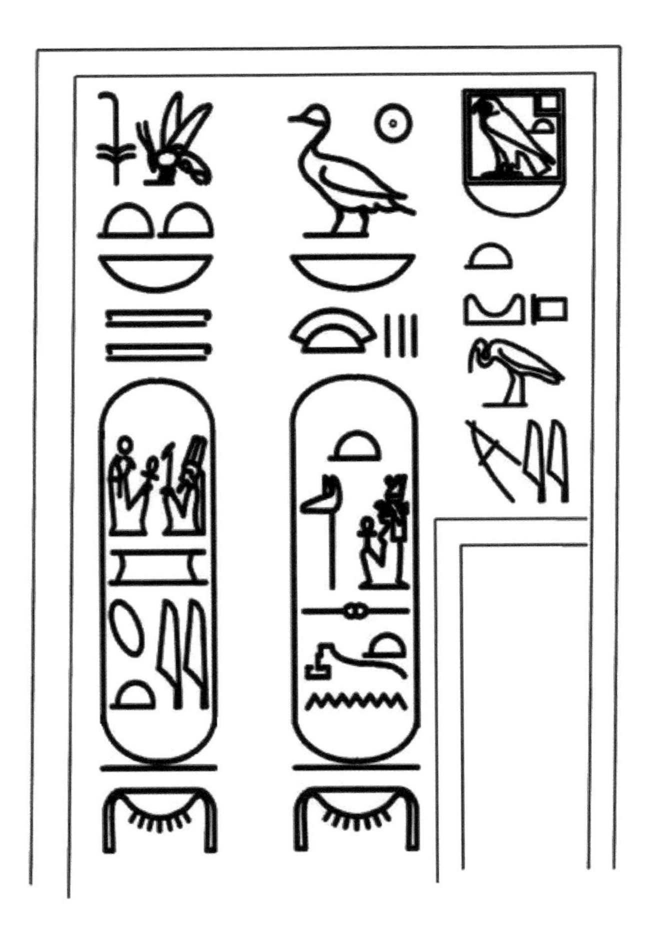

Figure 9: Inscriptions on the left side of the statue base (text D) and throne (text F)

TEXTS

A. Inscription on the belt (Figure 5):

s3t-rˁ-mry-imn

Satre-Meryamun[4]

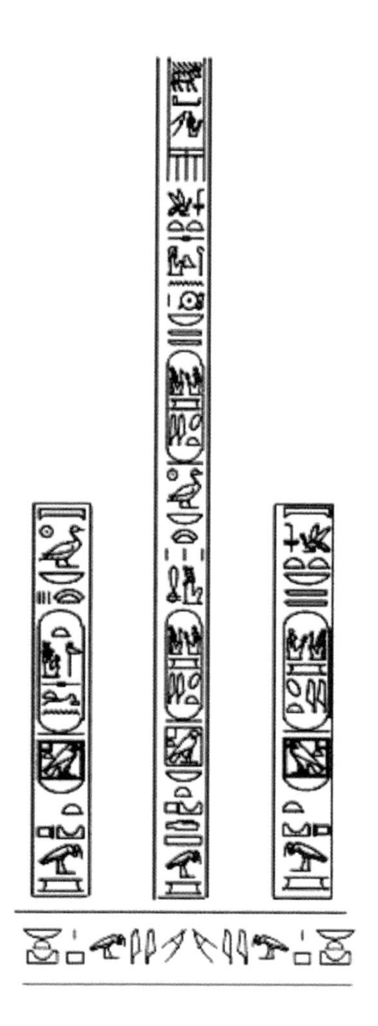

Figure 10: Inscriptions on the back of the statue base (texts C–D) and the back pillar (texts G–I)

B. Inscription on the garment (Figure 6):

niswt-bity nb tꜣwy (sꜣt-rꜥ-mry-imn) sꜣ-rꜥ nb ḫꜥw (tꜣ-wsrt-stpn-n-mwt) di [*ꜥnḫ?*]

King of Upper and Lower Egypt, Lord of the Two Lands, Satre-Meryamun, Son-of-Re, Lord of Diadems, Tausret-setepenmut, who gives [life?]…[5]

Figure 11: Inscription on the front of the base (texts C–D)

C. Inscription on the base, read from the center front leftward, to the back (Figures 7–8, 10–12):

> *ʿnḫ*[6] *ḥr kꜣ nḫt mry mꜣʿt nb ʿn m niswt mi itmw niswt-bity (sꜣt-rʿ-mry-imn) sꜣ-rʿ (tꜣ-wsrt-stp-n-mwt) mry ḥwt-ḥr nbt ḏw dšr*[7]
>
> May Horus, the strong bull beloved of Maat, live.[8] Beautiful lord as king like Atum, King of Upper and Lower Egypt, Satre-Meryamun, Son-of-Re, Tausret-setepenmut, beloved of Hathor, Mistress of the Red Mountain.

Figure 12: Inscriptions on the back of the statue base (texts C–D) and the bottom of the back pillar (texts G–I)

D. Inscription on base, read to the center front rightward, to the back (Figures 7, 9–12):

> *ꜥnḫ ḥr kꜣ nḫt mry mꜣꜥt nbty grg kmt wꜥf ḫꜣswt niswt-bity (sꜣt-rꜥ-mry-imn) sꜣ-rꜥ (tꜣ-wsrt-stp-n-mwt) mry ḥwt-ḥr nbt ḏw dšr*
>
> May Horus, the strong bull beloved of Maat, live. The Two Ladies: the one who founds Egypt and defeats the hill-countries,[9] King of Upper and Lower Egypt, Satre-Meryamun, Son-of-Re, Tausret-setepenmut, beloved of Hathor, Mistress of the Red Mountain.

E. Inscription on the right side of the block throne (Figure 8):

niswt-bity nb t3wy (s3t-rꜥ-mry-imn)
s3-rꜥ nb ḫꜥw (t3-wsrt-stp-n-mwt)
mry ḥwt-ḥr nbt ḏw dšr

King of Upper and Lower Egypt, Lord of the Two Lands, Satre-Meryamun,
Son-of-Re, Lord of Diadems, Tausret-setepenmut,
beloved of Hathor, Mistress of the Red Mountain.

F. Inscription on the left side of the block throne (Figures 9, 13):

niswt-bity nb t3wy (s3t-rꜥ-mry-imn)
s3-rꜥ nb ḫꜥw (t3-wsrt-stp-n-mwt)
mry ḥwt-ḥr nbt ḏw dšr

King of Upper and Lower Egypt, Lord of the Two Lands, Satre-Meryamun
Son-of-Re, Lord of Diadems, Tausret-setepenmut,
beloved of Hathor, Mistress of the Red Mountain.

G. Inscription on the back pillar (middle) (Figure 10):

k3 nḫt mry m3ꜥt niswt-bity sḫḳ3.n rꜥ nb t3wy s3t-rꜥ-mry-imn
s3-rꜥ nb ḫꜥw mi itmw s3t-rꜥ-mry-imn mry ḥwt-ḥr nbt ḏw dšr

[...] strong bull beloved of Maat, King of Upper and Lower Egypt, whom Re caused to ruler, Lord of the Two Lands, Satre-Meryamun, Son-of-Re, Lord of Diadems like Atum, Satre-Meryamun, beloved of Hathor, Mistress of the Red Mountain.

H. Inscription on the back pillar (right) (Figures 10, 14):

niswt-bity nb t3wy (s3t-rꜥ-mry-imn) mry ḥwt-ḥr nbt ḏw dšr

King of Upper and Lower Egypt, Lord of the Two Lands, Satre-Meryamun, beloved of Hathor, Mistress of the Red Mountain.

Figure 13: Inscriptions on the left side of the statue, throne (text F)

Figure 14: Inscription on the back pillar (upper portion of the right column) (text H)

I. Inscription on the back pillar (left) (Figure 10):

s3-rˁ nb ḫˁw (t3-wsrt-stp-n-mwt) mry ḥwt-ḥr nbt ḏw dšr

Son-of-Re, Lord of Diadems, Tausret-setepenmut, beloved of Hathor, Mistress of the Red Mountain.

Notes

1 Bakry, "Discovery," 17.
2 Bakry, "Discovery," 25.
3 Roehrig, "Forgotten Treasures," 58, 121 n. 27.
4 Lit.: "Daughter of Re, Beloved of Amun." This is Tausret's *niswt-bity* name.
5 It could be also translated "given [life]."
6 The *ˁnḫ* sign here has a double function and reads twice, for the two lines on the right and the left.
7 The text reads twice on the back base into two directions, to the right and the left, and the name of the goddess Hathor is written toward the end of the text on the right and left sides of the base to start the two texts on the back base.
8 Or "*Vive* Horus, Strong Bull Beloved of Maat."
9 Or "the foreign lands."

A Private Funerary Stela from the Excavation in Front of Karnak Temples

Mansour Boraik
Ministry of State for Antiquities, Luxor, Egypt

This article presents a funerary stela of New Kingdom date from the excavation carried out in front of the temples of Karnak by an Egyptian team directed by the author. Reused in the construction of a Roman Period bath, the stela features two scenes from funerary texts (the Amduat and Book of the Dead).

I dedicate this paper to Dr. Richard Wilkinson, who is one of the great scholars to work in Luxor. He has always been a great friend and supportive of our work there. Richard's work as the director of the University of Arizona Egyptian Expedition and mission at the temple of Tausret in Western Thebes has led to a deeper understanding of the history of that temple and of the reign of Queen Tausret. He has also enriched Egyptological literature with his books and publications, which have engraved his name in the history of Egyptology.

Description

Excavation in front of Karnak Temples revealed a great embankment of sandstone blocks, built to protect the temples from the danger of the river's annual flood (Figures 1 and 2).[1] It also brought to light two quays, the main location being to the south of the temple's tribune, with a secondary one to the north. Work there proved that the embankment does not form part of a basin such as that depicted in the tomb of Neferhotep (TT 49) from the New Kingdom. It may have functioned as a formal quayside in parallel to the stretch of embankment north and south of the first pylon tribune. Several staircases were built into the western face of the embankment, accompanied by many mooring loops (Figure 3) at different levels for embarkation of visitors' boats and ships. The embankment provided important clues as to the history of the river's location and level in ancient times.[2] That the Graeco-Roman structures found during excavations lack any erosion or evidence of flood confirms that the Nile has gradually migrated to the west subsequent to the completion of the embankment, where it remains to this day.

Figure 1: Artistic impression of Karnak West after the new excavations (all figures courtesy Ministry of State for Antiquities)

Figure 2: Artistic impression of the main quay of Karnak

Among the discoveries from late Roman times is a Roman bath (Figure 4) that was found north of the Ptolemaic bath discovered in 2007. The Roman bath covers 3,000 m^2, with many archaeological features having been discovered. Many blocks from the Pharaonic Period were discovered reused in the construction of this bath. Among the finds was the false door of Useramun, vizier during the reign of

Thutmose III, discovered at the bath's entrance.[3] The Roman bath complex was partially built over late Ptolemaic structures. Many mud-brick rooms were found adjacent to the north of the Roman bath and date this to the late Ptolemaic Period (Figure 8). A limestone stela, described below (Figures 9 and 10), was discovered inside one of the rooms. It was found with its inscribed surface facing down. Pottery and other artifacts found during excavation (Figures 5–7) date the bath to the third century CE and demonstrate the continued importance of the Karnak temples in the Roman Period.

DESCRIPTION OF THE STELA (FIGURES 9 AND 10)

The stela is of white limestone, with the following measurements: height, 51 cm; width, 27 cm; thickness, 10 cm. It is rectangular in shape and was prepared

Figure 3: The embankment found in front of Karnak

Figure 4: The area of the Roman bath

Figure 5: Amphoras found in the area of the Roman bath

Figure 6: Pottery from the third century CE

with incised borderlines at both sides and has a rounded top. The stela was cut from a reused block, as it has the remains of a sunk relief on its thickness showing part of two legs of a man wearing a short kilt. The stela itself was carved in three registers divided by two incised lines. The rounded upper part (lunette) is decorated in low sunk relief and depicts the sun god's boat with two oars at the stern. The scene also has two baboons praising the sun disk. According to Egyptian myth, the sun god in his barque knows his way through the darkness of night to his own rebirth in the morning, having done so since the beginning of time. This depiction represents the first hour of the Amduat.[4]

The first register has decoration and text relief with internal details. It shows the owner of the stela, wearing a long kilt, facing right as he burns incense, while behind him is another person, maybe his son, but unfortunately this part of the stela is badly damaged. In front of them, the god Osiris sits on his throne and holds with his left hand a *heka* scepter. Behind Osiris stands the goddess Maat; her right hand is missing but her left grasps an *ankh* symbol. She is followed by the god Anubis, who holds the *was scepter* with the right hand and *ankh* symbol with the left. Above this register is a text in a condition too bad to decipher entirely:

Wsr nb nḥḥ ////// wrt ʾInpw

The second register has a scene of six figures facing right, in an adoring position. The figures are two men and four women who most likely represent the family of the deceased. In front of the figures is a stand holding incense. The first man on the right raises his hands in adoration. He has a shaved head and is wearing a long kilt. He is followed by a second man, wearing the same kind of kilt. This man raises his right hand in adoration and holds a lotus flower in his left hand. The four women behind them wear long garments that cover their shoulders. They raise their right hands in adoration and hold lotus flowers in their left ones. The second woman wears a perfume cone on her head. The figures are mentioned by their names. Most likely they are offering in the presence of the deceased. The text above the figures is hard to read because it is just scratched into the stone and is preserved in a bad condition.

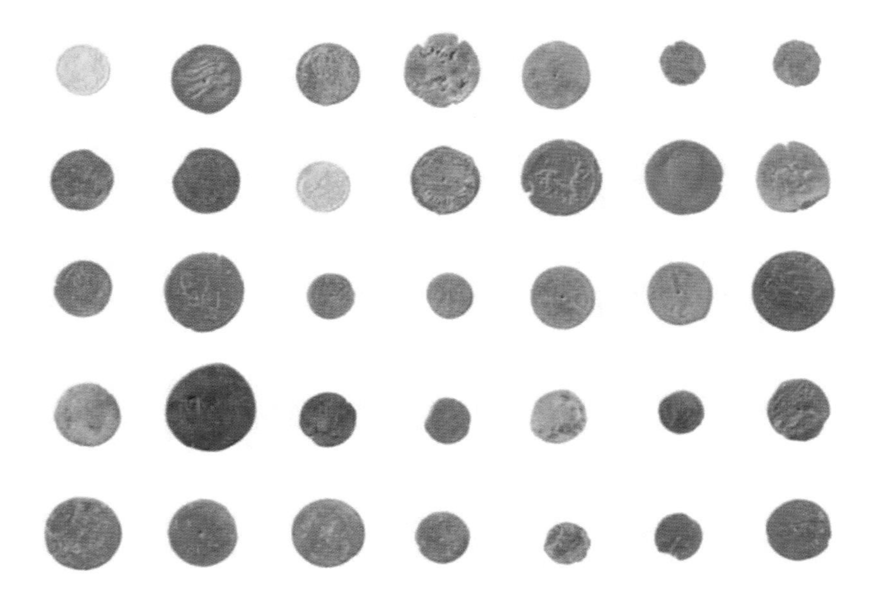

Figure 7: Roman Period coins

Figure 8: The Ptolemaic bath with embankment

The third register depicts the following (from right to left): two trees, from the second of which the goddess Nut appears, holding in her right hand a *hes* vase with purification water flowing toward four women. The first three women are represented kneeling, and the fourth at the end is standing. The lower part of this register is missing. The text above this scene is also damaged but has been deciphered as the following:

(above the two trees)
Nwt mis////// nṯrw nbt tꜢwy

(above the four women)
ḏd mdw in Wsr///// nbt pr ti3 b3kt Rʿ

(above the first woman)
ṯw///

This scene is chapter 57 of Book of the Dead, and it can be seen on the walls of many tombs in Western Thebes.

Date

The style of the stela and its design roughly indicate a New Kingdom date, evidenced by the clothes and religious scene. In addition, the workmanship is very poor, indicating the possibility of a late Ramesside Period date. During the Roman Period, the stela was relocated from the western Thebes to be used in the structures in front of Karnak temple.

Conclusion

Our excavation in front of the temples at Karnak has shed an important new light on the strategies used by the ancient Egyptians to protect one of the most important temples in history. The excavations have also presented new ideas about the west section from the embankment wall to the temple's first pylon and have revealed many archaeological remains from the Dynastic Period to the Byzantine Period.

Figure 9: Photograph of the Ramesside stela

Figure 10: Epigraphic drawing of the Ramesside stela

NOTES

1. I would like to give thanks those who shared in this excavation: Salah El-Masekh and Warda El-Nagar, and also to Ibrahim Soliman, director of Karnak Temples.
2. Mansour Boraik, "Excavation of the Quay and Embankment in front of Karnak Temples: Preliminary Report," *CdK* 13 (2010): 79–100.
3. Mansour Boraik, "A Granite False Door of Useramun," *Memnonia Cahier Supplementaire* 2 (2010): 181–191.
4. Theodor Abt and Erik Hornung, *Knowledge for the Afterlife: The Egyptian Amduat—A Quest for Immortality* (Zurich: Daimon Verlag, 2003), 24–27.

Some Observations on the Valley of the Kings in the Twentieth Dynasty

Edwin C. Brock
Royal Ontario Museum, Toronto

KV 19 is proposed as originally intended for Ramesses VIII. Several hitherto unnoticed details of KV 9 are explored: evidence of the original decorative program begun under Ramesses V remains; the height of the approach to corridor G has been altered; grooves scratched in the walls of upper corridors B, C, and D may not be iconoclastic. Finally, a correction is made regarding a now-lost graffito recorded by Champollion in that same tomb.

I wish to offer some observations concerning two Twentieth Dynasty tombs in the Valley of the Kings to my colleague Richard Wilkinson, whose interest in this site is well known. Some of these observations are based on material further elaborated upon here, namely KV 19, while the other contributions arose from my three seasons of work in KV 9 during my work with the ARCE-sponsored project to reconstruct the inner sarcophagus of Ramesses VI.

THE "LOST" TOMB OF RAMESSES VIII

The concept of "lost tombs" is admittedly a romantic image, conjuring fantasies of hidden treasures and adventurous explorers as dealt with by the popular view of archaeology depicted by the visual media. Indeed, there are still tombs in the Valley of the Kings whose ownership is either unidentified or uncertain, due to either the lack of textual evidence or the loss of archaeological remains. While between ten and fourteen tombs were known to ancient visitors to the Valley,[1] archaeological investigations in the first quarter of the nineteenth century, followed in the last decade of that century and the first quarter of the twentieth century, resulted in the identification of sixty-two tombs. Thanks to recent work in the Valley in the past three decades by various missions, numerous tombs have been re-examined, while in the past decade, two new tombs have been found (i.e., KV 63, KV 64).

Little is known of Ramesses VIII, one of the more shadowy rulers following Ramesses III.[2] His parentage can only be guessed at, based largely on his presence as a crown prince and later as king in the procession of princes inscribed on the west wall of the second courtyard in the temple of Ramesses III at Medinet Habu.[3] Few inscriptions, and even fewer monuments, of his survive.[4] There does not seem to be evidence of any proscription of his name from the few attested inscriptions that do mention him. The length of his reign is uncertain although likely less than two years.[5] The possible existence of a tomb for him has remained unattested, and it might be suggested that due to the ephemeral nature of his reign there was not time enough to construct one for him in the Valley of the Kings.

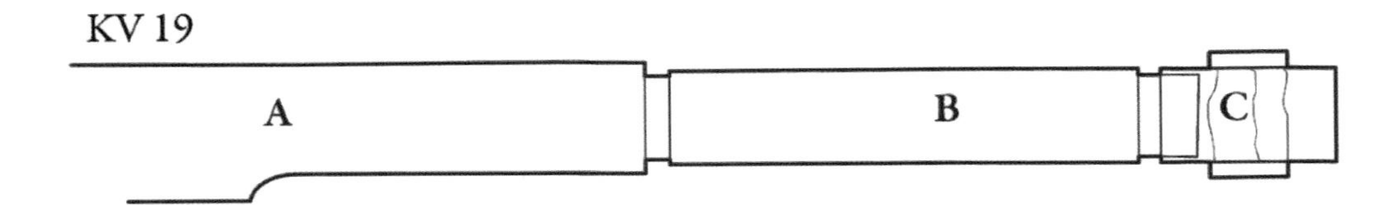

Figure 1: Simplified plan of KV 19, the tomb of Prince Ramesses-Montuherkhepeshef, after Theban Mapping Project, "KV 19 (Mentuherkhepeshef)," http://www.thebanmappingproject.com/sites/pdfs/kv19.pdf and Nicholas Reeves and Richard H. Wilkinson, *The Complete Valley of the Kings* (London: Thames and Hudson, 1996), 171

Evidence for one possible site for this tomb has always been visible but apparently little noticed.[6] Several years ago, while documenting tombs in a survey of the Valley of the Kings,[7] I chanced to note a significant detail in the dedication inscriptions painted on the entrance jambs of KV 19, the tomb of Prince Ramesses-Mentuherkhepeshef[8] (Figure 1). Each of these texts, sketched in red paint, appears as a single column on the north and south reveals of the entrance jambs,[9] framed on each side by a border of three vertical lines. They read: *dỉw m ḥsw nt ẖr nỉswt n ỉry pꜥt sꜣ nỉswt sš nỉswt ỉmy-r mšꜣ wr rꜥ msw s mntwḥr ḫpšf mꜣꜥ ḫrw* ("Given as a royal favor to the king's son, royal scribe, great overseer of the army Ramesses-Mentuherkhepeshef, true of voice"). The texts are not identical in orthography, either in the writing of the dedication formula or the prince's names and titles, probably influenced by space considerations and apparently being the work of two different artists. This is a phenomenon visible in the writing of the names and titles of the prince in corridor B as well, although possibly not by the same artists who sketched the original dedication texts on the entrance jambs. The example of the name on the north jamb appears more fully written (Figure 2a), with the squatting

Figure 2a: KV 19, B gate, north jamb, reveal, lower. Detail showing prince's name with original Seth animal. (E. C. Brock)

Figure 2b: **KV 19, B gate, south jamb, reveal, lower. Detail showing prince's name with original Seth animal. (E. C. Brock)**

figure of hawk-headed sun god (GSL C2)[10] holding a *wꜣs* scepter in the prefix "Ramesses" and the *ḫpš* sword (GSL T16) placed vertically behind the elements *mntwḥr*. All of these elements are placed above the horned viper glyph (GSL I9), with the seated figure determinative (GSL A51, but with a block throne) below the viper, followed by *mꜣʿ ḫrw* (GSL Aa11, P8, Y1, all written vertically). On the south jamb (Figure 2b), only the sun disk (GSL N5) is used for the first syllable of the "Ramesses" prefix, while the ox foreleg (GSL F24) is written for *ḫpš*, and *ḥr* is omitted, as is the epithet *mꜣʿ ḫrw*. In the two instances of the writing of the prince's name, the element *mntw* is shown as a squatting hawk-headed figure crowned with the disk and double plumes characteristic of that deity (GSL C10). Closer examination of these figures, however, shows them to be palimpsest, with traces of an earlier figure visible beneath. This earlier figure is the crouching Seth animal (GSL E20).[11] Note also in the original text that the group *ḫpš=f* was written farther to the right and redrawn slightly larger in the later version to better fill the space behind the Montu figure.

It is only here that any changes of the names of the tomb owner are visible. In all other examples in the tomb decoration (B gate thicknesses and corridor B), the name of the prince Ramesses-Mentuherkhepeshef appears without any traces of alteration, indicating that the decoration was carried out on behalf of this prince, a son of Ramesses IX, during that king's reign.[12] Additional dedication texts original to Mentuherkhepeshef occur at the beginning of the three-column inscription on the thickness of the south jamb of B gate and in the first corridor on the north wall behind the figure of Osiris, and on the south wall behind the figures of Ptah and Thoth.[13]

As with many of the royal tombs of the Twentieth Dynasty in the Valley of the Kings (e.g., KV 1, KV 2, KV 6, KV 9), the entrance to KV 19 is cut into the end of a rocky spur projecting from the east face of the cliffs that surround the valley.[14] The cutting of the tomb is unfinished, with work abandoned in the second corridor (C) beyond a pair of rectangular recesses cut into either wall just beyond the door jambs.[15] These two recesses are an important architectural detail, however, as they are found only in kings' tombs of the Twentieth Dynasty, not in those of queens, princes, or princesses.[16] They represent the final vestige of what began in royal tombs of the early to mid-Eighteenth Dynasty as a chamber (C) with a descending stairway cut into the floor. Examples, in chronological order, are seen in KV 20, KV 38, KV 35, KV 42, KV 34, and KV 35, and are designated as chamber C, following the system of Elizabeth Thomas[17] and subsequently the Theban Mapping Project.[18] Later in the Eighteenth Dynasty, from the reign of Thutmose IV (KV 43) onward, this feature developed into attenuated recesses, trapezoidal in profile, decreasing in size over time, a trend continuing into the Nineteenth Dynasty as far as the reign of Amenmesse (KV 10).[19] In royal tombs from the reign of Sethnakht and Ramesses III onward (KV 11, KV 2, KV 9, KV 1, KV 6, KV 18), it appears as a rectangular niche at the beginning of the second corridor (C).

Thomas indicated that the dimensions of the KV 19 tomb entrance and completed corridor and associated gates reflect the development of royal tomb construction at this period and are within the parameters of similar architectural features in other royal tombs immediately preceding and following this one.[20] The dimensions for the first corridor (B) and first and second gates (B, C), as well as C corridor niches for mid- to late Twentieth Dynasty royal tombs in the Valley of the Kings, in chronological order, are presented in Table 1.[21]

	KV 2	KV 9	KV 1	KV 19	KV 6
A entry width	3.66 m	3.65 m	3.69 m	3.69 m	3.76 m
B gate height	3.6 m	3.6 m	3.99 m	3.8 m	4.62 m
B gate width	2.78 m	2.76 m	2.81 m	2.81 m	2.70 m
B corridor height	4.23 m	3.84 m	4.04 m	3.77 m	4.47 m
B corridor width	3.16 m	3.17 m	3.17 m	3.14 m	3.22 m
B corridor length	15.17 m	14.014 m	15.28 m	15.3 m	15.33 m
C gate height	3.86 m	3.49 m	(J) 3.69 m	3.43 m	3.92 m
C gate width	2.72 m	2.81 m	—	3.74 m	2.76 m
C corridor height	4.23 m	3.65 m	(J) 3.94 m (original)	3.6 m	4.11 m
C corridor width	3.15 m	3.18 m	(J) 3.14 m (original)	3.14 m	3.22 m
C recesses height	1.65 m	1.06 m	—	1.05 m	1.06 m
C recesses length	2.64 m	2.58 m	—	2.52 m	2.62 m
C recesses depth	0.52 m	0.52 m	—	0.53 m	0.54 m

Table 1: Dimensions for the first corridor (B) and first and second gates (B, C), and C (J) corridor niches for mid- to late Twentieth Dynasty royal tombs in the Valley of the Kings

The only other prince's tomb of the Twentieth Dynasty identified in the Valley of the Kings is KV 3, belonging to an unidentified son of Ramesses III.[22] The dimensions of the corresponding gates and corridor are smaller than in KV 19 (B gate: height, 2.61 m; width, 2.13 m; B corridor: height, 3.13 m; width, 2.73 m; length, 9.72 m; C [F] gate: height, 2.8 m; width, 2.12 m).

Thus, the original dedicatee for KV 19 was the prince Ramesses-Sethherkhepeshef, apparently for whom another tomb was also cut and decorated in the Valley of the Queens (QV 43).[23] It is usually accepted that these two are the same individual, one of the sons depicted and named in the Medinet Habu procession of princes. At least one scholar, however, believes that there were two princes bearing this name; one, the owner of KV 19, was the son of the owner of QV 43.[24]

Some questions are raised by this reconstruction of usage of the tomb. If KV 19 was started for Prince Sethherkhepeshef as a royal favor, who, then, was the king who provided this tomb? From chronological considerations, likely candidates are either Ramesses VI or Ramesses VII. At first, the latter might seem the stronger candidate for the role of donor, especially given the Louvre ostracon 497, dated to that king and bearing a dedication formula to a "son whom he loves, great overseer of the army ('generalisimo') first king's son of his majesty, Ramesses, true of voice" on its verso.[25] It should be pointed out, however, that the figure of the king on the verso, possibly an artist's sketch for scenes in KV 1, is not original to the ostracon. The image of the king on the verso is painted in red over the three faded columns of text bearing the dedication formula. Note that the paleography of the glyphs in black on the verso text is similar to the glyphs sketched in red on the entry jambs of KV 19. This ostracon appears to be the principal evidence for positing a son ("Ramesses D") of Ramesses VII, who predeceased him, but given the observed disassociation of the text and figures, this evidence is less compelling.[26]

After the tomb was taken over for the use of Prince Mentuherkhepeshef in the reign of Ramesses IX, was that prince actually buried in this unfinished sepulchre? The modest pit cut into the floor once covered with limestone slabs[27] seems unworthy of the prince, particularly when compared to the sarcophagi provided for Twentieth Dynasty queens and princes both in the Valley of the Queens and this valley as well.[28]

Finally, the vexing question that opened this discussion—where ultimately, was Ramesses VIII buried at the end of his apparently brief reign?—remains unanswered. While it tentatively had been suggested that KV 6 may have been begun by Ramesses VIII,[29] it seems most unlikely that a second tomb would have been started when a well-advanced commencement for this king already existed. Ultimately, like the instances of Ramesses X and Ramesses XI, it may be that Ramesses VIII never was buried in the Valley of the Kings. If a burial had been made, it might have been in Per-Ramesses,[30] although as yet no evidence from of royal burials at this site has been adduced.

Observations on Some Decorative and Architectural Alterations to KV 9

As stated before, during my work on the reconstruction of the inner sarcophagus of Ramesses VI, I had the opportunity to closely examine various details of the decoration and architectural details of this tomb. It has long been recognized that the decoration of KV 9 (Figure 3), begun during the reign of Ramesses V, was altered when Ramesses VI took over the tomb, following the untimely death of his nephew.[31] The recognized extent of these changes included alterations of the cartouches where they were inscribed on the door jambs of the entry and the first five corridors. In addition, Abitz has noted some significant thematic decorative changes, such as on the rear wall right of the doorway from chamber E to pillared hall F, where traces of an *iwn-mwt-f* priest could be discerned under the later plaster bearing texts of the Book of Caverns.[32] In royal tombs of the previous dynasty, beginning with KV 8 (the tomb of Merenptah), Anubis and the *iwn-mwt-f* priest were depicted here.[33] This was changed in the subsequent reigns to two figures of the priest, placed on either side of the exit wall of this chamber, the so-called shaft chamber (although, as with all royal tombs from KV 10 onward, with the exception of KV 11, no shaft was ever cut here).[34] Abitz was uncertain of traces of a companion figure to the left of the door,[35] but now these are clearly discernible where plaster has fallen away. Here, beneath plaster bearing the ninth and tenth gates of the Book of Gates, are the forward leg of the priest and the extended leopard paw held in the priest's hand (Figure 4). Additional unnoticed instances of alteration of the decorative program now are visible on the inner thicknesses of the succeeding gate (F), again where the later plaster has fallen away. In the lower portion of the south and north inner thicknesses a rectangular shrine with cavetto cornice is evident (Figure 5).[36] Comparison with Piankoff's photographs indicates that this loss of plaster postdates the 1954 publication of the tomb.[37]

Evidence of another unremarked significant change of the decorative program can be seen in the first corridor (B) on the south side, where the initial scene of the

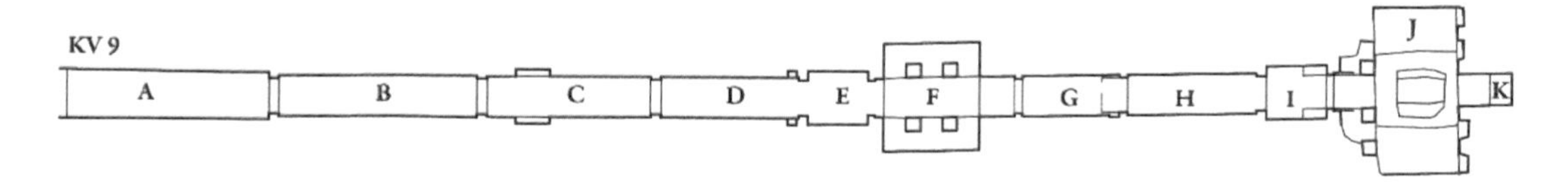

Figure 3: Simplified plan of KV 9, the tomb of Ramesses V and Ramesses VI, after Theban Mapping Project, "KV 9 (Ramesses VI and Ramesses VI)," http://www.thebanmappingproject.com/sites/pdfs/kv09.pdf and Nicholas Reeves and Richard H. Wilkinson, *The Complete Valley of the Kings* (London: Thames and Hudson, 1996), 164

Figure 4: KV 9, E west wall, south half. Detail showing traces of original figure of priest, with leopard's paw and forward leg. (E. C. Brock)

Figure 5: KV 9, F gate, north jamb, inner thickness. Detail showing traces of original image of shrine. (E. C. Brock)

Book of Gates is shown, depicting the sun god passing through the western horizon into the underworld.[38] Close examination of the lower register of this part of the scene, however, reveals the remains of an earlier decorative program where the later plaster of Ramesses VI has fallen away. What is revealed are elements of the opening vignette of the Litany of Re, found in this location in previous Ramesside tombs of the Nineteenth and Twentieth Dynasties, from the tomb of Sety I (KV 17) onward.[39] The visible element of this opening vignette of the Litany includes the foreleg of a crocodile between the heads of the first and second standing figures in the bottom register and the ear and horns that form the head of an antelope between the third and fourth standing figures in the bottom register[40] (Figure 6). This would suggest the possibility that the original decorative program of the tomb under Ramesses V followed the tradition of the Nineteenth and early Twentieth Dynasties of including the Litany of Re in the first two corridors. It is not possible to know how much of this composition was inscribed on the walls of the first two corridors of this tomb, since no other traces are visible beneath the plaster bearing the later phase of decoration under Ramesses VI, namely the Book of Gates on the south wall and the Book of Caverns on the north. This change in decorative program for royal tombs can be seen to coincide with the "usurpation" of the tomb by Ramesses VI, briefly giving prominence to the Books of Gates and Caverns, here completely rendered for the first time since the decoration by Merenptah of the entrance passage of the Osireion at Abydos.[41]

The second alteration that I wish to discuss concerns some hitherto unnoted architectural alterations in the approach to corridor G, the corridor following the

Figure 6: KV 9, B corridor, south wall. Detail showing traces of original opening vignette of the Litany of Ra, with crocodile foreleg and antelope head. (E.C. Brock)

descent in the first pillared hall F. The soffit (underside) of the "overhang" before gate G, near the floor level of hall F, is not horizontal but exhibits a surface that slopes down from front to rear. The decorated surface of the end of the descent that passes beneath the soffit until the G gate displays three vultures flying toward the tomb entrance (east).[42] This surface was all originally horizontal from its front edge to the lintel of gate G. Although much of the plaster on which the first vulture was painted was lost, enough remains at the wingtips to show that it was executed in a cruder style than the other two vultures farther in, and the plaster on this sloping surface itself is rougher. The overall impression is that this sloping surface was cut, plastered and painted sometime after the remainder of the soffit had been decorated.[43] At the front edges of this sloping surface, at least 0.25 m of the original surface has been cut away (Figure 7). In fact, toward the center of the soffit even more of the stone has been lost, perhaps from rock fall, as shown in earlier photographs made before Egyptian conservation efforts in the last decade of the last century filled this area in. This is readily visible in Piankoff's view of the central part of the rear (west) wall of F, showing loss of the bottom of the double image of Osiris enthroned in a shrine.[44]

Figure 7: KV 9, F descent, overhang. Detail showing cut back at south end of soffit. (E. C. Brock)

Figure 8: KV 9, F descent, north side. View showing rough cutting to lower surface of descent ramp. (E. C. Brock)

The sloping floor of this passage leading into corridor G also has been cut lower, as seen by the rough surface of the bottom of the walls on either side (Figure 8). As a result, the height of this passage has been increased by 0.45 m from its original height of 3.2 m. This raises the question of why this alteration was needed. Unlike alterations in the widths of gates of the passageways of tombs to accommodate the introduction of sarcophagi, as for example in the tombs of Thutmose IV (KV 43) and Merenptah (KV 8), to allow for an unexpected increase in width of the sarcophagus, this was not the case in KV 9. The fragmentary state of the outer sarcophagus box makes estimates of its original height difficult, although the box floor is nearly 1 m thick. The maximum height of the reconstructed inner box and lid is 1.85 m, meaning the minimum height of the outer box likely would have been 2.85 m and thus unlikely to have been so great as to necessitate the additional height created by the noted alterations in the approach to corridor G. In fact, ramps have been cut into the floors at the ends of the upper corridors (B–E) in order to increase the distance below the soffits of the gates (also present at the ends of G and H corridors).

A possible explanation may be found at the entrance to the tomb of Tutankhamun (KV 62). The soffit of the entrance lintel also exhibits a cut-back sloping down from the front to the rear, increasing the height to 2.06 m above the bottom entry step and 1.91 m at the far end to the floor. Measuring from the soffit to the entry steps, perpendicular to the plane of the slope, however, gives a distance of approximately 1.7 m. Using the same mode of measuring perpendicular to the planes of the floor and ceiling of corridor B gives a distance of approximately 1.81 m (instead of the vertical distance of 1.98 m). Note that there has been no similar cutting down of the floor of the entrance, but the height of corridor is 1.98 m, and the height of the entry into the antechamber is 1.97 m. Such a cutting might have been needed to allow introduction of the panels of the shrines that surrounded the sarcophagus. The shrines were made in sections, and the height of the outermost shrine panels (exclusive of cornice, roof, and dado elements) are 1.67 m high.[45] There might be a possibility that shrines also surrounded the sarcophagus of Ramesses VI, as seems to have been done in the tomb of Ramesses IV (KV 2) as the Turin papyrus depicts a group of shrines surrounding the sarcophagus.[46] If this was so, it might account for the cutting of the soffit and descent ramp to allow passage of shrine panels into the lower corridors leading to the burial chamber.

Another unremarked alteration to the decoration of the tomb also may be noted on the walls of the upper corridors, C and D (Figure 9). This takes the form of parallel vertical grooves cut into the decorated and inscribed plaster surfaces. These grooves do not appear to be the work of iconoclastic efforts by Coptic anchorites inhabiting the tomb. The iconoclastic destruction of figures is often characterized by damage that suggests an attempt to "disempower" the images by attacking the head or eyes and mouth, the arms and hands, legs and feet, and the genital area. The time period of these attacks are harder to identify, as they could also predate Christian reuse of the tombs. There seems to be an awareness demonstrated of the perceived spiritual power or "*baraka*" inherent in the images and texts. The gouging of the vertical grooves, however, seems less an effort at iconoclasm but still may indicate an awareness of spiritual power residing in the "sacred texts." A similar phenomenon is visible on the walls of Theban temples where vertical grooves have been gouged into the sandstone surfaces.[47] These grooves are the result of an ancient popular folk practice of obtaining powdered stone for magical/medical purposes for cures and to enable fertility. If this is another example of the belief in the efficacy of the graven image and text in the case of KV 9, it should be noted that the majority of the examples of gouges occur on the parts of the corridor walls where numerous text columns from the Book of Caverns and the Book of Gates are found [48]

Figure 9: KV 9, gouges. (E. C. Brock)

The final item concerning the tomb of Ramesses VI is a later addition, incorrectly located in the literature dealing with this tomb, and now gone missing. Following the robbery or robberies of this tomb, as well as others in the Twentieth Dynasty, official investigations were made. In some instances these inspections were recorded in the tombs, including names of the officials involved and even the dates. In the case of KV 9, a hieratic inscription of seven lines recorded a visit by the scribes

Amenhotep and his son Amennakht in regnal year 9 of Ramesses IX.[49] This text was recorded by Champollion, who fortunately included a crude sketch of part of the diagonal limb of a figure giving a context for the location of the text.[50] The citation for this graffito in Porter and Moss[51] associates it with the ceiling of the burial chamber depicting the figures of Nut and the Books of Day and Night. Aside from the incongruity of the visitors somehow gaining access to the vaulted ceiling of this chamber to inscribe a graffito, no traces of this inscription are visible here. In fact no traces of this graffito are visible anywhere in the tomb, and I have been unable to determine how the ascription of its location to the burial chamber ceiling came about. Champollion's publication of the graffito bears no indication of location and occurs between the depiction of the Books of Day and Night and their accompanying texts on the ceilings of corridors D and E and pillared hall F, not in any way in association with the decoration of the burial chamber and its ceiling. A clue to its location, however, is provided by Champollion's sketch of the diagonal limb associated with the hieratic text. On the rear wall of the niche (K) behind the burial chamber, a figure with two diagonal limbs depicts a variation of the terminal scene of the Book of Gates showing Nun lifting the solar barque out of the waters of chaos at dawn.[52] While there are numerous graffiti inscribed on this wall, mostly in Greek and Coptic, the graffito in question does not appear. The only other depiction of such a figure at the appropriate scale is located on the south side of the rear wall of the first pillared hall (F), again in the terminal scene of the Book of Gates, namely the large figure of Nun lifting the sun barque.[53] There is a large diagonal break in the wall with subsequent loss of plaster running between the diagonally upraised arms of the figure, exactly in the location where the inspection graffito would be expected. This would have been a vertical surface at the appropriate height for writing an inscription and well visible to anyone entering the chamber. Unfortunately, due to the loss of plaster here, no traces of the text are now visible, nor do they appear in any photographs of this wall. The outlines of the missing plaster section to the right of the north arm of the Nun figure is suspiciously regular and stops exactly at the edge of the scene, suggesting that some of the plaster might have been purposefully removed. The date for this loss of the plaster surface must predate Piankoff's publication, which shows the crack and loss of plaster. It is also possible that some loss of decoration had already occurred when Champollion visited the tomb, as his sketch of the scene omits some elements, including the head and shoulders of the figure of Nun and the central group of figures on the solar boat.[54]

NOTES

1 Elizabeth Thomas, *Royal Necropoleis of Thebes* (Princeton: n.p., 1966), 51–52. The minimum number of ten refers to those tombs bearing ancient visitors graffiti; see Jules Baillet, *Inscriptions grècques et latines des tombeaux des rois ou syringes à Thèbe,* MIFAO 42 (Cairo: Institut français d'archéologie orientale, 1920–1926), viii.

2 Kenneth A. Kitchen, "Ramesses V–XI, 20th Dynasty," *LÄ* V, 124–125, 127, n. 45–53.

3 PM I²:2, 502–503 (107, 107). For recent reviews of the depictions of the procession of princes in Medinet Habu with references to previous studies, see Steven R. Snape, "The Legacy of Ramesses III and the Libyan Ascendency," in Eric H. Cline and David O'Connor (eds.), *Ramesses III: The Life and Times of Egypt's Last Hero* (Ann Arbor: University of Michigan Press, 2012), 406–414.

4 *KRI* VI, 438–448.

5 Kitchen, "Ramesses V–XI," 124–125

6 Thomas, *Royal Necropoleis*, 131, 151–152, did note the possibility of KV 19 being started for the prince who became Ramesses VIII, based mainly on architectural dimensions. No mention of the dedication inscription discussed here was made. I first drew attention to this altered text in a brief note in 1995 (Edwin Brock, "The Clearance of the Tomb of Ramesses VII," in Richard H. Wilkinson (ed.), *The Valley of the Sun Kings: New Explorations in the Tombs of the Pharaohs* (Tucson: University of Arizona Egyptian Expedition, 1995), 64–65, n. 13. Nicholas Reeves and Richard H. Wilkinson, *The Complete Valley of the Kings* (London: Thames and Hudson, 1996), 167, 170, also make mention of the possibility of this tomb being initiated for Ramesses VIII as prince, ascribing this observation to me, in part due to my comments on this dedication text. Aidan Dodson, *After the Pyramids: The Valley of the Kings and Beyond* (London: Rubicon, 2000), 132–133, also notes the same possibility, credited to me.

7 This was part of a project with the California Institute of Science, sponsored by the American Research Center in Egypt and directed by John Rutherford in 1996. It was tasked with a survey of Valley of the Kings tombs for flood protection recommendations following the floods of October and November 1994.

8 PM I²:2, 546. For images of this text on the southern entrance jamb, see Theban Mapping Project, "Image 16250," http://www.thebanmappingproject.com/database/image.asp?ID=16250, and Theban Mapping Project, "Image 16251," http://www.thebanmappingproject.com/database/image.asp?ID=16251. Other dedication texts for Twentieth Dynasty princes are known, e.g., two sons of Ramesses III in

the Valley of the Queens, Khaemwaset (QV 44) (Fathi Hassanein and Monique Nelson, *La Tombe du Prince Khaemouaset [VdR no 44]*, Centre d'étude et documentation sur l'ancienne Ègypte collection scientifique 72, Vallée des Reines [Cairo: Conseil supérieur des antiquités, 1997], 57, 63, 110,114; Hassanein and Nelson, *La Tombe du Prince Amon-(Her)-Khepechef* [Cairo: Centre de documentation et d'études sur l'ancienne Egypte, 1976], 72, 86, 105, 114, 114; Janine Monnet, "Remarques sur la famille et les successeurs de Ramsès III," *BIFAO* 63 [1965]: 211; Edward Wente, "A Prince's Tomb in the Valley of the Kings," *JNES* 32.1 [1973]: 228). For other New Kingdom examples of the dedication text phrase, see *Wb* III, 158: B. II.6–7, and *Wb Belegstellen* III, pt. 1:34 (158:6–7), pt. 2:47 (158:7). See also Alan H. Gardiner, *Egyptian Grammar* (third edition, revised; Oxford: Oxford University Press, 1957), 121 §158 on the phrase *nt ẖr niswt*.

9 *Theban Mapping Project*, s.v. "Image 16250," http://www.theban mappingproject.com/atlas/database/image.asp?ID=16250, and *Theban Mapping Project*, s.v. "Image 16251," http://www.thebanmapping project.com/atlas/database/image.asp?ID=16251.

10 All citations of glyphs refer to the examples in the sign list of Gardiner's *Grammar*, 438–547 (here abbreviated GSL).

11 This figure of the crouching Seth animal recently has been commented on by E. Cruze-Uribe, "*stḫ ꜥꜣ pḥty* 'Seth, God of Power and Might,'" *JARCE* 45 (2004): 217–218, n. 85, fig., 17, photo 7, where I am credited with this observation.

12 This is clearly indicated by the presence of this king's prenomen inscribed on the belt of the figure of Thoth, second scene on the south side of corridor, cf. PM I²:2, 546 (3), *KRI* VI, 465 (h); *Theban Mapping Project*, s.v. "Image 15537," http://www.thebanmappingproject.com/ database/image.asp?ID=15537.

13 *Theban Mapping Project*, s.v. "Image 15502," http://www.thebanmap pingproject.com/database/image.asp?ID=15502, *Theban Mapping Project*, s.v. "Image 15521," http://www.thebanmappingproject.com /database/image.asp?ID=15521, *Theban Mapping Project*, s.v. "Image 15523," http://www.thebanmappingproject.com/database/image.asp? ID=15523.

14 The entryway (A) was actually begun as a cutting through the top of the shaft of KV 60. See *Theban Mapping Project*, s.v. "Image 13695," http: //www.thebanmappingproject.com/database/image.asp?ID=13695.

15 A view of this feature may be seen at *Theban Mapping Project*, s.v. "Image 16258," http://www.thebanmappingproject.com/database/ image.asp?ID=16258.

16 For examples see plans and sections in Kent R. Weeks (ed.), *Atlas of the Valley of the Kings, Study Edition* (Cairo: American University in Cairo Press, 2003), 26–27 (KV 2, Ramesses IV), 30–33 (KV 4, Ramesses XI), 42–45 (KV 6, Ramesses IX), 54–57 (KV 9, Ramesses V/VI), 62–65 (KV 11, Ramesses III), 84 (KV 18, Ramesses X), 85 (KV 19, Ramesses Mentu-herkhepeshef).

17 Thomas, *Royal Necropoleis*, 98 n. 39, 273–286.

18 Walton Chan, "Topographic and Architectural Drawings," in Kent R. Weeks (ed.), *Atlas of the Valley of the Kings, Study Edition* (Cairo: American University in Cairo Press, 2003), 7.

19 The lack of this feature in KV 14, the tomb of Queen Tausret, perhaps was due to its inappropriateness during the first phase of construction of this tomb while Tausret was still the royal consort of Sety II. See Hartwig Altenmüller, "Bemerkungen zu den neu gefundenen Daten im Grab der Königin Twosre (KV 14) im Tal der Könige von Theben," in C. Nicholas Reeves (ed.), *After Tut'ankhamûn: Research and Excavation in the Royal Necropolis at Thebes* (London and New York: Kegan Paul, 1992), 141–164. It is strange that this feature is absent from the tombs of Sety II (KV 15) and Siptah (KV 47). It cannot be determined now if KV 1, the tomb of Ramesses VII, had been provided with these niches, as this corridor was enlarged to serve as the burial chamber since the tomb was unfinished at the king's death (Brock, "Clearance," 47–50).

20 Thomas, *Royal Necropoleis*, 152.

21 Dimensions of these components in each of the relevant tombs are available at the individual links at *Theban Mapping Project*, "Sites in the Valley of the Kings," http://www.thebanmappingproject.com/sites/.

22 PM I^2:2, 500–501, wrongly cited as "abandoned tomb of Ramesses III." Although the presence of a frieze of cartouches of Ramesses III in the first corridor (B) gives a general date, no identifying texts survive for the prince whose figure accompanies the king. See Wente, "Prince's Tomb," 234 for suggestion that KV 3 was made for the prince Ramesses who became Ramesses IV.

23 PM I^2:2, 753–754.

24 Christian Leblanc, "Une nouvelle analyse de la double théorie des princes du temple de Ramsès III, à Medinet Habou," *Memnonia* 12/13 (2001–2002): 191–218, pl. XVIII; Christian Leblanc, "La véritable identité de Pentaouret, le Prince 'Maudit,'" *RdÉ* 52 (2001): 151–171, pls. XXIII–XXVII.

25 Jeanne Vandier d'Abbadie, "Un monument inédit de Ramsès VII au Musée du Louvre," *JNES* 9 (1950): 134–136; *KRI* VI, 389 (11). For color views of this ostracon, see Guillemette Andreu (ed.), *Les artistes de pharaon. Der el-Médineh et la Vallée des Rois* (Paris: Brepols, 2002), 174–175 (cat. 118).

[26] Kenneth Kitchen, "Ramessses VII and the Twentieth Dynasty," *JEA* 58 (1972): 185, n. 6; Aidan Dodson and Dyan Hilton, *The Complete Royal Families of Ancient Egypt* (London: Thames and Hudson, 2004), 186, 191, 194.

[27] Edward Ayrton, "The Tomb of Ramses Mentuherkhepshef (No. 19)," in Theodore M. Davis, *The Tomb of Siptah; The Monkey Tomb and the Gold Tomb* (London: Archibald Constable, 1908), 23. For a view of this feature, see *Theban Mapping Project*, s.v. "Image 16259," http://www.thebanmapingproject.com/database/image.asp?ID=16259.

[28] In the Valley of the Queens, PM I²:2, 753 (QV 42, Paraherwenemef), 755 (QV 44, Khaemwaset), 756 (QV 51, Isis), 761 (QV 55, Amenherkhepeshef), 765. Also add QV 52, Queen Tyti, for whom fragments of a sarcophagus recently have been found: S. Mohammed Sayed and Angelo Sesana, "Les vestiges du mobilier funéraire de la reine Tyti, retrouvés dans la tombe nº 52de la Vallée des Reines," *Memnonia* 6 (1995): 215–228, pls. XL–XLI. In the Valley of the Kings, KV 10: granite sarcophagus lid of Queen Takhat, Edwin Brock, "The Sarcophagus Lid of Queen Takhat," in Zahi Hawass and Lyla Pinch Brock (eds.), *Egyptology at the Dawn of the Twenty-First Century. Proceedings of the Eighth International Congress of Egyptologists Cairo, 2000* I (Cairo and New York: American University in Cairo Press, 2003), 97–102; KV 13: anthropoid granite sarcophagi for prince Amenherkhepehsef and Mentuherkhepeshef, Hartwig Altenmüller, "Dritter Vorbericht über die Arbeiten des Archäologischen Instituts der Universität Hamburg am Grab des Bay (KV13) im Tal der Könige von Theben," *SAK* 21 (1994): 1–18, taf. I–II.

[29] Elizabeth Thomas, "Ramesses III: Notes and Queries," *JEA* 45 (1959): 101, n. 7; this suggestion subsequently was withdrawn, Thomas, *Royal Necropoleis*, 131, n.110. Thomas's original suggestion has been echoed more recently by Dodson, *After the Pyramids*, 133.

[30] Tentative suggestion by Thomas Schneider, "Ramses X.: Person und Geschichte," in Hanna Jenni (ed.), *Das Grab Ramses' X. (KV 18)*, Aegyptiaca Helvetica 16 (Basel: Schwabe, 2000), 108.

[31] These have been extensively documented by Friedrich Abitz, *Baugeschichte und Dekoration des Grabes Ramses VI.*, Orbis Biblicus et Orientalis 89 (Freiburg and Göttingen: Universitäts Verlag, Vandenhoeck & Ruprecht, 1989), 40–48.

[32] Abitz, *Baugeschichte*, 40, 42 Abb. 7, 43.

[33] For this figure in the context of New Kingdom royal tombs, see: Ute Rummel, *Iunmutef. Konzeption und Wirkungsbereich eines altägyptischen Gottes*, Deutches Archäologisches Institut, Abteilung Kairo, Sonderschrift 33 (Berlin: De Gruyter, 2010), 134–144, 322–344.

[34] For a summary of the occurrences and interpretations of the function of this feature, see: Elizabeth Thomas, "The 'Well' in Kings' Tombs of Bibân el-Molûk," *JEA* 64 (1978): 80–83.

[35] Abitz, *Baugeschichte*, 43 n.1.

[36] Perhaps supporting a figure of the Anubis animal or some other therioform protective deity, such as are found in KV 11 and some of the tombs in the Valley of the Queens. See Friedrich Abitz, *Ramses III. in den Gräbern seiner Söhne*, Orbis Biblicus et Orientalis 72 (Freiburg and Göttingen: Universitätsverlag, Vanderhoeck & Ruprecht, 1986), 80–93.

[37] Alexander Piankoff, *The Tomb of Ramesses VI*, Bollingen Series 40.1 (New York: Pantheon Books, 1954), pls. 28, 57a.

[38] PM I^2:2, 511 (2). Piankoff, *Tomb of Ramesses VI*, 141–143, fig. 30, pl. 36. This scene, termed the "First Hour" in Eric Hornung, *The Ancient Egyptian Books of the Afterlife*, translated by David Lorton (Ithaca and London: Cornell University Press, 1999), 55–66, might better be understood as the expanded first gate of the composition.

[39] E. Hornung, *Das Buch der Anbetung des Re im Westen (Sonnenlitanei), Teil II, Ubersettzung und Kommentar*, Aegyptiaca Helvetica 3 (Geneva: Aegyptiaca Helvetica, 1976), 55.

[40] Visible but not commented on previously in Piankoff, *Tomb of Ramesses VI*, pl. 37 (bottom, center).

[41] PM VI, 29, (1)–(2) (incorrectly identified as Book of Gates instead of Book of Caverns); (5)–(6).

[42] Piankoff, *Tomb of Ramesses VI*, pl. 172 (omitting first vulture).

[43] Piankoff, *Tomb of Ramesses VI*, pls. 74, 88.

[44] Piankoff, *Tomb of Ramesses VI*, pl. 35.

[45] Carter object cards 207-04 and 207-17 (Griffith Institute, "Carter Archives - 207," *Tutankhamun: Anatomy of an Excavation: The Howard Carter Archives*, http://www.griffith.ox.ac.uk/gri/carter/207.html); see also Martha R. Bell, "Notes on Exterior Construction Signs from Tutankhamun's Shrines," *JEA* 76 (1990): 107–124.

[46] Howard Carter and Alan H. Gardiner, "The Tomb of Ramesses IV and the Turin Plan of a Royal Tomb," *JEA* 4 (1917): 130–158.

[47] Jitse H. F. Dijkstra, *Syene I: The Figural and Textual Graffiti from the Temple of Isis at Aswan* (Mainz am Rhein: Von Zabern, 2012), 27–28; Claude Traunecker, "Une pratique de magie populaire dans les temples de Karnak," in Alessandro Rocatti and Alberto.Siliotti (eds.), *La Magia in Egitto ai Tempi dei Faraoni* (Milan: Rassenga internazionale di cinematogafia archeologica: arte e natura libri, 1987), 221–242.

48 Piankoff, *Tomb of Ramesses VI*, pls. 15–17, 43, 45–47.

49 *KRI* VI, 658–659; Cyril Aldred, "More Light on the Ramesside Tomb Robberies," in John Ruffle, Gaballa. A. Gaballa, and Kenneth A. Kitchen (eds.), *Orbis Aegyptiorum Speculum: Glimpses of Ancient Egypt: Studies in Honour of H. W. Fairman* (Warminster: Aris & Phillips Ltd., 1979), 92, n. 6–8. For the scribe Amenhotep, see: Cathleen Keller, "How Many Draughtsmen Named Amenhotep? A Study of Some Deir el-Medina Painters," *JARCE* 21 (1984): 119–129; Keller, "Un artiste égyptien à l'oeuvre: le dessinateur en chef Amenhotp," in Guillemette Andreu (ed.), *Deir el-Médineh et la Vallée des Rois. La vie en Égypte autemps des pharaons du Nouvel Empire* (Paris: Editions Kheops, Musée du Louvre, 2003), 83–114; Benedict G. Davies, *Who Was Who at Deir el-Medina: A Prosopographic Study of the Royal Workmen's Community* (Leiden: Nederlands Instituut voor het Nabije Oosten, 1999), 112–113; Miroslav Barwik, *Twilight of Ramesside Egypt* (Warsaw: Agade, 2011), 24–27.

50 J.-F. Champollion, *Monuments de l'Égypte et de la Nubie. Notices Descriptives* II (Paris, 1879), 635. This hieratic graffito was transcribed by W. Spiegelberg, *Ägyptische und andere Graffiti (Inschriften und Zeichnungen) aus der Thebanischen Nekropolis* (Heidelberg: Winter, 1921), 92.

51 PM I^2:2, 517.

52 Piankoff, *Tomb of Ramesses VI*, pl. 124.

53 Piankoff, *Tomb of Ramesses VI*, 222–224, fig. 79, pl. 62. For a view of the wall following SCA restoration, see *Theban Mapping Project*, s.v. "Image 16304," http://www.thebanmappingproject.com/database/image.asp?ID=16304.

54 Champollion, *Monuments* II, 541.

Curious Nautical Details from the Eleventh Dynasty Temple at Deir el-Bahri

Noreen Doyle
University of Arizona Egyptian Expedition

Several fragmentary boat scenes from the temple of Mentuhotep present puzzling nautical details not seen elsewhere in pharaonic iconography. These include a watercraft with possibly three quarter rudders and unusual groupings of rope. Comparison with Old and New Kingdom iconography suggests that these parallel other boats that appear in earlier and later royal monuments. An explanation for ceremonial barques with hogging trusses is also offered.

Some years ago, my survey of Egyptian nautical iconography brought to my attention a relief fragment in the collection of the Yale Peabody Museum of Natural History, YPM 6777. This piece of a pharaonic jigsaw puzzle has haunted the back of my mind since that time: there are no fragments of which I am aware that join with it. I will caution that this paper will present no grand conclusions—the puzzle remains fundamentally unsolved. Nonetheless, I feel it worthwhile to shine some additional light on this and several other fragments of nautical iconography from the temple dedicated to the king whose reign assured the importance of ancient Luxor, which in turn led to the founding of the Valley of the Kings as a royal necropolis. I hope that Professor Wilkinson, who has devoted so much of his career to the valley and and to the analysis of pharaonic iconography, will appreciate the following interpretive efforts.

The men stand on a raised platform (painted a faint reddish-brown) that provides a flat baseline above the steeply curving sheer[2] of a boat. Separate and forward of this platform is a structure indicated by a vertical post that has been given tan and reddish-brown horizontal stripes. This appears to be part of a deck cabin, which also has incised horizontal elements; these are, like most of the rest of the cabin, again painted reddish-brown. The lower portion of the cabin, below the horizontal lines, is tan.

The fragment of scene remaining on YPM 6777, derived from the Eleventh Dynasty temple at Deir el-Bahri, depicts part of a watercraft and its crew (Figure 1).[1] Three sailors are preserved from the waist down: each wears a short kilt, once painted white. Their legs (which the sculptors have given calf muscles) and feet

Figure 1: YPM 6777, fragment of relief showing three helmsmen. Eleventh Dynasty, temple of Mentuhotep, Deir el-Bahri (drawing by Noha Bolbol after G.D. Scott, *Ancient Egyptian Art at Yale* [New Haven: Yale University Art Gallery, 1986], 64 no. 30)

are painted a reddish-brown. The fragment contains no trace of their hands, which are engaged in activity above waist level.

The sheer of the hull is indicated by four incised parallel lines that rise sharply toward the left, i.e., the stern. These four lines define three stripes, all of which are painted what now appears to be a faint reddish-brown. There is an object at the far left of the relief, just above the sheer, which is interrupted by the break in the stone. The object has been described as "an animal head that decorated the stern."[3]

The platform occupied by the men also supports three thick posts painted tan and "orange,"[4] a brighter shade than the reddish-brown used for the skin of the crew. In front of each post is another vertical element, painted reddish-brown. These extend from the break in the stone to "midair" and are certainly tillers in the (missing) hands of the helmsmen.

The stern platform is a feature of two-dimensional iconography.[5] It does not appear in models of the period, even when they have an exaggerated sheer;

Egyptian artists commonly exaggerated the curvature of the sheer,[6] as if doing so intensified the "ship-ness" of the representation. This leaves open the question of whether actual boats had such a platform or if the artist was merely providing a baseline upon which the helmsman can sit or stand, perhaps elevating an element of the hull that was in reality hidden by the sheer strake or bulwark.[7] Middle Kingdom examples lack the kind of construction details that their (uncommon) Old Kingdom counterparts sometimes possess.[8] Usually these platforms (or baselines?) occupy space abaft the rudder stanchion—between it and the rising sheer (see Figure 8 for a Middle Kingdom example). For YPM 6777, however, this platform begins a short distance abaft the cabin, and the three rudder stanchions rise from it.

How are these rudder stanchions—and the rudders associated with them—meant to be "read"? That is, what three-dimensional reality or concept did the ancient artist intend to convey to the viewer?

Middle Kingdom steering gear descended from that in use during the Old Kingdom and broadly resembled that used later, during the New Kingdom.[9] A variety of steering gear was in use during the early Middle Kingdom. All were forms of rudder, which is distinguished from a steering oar by being "permanently mounted and turn[ed] about a fixed axis."[10] In other words—in the cases to be discussed here—a rudder is supported at two points (by a stanchion and by a beam or other element of the hull) and thus can be only turned about its axis (by means of a tiller), whereas a steering oar, if given any structural support other than the hands of its operator, is fixed at only one point on the hull and thus may, at least hypothetically, be more freely moved in operation. After the Fifth Dynasty, steering oars appear in art only as archaisms.[11]

Middle Kingdom boats employed either of two general kinds of rudder, both supported by a stanchion but distinguished by their placement: quarter or axial. Axial rudders are mounted along the axis of a vessel, that is, directly over the stern, following the centerline of the hull. From two-dimensional representations and from models it is evident that such rudders rested against a shallow groove in the sternpost (Figure 2). Quarter rudders, which are usually but not always encountered in pairs,[12] are in almost all cases supported by a beam (crosspiece) that extends outboard over the sheer (Figure 3).[13] Such arrangements are also known from the boats found in association with the pyramid of Senwosret III at Dahshur.[14]

Figure 2: Wall painting depicting a funerary procession of a funerary barge with quarter rudders towed by a boat with an axial rudder. Twelfth Dynasty, Senwosret II; Beni Hasan, tomb of Khnumhotep (after Percy E. Newberry, *Beni Hasan I* [London: Egypt Exploration Fund, 1893], pl. 29)

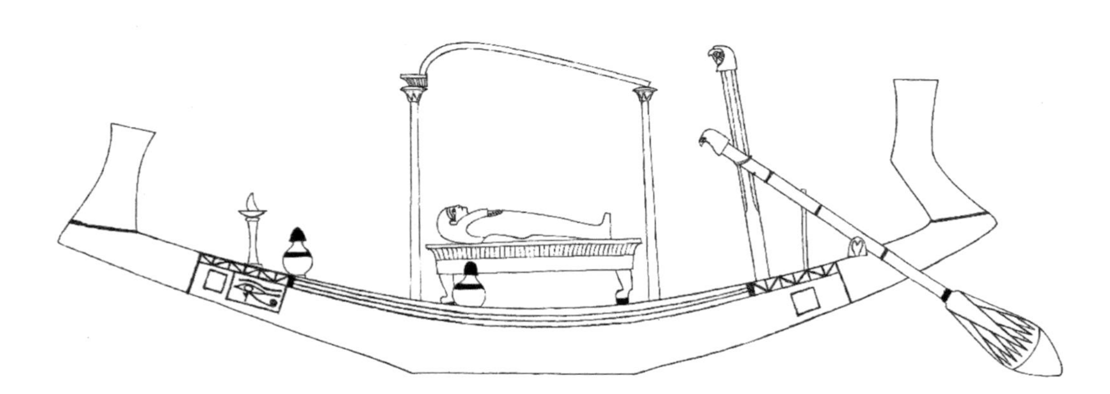

Figure 3: BM 9525, Middle Kingdom model funerary barge. Eleventh or Twelfth Dynasty (after S. R. K. Glanville, *Catalogue of Egyptian Antiquities in the British Museum II: Wooden Model Boats* [London: British Museum, 1972], 14 fig. 13a)

Is it possible that the three helmsmen are on different boats, i.e., that each is operating an axial rudder? Artists in the New Kingdom often showed crowded river scenes with boats moored, or being operated, close together.[15] In these scenes, the hull of the "near" boat obscures another (or others). Although artists showed boats this way even in some Predynastic representations,[16] this was not the case in the Old Kingdom, and this convention is rare in the Middle Kingdom. In the tomb of Djehutyhetep at Deir el-Bersha, a painted scene depicts three moored boats (with gangplanks) at the forefront of a procession.[17] Two bows extend noticeably beyond that of the "near" boat. Only two sets of steering gear of the three boats are shown (or survive), and these are separated by a considerable distance; the second boat's axial rudder is obscured behind the cabin of the first. There is no sharing of a "groundline," much less the appearance of sharing a structural one as the three helmsmen of YPM 6777 seem to do. It seems highly unlikely, therefore, that these three helmsmen are aboard different boats.

Behind the last helmsman of YPM 6777, at the level of the sheer (which is not preserved at that point due to a break in the block), is an "animal head," which, in Scott's interpretation, "decorated the stern."[18] An eye is clearly visible, and, despite the damage to the front of the face, it is quite clearly a falcon's head. What kind of ornamentation is this?

Scott's brief description seems to indicate that he means it to be a style of stern ornamentation that appears, for example, on sacred barques, in which both bow and stern have forward-facing heads of anthropo- or zoomorphic gods. Boats of this type are best known from New Kingdom examples, most notably from the various grand festivals at Luxor in which divine cult images traveled among the temples in full-sized vessels and/or portable barques. No representation of a boat of this type from the Middle Kingdom is known to me, although they were in use during the Old Kingdom, when they appear in a royal procession on the causeway of Sahure at Abusir.[19] They are not yet divine boats. The preserved names relate these boats directly or indirectly with the king: ("doubled" boat—to be described in more detail below—with indeterminable but probably falcon heads crowned with horns and uraei) *Sahure's Palace*; (boat with lioness head) *One Who Revives the* Rekhyt-*People*; (boat with falcon head crowned with horns and uraeus) *Great Mansion of the Feast of the Two Lands*; (boat with "jackal" head) *Great Mansion of the United Gods*; (boat with "jackal" head) *Great Mansion That Satisfies the Gods.* The names of their crews and gangs of sailors depicted running in the subsidiary registers do likewise: e.g., "crew of the retainers of Sahure, Pacifier of the Two Lands," "crew of the gang of Horus, Nebkhau" [i.e., Sahure], "crew of the beloved ones of the great Sahure," "crew of the retainers of Sahure 'Horus Lord of Beauty.'"

There is a depiction of a divine boat (in addition to one of a portable barque) among the published fragmentary reliefs from Mentuhotep's temple. The boat, in which the king stands and either punts with a pole or guides with an archaic steering oar, is papyriform, with a shrine forward of and a throne abaft him.

Dieter Arnold remarks on the fact that both the shrine and the throne are empty: this image of the divine boat does not contain a cult image of the god.[20] An image of a sphinx seeming to represent the king stands on the decorative tip of the boat's stem. The aforementioned portable barque (likely related to the Sokar festival) is less well preserved; only its papyriform shape and that it stands on a sledge can still be discerned.[21]

This does not preclude, of course, other boats of a divine or other ritual nature from having the anthropo/zoomorphic ends, but YPM 6777 presents another difficulty in that regard. Such an interpretation of the form of the boat would present a considerable difficulty if one considers where the rudder stocks must be. While it is possible to *imagine* such a stern ornamentation accommodating a single axial rudder (for example, with a groove supporting the stock on the back of the head), there is no example known to me from any period; no axial rudder is associated with a figural stern. Figural sterns are associated only with quarter rudders.

Far more likely, the falcon image on YPM 6777 is set on a crosspiece. Such ornaments occur, for example, on two models in the British Museum, BM 9524[22] and BM 9525 (Figure 3).[23] Although dated in publication to the Twelfth Dynasty, these models, of unknown provenience, could as well belong to the late Eleventh.[24] They represent papyriform funeral barges, each equipped with columns supporting a roof, mummy, and offering table with jars or jars and an incense burner, in addition to female mourners and a single helmsman. Although in the relief the falcon head faces forward, in the models the heads face outboard. That these are the carved ends of the crosspieces rather than elements pegged onto the upper surface indicates that this orientation is original and not the result of an error during modern reassembly. Actual examples are known from the boats found at the pyramid complex of Senwosret III at Dahshur (Figure 4).[25] Such falcon heads also appear on New Kingdom portable barques and sacred river barges in association with quarter rudders, their position suggesting placement on a crosspiece. They do not appear on the accompanying tow-boats, even those that have quarter rudders.[26]

On YPM 6777, what may be the trace of a rudder stock appears just above and behind the falcon head.[27] There are, however, *three* helmsmen, *three* tillers, and *three* rudder stanchions, all evidently aboard a single vessel. What is their arrangement? Are they one behind another or side by side? As Heinrich Schäfer has observed, "We *cannot deduce the spatial relationships of the original from any representation with*

Figure 4: Falcon decoration from one of the Dahshur Boats in the Egyptian Museum, Cairo. Twelfth Dynasty, Senwosret III; pyramid complex of Senwosret III, Dahshur (from Pearce Paul Creasman, "A Further Investigation of the Cairo Dahshur Boats," *JEA* 96 [2010], 111 fig. 9)

non-overlapping figures" (italics in the original).[28] Nonetheless, other representations of steering gear might provide clues.

In the Old Kingdom, paintings and relief of watercraft commonly show two or more helmsmen with their steering oars on one side of a boat. There is always, however, the question of how many helmsmen/steering oars are meant to exist and where: has the artist represented the entire complement on the one side or does he intend to imply each figure (and his equipment) as half of a pair? The greatest number of steering oars—thirteen (for twenty six?)—appears on a sailing vessel depicted at the causeway of Sahure at Abusir. The king, who is shown on an enormous scale relative to the rest of the crew, stands on a platform at the stern, abaft these helmsmen, operating the sail.[29]

These Old Kingdom examples all represent helmsmen with steering oars, which do not have stanchions. Rudders—which probably evolved out of the helmsman's practice of steadying the steering oar against the myke (a.k.a. mast crutch) used to support an unstepped mast[30]—complicated the artist's job. First appearing in the iconography of the Sixth Dynasty, rudders could be mounted either over the stern by means of a transom (made of one or more boards) fitted between a pair of outboard bulwarks (wings)[31] or at the quarters by means of a crosspiece. Old Kingdom artists showed a bewildering variety of arrangements between the elements of equipment and operator, some of which resulted from artistic license or error: one helmsman, one tiller, one rudder, one stanchion; one helmsman, one tiller, two rudders, one stanchion; one helmsman, two tillers, two rudders; two stanchions; etc.[32] Models of this period possess simply two stanchions.[33]

By the Middle Kingdom, steering gear is depicted more regularly. Axial rudders are represented, naturally enough, as a single stanchion, rudder, and helmsman. Pairs of quarter rudders in this period (with either one or two helmsmen to operate them) appear to be an archaizing feature of papyriform boats, such as funerary barges.[34] More everyday working boats—including those that tow funerary barges—possess axial gear. This is not true in later periods. Some New Kingdom "traveling boats"—those meant for the private transport of grandees—carry a pair of quarter rudders,[35] as do the Punt expedition ships of Hatshepsut.[36]

More than a single pair of quarter rudders on a vessel is known to me to occur only once in the iconography: the obelisk barge of Hatshepsut (Figure 5). Here the artist unequivocally depicted two pairs of quarter rudders/stanchions/ [helmsmen].[37] The crosspiece on which each rudder rests differs from that seen in the Middle Kingdom; this new development, which appears in two-dimensional art as a hook seeming to hang down over the side of the hull, probably represents a crosspiece of the sort found on some of the model boats from Tutankhamun's tomb (Obj. Nos. 308, 311) (Figure 6); these have near each end a hook-like form created by a deep, rounded notch in the rear face of the beam,[38] which draftsmen working in two dimensions showed from above. The stock of the rudder rests in the notch. The obelisk barge possesses no ornamentation on its two crosspieces, and in fact this kind of hooked crosspiece never seems to sport decoration, even when the boat is a ritual or "mythological" one. Ornamentation of the obelisk barge is confined to the incurving papyriform stern and a [Wepwawet?] standard at the bow. A plain forecastle stands at the bow, abaft the standard; any decoration it (or, indeed, the hull) might have had in paint has not survived.[39]

It is not impossible that the fragment of cabin on YPM 6777 is the fragment of something else, such as a large architectural element with wooden framework for its transportation. Hatshepsut's obelisk barge is the best known example, but others exist from the Old Kingdom as well.[40] The association between the falcon heads and ceremonial boats does make this hypothesis highly unlikely. Nonetheless, the similar association between papyriform stem and/or stern and ceremonial vessels serves as a caution: the determinative of the obelisk barge in the text accompanying Hatshepsut's fragmentary relief portrays just such a "ceremonial" stern on this huge working vessel.[41]

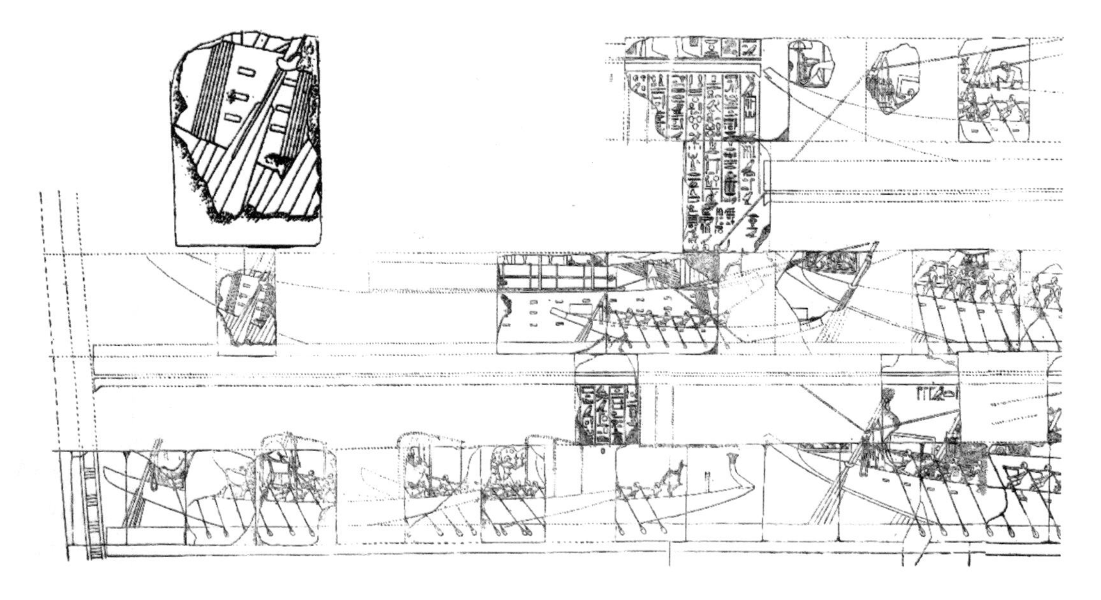

Figure 5: Relief depicting the obelisk barge of Hatshepsut; inset: detail of quarter rudders. Eighteenth Dynasty, temple of Hatshepsut, Deir el-Bahri (after Edouard Naville, *The Temple of Deir el Bahari VI: The Lower Terrace, Additions and Plans* [London: Egypt Exploration Fund, 1908], pl. 154)

Regarding the helmsmen of YPM 6777, there remains one last, if highly speculative, possibility for their spatial arrangement: namely that the helmsmen are side by side and all three rudders rest on the same crosspiece: one at starboard, one at port, and the third between them, along the axis of the boat. Such a hypothesis presupposes either a nonfigural stern with a transom or, far less likely, a "doubled" figural stern, in which the hull splits at bow and at stern, with each resulting end terminating in a figure. Such a vessel appears among Sahure's fleet of ceremonial watercraft depicted at Abusir, which were mentioned previously.[42] All of these boats (among which is a hull with a "tripled" figural stern) are steered by four or five (pairs, surely) of steering oars mounted at the quarters. Hypothetically, such a boat could be outfitted with a row of three rudders across its breadth.

Regardless of the arrangement—or, indeed, of the precise number—of the helmsmen, there is a possible explanation other than spectacular size for the unusual complement shown on YPM 6777.

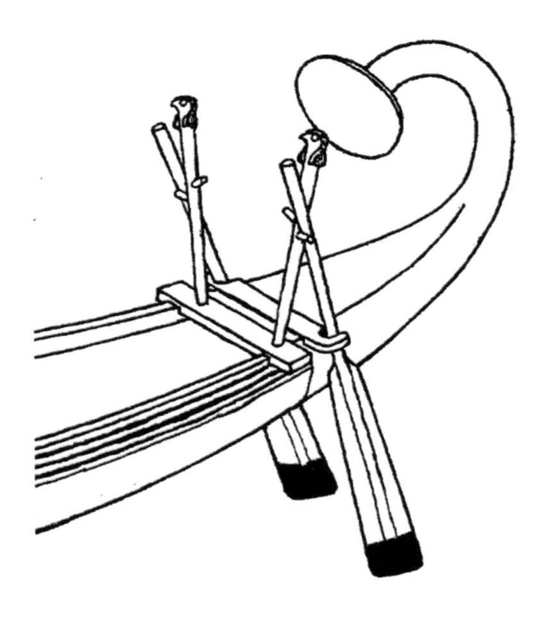

Figure 6: Stern of model boat (Obj. No. 308), showing crosspiece and quarter rudders. Eighteenth Dynasty, KV 62, Tutankhamun (after Dilwyn Jones, *Model Boats from the Tomb of Tut'ankhamun* [Oxford: Griffith Institute, 1990], pl. 34

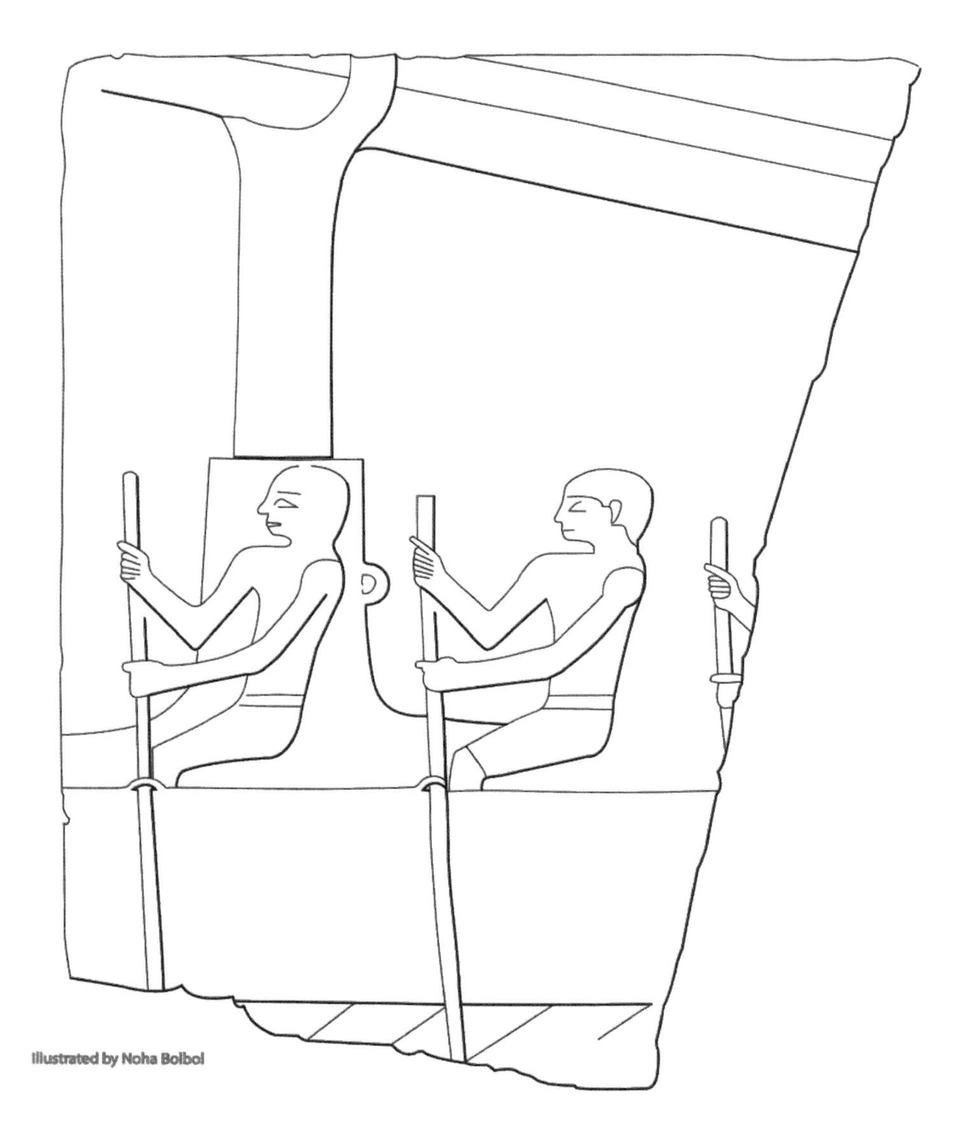

Figure 7: YPM 6772 A, fragment of relief depicting oarsmen, myke, and unstepped mast. Eleventh Dynasty, temple of Mentuhotep, Deir el-Bahri (drawing by Noha Bolbol after Scott, *Ancient Egyptian Art*, 62 no. 28)

I have argued elsewhere that archaizing of the sailing rig occurred during the Old and Middle Kingdoms, with bipod masts being used for ceremonial boats long after the pole mast had eclipsed them on working watercraft.[43] As remarked previously here, quarter rudders were confined to papyriform ceremonial boats during the Middle Kingdom, while working watercraft employed more "modern" stern-mounted gear. This also means that Middle Kingdom working boats had only a single rudder and helmsmen. Quarter rudders are ordinarily confined to a single pair, but this was by no means the case with steering oars, the placement of which is echoed by quarter rudders. Old Kingdom watercraft frequently possessed two or more pairs of steering oars, which were archaic technology by the Middle Kingdom. Thus YPM 6777's unusually large number of helmsmen—whatever their arrangement (over stern or quarters) or number (three or six)—was very possibly an archaizing feature of a ceremonial boat.

No trace of how the boat portrayed in YPM 6777 is propelled survives. It might have been rowed, sailed, or towed. Other relief fragments from Mentuhotep's temple do include means of propulsion. YPM 6772[44] shows five oarsmen plying their oars but no features of the vessel other than a flat sheer. YPM 6772 A[45] preserves two complete oarsmen and the hands of a third (Figure 7). This fragment shows an unstepped mast and perhaps the yard or boom supported in a myke (mast crutch). The myke has been stepped in place of the mast in the tabernacle (a support structure surrounding the lower portion of the mast). It is held in place by a pin that would pass through the eye shown on the tabernacle. Removing the pin would allow the mast or myke to be tilted in or out of place. This device appears, for example, among the roughly contemporaneous models of Meketre (TT 280).[46] Despite this nautical detail, the rowers of YPM 6772 A "are rendered summarily," in contrast with the helmsmen in YPM 6777.[47]

As Elke Noppes realized, YPM 6772 A joins very well to a relatively extensive relief (Figure 8).[48] This relief retains some of its paint and shows an additional four oarsmen abaft (i.e., to the left of) those on YPM 6772 A. The stern of the boat is quite damaged, but clearly it had a helmsman operating an axial rudder. A tow rope runs from this boat to another, much larger, vessel with a very different form of hull. Unfortunately, the larger boat's bow is insufficiently preserved to reveal any ornamentation other than the *wedjat* eye on the hull (Figure 9).[49] While a funerary context cannot be ruled out, this may have portrayed a scene from the Beautiful Festival of the Valley, a ceremony perhaps inaugurated by Mentuhotep. Hatshepsut also depicted this festival (as well as the Festival of Opet) on her own monument at Deir el-Bahri.[50]

Several other relief fragments from Mentuhotep's temple include elements of rigging. YPM 6779[51] shows a mast, boom, (lowered) yard, and associated rigging, all entirely ordinary. Two other fragments published by Naville are more

Figure 8: YPM 6772 A joined with reliefs in situ (photomontage reconstruction by Elke Noppes, modified by the author with the epigraphic drawing by Noha Bolbol, above)

interesting (Figure 10).[52] To judge by the style and by the quality of execution, these are not from the same scene as YPM 6777. Both seem closer in style to YPM 6772 A and 6772 B but might not belong with each other: the artist of Figure 10b has indicated the twists of the rope, a detail missing from the other fragment (Figure 10a) and from YPM 6779 (not illustrated here). But both of the reliefs in Figures 10 show the same nautical element: masses of rope fastened about an eye cleat by means of a belaying pin.

What these represent is difficult to say. In some respects they resemble the masses of backstays (ropes, fastened near the stern, that help to support a mast) seen in some Old Kingdom representations.[53] In the Middle Kingdom, backstays are far fewer in number, perhaps no more than two pair (as seen, for example, in Figure 2). Furthermore, the rigging in Figures 10a and 10b is considerably more robust than one sees in other examples.

The angle of rise also differs: while the Old Kingdom backstays tend to rise at an angle of roughly 45 to 60 degrees (as measured from horizontal), what appears in these two Middle Kingdom reliefs from Deir el-Bahri is vertical or nearly so. In

Figure 9: Relief showing boat being towed in procession by boat in Figure 8 (photograph by Elke Noppes)

this respect they more closely resemble, as Shelley Wachsmann has observed, the lateral trusses used to support the bipod masts aboard some Old Kingdom vessels and the pole masts of Hatshepsut's seagoing ships.[54] Cables also appear to secure the steering gear aboard two of Hatshepsut's "fleets": the seagoing Punt ships and their support boats (the latter of which have axial rudders); and the obelisk barge (probably), its tow-boats, and an accompanying royal vessel with falcon-headed stern (Figure 5). A small difference between some of these and their apparent Middle Kingdom parallels is the shape of the wooden element. In the Middle Kingdom reliefs, this object takes the form of a modern belaying pin: one end blunt and round, the other end tapered to a point. Old Kingdom iconography tends to show a straight, flat-ended stick, more appropriate for tightening the braids (as a Spanish windlass) rather than for securing them (as a belaying pin). The objects portrayed in Hatshepsut's Punt relief, however, have a belaying pin form but apparently a Spanish windlass function.

b

Figure 10: Reliefs showing ropes fastened to eye cleats by means of belaying pins. Eleventh Dynasty, temple of Mentuhotep, Deir el-Bahri (from Edouard Naville and H. R. Hall, *The XIth Dynasty Temple at Deir el-Bahari III* [London: Egypt Exploration Fund, 1913], pl. 13.7)

Furthermore, the Old and New Kingdom support cables are either braided, crossed (artistic shorthand for a braid?), or seized, as these Middle Kingdom cables appear not to be. There is no trace of a mast or stanchion associated with either Figure 10a or Figure 10b. Particularly for the former, where a cabin or some other large object is clearly visible to the left (i.e., probably forward) of the cables, it is difficult to visualize how these could be associated with masts except as masses of backstays (though again I point out that the angle seems wrong for such a purpose; the arrangement would have to be markedly different from those seen elsewhere in the iconography).

Their seemingly ephemeral nature (i.e., the belaying pin, which, when pulled, would release the knot) makes association with a hogging truss unlikely. Might they be for securing a large item of cargo whose edges exist beyond the bounds of the fragments? Could some aspect of their representation (perhaps the shape of the wooden element) be the result of misinterpretation of an earlier model or some other artistic error? Or do they simply serve a purpose lacking more firmly identifiable earlier or later parallels?

The fragmentary nature of the nautical reliefs from Mentuhotep's temple at Deir el-Bahri presents more questions than answers. The most secure conclusion that can be drawn at present is that the temple's decoration included scenes featuring boats that differ significantly from those that appear in private tombs of the period as either wall paintings or models. They also, in some details, differ significantly from boats of earlier and later periods. Ironically, in this general way they parallel better-preserved representations of watercraft that are unique in the artistic record, found in the royal monuments of both earlier and later rulers: for example, the double- and triple-hulled royal boats of Sahure's pyramid complex at Abusir and the obelisk barge of Hatshepsut's temple at Deir el-Bahri.

Do any of these Eleventh Dynasty fragments represent "working" vessels, perhaps seagoing or for transport of monumental architectural elements? It is impossible, at present, to say. It is tempting to believe that Mentuhotep included such scenes in his design program, as did his Old Kingdom predecessors: the human figure preserved in Figure 10a echoes the worshipful Egyptian crew and foreign passengers aboard Sahure's and Unas's seagoing fleets (Figure 11). And it seems only natural that such scenes might have inspired Hatshepsut, who was clearly offering herself as a successor to Mentuhotep,[55] to so notably include scenes of similar accomplishments in her own temple. While inspiration for her scenes has been attributed directly to Sahure,[56] the Eleventh Dynasty fragments from Deir el-Bahri hint that another influence might have existed much closer at hand.

Very little of the Eleventh Dynasty temple decoration from which we might reconstruct Mentuhotep's scenes remains. Even so, it is hoped that future publication of additional material—and new analysis of that which is already known—may continue to yield fragments to fit into the puzzle, so that we may gain a better understanding of the spectrum of watercraft in use during the Middle Kingdom.

Figure 11: Relief showing Old Kingdom seagoing ship (with hogging truss and with unstepped mast cradled in a myke) and its worshipful crew. Fifth Dynasty, causeway of Sahure, Abusir (after Ludwig Borchardt, *Das Grabdenkmal des Königs S'ahu-Re Band 2: Die Wandbilder: Abbildungsblätter* [Leipzig: Hinrichs, 1913], pl. 13)

A Thematically Related Postscript

Seemingly unrelated (except by nautical theme) to any of the reliefs discussed in detail above is a highly fragmented yet reconstructible scene (Figure 12) of four (or more?) crewless, papyriform vessels with straight, vertical bows and inward-turned sterns, i.e., Reisner's Type V Form 1.[57] Each has a very curious feature for a boat of this design: a hogging truss. This is supported by three forked stanchions.

The purpose of such a truss is to keep the ends of a boat from hogging (sagging). At this period in time, Egyptian boats were constructed without a keel, making such a device necessary under certain conditions.[58] Ordinarily, hogging trusses appear—

in the iconography—only on seagoing vessels[59] (Figure 11) and on boats carrying either cattle[60] or extraordinarily heavy loads of stone (Figure 5).[61] Notably and exceptionally, the vessels shown here are of a ceremonial form (cf. Figure 3).

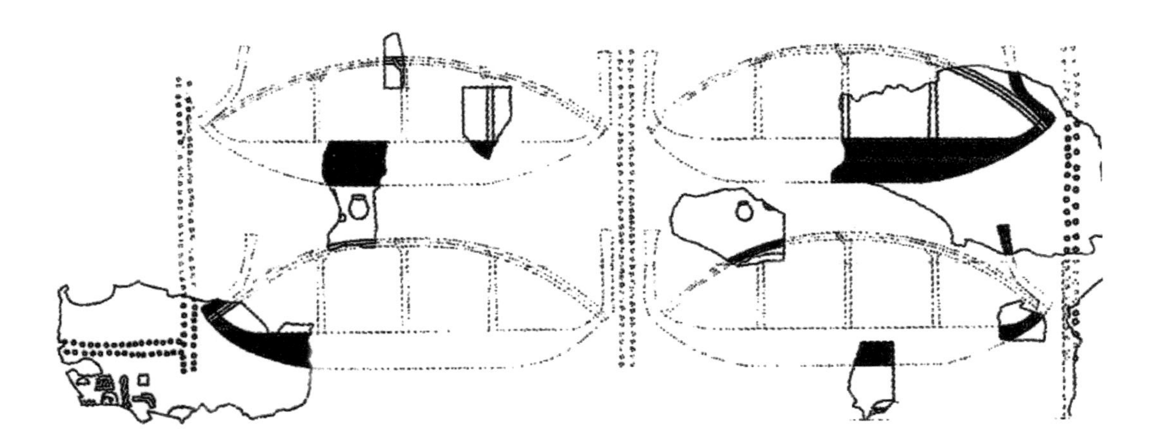

Figure 12: Relief depicting a scene of boats with hogging trusses. Eleventh Dynasty, temple of Mentuhotep, Deir el-Bahri (after Dieter Arnold, "A Boat Ritual of Mentuhotep Nebhepetra," in Z. Hawass and J. Houser Wegner [eds.], *Millions of Jubilees: Studies in Honor of David P. Silverman* [Cairo: Supreme Council of Antiquities, 2010], 44 fig. 1)

Arnold proposes or cites several possible interpretations of the scene, which has the additional oddity of taking place not on water but on sand. The precise nature of the ceremony depicted must, as Arnold remarks, remain speculative.[62] Given the evidence at hand, I am nonetheless inclined toward his fifth suggestion, which he summarizes wisely as a question: "Did the Mentuhotep relief depict ceremonies in connection with the burial of four funerary barques at the desert edge?"[63]

At least no mystery needs to surround the presence of the hogging trusses. The boats are not buoyed by water. To prevent the sagging of their unsupported ends, which would damage their structural integrity, the hulls have been outfitted with the trusses. Such an arrangement also appears in a New Kingdom image depicting working boats being towed along a mud slipway, perhaps to bypass the unnavigable stretch of the Nile at Mirgissa (Figure 13).[64]

This indicates that the hulls depicted in this scene were not built to withstand such circumstances. Instead, the boats depicted in Figure 12 had been constructed for use on the water and, being pressed into service for this sand-borne ceremony, were adapted accordingly.

Figure 13: Boats equipped with hogging trusses, dragged across mud. Eighteenth Dynasty, Tutankhamun, TT 40 [Amenhotep/Huy] (after Nina M. Davies and Alan H. Gardiner, *The Tomb of Huy, Viceroy of Nubia in the Reign of Tut'ankhamun [No. 40]* [London: Egypt Exploration Society, 1926], pl. XVIII)

NOTES

1. Gerry D. Scott III, *Ancient Egyptian Art at Yale* (New Haven: Yale University Art Gallery, 1986), 64–65 (No. 30); Elke Noppes, "Yale Peabody Museum of Natural History," *Mentuhotep Nebhepetre* (updated 11 September 2009, http://www.mentuhotep.de/museen/yale.htm).
2. Most of the nautical terminology used here may be found in the glossary of J. Richard Steffy, *Wooden Ship Building and the Interpretation of Shipwrecks* (College Station: Texas A&M University Press, 1994), 266–298.
3. Scott, *Ancient Egyptian Art*, 65.
4. Scott, *Ancient Egyptian Art*, 65.

[5] E.g., Percy Newberry, *Beni Hasan I* (London: Egypt Exploration Fund, 1893), pls. 14, 16; Norman de Garis Davies and Alan H. Gardiner, *The Tomb of Antefoker, Vizier of Sesostris I, and of His Wife, Senet* (London: Egypt Exploration Society, 1920), pl. 18.

[6] Shelley Wachsmann, *The Gurob Ship-Cart Model and its Mediterranean Context* (College Station: Texas A&M University Press, 2013), 65.

[7] Sometimes artists do conceal the feet within the hull (e.g., Percy Newberry, *El Bersheh* I [London: Egypt Exploration Fund, n.d.], pl. 18], a convention that becomes common during the New Kingdom; e.g., the Punt expedition ships of Hatshepsut and fleet towing the obelisk barge—but not, interestingly, the obelisk barge itself. Does this indicate that on some vessels the deck was essentially flush with the sheer strake? (For a discussion of bulwarks and other terminology, including the structural function of the upper planks of a hull, see Steve Vinson, "On *Ḥry.t*, 'Bulwark,' in P. Anastasi IV, 7/9–8/7," *ZÄS* 124 [1997]: 156–162.)

[8] E.g., Junker, H. *Giza IV. Die Mastaba des K3jmᶜnḫ (Kai-em-anch)* (Wien: Hölder-Pichler-Tempsky, 1940), pl. 3, which shows an apparent support stanchion as well as a hanging knee (but note as well the absence of such detail in the very similar vessel immediately behind it, seen in pl. 4). Sahure, shown at an outsized scale maneuvering the sail of a papyriform boat, stands on a similar kind of platform in a relief from Abusir (Tarek El Awady, *Abusir XIV: Sahure—The Pyramid Causeway: History and Decoration Program in the Old Kingdom.* [Prague: Charles University in Prague, 2009], 136–137 fig. 78, pl. 1).

[9] An overview of steering gear and its development from the Old through New Kingdoms may be found in Noreen Doyle, "Iconography and the Interpretation of Ancient Egyptian Watercraft" (master's thesis, Texas A&M University, 1998), 77–150. See also William Edgerton, "Ancient Egyptian Steering Gear," *American Journal of Semitic Languages and Literature* 43.4 (1927): 255–265.

[10] J. Richard Steffy, *Wooden Ship Building and the Interpretation of Shipwrecks* (College Station: Texas A&M University Press, 1994), 280; Doyle, "Iconography," 81. Some make a different distinction by classifying what I define here to be a steering oar as a rudder if its size makes it not useable for rowing: Samuel Mark, "A Different Configuration for the Quarter-Rudders on the Khufu I Vessel (c. 2566 BC), and Egyptian Methods of Mounting Quarter-Rudders and Oars in the 4th and 5th Dynasties," *IJNA* 41.1 (2012): 84–93.

[11] Doyle, "Iconography," 99.

[12] The "sporting boat X" of Meketre (Eleventh Dynasty; temp. Mentuhotep) has a single rudder mounted at the starboard quarter (Herbert E. Winlock, *Models of Daily Life in Ancient Egypt: From the Tomb of Meket-Re at Thebes* [Cambridge, Mass.: Metropolitan Museum of Art, 1955], 65, fig. 82).

[13] Again, "sporting boat X" of Meketre provides the exception. Although conventionally mounted to a rudder stanchion, its lower portion is supported by a spur (or, to use Winlock's description, a "hook") of wood lashed to the hull mounted at the starboard quarter (Winlock, *Models of Daily Life*, 65, fig. 82; Doyle, "Iconography," 113).

[14] Pearce Paul Creasman, "A Further Investigation of the Cairo Dahshur Boats," *JEA* 96 (2010), 111–112. For a discussion of the mounting of (primarily) Old Kingdom steering gear, see Mark, "Different Configuration," 86–93.

[15] E.g., TT 57, tomb of Khaemhat (temp. Amenhotep III): *LD* V: pl. 76b; TT 162, tomb of Kenamun (Eighteenth Dynasty): Norman de Garis Davies and R. O. Faulkner, "A Syrian Trading Venture to Egypt," *JEA* 33 (1947): pl. VIII; tomb of Maya at Amarna (temp. Akhenaten): Norman de Garis Davies, *The Rock Tombs of El Amarna V* (Oxford: Oxford University Press, 1908), pl. V.

[16] Heinrich Schäfer, *Principles of Egyptian Art*, edited by Emma Brunner-Traut, translated and edited by John Baines (Oxford: Clarendon Press, 1974), 170–171.

[17] Percy E. Newberry, Francis Ll. Griffith, and George W. Fraser, *El Bersheh Part 1 (The Tomb of Tehuti-Hetep)* (London: Egypt Exploration Society, 1895), pls. 12, 18.

[18] Scott, *Ancient Egyptian Art*, 65.

[19] See El Awady, *Abusir XVI*, 135–154 and pls. 1–4 for a description of Sahure's "royal fleet."

[20] Dieter Arnold, *Der Tempel des Königs Mentuhotep von Deir el-Bahari 2. Die Wandreliefs des Sanktuares* (Mainz am Rhein: Von Zabern, 1974), 26–27. Might this imply the presence of Amun as the "invisible"?

[21] Arnold, *Tempel des Königs Mentuhotep* 2, 28–29, pl. 32.

[22] S. R. K. Glanville, *Catalogue of Egyptian Antiquities in the British Museum II: Wooden Model Boats* (London: British Museum, 1972), 10–13, figs. 10–12, pl. IIIa.

[23] Glanville, *Wooden Model Boats*, 13–16, figs. 13–15, frontispiece, pl. IIIb.

[24] They compare well in their general qualities with, for example, the boat models from Tomb 10A at Deir el-Bersha, dated to the late Eleventh/early Twelfth Dynasties (Rita Freed, Lawrence M. Berman, Denis M. Doxey, and Nicholas S. Picardo, *The Secrets of Tomb 10A: Egypt 2000 BC* [Boston: Museum of Fine Arts Publications, 2009], 183–188).

[25] Creasman, "Further Investigation," 110, 111 fig. 9; Pearce Paul Creasman, "The Cairo Dahshur Boats" (master's thesis, Texas A&M University, 2005), 107–113.

[26] E.g., the portable barques of Amun, Mut, Khonsu, and the king in the Festival of Opet procession (e.g., Epigraphic Survey, *Reliefs and Inscriptions at Luxor Temple 1: The Festival Procession of Opet in the Colonnade Hall with Translations of Texts, Commentary, and Glossary*, OIP 112 [Chicago: Oriental Institute at the University of Chicago, 1994], pls. 6–9, 11–16, 36, 39, 40, 56–58, 76–78 [river barge], 79–81, 108, 110–111. Their portrayal is not consistent, however, and some of the heads appear to be associated with the ends of bulwarks rather than crosspieces; cf. pls. 43, 46–48, 55–58, 63–64, 66–67, 76–78 [portable barque], 79, 86, 103). Tow-boats with quarter rudders but no falcon heads: pls. 17, 27–30; cf. the also "falconless" quarter rudders of the sailing vessels, e.g., pl. 34.9. Throughout these same scenes (and others), falcon heads appear as decorative elements elsewhere, e.g., as terminals of bulwarks. Human heads similarly appear on some New Kingdom funerary boats (e.g., TT 82, Nina de Garis

Davies and Alan H. Gardiner, *The Tomb of Amenemhet* [No. 82] [London: Egypt Exploration Fund, 1915], pl. 12); TT 100, Norman de Garis Davies, *The Tomb of Rekh-Mi-Re at Thebes* [New York: Metropolitan Museum of Art, 1943], pl. 80).

27 An attempt to reconstruct my then understanding of Scott's suggestion appears in Doyle, "Iconography," 117 fig. 6-48, which shows (with a question mark) an inward-swept stern that sheltered the falcon head in a manner vaguely parallel to what appears at the bow of an Old Kingdom "hedgehog boat." It should be noted that neither I nor Noha Bolbol, the epigrapher who kindly rendered it for me based on the published photograph, have examined the relief in person, leaving open to particular question any interpretation of this area of the relief.

28 Schäfer, *Principles*, 172; he discusses "figures juxtaposed without overlapping" in depth on pages 172–173 (§ 4.3.7).

29 El Awady, *Abusir XVI*, pl. 1.

30 Doyle, "Iconography," 103.

31 Doyle, "Iconography," 92, 102 figs. 6-27 and 6-28, 147 n. 114. I remain grateful to Frederick Hocker's recommendation of this terminology (personal communication).

32 Doyle, "Iconography," 108 fig. 6-37, 110.

33 Doyle, "Iconography," 110.

34 There are rare exceptions: e.g., the *single* quarter rudder, mounted on the starboard side, of Meketre's model "sporting boat X" (Winlock, *Models of Daily Life*, fig. 82).

35 E.g., Davies, *Rekh-Mi-Re*, pl. LXVIII; Tutankhamun Obj. Nos. 276, 284, 306, 309, 310, 314, 336 (Dilwyn Jones, *Model Boats from the Tomb of Tut'ankhamun* [Oxford: Griffith Institute, 1990], 28-42, pls. 15–23, 25); also on the warships of Ramesses III depicted in battle against the Sea Peoples at Medinet Habu (Doyle, "Iconography," 126, 127 fig. 6-56; Harold H. Nelson, "The Naval Battle Pictured at Medinet Habu," *JNES* 2 [1943], fig. 4).

36 Edouard Naville, *The Temple of Deir el Bahari III: End of Northern Half and Southern Half of the Middle Platform* (London: Egypt Exploration Fund, 1898), pls. 73–75. The rougher waters of the Red Sea may have been too much for New Kingdom axial rudders. Unlike their Middle Kingdom predecessors, New Kingdom axial rudders were fixed between two protruding wooden elements at the stern (see Figure 13; note that the rudders have been removed from the vessels in this painting). Placement of the rudder stock through these "tines" may have endangered the structural integrity of the hull (or at least the rudder itself) during rough seas. Quarter rudders of one form or another were the standard seafaring steering gear for centuries until the development of the pintle and gudgeon by Northern European shipwrights; see Lawrence V. Mott, *The Development of the Rudder: A Technological Tale* (College Station: Texas A&M University Press, 1997) for a thorough discussion.

[37] The determinative for the boat in the accompanying inscription shows only a single rudder (implying one pair; Edouard Naville, *The Temple of Deir el Bahari VI: The Lower Terrace, Additions and Plans* [London: Egypt Exploration Fund, 1908], pl. 154); see also redrawing in Björn Landström, *Ships of the Pharaohs* (Garden City: Doubleday, 1970), 128 fig. 382.

[38] Jones, *Model Boats*, pls. 34–35 (Obj. Nos. 308, 311). This differs slightly from the squared notches seen, for example, in some Middle Kingdom models, such as CG 4917 (George Andrew Reisner, *Catalogue Général des Antiquités Égyptiennes du Musée du Caire, Nos. 4798–4976 et 5034–5200. Models of Ships and Boats* [Cairo: Institut français d'archéologie orientale, 1913], 74 fig. 275). Some New Kingdom vessels have an additional projection of wood that "locks in" the stock (Tutankhamun Obj. No. 284; Jones, *Model Boats*, pl. 32; for a brief discussion, see Doyle, "Iconography," 120).

[39] Notice that the accompanying tow boats have ornamental forecastles and sterncastles, showing the king as a lion, bull, or sphinx (Naville, *Deir el Bahari VI*, pl. 154). Amidship of each is a long cabin; a smaller, partly open-sided structure occupies the deck between the cabin and the helmsmen. The steering gear for each boat consists of a single pair of quarter rudders with the hook-like (i.e., notched) crosspiece.

[40] Papyriform columns (with shipping timbers): Selim Hassan, "The Causeway of Wnis at Sakkara," *ZÄS* 80 (1954), 137; sarcophagus and lid (with shipping timbers): Charles Boreux, *Études de nautique égyptienne: L'Art de la navigation en Égypte jusqu'à la fin de l'Ancien Empire* (Cairo: Institut français d'archéologie orientale, 1925), 489 fig. 190. Unfortunately, the stern of the boat carrying the twin papyriform columns has not survived (and the boat ahead of it, of which only the stern remains, appears to carry an altogether different cargo), so the number of its steering oars cannot be determined. The boat carrying the sarcophagus of Senedjemib has two men at the stern who hold either steering oars or punting poles.

[41] Naville, *Deir el Bahari VI*, pl. 154; Landström, *Ships of the Pharaohs*, 128 fig. 382.

[42] El Awadi, *Abusir XVI*, 142–146, pls. 2–3.

[43] First proposed in Doyle, "Old Kingdom Sailing Rigs and Later Bipod Masts: A Reevaluation from the Iconographic Evidence" (master's thesis, University of Liverpool, 2003), 65–70, and later in "The Persistence of the Bipod Mast and the Transience of the Tripod" (paper delivered at the fifty-seventh annual meeting of the American Research Center in Egypt, Jersey City, New Jersey, April 28–30, 2006). A publication on this topic is in preparation.

[44] Scott, *Ancient Egyptian Art*, 63 (No. 29).

[45] Scott, *Ancient Egyptian Art*, 62 (No. 28).

[46] Winlock, *Models of Daily Life*, pls. 78, 85.

[47] Scott, *Ancient Egyptian Art*, 62; he contrasts this with the quality of the relief in YPM 6777 (p. 65).

[48] Elke Noppes, "Yale Peabody Museum."

[49] This ornamentation, with this placement, appears on Old Kingdom royal vessels (e.g., Boreux, *Études*, 375 fig. 148). In the Middle Kingdom, it appears especially on papyriform funerary boats (e.g., here, Figure 3).

[50] Edouard Naville, *The Temple of Deir el Bahari V: The Upper Court and Sanctuary* (London: Egypt Exploration Fund, 1906), 3–5, pls. 122, 124–126; Ann Macy Roth, "Hatshepsut's Mortuary Temple at Deir el-Bahri: Architecture as Political Statement," in Catharine H. Roehrig (ed.), *Hatshepsut: From Queen to Pharaoh* (New York: Metropolitan Museum of Art, 2005), 150.

[51] Scott, *Ancient Egyptian Art*, 64–65 (No. 31).

[52] Edouard Naville and H. R. Hall, *The XIth Dynasty Temple at Deir el-Bahari III* (London: Egypt Exploration Fund, 1913), pl. 13.7; Shelley Wachsmann, *Seagoing Ships and Seamanship in the Bronze Age Levant* (College Station: Texas A&M University Press, 1998), 251 fig. 11.5A–B.

[53] For example, the tomb of Mereruka (Sixth Dynasty, temp. Teti–early Pepy I); Prentice Duell, *The Mastaba of Mereruka* (Chicago: University of Chicago Press, 1938), pls. 140–144.

[54] Wachsmann, *Seagoing Ships*, 250. Old Kingdom examples include, among others, images of boats of Fourth to Fifth Dynasty date from Giza, found reused at Lisht (Hans Goedicke, *Re-used Blocks from the Pyramid of Amemenhet I at Lisht* [New York: Metropolitan Museum of Art, 1971], 107 no. 61, 111 no. 62, 113 no. 63) and the Punt ships of Unas (Hassan, "Causeway of Wnis," 139 fig. 2). At least some of these are representations of seagoing vessels, but river boats also appear with such trusses for their bipod masts: e.g., at Saqqara, the Fifth Dynasty tombs of Khnumhotep (Hilda Petrie, *Seven Memphite Tomb Chapels* [London: Bernard Quaritch, 1952], pl. 17.6]) and Tii (Lucienne Épron, François Daumas, Georges Goyon, and Pierre Montet, *Le Tombeau de Ti* [Cairo: Institut français d'archéologie orientale, 1939], pl. 49).

[55] E.g., Roth, "Hatshepsut's Mortuary Temple," 147.

[56] Roth, "Hatshepsut's Mortuary Temple," 149.

[57] Dieter Arnold, "A Boat Ritual of Mentuhotep Nebhepetra," in Z. Hawass and J. Houser Wegner (eds.), *Millions of Jubilees: Studies in Honor of David P. Silverman* (Cairo: Supreme Council of Antiquities, 2010), 43–47.

[58] For related pharaonic boatbuilding practices, see Creasman, "Cairo Dahshur Boats"; Creasman, "Further Investigation"; Frederick M. Hocker, "Appendix: Did Hatshepsut's Punt Ships Have Keels?" in Wachsmann, *Seagoing Ships*, 245–246; Shelley Wachsmann, *Seagoing Ships*, 215–243; and Cheryl A. Ward, *Sacred and Secular: Ancient Egyptian Ships and Boats* (Philadelphia: Archaeological Institute of America, 2000).

[59] Old Kingdom (Sahure): Ludwig Borchardt, *Das Grabdenkmal des Königs S'ahu-Re Band 2: Die Wandbilder: Abbildungsblätter* (Leipzig: Hinrichs, 1913), Bl. 12–13; (Wenis): Hassan, "Causeway of Wnis," 139 fig. 2; Wachsmann, *Seagoing Ships*, 15 figs. 2.7–2.8. New Kingdom (Hatshepsut): Naville, *Deir el Bahari III*, pls. 69–75. Cf. Arnold, "Boat Ritual," 43.

[60] TT 40 (Huy; temp. Tutankhamun): Nina M. Davies, *The Tomb of Huy, Viceroy of Nubia in the Reign of Tutankhamun* (London: Egypt Exploration Society, 1926), 34 fig. 5, pl. XXXII.

[61] New Kingdom (Hatshepsut): Naville, *Deir el Bahari VI*: pls. 153–154. Cf. Arnold, "Boat Ritual," 43.

[62] Arnold, "Boat Ritual," 45–46.

[63] Arnold, "Boat Ritual," 46.

[64] TT 40 (Huy; temp. Tutankhamun): Doyle, "Iconography," 32 fig. 2-2; Pearce Paul Creasman and Noreen Doyle, "Overland Boat Transportation during the Pharaonic Period: Archaeology and Iconography," *JAEI* 2.3 (2010), 19–20.

Some Remarks on the Funerary Equipment from the Tomb of Amenhotep III (KV 22)[1]

Nozomu Kawai
Institute of Egyptology, Waseda University, Tokyo

The burial equipment of Amenhotep III—particularly the fragmentary remains of the sarcophagus, coffin(s), canopic equipment, and shabtis—is reviewed in light of re-excavation of KV 22 by the Waseda University Egyptian Expedition. Also reviewed are shabtis of Queen Tiye from the king's tomb and a grafitto in its burial chamber and what they say about the dates of their creation and the presence of Tiye's burial in her husband's tomb.

It was in 1994 when I first met Richard H. Wilkinson at the International Symposium on the Valley of the Kings at the University of Arizona, which he organized. It was my first journey to the United States, and I clearly remember how impressed I was by the scholarship at the symposium. Although I was just a graduate student from Japan, I received great hospitality while I was there. Since then I have seen Richard in the US and Egypt occasionally, and he always shows me his kind friendship. This article is dedicated to Richard as a token of my gratitude for his wonderful hospitality and friendship.

The tomb of Amenhotep III was one of the most magnificent of the Eighteenth Dynasty, and as such it might have contained some of the richest funerary equipment of all the New Kingdom royal tombs.[2] Although the remnants of the original burial assemblages are largely missing, re-clearance of the tomb by the Waseda University Egyptian Expedition under the direction of Professors Sakuji Yoshimura and Jiro Kondo has yielded thousands of fragments of the original funerary equipment.[3] I have worked with them since the beginning of the project and have also investigated the objects from Amenhotep III's tomb stored in museums and collections around the world. I aim to prepare a catalog of these objects as a part of the final publication of the tomb.[4]

In light of the recent work in the tomb by Waseda University and my own investigations, I will present the characteristics of the basic funerary equipment for the burial of Amenhotep III. I will then discuss the objects for the burial of Queen Tiye found in the tomb, as well as her reburial.

THE TOMB OF AMENHOTEP III AND THE HISTORY OF ITS EXPLORATION

The tomb of Amenhotep III is located in the western branch of the Valley of the Kings and is now numbered as KV 22. As the foundation deposits in front of the tomb contain faience plaques inscribed with the name of Amenhotep III's father, Thutmose IV,[5] it is likely that the tomb was originally constructed for the latter king.[6] Presumably Amenhotep III was forced to alter his burial plan when Thutmose IV died prior to the completion of the cutting of KV 22.[7] Thutmose IV was eventually buried in KV 43. Ultimately, it was Amenhotep III for whom KV 22 became the final resting place.

The basic tomb plan (Figure 1) follows that of its immediate predecessors, with the principal exception being that the entrance to the burial chamber, rather than being on the main axis, is instead at one end of a side wall of the antechamber. It has also two pillared chambers opening off the crypt of the burial chamber, each with its own annex. Room Je at the end of the chamber seems to have been originally intended for the burial of Queen Tiye,[8] although ultimately she appears to have been buried in the royal tomb at Amarna.[9] The second complex, Room Jd, on the other hand, preserves traces of enlargement out of the standard subsidiary chamber.[10] As this is a later addition to the tomb plan, it has been assumed that the chamber was intended for Sitamun, Amenhotep III's eldest daughter, who obtained the title of queen in the first *Sed* Festival of Amenhotep III.[11]

Scholars and visitors brought a number of funerary objects of Amenhotep III to Europe. Many objects, mainly stone shabtis found by Napoleon Bonaparte's expedition, were drawn in the *Description de l'Égypte* (Figure 2) and exhibited at the Musée d'Louvre in Paris.[12] Despite a superficial clearance of KV 22 said to have been carried out by Theodore Davis, the first scientific archaeological works were undertaken by Howard Carter under the sponsorship of the fifth Earl of Carnarvon from February to March 1915.[13] The finds by Carter's excavations are now stored in Highclere Castle in Newbury, England, and the Metropolitan Museum of Art in New York.[14]

Although Howard Carter noted that he made a complete clearance of the tomb, heaps of debris containing small fragments of the funerary equipment still remained inside and outside of the tomb when the Waseda University team started clearance in 1989. Since then, excavations have been carried out inside and outside

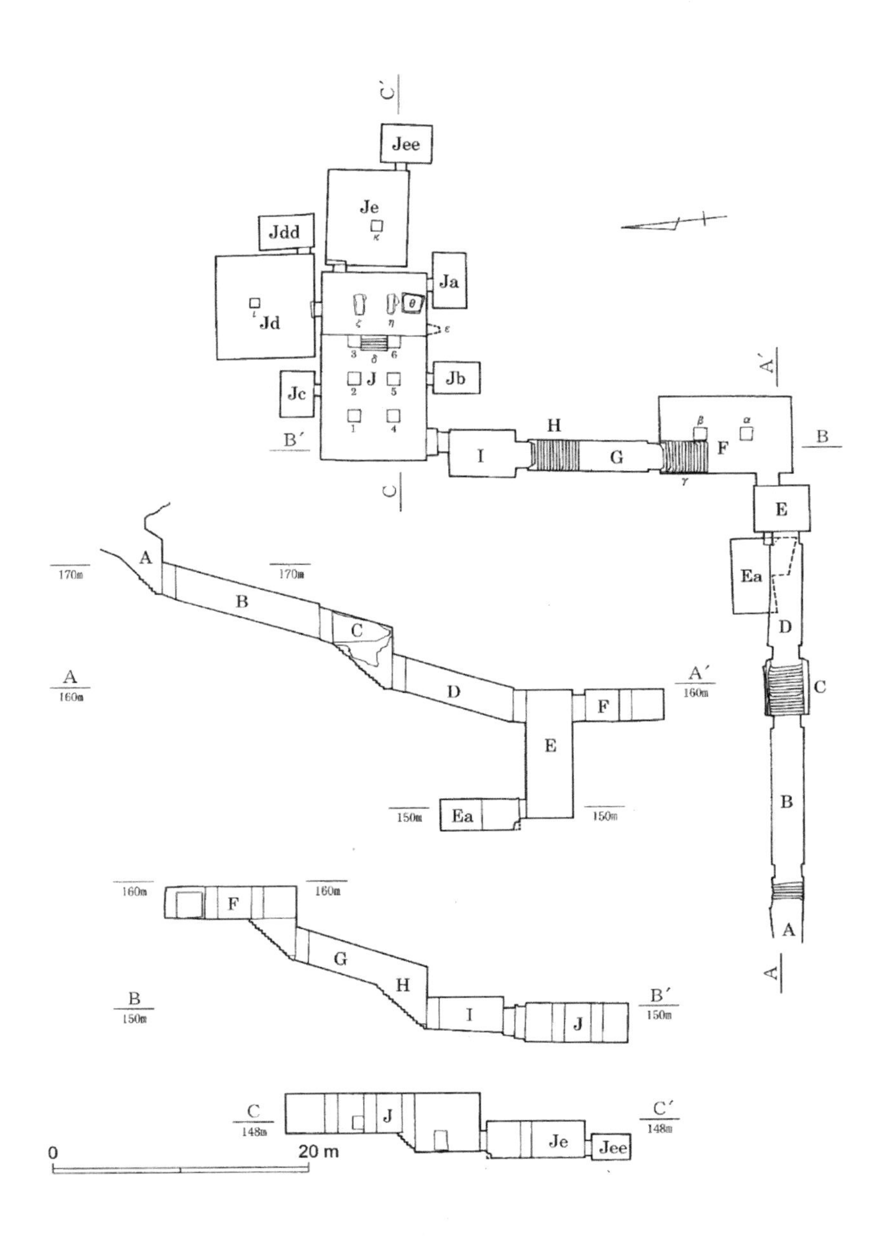

Figure 1: Plan of KV 22, the tomb of Amenhotep III (after S. Yoshimura [ed.], *Research in the Western Valley of the Kings, Egypt–The Tomb of Amenophis III (KV22)*; Tokyo: Chuo Koron Bijutsu Shuppan, 2008, fig.10)

the tomb, yielding thousands of fragments of funerary objects.[15] Now the Waseda team has focused on conservation of the wall paintings under the auspices of UNESCO, while documentation of the wall scenes after conservation and study of the objects from the tomb have been undertaken at the same time.[16]

Figure 2: Drawings including shabtis from the tomb of Amenhotep III in *Description de l'Egypte* (after *Description de l'Égypte* II, pl. 81)

FUNERARY EQUIPMENT FOR THE BURIAL OF AMENHOTEP III

The burial goods of the tomb of Amenhotep III seem to have been largely disturbed and scattered when the Waseda University team began its work. For example, fragments of a canopic chest and shabtis were uncovered outside the tomb. Thus, it is impossible to reconstruct the original locations of the finds in the tomb. However, we can at least try to reconstruct general components and features of Amenhotep III's funerary equipment even from tiny fragments. Following is the description of the major objects for the burial of this king in light of our recent work on the finds from his tomb.

SARCOPHAGUS OF AMENHOTEP III[17]

Eighteenth Dynasty kings were buried in magnificent stone sarcophagi capable of containing a number of anthropoid coffins, one nested within the other. In size the sarcophagus had grown tremendously toward the end of the dynasty; the lid was now vaulted, and its outline was no longer that of a simple box: the head end was rounded so that the plan assumed the shape of a cartouche. That the entire box of Amenhotep III's sarcophagus should have disappeared without a trace is mysterious. Its granite lid, broken into more than fifty pieces, still lines the sarcophagus chamber. We turned them upright and gathered the small fragments together in one place.

This lid appears to have originally been 300 cm in length and 134 cm in width. The central column contains the familiar prayer addressed by Amenhotep III to the goddess Nut. Eight horizontal bands consist of dedications of the king to the eight deities. Incised on the under surface are two significant innovations. The figure of the goddess Nut is winged for the first time, and two *wedjat* eyes that were previously accouterments on the side of the box have been moved to the undersurface of the lid, so that the king's mummy, resting on its back, could see out of them (Figure 3).[18] Notably, we found that a little gold still remained on several parts of the upper surface of the lid.[19] Our clearances found not one single fragment of the sarcophagus box.

ROYAL COFFINS[20]

Several fragments from the royal coffin (or coffins) were recovered (Figure 4). They have an inlayed *rishi*-pattern decoration resembling those of other royal coffins of the Eighteenth Dynasty; some represent the distal portion of the encircling wing of one of the protective goddesses, indicating that the original appearance was similar to that of the second coffin of Tutankhamun.[21] Remnants of the original gold leaf once covered in *rishi* decoration are observed on some fragments, but most were apparently stripped away by robbers in antiquity. Although we have uncovered only small fragments of royal coffin during our clearance, it is certain that Amenhotep III seems to have been buried in a type of coffin similar to that of Tutankhamun.

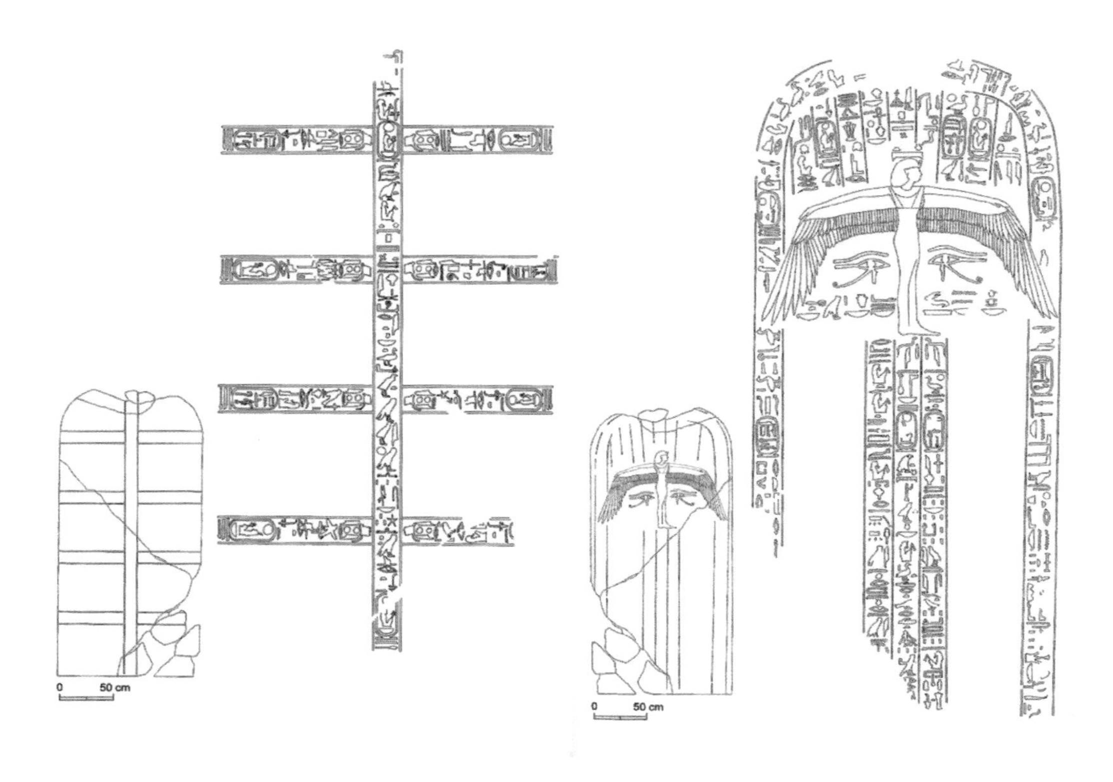

Figure 3: Drawings of the lid of the sarcophagus of Amenhotep III, after Yoshimura (ed.), *Research in the Western Valley of the Kings*, figs. 133–134

CANOPIC EQUIPMENT[22]

Although the canopic equipment of Amenhotep III had been largely unknown prior to our excavation, we uncovered a number of fragments that have enabled us to reconstruct its original appearance. Notably, several wooden fragments of a head wearing the *khat* headdress in the same scale proved that the four protective goddesses were attached to the canopic shrine of Amenhotep III, just as on that of Tutankhamun (Figures 5 and 6). The canopic chest of Amenhotep III is made of calcite, decorated with protective goddesses stretching their arms at its four corners, following the type of royal canopic chest initiated by Amenhotep II.[23]

Figure 4. Fragments of the royal *rishi* coffins of Amenhotep III

Unlike those of Tutankhamun and Horemheb, however, the legs of the protective goddesses at each corner were separated on each side, as on that of Amenhotep II. A fragment of a stopper showing the back of the king's *nemes* headdress proves that the stopper represented the head of the king (Figure 7). This evidence reveals that the assemblage of Amenhotep III's canopic equipment is similar to that of Tutankhamun.

SHABTIS OF AMENHOTEP III

The shabtis of Amenhotep III have survived in fairly large numbers and in various materials, including wood, faience, and several kinds of ornamental stone. The number, quality, and diversity of the shabtis from the tomb of Amenhotep III are remarkable compared to previous Eighteenth Dynasty royal tombs, including our excavated material: a total of over eighty in various states of preservation are known and stored in collections all over the world.[24] We also found a number of fragments of shabti figures made of a variety of materials, such as cedar, calcite, serpentine, and faience, in the course of the excavation (Figure 8). By comparing these to the king's shabtis in collections, we are able to understand the basic composition of the type of the shabtis from his tomb.

Figure 5: Fragments of the heads of the protective goddesses from Amenhotep III's canopic shrine

As for the stone examples, they can be grouped into four major types in terms of material: red granite, granodiorite, serpentine, and calcite. As Betsy Bryan noted, they represent red, black, and white, associated, respectively, with solarization, rejuvenation, and the Osiris mummy; she has also pointed out that these colors of the stone shabtis match those ordained by Amenhotep III for his funerary temple statuary.[25]

The first shabti group is of red granite. This type tends to be very tall, ranging from 60 to 70 cm in height. Red granite shabti figures wear the *nemes* headdress, white crown, and double crown. As the red granite sarcophagus was introduced for the burial of Amenhotep III, so he introduced this material for the fashioning of shabtis for the first time. This was probably due to his strong connection with the

Figure 6: Fragments of the canopic chest of Amenhotep III, showing the parts of one of the protective goddesses

solar cult.[26] The facial features of the red granite shabtis also express characteristics of this king's image in more detail than do other stone shabtis.

As for the granodiorite shabtis of Amenhotep III, examples were very few compared to other stones. However, the details are quite similar to those of the red granite shabtis probably because, as Bryan pointed out, both are of hard stone carved by the same workshop.[27]

Calcite shabti figures measure approximately 40 cm in height. This type also wears the *nemes* headdress, white crown, and double crown, like the examples of the red granite shabtis. Calcite shabtis tend to be lightly carved, and their facial features originally relied heavily on paint. The round shape and oblique almond eyes are very distinctive features of Amenhotep III.

Serpentine shabti figures seem to be the most numerous of the stone shabtis of this king. This type wears various styles of headdress, such as the *khat* headdress, Nubian wig, *nemes* headdress, and the *nemes* headdress surmounted by the double crown.

Figure 7: A fragment of a canopic stopper of Amenhotep III, showing the back side of a king's *nemes* headdress

Figure 8: Major fragments of the shabtis of Amenhotep III found by the Waseda University Egyptian Expedition

A pattern is apparent in the stone shabtis of Amenhotep III. The shabtis wearing the *nemes* headdress normally hold *ankh* signs in both hands, while those wearing either the double crown or white crown hold the crook and flail.

Wooden shabtis are the largest number among the shabti figures of Amenhotep III. As far as I have examined them, Amenhotep III's wooden shabti figures do not wear the *nemes* headdress. They normally wear either a blue crown, a red crown, a white crown, or a Nubian wig. Furthermore, they are made of either ebony or cedar. Ebony shabti figures are of a large scale, approximately 40 cm in height. An example in the Metropolitan Museum of Art is a masterpiece.[28] It has eyes inlaid with colored glass and rimmed with gold, and it bears an inscription—a long version of the shabti text especially composed for Amenhotep III—inlaid with yellow paste. The headdress of this piece is now missing, but it seems that it was made of another material, most probably faience. Smaller-scale wooden shabtis are made of cedar. No complete shabti, however, made of cedar remains. Most of the faces of the wooden shabtis of Amenhotep III had inlaid eyes, but some are modeled and painted. There are some fragments of wigs with a yellow band made of faience from Waseda University excavations.[29] Probably they were originally parts of wooden shabtis, since there is no body of a faience shabti of Amenhotep III, as far as I have investigated.

MISCELLANEOUS OBJECTS

A great number of fragments of funerary objects have been found in the course of our excavation since 1991. Other than the major funerary equipment just mentioned above, they include miniature coffins, magical bricks, statuary, model boats, sandals, furniture, faience ornaments and vessels, pieces of inlay, glass vessels, stone vessels, decorated pottery, among others. The detailed catalogue of these objects will be presented in the future publication.[30]

SHABTI FIGURES OF QUEEN TIYE AND HER REBURIAL IN THE TOMB OF AMENHOTEP III (KV 22)

A complete shabti and shabti fragments belonging to Queen Tiye were also found in the tomb of Amenhotep III by Napoleon's expedition (Figure 9) and by Howard Carter.[31] Carter stated that Queen Tiye had actually been buried in the tomb of Amenhotep III.[32] The shabti and fragments are made mainly of calcite, steatite, or faience. A piece bears the titles of not only *ḥmt nswt wrt* "great royal wife" but also *mwt nswt* "king's mother,"[33] indicating she was also the mother of a king (apparently Akhenaten) when they were manufactured. Furthermore, one shabti is inscribed with *mwt nswt n wʿ-n-rʿ Ty ʿnḫ.ti* "the mother of Waenre, Tiye, may she live."[34] This evidence clearly indicates that these shabti figures were manufactured during the reign of Akhenaten. In fact, the gilded shrine for the burial of Queen Tiye from KV 55 has exactly the same inscription (Figure 10),[35] suggesting that Akhenaten commissioned the shabti for the same purpose at almost the same time.

Nicholas Reeves believes that the shabti fragments inscribed with the text "king's mother (of Waenre)" would be easier to explain if the reigns of Amenhotep III and Amenhotep IV-Akhenaten were at one stage concurrent.[36] Rolf Krauss and Maarten Raven supposed that these shabtis are votive, like the shabtis dedicated to Tutankhamun by Nakhtmin and Maya.[37] Reeves noted that if there were no

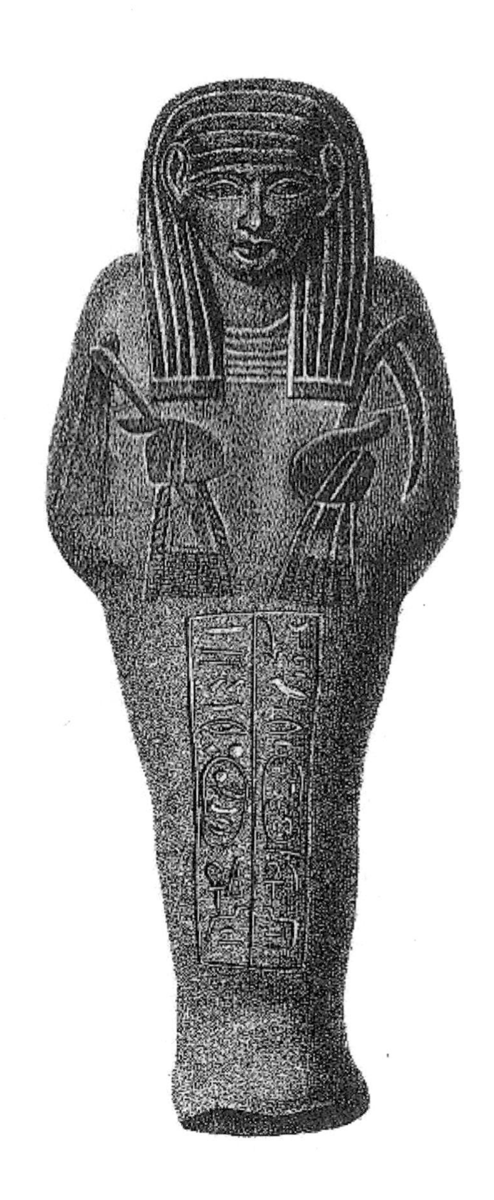

Figure 9: A shabti of Queen Tiye found in KV 22 by Napoleon's expedition (after *Description de l'Égypte* II, pl. 80.6)

coregency between Amenhotep III and his son, these would have to be interpreted not as shabtis for the queen's use in the next world but as votive images offered by the queen for her dead husband's burial.[38] On the other hand, Marc Gabolde and Marianne Eaton-Krauss believe that Queen Tiye was reburied in the tomb of

Figure 10: Inscriptions from the gilded shrine of Queen Tiye from KV 55 (after T. M. Davis et al., *The Tomb of Queen Tiyi* [London: Constable and Co., 1910], pl. 35)

Figure 11: Side of the gilded shrine of Queen Tiye from KV 55 (after Davis et al., *Tomb of Queen Tiyi*, pl. 33)

Amenhotep III as her husband had originally intended by making a burial chamber for her behind Amenhotep III's own burial chamber, her corpse and funerary equipment having been transferred from the royal tomb at Amarna to Thebes after the abandonment of Akhetaten.[39]

A complete shabti figure of Queen Tiye made of steatite found by Napoleon's expedition has two columns of inscriptions on its surface containing the throne name of Amenhotep III and the name of Queen Tiye (Figure 9).[40] Stylistically it dates to the Amarna period, and "Osiris" is not written before the names of the king and queen, unlike the shabtis of Amenhotep III. As Christiane Ziegler and Eaton-

Krauss rightly noted, the use of phonetic characters instead of a figure for the *maat* element in Amenhotep III's throne name shows that it was made after Amenhotep III's death.[41] This is also observed on the sarcophagus of Queen Tiye found in the royal tomb at el-Amarna[42] and on her gilded shrine found in KV 55 (Figure 11).[43] A fragment of a foot of a wooden shabti found by the Waseda University Egyptian Expedition has the tip of the *ankh* sign presumably attached to the sun disk, which was particularly used during Akhenaten's reign (Figure 12). The text ends with *nḥḥ* "forever," showing that the original text might have been dedicated to Queen Tiye on the basis of the text "king's mother Tiye, may she live forever" inscribed on a shabti fragment of Queen Tiye.[44] A parallel can be found on her gilded shrine from KV 55.[45] Therefore, it can be assumed that this wooden shabti was also made during Akhenaten's reign.

Two fine faience faces of a queen from our excavation also seem to represent Tiye (Figure 13), since at least one of these could be joined to a fragmentary body of the queen's shabti now at Highclere Castle.[46] It is now exhibited there with the cast of a face and neck slotted neatly into the recess at the top, flanked by blue faience lappets of a tripartite wig. The top of the frame for two columns of inscription is preserved.

Figure 12: A foot of a shabti of Queen Tiye (?) found in KV 22 by the Waseda University team

Figure 13: Two faces in yellow faience found in KV 22 by the Waseda University team

Although it is very difficult to read the text, I was able to identify a part of *ḥmt nswt* "king's wife," which confirms the identification of the shabti.[47] One of the two faience faces has a pierced ear, which, according to Eaton-Krauss, is a feature favored during the Amarna period,[48] and this also indicates that it was made during Akhenaten's reign. The same feature is observed on the ears of a calcite head of Queen Tiye in Chicago, which was recently identified by Eaton-Krauss.[49]

Evidence so far suggests that the shabti figures of Queen Tiye were made during Akhenaten's reign and after the death of Amenhotep III. Thus, they do not seem to have been votive images offered by Queen Tiye to the burial of Amenhotep III. Instead, they indicate that the queen's burial was transferred from the royal tomb at Amarna to the tomb of Amenhotep III after Akhenaten's death. When did this event take place? Marianne Eaton-Krauss suggested that this was done toward the end of Smenkhkare's reign,[50] while Marc Gabolde believes that Queen Tiye was reburied in the tomb of Amenhotep III during Tutankhamun's reign.[51]

The Waseda University team also found a graffito with the regnal year date of an unnamed king between the antechamber and the staircase in the tomb of Amenhotep III (Figure 14). It reads *ḥꜣt-sp* 3 *ꜣbd* 3 *ꜣḫt sw* 7 "Year 3, 3rd month of *akhet*

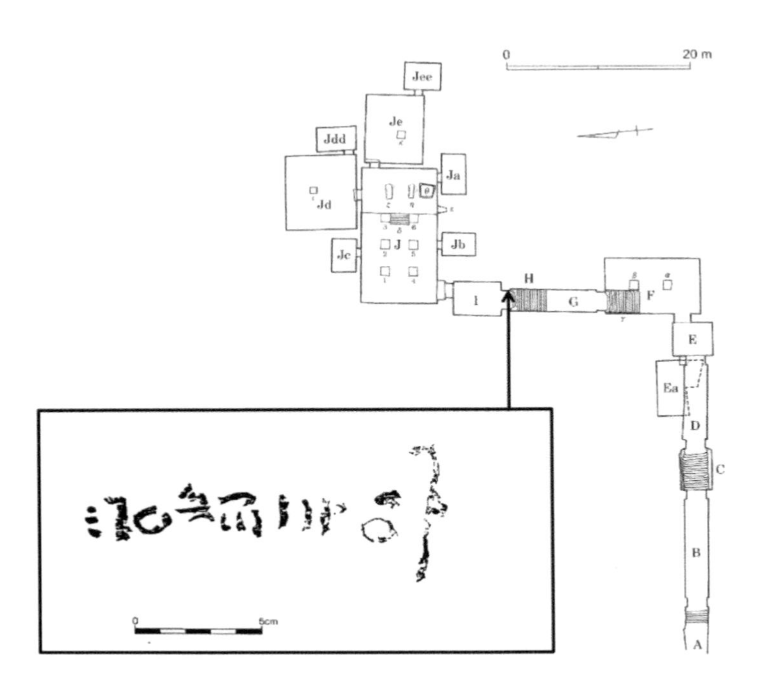

Figure 14: The year 3 graffito in the tomb of Amenhotep III and its location

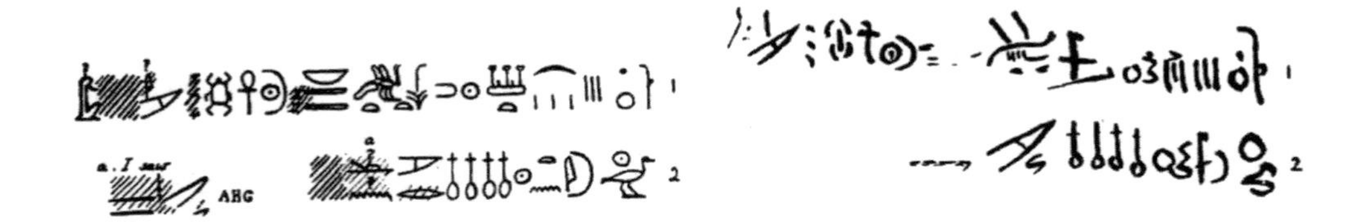

Figure 15: The year 3 graffito of Pawah in the tomb of Pairi (TT 139), after Gardiner, "The Graffito from the Tomb of Pere," *JEA* 14 (1928), pl. fig. 1

season, day 7."[52] As Eaton-Krauss suggested, this graffito seems to have been associated with the date of the reburial of Queen Tiye.[53]

Nicholas Reeves and Richard Wilkinson, however, suggested that the graffito was written at the time the tomb was closed, following the interment of Amenhotep III, and also noted this as possible evidence of a co-regency between Amenhotep

III and Amenhotep IV-Akhenaten.[54] Eaton-Krauss, however, suggested that the year 3 graffito could be related to the preparation for the reburial of Queen Tiye in KV 22 toward the end of Smenkhkare's reign.[55] Marc Gabolde believes that the year 3 graffito in KV 22 was written a few days before the graffito of Pawah in year 3 of King Neferneferuaten in the tomb of Pairi (TT 139) (Figure 15)[56] due to the similarity of paleography and close dates of the events, and he suggests that the graffito in KV 22 is the date of the reburial of Queen Tiye in the tomb of Amenhotep III during Neferneferuaten's year 3.[57]

Another possibility is that the year 3 graffito records the date of work at a particular part of the tomb,[58] but this year 3 seems to have been too early to finish that part of the royal tomb in Amenhotep III's reign, even though his father Thutmose IV had already excavated it.

In the tomb of Thutmose IV, a graffito with the year 8 of Horemheb is written on the wall of the antechamber, which is close to the door of the burial chamber. This graffito mentions the renewal of Thutmose IV's burial ordained by Maya, overseer of the treasury and overseer of the royal necropolis.[59] This graffito was written on the wall of the antechamber where there was no painting, while the walls of the antechamber in the tomb of Amenhotep III were completely decorated. It can be assumed, then, that the year 3 graffito in Amenhotep III's tomb was written in an empty space closest to the entrance to the burial chamber; it is also likely that the year 3 graffito was written after a later activity associated with the burial. Therefore, I suggest that the year 3 graffito was written on the date of the reburial of Queen Tiye. The location of the year 3 graffito in KV 22 is thus quite similar to that of the year 8 graffito in KV 43, because both were written on the empty wall closest to the door to the burial chamber. Like the graffito with the year 8 of Horemheb in the tomb of Thutmose IV, the year 3 graffito in the tomb of Amenhotep III might relate to the restoration activity of the tomb from the heretical period of Akhenaten's reign. Indeed, the reburial of Queen Tiye in the tomb of Amenhotep III could be seen as a "restoration" of the tomb after the Amarna period.

The paleography of the year 3 graffito appears to be late Eighteenth Dynasty. It resembles those of both the graffito of Pawah listing year 3 of King Neferneferuaten in TT 139 and the wine-jar dockets from the tomb of Tutankhamun.[60] Since Neferneferuaten had already returned to the worship of Amun, as the graffito of Pawah mentions, it is not unlikely that the year 3 graffito in KV 22 was written during King Neferneferuaten's reign for either the inspection of the tomb for the reburial of Queen Tiye or for the purpose of Queen Tiye's actual reburial, as Eaton-Krauss suggests, or for Queen Tiye's actual reburial, as Gabolde suggests. However, Neferneferuaten's successor, Tutankhaten, seems to have ascended to the throne in Akhetaten,[61] and the court left Amarna only around year 2 of his reign.[62] Therefore, it is more reasonable to assume that the transfer of the burial of Queen Tiye from the royal tomb at Amarna to the tomb of Amenhotep III was undertaken in Tutankhamun's year 3.

Although the funerary shrine of Queen Tiye was installed in KV 55, I assume that the shrine was probably intended to be brought to KV 22. Presumably the plan was changed either due to the difficulty of installing such a large object in KV 22, which already contained a large amount of funerary equipment belonging to Amenhotep III when the reburial of Queen Tiye took place, or due to an unknown religious reason, since the shrine still bore images of the Aten. Furthermore, numerous seal impressions carrying the prenomen of Tutankhamun were found in KV 55, where the funerary shrine was placed.[63] Reeves and Gabolde have argued that the reburial of the Amarna royal family took place under Tutankhamun's reign.[64] Recent investigation of DNA of the royal family of the late Eighteenth Dynasty by Zahi Hawass and his team proved that Queen Tiye is Tutankhamun's grandmother, suggesting the intimate relationship between them.[65]

Therefore, I suggest that the reburial of Queen Tiye in the tomb of Amenhotep III was made in year 3 of Tutankhamun as he buried his father Akhenaten in KV 55.

Notes

1. The earlier version of this paper was presented at the International Symposium "Valley of the Kings since Howard Carter," sponsored by the Supreme Council of Antiquities and held in Luxor, Egypt, on November 4, 2009. This paper was a part of the result of my research funded by the Grant-in-Aid of the Japan Society for the Promotion of Science, which enabled me to participate in the symposium. I am grateful to Zahi Hawass, then Vice Minister of the Ministry of Culture, for inviting me to the international symposium "Valley of the Kings since Howard Carter," and to the staff of the symposium. I would like to thank Professor Emeritus Sakuji Yoshimura and Professor Jiro Kondo for permission to work and present material from the excavations at the tomb of Amenhotep III by the Waseda University Egyptian Expedition.
2. Cf. N. Reeves and R. H. Wilkinson, *The Complete Valley of the Kings* (London: Thames and Hudson, 1996), 113–114.

3 See J. Kondo, "A Preliminary Report on the Re-clearance of the Tomb of Amenophis III (WV 22)," in C. N. Reeves (ed.), *After Tutankhamun: Research and Excavations in the Royal Necropolis at Thebes* (London and New York: Kegan Paul, 1992), 41–54; J. Kondo, "The Re-clearance of Tombs WV 22 and WV A in the Western Valley of the Kings," in R. H. Wilkinson (ed.), *Valley of the Sun Kings: New Explorations in the Tombs of the Pharaohs* (Tucson: University of Arizona Egyptian Expedition, 1995), 25–33; S. Yoshimura and J. Kondo, "Excavating the Tomb of Amenophis III," *Egyptian Archaeology* 7 (1995), 17–18; S. Yoshimura and J. Kondo, "The Tomb of Amenophis III: Waseda University Excavations 1989-2000," *ASAE* 78 (2004), 205–209; N. Kawai, "Objects from KV22," in S. Yoshimura (ed.), *Research in the Western Valley of the Kings, Egypt – The Tomb of Amenophis III (KV22)* (Tokyo: Chuo Koron Bijutsu Shuppan, 2008), 139–204, 262–266 (English summary).

4 This is the project funded by the Japan Society for the Promotion of Science through its Grant-in-Aid for Scientific Research. The final publication of the objects from the tomb of Amenhotep III will include those stored in museums and collections around the world. I have studied the objects from the tomb of Amenhotep III in the following museums and collections: Metropolitan Museum of Art, New York; British Museum, London; Petrie Museum of Egyptian Archaeology, University College London; Myers Collection, Eton College; and Highclere Castle, Newbury. I would like to thank Dorothea Arnold, Catharine Roehrig, Diana Craig Patch (Metropolitan Museum of Art), W. Vivian Davies, John H. Taylor (British Museum), Stephen Quirke (Petrie Museum of Egyptian Archaeology), Nicholas Reeves (then Eton College), the eighth Earl of Carnarvon, and Lady Fiona Carnarvon (Highclere Castle) for the permission to work with the objects in the aforementioned collections.

5 H. Carter, MSS, GI I. A. 139 (1–4), I. J. 386 (nos 5–58).

6 C. N. Reeves, *Valley of the Kings: Decline of a Royal Necropolis* (London: K. Paul International, 1990), 39, n. 74.

7 M. Eaton-Krauss, "Review of N. Reeves and R. H. Wilkinson, *The Complete Valley of the Kings*," *BiOr* 56.3–4 (1999): 333; T. Kikuchi, "Wall Decoration," in Yoshimura (ed.), *Research in the Western Valley of the Kings*, 133, 261–262 (English summary).

8 W. C. Hayes, *Royal Sarcophagi of the XVIIIth Dynasty* (Princeton: Princeton University Press, 1935), 124–127.

9 For the burial of Queen Tiye at the Royal Tomb at Amarna, see M. J. Raven, "A Sarcophagus for Queen Tiye and Other Fragments from the Royal Tomb at el-Amarna," *OMRO* 74 (1994): 7–20; E. C. Brock, "The Sarcophagus of Queen Tiy," *JSSEA* 26 (1999): 8–21; M. Gabolde, *D'Akhenaton à Toutankhamon* (Lyon: Université Lumière-Lyon 2, Institut d'archéologie et d'histoire de l'antiquité, 1998) 126, 129, 134–138.

10 For the details of the enlargement of Room Jd for the burial of Sitamun, see N. Kawai, "Architecture of KV22," in Yoshimura (ed.), *Research in the Western Valley of the Kings*, 51–54, 256 (English summary).

11 Hayes, "Inscriptions from the Palace of Amenhotep III," *JNES* 10 (1951): fig. 9, label type 95.

12 *Description de l'Égypte* III, 193; X, 218.

13 Carter, MSS, GI I. A. 138, 139, 140, I. J. 386.

14 For the collections at Highclere Castle, see N. Reeves, *Ancient Egypt at Highclere Castle* (Newbury, Berkshire: Highclere Castle, 1989); N. Strudwick, *The Legacy of Lord Carnarvon: Miniatures from Ancient Egypt and the Valley of the Kings* (Laramie, Wyoming: University of Wyoming Art Museum, 2001); Lady Fiona Carnarvon, *Egypt at Highclere: The Discovery of Tutankhamun* (Newbury, Berkshire: Highclere Castle, 2006). For the collections in the Metropolitan Museum of Art, see W. C. Hayes, *The Scepter of Egypt: A Background for the Study of the Egyptian Antiquities in the Metropolitan Museum of Art 2. The Hyksos and the New Kingdom (1675–1080 B.C.)* (New York: Harper, 1959).

15 See note 4 in this article.

16 For the result of the first and second phase of the conservation, see S. Yoshimura and J. Kondo (eds.), *Conservation of the Wall Paintings in the Royal Tomb of Amenophis III—First and Second Phase Report* (Paris and Tokyo: UNESCO and Waseda University, 2004).

17 Hayes, *Royal Sarcophagi*, 27–30, 123–132, 170–171, pl. XVI; Kawai, "Objects from KV22," 139–142, figs. 133–135, pls. 30, 53, 54.

18 Hayes, *Royal Sarcophagi*, 129, n. 75, 132.

19 Kondo, "Preliminary Report," 45.

20 Kawai, "Objects from KV22," 142–143, 178, fig. 140, 263, pl. 31.

21 Cf. Z. Hawass, *King Tutankhamun: The Treasures of the Tomb* (London: Thames and Hudson, 2007), 103–105, 107–108.

22 Kawai, "Objects from KV22," 144–145, 180–181, figs. 142–143, 263, pl. 31.

23 Cf. A. Dodson, *The Canopic Equipment of the Kings of Egypt* (London: Kegan Paul International, 1994), 48–68, pls. XVIII–XXIX.

24 C. Strauss-Seeber once counted about sixty shabtis of Amenhotep III; see C. Strauss-Seeber, "Kriterien zur Erkennung der königliche Rundplastik Amenophis'III," in L. M. Berman (ed.), *The Art of Amenhotep III: Art Historical Analysis* (Cleveland: Cleveland Museum of Art, 1990), 14. However, I have counted more than eighty, including the pieces from Waseda University excavations and others.

25 B. M. Bryan, "67. Shawabty of Amenhotep III," in A. P. Kozloff and B. M. Bryan, *Egypt's Dazzling Sun: Amenhotep III and His World* (Cleveland: Cleveland Museum of Art, 1992), 325.

26 Cf. Bryan, "68. Shawabty of Amenhotep III," in Kozloff and Bryan, *Egypt's Dazzling Sun*, 326.

27 Cf. Bryan, "67. Shawabty of Amenhotep III," in Kozloff and Bryan, *Egypt's Dazzling Sun*, 325.

28 Hayes, *Scepter of Egypt* 2, 241–242, fig. 146.

29 Kawai, "Objects from KV22," 151, nos. 53–54, pl. 32.

30 As for the major miscellaneous objects, see Kawai, "Objects from KV22," 151–175, figs. 147–165, pls. 32–36, 55–60.

31 As for the list of Queen Tiye's shabtis from the tomb of Amenhotep III (KV22), see C. Ziegler, "Notes sur la Reine Tiy," in C. Berger, G. Clerc, and N. Grimal (eds.), *Hommages à Jean Leclant 1, Études Pharaoniques* (Cairo: Institut français d'archéologie orientale, 1994), 542–48; Gabolde, *D'Akhenaton à Toutankhamon*, 139–141; M. Eaton-Krauss, "The Head from a Shabti of Queen Tiye in Chicago," *Orientalia* 75.1 (2006): 88–89.

32 H. Carter and A. C. Mace, *The Tomb of Tut.Ankh.Amen* I (London: Cassell, 1923), 121.

33 Aubert collection, a fragment of the legs of a shabti, in calcite. J. F. Aubert and L. Aubert, *Statuettes égyptiennes: chaouabtis, ouchebtis* (Paris: Librairie d'Amérique et d'Orient, 1974), 52–53, pl. 6 (12–13).

34 Louvre E 21438, a fragment of the legs of a shabti, in calcite. J.-L. Bovot, *Les serviteurs funéraires royaux et princiers de l'ancienne Égypte* (Paris: Réunion des musées nationaux, 2003), 216–217.

35 T. M. Davis et al., *The Tomb of Queen Tiyi* (London: Constable and Co., 1910), 13, pl. XXXI.

36 N. Reeves and R. H. Wilkinson, *The Complete Valley of the Kings: Tombs and Treasures of Egypt's Greatest Pharaohs* (London: Thames and Hudson, 1996), 110.

37 R. Krauss, *Das Ende der Amarnazeit* (Hildesheim: Gerstenberg, 1978), 99–100; M. Raven, "A Sarcophagus for Queen Tiy and Other Fragments from the Royal Tomb at el-Amarna," *OMRO* 74 (1994): 418.

38 Reeves and Wilkinson, *Complete Valley of the Kings*, 110.

39 Gabolde, *D'Akhenaton à Toutankhamon*, 138–145; Eaton-Krauss, "Review of N. Reeves and R. H. Wilkinson," 334.

40 Ziegler, "Notes sur la Reine Tiy," 543–544, fig. 3.

41 Ziegler, "Notes sur la Reine Tiy," 544–545; Eaton-Krauss, "Head from a Shabti," 89–90.

42 Gabolde, *D'Akhenaton à Toutankhamon*, pls. XVIII, XX.

43 Davis et al., *Tomb of Queen Tiyi*, pls. XXXI-XXXII.

44 Ibid.

45 Cf. Ziegler, "Notes sur la Reine Tiy," 547.

46 Kondo, "Preliminary Report," 47–48, pl. VIII; Yoshimura and Kondo, "Excavating the Tomb of Amenophis III," 17.

47 I am grateful to the eighth Earl of Carnarvon and Lady Fiona Carnarvon for allowing me to examine the shabti of Queen Tiye at Highclere Castle in September 2009.

48 Eaton-Krauss, "Head from a Shabti," 90.

49 Eaton-Krauss, "Head from a Shabti," 90, Tab. IX, X.

50 Eaton-Krauss, "Review of N. Reeves and R. H. Wilkinson," 334.

51 Reeves and Wilkinson, *Complete Valley of the Kings*, 113, 115.

52 Kondo, "Re-clearance of Tombs WV 22 and WV A," 29–30.

53 Eaton-Krauss, "Review of N. Reeves and R. H. Wilkinson," 334.
54 Reeves and Wilkinson, *Complete Valley of the Kings*, 113, 115.
55 Eaton-Krauss, "Review of N. Reeves and R. H. Wilkinson," 334.
56 A. H. Gardiner, "The Graffito from the Tomb of Pere," *JEA* 14 (1928): 10–11.
57 Personal communication with Marc Gabolde.
58 This sort of graffito can be found in other royal tombs in the Valley of the Kings. For example, see H. Altenmüller, "Bemerkungen zu den neu gefundenen Daten im Grab der Königin Twosre (KV14) im Tal der Könige von Theben," in Reeves (ed.), *After Tutankhamun*, 141–164.
59 T. M. Davis et al., *The Tomb of Thoutmôsis IV* (London: Constable and Co., 1904), xxxiii f., with fig. 7.
60 J. Černy, *Hieratic Inscriptions from the Tomb of Tutankhamun*, Tutankhamun Tomb Series 2 (Oxford: Griffith Institute Press, 1965).
61 A. Dodson believes, however, that Neferuneferuaten and Tutankhaten were coregent for three years. See, A. Dodson, *Amarna Sunset: Nefertiti, Tutankhamun, Ay, Horemheb and the Egyptian Counter-Reformation* (Cairo: American University in Cairo Press, 2009), 47–52.
62 Cf. B. J. Kemp, "The Amarna Workman's Village in Retrospect," *JEA* 73 (1987), 42.
63 Reeves, *Valley of the Kings*, 44, pl. II.
64 Reeves, *Valley of the Kings*, 44, pl. II; Gabolde, *D'Akhenaton à Toutankhamon*, 262–263.
65 Z. Hawass et al., "Ancestry and Pathology in King Tutankhamun's Family," *Journal of American Medical Association* 303-7 (2010): 638–647.

The Debate over Egyptian Monotheism: Richard H. Wilkinson's Perspective

Nanno Marinatos
University of Illinois at Chicago

Interpretations of Amarna-era monotheism are products of their historical and cultural contexts. The examples examined are those of Arthur J. Evans, James Henry Breasted, Erik Hornung, and Richard H. Wilkinson.

Egyptian monotheism has preoccupied Egyptologists since the discovery of the Amarna texts at the end of the nineteenth century. But although the content of Akhenaten's hymns has been clear enough to the specialists, the evaluation of the Amarna religion and its monotheism has varied. In the following brief essay in honor of Richard H. Wilkinson, I will make an attempt to put his work on Egyptian religion into a historical perspective.

Monotheism is not an ancient word. According to Jan Assmann, it was invented in the seventeenth century to distinguish Judaism, Christianity, and Islam from the idolatrous religions of the "other."[1] Since it was a tool of polemics against idolatry, the monotheism propounded by Akhenaten was at first regarded in a positive light and as a mark of civilization. Let us take a brief look at two scholars—one dealing with Egypt, the other with Minoan Crete—in the period just before and between World Wars I and II.

In 1912, the American Egyptologist James H. Breasted in his *Development of Religion and Thought in Ancient Egypt* suggested that the principal features of monotheistic religion were justice and ethics and that they were rooted already in the Pyramid Texts of the Old Kingdom. The development (toward improvement) ended with the Amarna age and was analogous to the development of the religion of the Hebrews.[2] Later, Breasted produced another book, *The Dawn of Conscience,* in which he argued more fully that Amarna religion was a precursor of Judeo-Christian-Islamic monotheism.[3] This was a very influential work, which had an impact even on Sigmund Freud, as Jan Assmann explains in *Moses the Egyptian.*[4]

At the same time as Breasted was writing, his British colleague and friend, the excavator of Knossos, Arthur Evans, produced his own version of monotheism applied to Minoan religion. Indeed, it was only after the end of World War I that

Evans made important revisions to his interpretation of Minoan cult and arrived at the conclusion that one goddess embodied all others. Previously he had explained the images of Crete with the aid of the anthropological theory of primitive religious animism as outlined by E. B. Tylor in 1877.[5] However, by 1932 Evans was convinced that Crete had a highly civilized religion, and he wrote: "It seems to me that we are in the presence of a largely Monotheistic cult, in which the female form of divinity held a supreme place."[6] Note that nowhere did he deny polytheism. He assumed that one single female deity held the supreme position in the pantheon and she embodied all the other female deities, who were her manifestations. He was led to this view by the observation that the images of goddesses were not diversified enough to warrant distinct *personas*. Quite the opposite was the case: all iconographical variations of the female conformed to a basic formula.

How was it possible that such a civilized and advanced religion existed at such an early period of mankind? Evans imagined two possibilities. The first was that unity of deity (we would call it *monism* today) was due to a relic of a primeval deity of Neolithic times, when one single matriarchal goddess prevailed. Yet, such a relic did not fully explain the complex character of the goddess, who, as Evans came to realize, was mistress of both heaven and the underworld. A second possibility was more likely: Crete developed its theological monism under the impact of Egypt. He wrote:

> Clearly the Goddess was supreme, whether we are to regard her as substantially one being of varied aspects, celestial, terrestrial, or infernal, or partly differentiated divine entities. As a working hypothesis the former view has been here preferred.[7]

Of the striking affinity between the Minoan goddess to Egyptian Hathor and Isis he wrote in 1921:

> How much of the spiritual being of the Egyptian Mother Goddess may not have been absorbed by her Minoan sister? [...] A curious sympathy with the cycle of the Egyptian Mother Goddess was in fact afforded by the subject of certain animal reliefs found in the Temple repository.[8]

Thus, Evans and Breasted arrived at similar conclusions about monotheism as regarded the ancient religions they studied, and it is no accident that the two men corresponded and exchanged views. Breasted wrote in 1927 that Evans recognized the role of ancient Egypt in the development of human history.[9] At the core of their conception of monotheism were ethics and justice. Breasted dedicated an entire chapter to ethical monotheism in his *Development of Religion and Thought in Ancient Egypt*.[10] The solar deity, Aten, he stated, united the entire inhabited world as well as the cosmos in one entity, and his epithet was "a mother, profitable to gods and men." The father and mother of mankind was a deity of utter kindness and solicitude for mankind.[11] Breasted also stated that "the obligation to a moral life" was dictated by the sun god.[12]

Similarly, Evans wrote in 1932:

> Surveying the whole field it may be confidently said that, so far as the evidence goes, of all of these kindred religious systems, that of ancient Crete and of the Minoan world stands out as the purest and best.[13]

The two men, who were almost exact contemporaries, evidently believed in the goodness of civilization and projected this to the cultures they studied and admired.

Before we reflect on the time period in which they wrote, we must make a small digression on Evans. He did not take the phenomenon of civilization for granted, nor did he think that it was the inevitable product of the betterment of human development. Compared to the vast history of mankind, reaching back to hundreds of thousands of years and geological times, civilization was like a diamond lost in the grains of desert sand. He had learned this from his father, John Evans, an acquaintance of Charles Darwin. In *Descent of Man*, Darwin expressed the pessimistic opinion that although mankind's intellectual faculties were gradually perfected through natural selection, there existed no guarantees of constant progress. Reversion could always occur: "We must remember that progress is no invariable rule."[14] This was one more reason to appreciate the civilizations of Egypt and Minoan Crete.

One wonders, though, whether it was entirely due to accident that they formulated these thoughts around the period of the First World War and in the inter-war years. These times were marked by social unrest, contestation of traditional values, revolutionary political movements, atheism, bolshevism, communism, feminism, and (not too far in the horizon of the future) fascism. Traditional aesthetics in art had been challenged by expressionist painters in Germany and the cubism of Picasso and Braque in Paris. The cinema of the Weimar Republic in Berlin had utilized artificial expressionist sets and characters of insane criminals, prostitutes, and socially troubled masses. Seen against this backdrop, it almost seems as though Breasted and Evans unconsciously defended the boundaries of their civilization as they knew it and found echoes of it in ancient monotheistic traditions.

But the world was moving on. Breasted died in New York City in 1935 of a *Streptococcus* infection after returning from Egypt—this was the time of Hitler's highest popularity in Germany. Evans died at his home at Youlbury, near Oxford, six years later. During his last days, in the summer of 1941, he was told that Crete was bombarded by the Germans and that the Herakleion Museum (where all the antiquities of Minoan Crete were stored) had been hit by explosives. His lifetime's work was destroyed—or so he thought. Both men felt that they defended the possibilities of civilization.

Our times appear to have different concerns. After the Second World War, Akhenaten's religion appears more dogmatic than moral. Eberhard Otto (1953) called the pharaoh ambitious, egocentric, ugly, and despotic.[15] Barry J. Kemp feels that "Akhenaten's kingship provides an unintended caricature of all modern leaders who indulge in the trappings of charismatic display."[16] Jan Assmann sees Akhenaten as the inventor of a counter-religion that traumatized Egyptian society and created a memory of Egypt as a land of despotism and hubris.[17]

It is no accident that the twentieth century has been more attracted to the other side of Egyptian religion, its pluralism. Erik Hornung, in a groundbreaking monograph with the subtitle *The One and the Many*, avoids the term *monotheism* to describe Egyptian religion and uses instead *henotheism*, a term he borrows from the nineteenth century historian of religion, Max Müller.[18] Hornung reconciles the one and the many by reference to the special qualities of Egyptian logic of classification, a logic that differs from Christian systematic theology and yet is entirely valid. The unity of a god exists as a concept but may be diversified in his/her manifestations or forms. For example, the mother goddess may be split to the lioness Sekhmet and the cow Hathor, thereby expressing *both* the maternal tenderness of the cow *and* the wildness of the lioness, all in one.[19] This is remarkably close to what Evans envisaged for the Minoan goddess, except that Hornung does not use the term *monotheism*, which is reserved only for the exclusive religion of Akhenaten.[20]

Wilkinson's work is much indebted to Hornung, since both scholars take images seriously as expressions of belief. But it is Wilkinson to whom we owe several pictorial dictionaries of images and a systematization of the conceptual and visual apparatus of Egyptian religious pluralism.[21] Wilkinson writes:

> Despite the fact that the Egyptian pantheon appears to the outside observer to be filled with a veritable menagerie of gods, goddesses and other beings in an almost mindless variety of manifestations, for the most part Egyptian deities were conceived in logical types consisting of human (anthropomorphic), animal (zoomorphic), hybrid and composite forms.[22]

Later in the same book, he continues:

> As god or a goddess who might well be described as a cosmic or "ancestral" or "underworld" deity could at the same time also be a deity associated closely with creation or kingship or any number of other aspects of existence [...] [T]he many gods and goddesses included have been grouped by their appearances.[23]

These works have been invaluable sources to many scholars outside the field of Egyptology, including the present author, because classification and analysis are the first rules of science.[24] By correlating forms and conceptual categories, Wilkinson demonstrated not only the pluralism and unity of Egyptian religion but the special place that Akhenaten's reform held in this tradition.

> Rather than its radical focus on one god [...] it was a dogmatic exclusiveness that set the religion of Akhenaten apart and that ultimately made his theology unacceptable to most Egyptians. It would only be with the eventual rise of Christianity and Islam that such exclusivity in the worship of the One would take hold, and in so doing, would historically spell the end for Egypt's Many.[25]

This brief overview of the debate over monotheism shows a shift of values. Breasted and Evans were defending the goodness of their civilization through the concept of monotheism because they equated it with morality and justice. But Egyptologists today have learned to distrust dogma because it leads to fanaticism and possibly violence. Wilkinson outlines the ethical elements in Egyptian religion but does not confine them to the aesthetics and exclusive dogma of Akhenaten's reign.

NOTES

1 Jan Assmann, *Moses the Egyptian: The Memory of Egypt in Western Monotheism* (Cambridge, Mass., and London: Harvard University Press, 1997); Jan Assmann, "Monotheism and Polytheism," in S. Isles Johnston (ed.), *Religions of the Ancient World* (Cambridge, Mass.: Harvard University Press, 2004), 17–31.

2 James Henry Breasted, *Development of Religion and Thought in Ancient Egypt* (New York: C. Scribner's Sons, 1912), xv, 312–343.

3 James Henry Breasted, *The Dawn of Conscience* (New York and London: C. Scribner's Sons, 1933).

4 Assmann, *Moses the Egyptian*, 144–167.

5 Edward Burnett Tylor, *Primitive Culture: Researches into the Development of Mythology, Philosophy, Religion, Art, and Custom* 2 (1871; reprint, New York: Henry Holt & Co., 1877); Arthur J. Evans, "The Mycenaean Tree and Pillar Cult and its Mediterranean Relations," *JHS* 21 (1901): 99–204.

6 Arthur J. Evans, 1932. "The Earlier Religion of Greece in the Light of Cretan Discoveries," in Warren R. Dawson (ed.), *The Frazer Lectures 1922–1932 by Diverse Hands* (1932; reprint, Freeport, N.Y.: N.Y. Books for Libraries Press, 1967), 41.

7 Arthur J. Evans, *The Palace of Minos at Knossos* III (London: MacMillan, 1930), 457.

8 Arthur J. Evans, *The Palace of Minos at Knossos* I (London: MacMillan, 1921), 510.

9 James Henry Breasted, "The New Crusade." *American Historical Review* 34.2 (1929): 215–236 (http://www.historians.org/info/aha_history/jhbreasted.htm).

10 Breasted, *Development of Religion*, 165–198, 312–343.

11 Breasted, *Development of Religion*, 318; see also 43. Even today Egyptologists find the term *henotheism* useful; see Erik Hornung, *Conceptions of God in Ancient Egypt: The One and the Many* (Ithaca, N.Y.: Cornell University Press, 1982), 24–26, 236–237.

12 Breasted, *Development of Religion*, 187–188.

13 Evans, "Earlier Religion of Greece," 287.

14 Charles Darwin, *The Descent of Man and Selection in Relation to Sex* (New York: A. L. Burt, 1874), 159; see also 41–49.

15 Cited by Erik Hornung, *Akhenaten and the Religion of Light* (Ithaca: Cornell University Press, 1999), 15.

16 Barry J. Kemp, *Ancient Egypt: Anatomy of a Civilization* (1989; reprint, London and New York: Routledge, 2006), 281.

17 Assmann, *Moses the Egyptian*, 6–39, see esp. 11.

18 Hornung, *Conceptions of God*, 237.

19 Hornung, *Conceptions of God*, 113.

20 Hornung, *Akhenaten*, 1–17, 94.

21 Richard H. Wilkinson, *Reading Egyptian Art: A Hieroglyphic Guide to Ancient Egyptian Painting and Sculpture* (London: Thames and Hudson, 1992); Wilkinson, *Symbol and Magic in Egyptian Art* (London: Thames and Hudson, 1994); Wilkinson, *The Complete Gods and Goddesses of Ancient Egypt* (London: Thames and Hudson, 1992).

22 Wilkinson, *Complete Gods and Goddesses*, 26.

23 Wilkinson, *Complete Gods and Goddesses*, 71.

24 Nanno Marinatos, *Minoan Kingship and the Solar Goddess* (Urbana/Champaign: University of Illinois Press, 2010).

25 Wilkinson, *Complete Gods and Goddesses*, 39.

The Tomb of the Vizier Amenhotep-Huy in Asasif (AT 28): Preliminary Results of the Excavation Seasons 2009–2012

Francisco J. Martín Valentín and Teresa Bedman
Institute of Studies of Ancient Egypt, Madrid

Evidence for the career of Amenhotep-Huy, who served as vizier of north and south under Amenhotep III, is examined. His tomb in Asasif, AT 28, is undergoing excavation by the Institute of Studies of Ancient Egypt, and an initial description of its architecture, finds (including relief fragments, a concubine figure, votive ears, and other objects), and later reuse is given.

It is our pleasure to contribute to these papers presented in honor of Professor Richard H. Wilkinson. He has conducted research and excavation in Egypt for the past twenty-five years, mainly in the Valley of the Kings, and most recently excavating the Theban temple of Tausret, a queen of the Nineteenth Dynasty who ruled Egypt as a king. His excavations and investigations at Thebes have a special connection with us and our current project in the Theban necropolis at Asasif, as we have both worked nearby in the field, and this gives a special sense to this paper.

Tomb number 28 at Asasif,[1] as cataloged by Friederike Kampp,[2] is located in the Theban necropolis, in the northern area of Asasif, before and below the Eleventh Dynasty tomb belonging Djar (TT 366) and adjacent to the Eighteenth Dynasty tomb of Kheruef (Figure 1).[3] In May 1978 it was identified by Andrew Gordon of the University of California, Berkeley and by Diethelm Eigner, as belonging to the Eighteenth Dynasty. Its owner was the Vizier Amenhotep, called Huy, who held his position during the reign of King Amenhotep III. The exploration of both researchers revealed the greatly impaired state of the monument and its unfinished status.[4]

The Vizier Amenhotep-Huy

Documents and monuments related to the vizier Amenhotep-Huy are scarce in comparison with referrals to other officials of the same period. The main reason for this darkness is, without doubt, persecution of his memory, which resulted in the destruction of his monuments.

Known documents related with the vizier Amenhotep are as follows:

(a) two inscriptions found at Malkata referring to the first *Heb Sed* of Amenhotep III (regnal year 30);[5]
(b) a stela (BM 138) containing a copy of the foundation decree of the funerary temple of Amenhotep-son-of-Hapu (regnal year 31);[6]
(c) various remains of monuments with inscriptions from the quarries of Gebel el Silsila;[7]
(d) Amarna Letter EA 71;[8]
(e) two statues from Bubastis, Cairo Museum CG 590 (Figure 2) and BM 1068;[9]
(f) relief in Amenhotep III's temple at Soleb.[10]

In view of the documents that we know so far, we can conclude that Amenhotep, called Huy, was a courtier of King Amenhotep III and that he held the position of northern vizier and later also that of vizier of the south, in Thebes.

The documents that we know correspond to regnal years 30, 31, and 35 of Amenhotep III. This means that, at least, we know that Amenhotep-Huy served as vizier during these years. The subject to discuss and clarify is the sequence of events in Amenhotep's career. Did it begin with his appointment as vizier of the south based in Thebes, or, alternatively, did he originally serve as northern vizier and assume his position as vizier of the south only after the disappearance of Ramose? In our opinion, for the moment, the second alternative is the most plausible, until we have learned more from our excavations in Asasif Tomb number 28.

The two jar inscriptions discovered in Malkata that bear his name[11] only demonstrate the presence of Amenhotep as vizier (without specifying southern or northern) in the ceremonies of the first jubilee (in year 30) of King Amenhotep III. On the other hand, it is perfectly logical and coherent that the northern vizier had to be present at such important ceremonies. Ramose was also present at the jubilee, as evidenced by a jar with his name tag found in Malkata.[12]

This evidence is confirmed by the joint presence of both viziers at the inauguration of the temple of Amenhotep III at Soleb. The fact that Amenhotep has been represented before Ramose may have less to do with protocol (Upper Egypt usually being mentioned before Lower Egypt) and more to do with his having held his office longer. On the other hand, we know that the predecessor of Ramose and

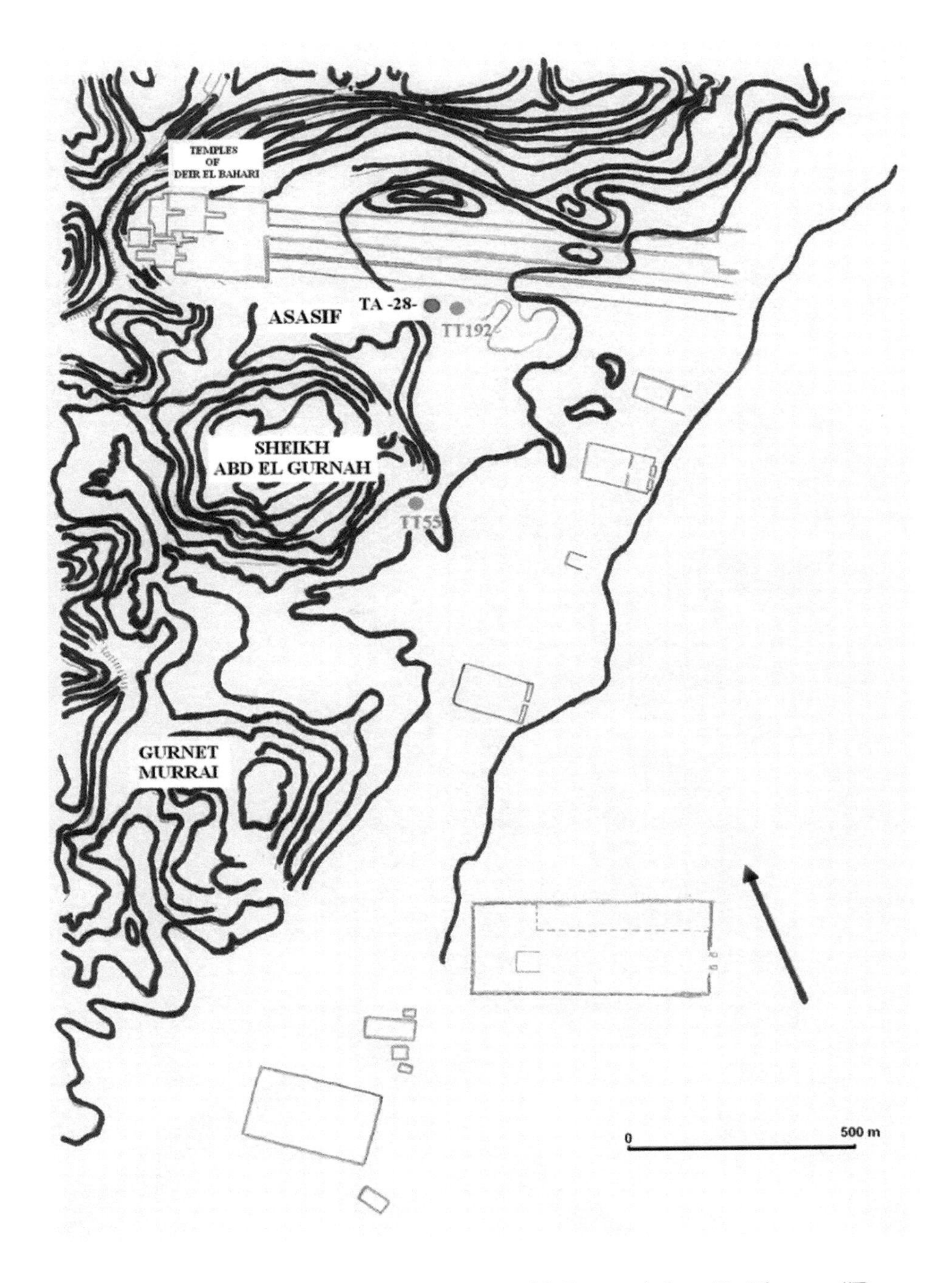

Figure 1: Location of Tomb 28 at Asasif, Luxor (after D. Eigner, "Das thebanische Grab des Amenhotep, Wesir von Unterägypten: die Architektur," *MDAIK* 39 [1983]: pl. 6)

Amenhotep as vizier, in this case of both north and south together, had been the high priest of Amun, Ptahmose. Therefore, it is plausible to think that, after Ptahmose, there were two viziers: one for Upper Egypt (Ramose) and another for Lower Egypt (Amenhotep).

The two statues from Bubastis,[13] found with the remains of another belonging to the Queen Tiye's steward, Kheruef, prove that both men left their testimonies in the temple of Bastet on the occasion of the preparations for the first jubilee of the king. Here, Amenhotep appears as northern vizier. The titles are typical for the northern civil service and are very similar to those of other officials of the north.

However, evidence exists that in year 31 Amenhotep-Huy appeared in Thebes as vizier to perform the rites for the foundation of the funerary temple of Amenhotep-son-of-Hapu.[14] As Ramose was not present, we can assume that he was no longer vizier of the south: it must be assumed that he resigned from his post as vizier of the south between years 30 and 31, and as a result Amenhotep-Huy assumed this role.

From texts inscribed in the quarries of the Gebel el Silsila[15] we know that, in year 35 of the reign, Amenhotep-Huy continued to occupy the post of vizier of the south (perhaps at the same time as that of the north, such as had also happened during Ptahmose's time as vizier); there was thus a period from year 31 until year 35 in which Amenhotep was unquestionably vizier of the south and probably at the same time vizier of the north, since we do not know of anyone else who might have held this position during this time.

Probably during this period of four to five years, his tomb was being excavated in the area of the Asasif, in the same part of the necropolis where the Queen Tiye's steward, another prestigious royal official, had built his own tomb (TT 192).[16] It is clear that Amenhotep was inspired by Kheruef's tomb to build his own, and that, because of the status of both, the excavation of Kheruef's would have been started some time before that of Amenhotep. This confirms that there was a moment of coincidence between Kheruef and Amenhotep in which Amenhotep held only the title of vizier of the north.

After Amenhotep III's year 35, we know nothing of Amenhotep. As a result, the end of his career as vizier of the north and south probably occurred at this time. We know that the next vizier of the south was Nakht, who lived in Akhetaten (Amarna), while in Memphis the vizier of the north was Aper-El,[17] who served in that capacity during the last two or three years of the reign of Amenhotep III.

Figure 2: Statue of Vizier Amenhotep-Huy from the Egyptian Museum, Cairo 590 (T. Bedman; © IEAE)

From the very damaged state of the monuments and documents that have come down to us, we have reason to suspect a persecution of the memory of Amenhotep-Huy by officials of Akhenaten. It also seems likely that the persecution of his memory and the destruction of his name, titles, and images would have taken place on the occasion of his dismissal or death, since we have detected special effort for the destruction of his personality and his *ka*. This implies that Amenhotep-Huy was perhaps one of the strongest adversaries against the new religious currents and, of course, a man closely linked with traditional cults of the Egyptian gods whose clergy would suffer severely because of the imposition of the only one god, the Aten.

The Tomb: A Description

Exploration carried out in the monument by the Institute of Studies of Ancient Egypt (IEAE)[18] has revealed its greatly damaged state and unfinished status. Until the beginning of our work, the tomb had never been excavated.

The tomb (Figure 3) begins with an outer courtyard, with an area of 528 m^2; the north and south faces are lined by columns, of which only one remains in a state of partial construction, excavated in the rock of the plateau. On the west façade of the courtyard are three hollows, two of which are windows; the central one is the entrance to the solar chapel, which has an area of 381 m^2.

The entrance is in a hollowed area in the rock mass, intended to be the original door leading into two lines of columns. On both sides, north and south, of the above-mentioned entry are two niches, probably devoted to statues of the deceased. The chapel was originally equipped with three rows of ten columns each, thirty in total, apparently all of the closed papyriform style. Only two of them still stand, seriously damaged, while fragments of the others must be among the debris covering the floor of the chamber to a depth of several meters. They were destroyed up to half of their shafts or completely. The chapel is wider than that of TT 192, belonging to Queen Tiye's steward, Kheruef, which is located practically next to AT 28.

Near the door were discovered fragmented shabtis and the remains of linen from mummy bandages. That shows the tomb was used after the Eighteenth Dynasty as a place for mummification and new burials, probably in late Ramesside times and the Third Intermediate Period.

The tomb belongs to the type built in the Theban necropolis during the reigns of the pharaohs Amenhotep III/Amenhotep IV. The general characteristics of these T-shaped tombs are: a courtyard and very spacious chapel/hall, the ceiling of which is supported by a large number of columns or pillars; a longitudinal hall that, in some cases, contains pillars or columns; then, a shaft with several changes of direction leading to a kind of tripartite chapel, and, beyond, to the burial chamber.

At Asasif Tomb 28 the entry and burial chamber, located in the bottom of the southwest corner of the chapel, should have existed. Unfortunately, the excavations carried out in this place during the season 2012 have shown that, although work was begun to build the shaft, it was abandoned unfinished.

In the courtyard of Asasif Tomb 28 there are other catalogued tombs, clearly belonging to periods later than the main monument (Figure 4). In the south wall of

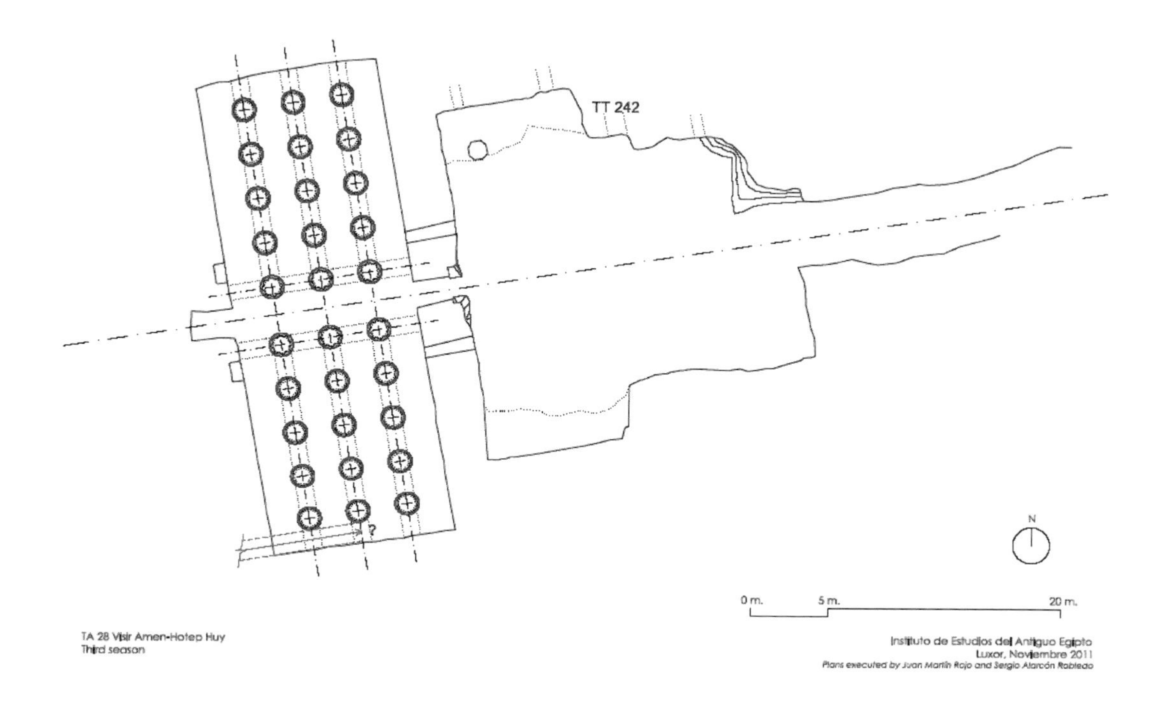

Figure 3: Plan of Asasif Tomb 28, belonging to Vizier Amenhotep-Huy (documentation of the Vizier Amen-Hotep, Huy [AT 28] Project) (T. Bedman; © IEAE)

the corridor to the courtyard is AT 268, and, in the northwestern part of the aforementioned courtyard, TT 244.

Moreover, there are five more tombs, without number: three in the south wall, one in the north wall of the courtyard, and one more close to the main entrance to the chapel of AT 28. Two of these were discovered during our excavations in 2010.

The study of the tomb itself and evidence from other funerary monuments of the same period have presented a series of data that are of great interest to gaining a better knowledge and appreciation of the AT 28 belonging to Vizier Amenhotep, called Huy.

Figure 4: New tomb discovered in 2010 at the north wall in the courtyard of Asasif Tomb 28 (T. Bedman; © IEAE)

FROM A GEOLOGICAL POINT OF VIEW

Tomb number 28 at Asasif is carved into the desert plateau, which is primarily made of limestone layers of the Serai Formation (early Eocene Period) and the Drunka Formation (Lower Eocene Period) of the Thebes Group. This type of sedimentary rock is composed of calcium carbonate with fossil mollusks such as echinoids and nummulitid foraminifera, and impurities of dolomite, quartz, iron oxides, and various clay minerals (all aluminum silicate compounds). The color of this rock is whitish gray when first exposed, and yellow or red when exposed to the elements over time.[19]

One of the reasons that the builders of the tombs chose the areas concerned to carry out excavations was precisely that this rock is relatively soft and easy to work. In fact, the porosity allowed the execution of reliefs with great skill; one just wetted the surface with water before proceeding to sculpt.

The drawback of this rock is that it developed in horizontal layers of different thickness, and because of this it has a low resistance to seismic disturbances. For that reason this stone is broken, both horizontally and vertically; its low hardness usually results in the excavated monuments arriving at a terrible state of destruction by natural causes.

This is the case of the Asasif Tomb 28. A simple external examination shows the great degradation of rock in which it was excavated (Figure 5).

The arrangement of the New Kingdom T-shaped tomb chapels, with the distribution of space in longitudinal and transverse halls, was typical for the Theban area during the Eighteenth Dynasty. This design differentiates them from tombs of other periods and other places in Egypt. In short, tombs of this type are usually composed with the following elements:

(a) a passage giving access to the courtyard of the tomb;
(b) a square courtyard, more or less regular;
(c) a transverse hall with its roof held aloft by columns or pillars;
(d) a longitudinal room with its roof held aloft by columns or pillars;
(e) an interior room with one or more holes or niches excavated in the wall for statues;
(f) access to the burial chamber, usually a shaft;
(g) a burial chamber with or without pillars.

From an Architectural Point of View

Asasif Tomb 28 establishes the evolutionary process of the design of the tombs in the Theban area during the reign of Amenhotep III. Indeed, it is observed how, from the beginning of the reign, tomb structures were expanded so that the monument became larger on all its parts.

Certainly they were experimenting with design. Sometimes they expanded the courtyard; at other times, the chapel devoted to the solar cult (usually transverse to the east-west axis of the tomb); and at yet other times, the longitudinal room devoted to the owner's funerary cult. This process concluded in the last third of the reign of Amenhotep III, giving rise to the construction of the largest Eighteenth Dynasty tombs in the Theban area. This style of great dimensions is closely linked

Figure 5: The tomb before the excavations in 2009 (T. Bedman; © IEAE)

with the classic religious constructions carried out during this part of the reign, particularly from the celebration of the first *Heb Sed* of Amenhotep III.

In this period, the use of columns and pillars to hold bigger rooms and higher ceilings increased, although these were, in effect, faux architectural structures, because the rooms were sculpted in the bedrock and the ceilings thus required no support. The style of these columns could be polygonal (up to thirty-six facets) or in closed papyriform style with up to eight segments in the capital and shaft.

The aforementioned architectural evolution can be observed in TT 48, belonging to Amenemhat Surero, in El Khokha, TT 55 of Ramose in Gurnah, and TT 192 of Kheruef in Asasif, which is the model followed by the designer and director of the construction of Asasif Tomb 28 of Amenhotep-Huy. It could be considered that these two tombs in Asasif (TT 192 and AT 28) were a first test of what would later become the temple-tombs of Deir el-Bahri, built during the Twenty-Fifth and

Figure 6: The chapel of AT 28, looking from the north, as seen in excavation season 2011 (T. Bedman; © IEAE)

Twenty-Sixth Dynasties in Asasif (Padiamenopet [TT 33], Montuemhat [TT 34], Harwa [TT 37], Padineith [TT 197], or Pabasa [TT 279]).

Asasif Tomb 28 is badly damaged (Figure 6), and its space had been used as cemetery and place for mummification during late Ramesside times and the Third Intermediate Period and as a habitation during the Coptic Period. In fact, the area where AT 28 is located also includes the frequent presence of burials from the Ramesside Period and Third Intermediate Period.

The work was started with finding the bedrock in the ground of the courtyard, in order to obtain the space required to install the door at the entrance of the tomb. The excavated area had a surface of about 72 m^2 around the entrance to the tomb, with a depth of 5–6 m.

Findings and Results of Excavations in the Seasons 2009–2012

During the excavation, numerous remains of bandages and human bones were found, as well as a multitude of small fragments of ceramic material or clay with stucco and paint and many poor-quality ceramic shabtis of small size (2~2.5 cm). They are all from the Third Intermediate Period. Also among the finds have been numerous fragments of stone with reliefs of the highest quality accompanied by fragmentary hieroglyphic texts, probably belonging to the lintel and jambs from the door of the tomb (Figure 7).

A remarkable find was a series of votive ears (around thirty-seven pieces) found in the top layers of debris without context level. At a depth of approximately 3.5 m below the first level were found remains of structure of adobe with an area of fire and ash (perhaps from a kitchen), probably from the Coptic Period. The same general area also yielded a female figure of ivory (Figure 8), 14 cm tall (register-book no. 514), nude, featuring a tripartite wig, painted eyes, and a sculpted necklace of shells (*Cypraea moneta;* cowrie) with the image of a cat, probably the goddess Bastet. This dates perhaps from the Third Intermediate Period.

Figure 7: Relief fragment with the coronation name of Amenhotep III (T. Bedman; © IEAE)

Another notable discovery was a block of limestone with reliefs and inscriptions (registry no. 956; Figure 9), which reveals the face of the vizier Amenhotep-Huy. This block is part of no. 339, discovered during the 2009 season.

In the Third Intermediate Period levels we have found remains of a bed of mud bricks with evidence of having been used for mummification of a body, along with dozens of bundles of linen containing natron. We have also found dozens of mud shabtis belonging to (Pa)-di-iry-khonsu, probably also from the Third Intermediate Period (Figure 10).

Figure 8: Concubine figurine, register book number 514. Ivory. Third Intermediate Period (T. Bedman; © IEAE)

On the east wall, inside the chapel, on the northern and southern door jambs, we discovered reliefs representing the goddesses Selket, Nephthys, Isis, and Neith receiving offerings from the vizier, as well as two of the four sons of Horus.

Inside the chapel of AT 28 there were also some pieces belonging to leather straps typical of the mummies of highs priests of Amun in the Third Intermediate Period,[20] with the effigy of King Osorkon I (Twenty-Second Dynasty) performing anointing for a goddess (who may be Neith) and further evidence of the mummification process (Figure 11).

Figure 9: Relief fragments with the face of Vizier Amenhotep-Huy. Register book nos. 339 and 956 (T. Bedman; © IEAE)

Figure 10: Shabti of (Pa)-di-iry-khonsu. Third Intermediate Period. (G. Cabanillas; © IEAE)

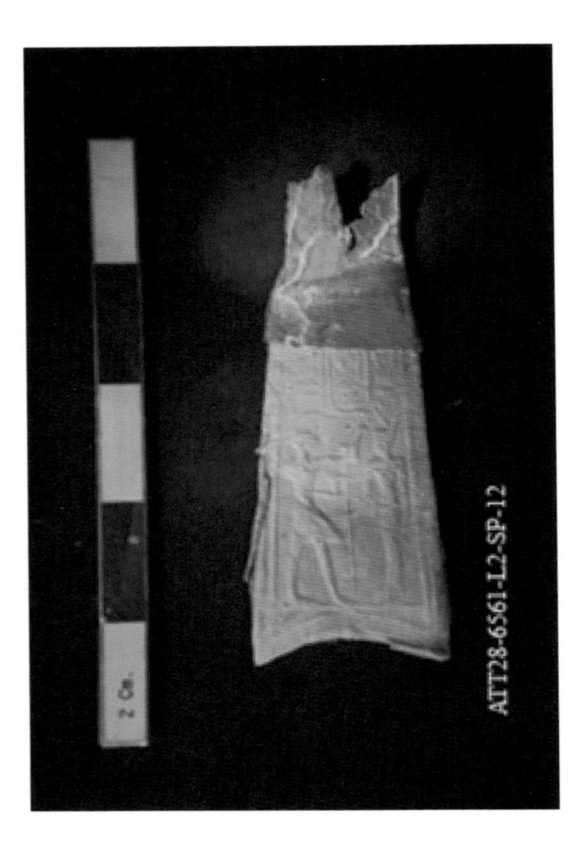

Figure 11: Fragment of leather strap with the effigy of King Osorkon I, Twenty-Second Dynasty (G. Cabanillas; © IEAE)

CONCLUSIONS

The work carried out by the Institute of Studies of Ancient Egypt during the field seasons of 2009–2012 in the Tomb 28 of Asasif has revealed the main features of the monument (Figure 12). The excavation has demonstrated that the site was the subject of multiple violations, including theft of the mummies buried in the tombs constructed in the courtyard of the AT 28. There have also been found reliefs from the walls of the tomb's interior chapel and its gateway, all of a high artistic quality and belonging to the reign of Amenhotep III.

In the late Ramesside Period and in the Third Intermediate Period, the tomb was used as a place for mummification; the monument was apparently regarded as a sacred place for the worship of the vizier Amenhotep-Huy as an intermediary between the people and the god Osiris.

The work to be carried out in the next seasons will consist of removing all remains from the chapel and looking for evidence of a shaft excavated at the time of the vizier Amenhotep-Huy, leading to the burial chamber, to see if both shaft and burial chamber ever existed.[21]

Figure 12: Asasif Tomb 28, looking from the southwest. Season 2012 (T. Bedman; © IEAE)

NOTES

1 D. Eigner, "Das thebanische Grab des Amenhotep, Wesir von Unterägypten: die Architektur," *MDAIK* 39 (1983): 39–50; A. Gordon, "The Tomb of the Vizier Amenhotep at Thebes," *MDAIK* 39 (1983): 72–80.

2 F. Kampp, *Die Thebanische Nekropole. Zum Wandel des Grabgedankens von der XVIII. bis zur XX. Dynastie* (Mainz am Rhein: Philipp von Zabern, 1996), 12.

3 D. Eigner, *Die monumentalen Grabbauten der Spätzeit in der tebanischen Nekropole. Untersuchungen der Zweigstelle Kairo des Österreichischen Archäologischen*

Institutes VI., (Wien: Verlag der Österreichischen Akademie der Wissenschaften, 1984), 3–4.

4 Gordon, "Tomb of the Vizier Amenhotep," 72.

5 W. C. Hayes, "Inscriptions from the Palace of Amenhotep III," *JNES* 10 (1951): 35–40, 82–104, 156–183, 231–242 (nos. 103 and 185).

6 A. Varille, *Inscriptions concernant l'architecte Amenhotep fils de Hapou*, Bibliotheque d'Étude 44 (Le Caire: Institut français d'archéologie orientale, 1968), 67–85

7 G. Legrain, "Notes d'Inspection, IV," *ASAE* 4 (1904): 197–212.

8 W. L. Moran, *Les Lettres d'El-Amarna. Correspondance diplomatique du pharaon* (Paris: Les Éditions du Cerf, 1987), 246–247

9 E. Naville, *Bubastis (1887-1889)*, Egypt Exploration Fund Memoirs 8 (London: Egypt Exploration Fund, 1891), 31–33 and pls. XIII and XXXV

10 M. Schiff Giorgini, *Soleb* V. *Le Temple. Bas-reliefs et inscriptions* (Le Caire: Institut français d'archéologie oriental, 1998), pl. 42.

11 Hayes, "Inscriptions," nos. 103 and 185.

12 Hayes, "Inscriptions," no. 96.

13 Naville, *Bubastis*, 31–33 and pls. XIII and XXXV.

14 Varille, *Inscriptions*, 67–85.

15 Legrain, "Notes d'Inspection," 197–212.

16 Oriental Institute, *The Tomb of Kheruef: Theban Tomb 192*, OIP 102 (Chicago: Oriental Institute of the University of Chicago, 1980).

17 A. Zivie, *Découverte à Saqqara. Le vizir oublié* (Paris: Éditions du Seuil, 1990).

18 F. J. Martín Valentín, "La Tumba de Kheruef (TT192). Indicios de una corregencia," *Boletín de la Asociación Española de Egiptología* 3 (1991): 213–240; Martín Valentín, "En torno a la Tumba de Ramose (Nº 55 de Sheikh Abd El Gurnah)," *Aegyptiaca Complutensia* 1 (1991): 57–78; Martín Valentín, *Amen-Hotep III. El esplendor de Egipto* (Madrid: Alderabán, 1998); Martín Valentín, "Indications et évidences d'une corégence entre Amenhotep III et Amenhotep IV dans la nécropole thébaine," in C. Eyre (ed.), *Proceedings of the 7th International Congress of Egyptologists*, 741–757 (Leuven: Peeters, 1998).

19 A. Lucas, *Ancient Egyptian Materials and Industries*, 4th edition (London: Histories and Mysteries of Man, 1962): 52–55; M.-P. Aubry et al., "Pharaonic Necrostratigraphy: A Review of Geological and Archaeological Studies in the Theban Necropolis, Luxor, West Bank, Egypt," *Terra Nova* 21.4 (2009): 237–256.

20 A. Niwiński, *21st Dynasty Coffins from Thebes: Chronological and Typological Studies* (Mainz am Rhein: Philipp von Zabern, 1988), 15 and fig. 15.

21 We would like to thank the Ministry of State for Antiquities in the person of Mohamed Ibrahim, and the SCA Permanent Committee in the persons of His General Secretary Mustapha Amin, and to Mohamed El Bialy, Adel Hussein, Mohmed Ismail, Mansour Boraik, Ibrahim Soliman, Mohamed Abd El Azinz, Noor Abd El Gafar, Fahty Yassin, and all those others who have helped us these years. We also want to thank the Fundación Gaselec, Xelram, Fundación 3M, Thales Spain, and our team, which has included the following: Gustavo

Cabanillas; José María Saldaña; María Dolores Corona; Ahmed Baghdady; Juan Martín Rojo; Sergio Alarcón; Mari Fe San Segundo; José Luis García-Vicioso; Lidia Montoya; Pilar Pujol; Naty Sánchez; Eva Palacios; Laura Escobar; Juan Friederichs; Ángel Ramirez; Guiomar Pastor; Esther Fernández; Silvina Vera; María José García; Sergio Portela; Mahmud Abdellahy; Yaser Abd el Rasik; Mohamed el Azab; Ali Farouk; Ana Queseda; Ahmed Nasser; Lourdes Narváez; Javier Cebadera; Mario Pérez; Raquel Pérez; and José Luis Rodríguez.

The Lords of the West in Ramesside Tombs

Teresa Moore
University of California, Berkeley

Five private Theban tombs from the Ramesside Period include scenes of the tomb owner venerating royalties, as well as high officials: TT 19 (Amenmose), TT 2 (Khabekhnet), TT 359 (Anhurkhau), TT 284 (Pahemnetjer), and TT 306 (Irdjanen). Each scene, including the identity of the subjects and the nature of their dress, is discussed individually and overall trends regarding selection of subjects, details of the iconography, and other aspects are examined.

"Pre has gone, his Ennead after him, and the kings likewise."
—Butehamun, "Letter to Akhtay's Coffin"[1]

A glance at the bibliography of Richard H. Wilkinson reveals his longstanding interest in the history of the Theban west bank. This study of an unusual theme in a small number of Theban tombs is dedicated to Professor Wilkinson in the hope that he may find it of interest.

Among the fifty or so private Theban tombs whose decoration features the images of deified royalty, five—TT 2, TT 19, TT 359, TT 284, and TT 306—are notable for scenes that include the tomb owner venerating two rows of individuals, who may include not only kings and queens but also royal children and even high officials. All of these tombs are Ramesside in date, but the scenes of offering to royal ancestors by private persons do have precursors in Eighteenth Dynasty art.

Several private stelae dating to the first half of the Eighteenth Dynasty honor two or more royalties, sometimes closely related, sometimes separated in time by a span of centuries. The stela of Qenamun (MMA 28.9.6), a priest of Amenhotep I, depicts the donor offering to that king and to Senwosret I;[2] a *wꜥb* priest of the mortuary temple of Thutmose III associated Thutmose III and Senwosret I on his stela (Cambridge EGA 3074.1943);[3] the "draftsman of Amun in every place," Amenemheb, dedicated a stela showing himself offering to Amenhotep I and Ahmose-Nefertari;[4] and Cairo stela CG 34034, damaged by Atenist erasures and later restored, featured Amun-Re, Amenhotep I, Ahmose-Nefertari, and Thutmose III.[5] Another group of deified royalties is found in the upper register of the stela of Nebsu, Cairo CG 30029: Amenhotep I, Ahmose-Nefertari, Sitamun, and Ahmose Sapair.[6] Likewise dated to the mid-Eighteenth Dynasty (specifically to the reign of

Thutmose III) is the stela of Padju from Upper Egypt, Cairo CG 34005.[7] Here, in the upper register, Amenhotep I and the prince Ahmose-Sapair are shown praising Montu, while the donor kneels in worship in the lower register. A generation or so later, a man called Sennefer dedicated a stela (Turin 1455) depicting (in the upper register) Thutmose I and Thutmose III, Amenhotep I and Ahmose-Nefertari, and (in the lower register) Amenhotep II and Ahmose-Sapair.[8] Of particular note is Sennefer's selection of both Ahmosid and Thutmosid family members for veneration and the iconographical variety on display: Amenhotep I wears the *ḫprš* with attached ribbons; Thutmose I, a combination of *3tf* and *nms*; Thutmose III, the *ḫprš*; and Amenhotep II, the boatman's circlet and *ibs* wig. Another group of royalties appears on the mid-Eighteenth Dynasty stela of Amenmen from Abydos (BM 297), in the lower register of which the donor adores Amenhotep I, accompanied by Ahmose-Nefertari and Sitkamose.[9] If the date is correct, then we have here another early example of the veneration of a group of royal ancestors.[10] The continuity of this motif at the end of the Eighteenth Dynasty is demonstrated by the stela of Smentaui and Huy (CGC 34037).[11] On this monument, in the upper register, King Ahmose and Queen Ahmose-Nefertari are enthroned on the left, and Amenhotep I and Ahmose-Nefertari on the right.

Among the Eighteenth Dynasty Theban tomb paintings are several depictions of deified royalty; perhaps the most famous of these is the painting of Amenhotep I and Ahmose-Nefertari in TT 181, the tomb of the sculptors Nebamun and Ipuky, dating to the reign of Amenhotep III. The chief scribe Neferhotep, who flourished at the very end of the Eighteenth Dynasty, commissioned a very similar depiction of the deified mother and son in his nearby tomb (TT 49).[12] But that of Amenemhat at Qurna (TT 53), dated to the reign of Thutmose III, depicted the tomb owner making an offering to female members of the Ahmosid family: Ahmose-Henuttameh, her mother Ahmose-Inhapi, and possibly Rai, the nurse of Queen Ahmose-Nefertari.[13]

Later in the Eighteenth Dynasty, probably during the reign of Amenhotep III, the gardener of divine offerings of Amun, Nakht, was buried in TT 161 at Dra Abu el-Naga.[14] To the right of his false-door stela, Nakht had himself shown making an offering to Amenhotep I and Prince Sapair; to the left of the stela, the tomb owner presents a large bouquet to Thutmose III. And on the right side wall, Nakht and his wife Tahemet offer to three deities seated in a kiosk: Osiris, Hathor, and Ahmose-Nefertari. In this tomb, too, we can perhaps see the germ of the idea that leads to the more extensive royal groupings of the Ramesside tombs.

THEBAN TOMB 19: AMENMOSE

Two of these latter monuments, the earliest of the five under discussion, date to the reign of Ramesses II. Here we will first examine TT 19, located in the northern part of the Dra Abu el-Naga necropolis. In the transverse hall, the tomb's only decorated chamber, the owner, Amenmose, First Prophet of Amenhotep of the Temenos (*wbꜣ*),[15] commissioned an impressive array of six scenes relating to the cults of deified royalty.[16]

In the second register on the left half of the rear wall, two priests, facing right, offer to a series of enthroned kings and queens.[17] Above them, columns were outlined, but the text was not filled in. On the right, the register is split to accommodate two rows of six kings each, while two enthroned queens have been placed on a separate ground line slightly above and in front of the upper row of kings. A cartouche was provided for the first queen, but her name was apparently never inscribed within it, although the epithet "true of voice" was appended. The second queen, who was depicted with black skin, is identified as "the God's Wife (Ahmose-Nefertari)|." One wonders what queen could have preceded her—possibly her mother, Ahhotep. On the other hand, perhaps the first lady is a distinct manifestation of Ahmose-Nefertari herself, her appearance inspired by a different cult statue.[18] In this connection it is worth noting that Smentaui and Huy, perhaps only a generation or so earlier, had depicted Ahmose-Nefertari twice on their stela, and the contemporary tomb of Khabekhnet at Deir el-Medina (see below) displays two local forms of the deified Amenhotep I in the same scene. Here in TT 19, both images wear the tripartite wig, vulture diadem, and modius; each of them holds a queenly flabellum in her right hand and has her left hand clenched as though holding an *ankh*.

The sequence of kings begins with Nebhepetre (Mentuhotep II). He is followed by Ahmose, Amenhotep (I), Aakheperkare (Thutmose I), Aakheperenre (Thutmose II), and Menkheperre (Thutmose III) in the first row, and by Aakheperure (Amenhotep II), Menkheperure (Thutmose IV), Nebmaatre (Amenhotep III), Djeserkheperure (Horemheb), Menpehtyre (Ramesses I) and Menmaatre (Sety I) in the second row. The founder of the Middle Kingdom seems to have been represented wearing the *ḫꜣ.t* or bag-wig headdress, as does Ahmose. Amenhotep I appears in the *ỉbs* wig and boatman's circlet. Of the remaining rulers, all but three are depicted with the *ḫprš*; the exceptions are Amenhotep II, Ramesses I, and Sety I. Each king holds the crook and flail in his right hand and an *ankh* in his left. The reason for the iconographical variation is obscure; perhaps they were based on the actual appearance of cult images. We may remark, however, that Amenhotep of the Temenos, as he appears during the Valley Festival and in the oracular consultation in this tomb, wears the *ḫprš*, and that the black-painted statue of Thutmose III within his barque shrine wears the *ibs* wig. The iconography of these two kings in the series may, therefore, be based on other statues.

THEBAN TOMB 2: KHABEKHNET

Roughly contemporary with the tomb of Amenmose is TT 2, belonging to the workman Khabekhnet, a son of Sennedjem, at Deir el-Medina.[19] Among the craftsmen's tombs, Khabekhnet's is remarkable for the number and variety of scenes depicting deified royalty.[20] On the north wall of the chapel, Khabekhnet and another man, who may be his brother Khonsu (or Khabekhnet shown a second time), are represented before two rows of deceased kings, queens, and princes: "Offering every good and pure thing—consisting of bread, beer, beef, fowl, wine, and milk—to your *k3s*, to the Lords of Eternity, by the Servant in the Place of Truth," in the upper register, and "offering every good and pure thing to your *k3s*, to the Lords of the West, by the Servant in the Place of Truth" in the lower register.[21] The kings are depicted wearing the *nms* and uraeus and holding the crook and flail; although their bodies are swathed, their arms are free. The queens wear the vulture and modius and hold flabella in their left hands; they may have held *ankhs* in their right hands. Among them, Ahmose-Nefertari is distinguished by the pair of tall plumes and the disk that have been added to her headdress. Princes wear sidelocks and long kilts.

In the upper of the two registers, the first figure is that of "the Lord of the Two Lands, (Djeserkare)|, the Lord of Diadems (Amenhotep)|." Behind him is his mother, "the Lady of the Two Lands, (Ahmose-Nefertari)|, may she live and endure!" Following them we find (Seqenenre)| (Tao-qen)|, the Lord (or Lady) of the Two Lands (Ahhotep)| (*sic*—the figure is that of a king), (Merytamun)|, a King's Sister whose name began with Ta-, a Mother of the God (Kasmut)|, the King's Sister (Sitamun)|, Prince (Siamun)|, the Royal Wife (Sitkamose)|, the Great Royal Wife (Henuttamehu)|, Royal Wife and Lady of the Two Lands [Tumerisi],[22] the Royal Wife and Lady of the Two Lands (Ahmose)|, and Prince Sapair.

The second row begins with the "Lord of the Two Lands (Nebhepetre)|, Lord of Diadems (Mentuhotep)|, given life like Re" and continues with (Nebpehtyre)|

(Ahmose)|, (Sekhentyenre)| (*sic*), (Wadjkheperre)| (Kamose)|, Prince (Binpu)|, Prince (Wadjmose)|, a Prince (Ramose)|, a (Prince Nebenkhal)| or similar, a Prince (Ahmose)|, and four more God's Wives: (Kamose)|, (Satirbau)|, (Takherdqai)|, and one whose name is lost.[23] As Redford notes, this sequence of royalties focuses on the family of Amenhotep I and, except for Prince Wadjmose (whose funerary chapel, close to the Ramesseum, was doubtless quite familiar to Khabekhnet and his colleagues), seems to exclude its Thutmosid successors.[24] Khabekhnet's series is striking both in its length and in its inclusion of personages who are attested nowhere else.

THEBAN TOMB 359: ANHURKHAU

For the Twentieth Dynasty representatives of the extended assemblage of royal figures, we return to Deir el-Medina and the tomb (TT 359) of Chief Workman Anhurkhau the Younger, dating to the reign of Ramesses IV.[25] In its subterranean outer chamber, on the wall to the right of the entrance, Anhurkhau, accompanied by his wife, Wabet, is depicted censing before two rows of enthroned, deified royal persons.[26] Since much of the painted plaster had disintegrated by the early twentieth century, the study of this painting owes much to the copy produced by Lepsius's expedition.[27]

The columns of text over the Chief Workman's figure read, "Offering incense to the Lords of Eternity, the Great Ones of Everlastingness (by) the Chief Workman in the Place of Truth and Overseer of Works in the Horizon of Eternity in which he rests, Anhurkhau, justified for eternity." Above Wab(et) the caption reads, "his sister, the Lady of the House, the Singer of Amun-Re, King of the Gods, Wab(et); her beloved daughter, Sherit(re) and her beloved daughter, Tuy."

The royalties whom the couple honors are enthroned upon daises in two rows, the upper row having eleven members, and the lower row, nine. Males are swathed like mummies; except for Amenhotep I, they wear the striped *nms*. The series also includes two princes who wear *ibs* wigs combined with the sidelock. Each queen wears a headdress comprising a wig, vulture diadem, and modius, and in her hands are the flabellum and *ankh*. Behind the last figure of the second row, the "Hereditary Prince and [King's Scribe] Huy, justified before the gods," (that is, Amenhotep-son-of-Hapu) is seated, holding his palette and brush at the ready.

For the identities of most of the individuals pictured here, the record made by Lepsius's expedition is essential. Amenhotep I occupies the preeminent position in the upper row, identified (in contrast to his brother kings) by both his cartouches written inside a rectangle: "(Djeserkare)| (Amenhotep)|." He is distinguished, as well, by his *ibs* wig and boatman's circlet, so that it is quite likely that he appears in his local manifestation "Amenhotep, Lord of the Town."[28] His father, "(Nebpehtyre)|," is seated behind him. Three queens follow Ahmose: his mother (Ahhotep)|, his daughter (Merytamun)|, and (Sitamun)|, a sister, niece, or cousin.[29] The king next in line is identified as (Siamun)|, perhaps the King's Eldest Son of that name who may have been a son of Kamose.[30] Seated behind him is a now-anonymous queen, probably (Sitkamose)|,[31] and then a queen who can be identified as Ahmose-Henuttamehu.[32] A queen (*Twrs*)| follows her, possibly Ahmose-Tu(m)erisi, another daughter of Seqenenre.[33] Another queen, whose name included the element "Ahmose," takes the tenth position in this row, which concludes with the young prince "Osiris Sapair."[34]

Ahmose-Nefertari occupies the first position in the lower row. After the great queen, we find "(Menpehtyre)|" Ramesses I, "(Nebhepetre)|" Mentuhotep II, "(Amenhotep)|,"[35] and "(Seqenenre)|" Tao II. Interrupting the sequence of kings is another prince, who holds a lotus in his left hand; according to Cherpion and Corteggiani, he is most probably to be identified with Wadjmose, as his position here corresponds to that of the same prince in the tomb of Khabekhnet.[36] Then we find "(Heqamaatre)|" Ramesses IV, under whom TT 359 was decorated, a king whose name is lost, and Thutmose I. Behind the last figure of the second row, the "Hereditary Prince and [King's Scribe] Huy, justified before the gods," (that is, Amenhotep-son-of-Hapu) is seated, holding his palette and brush at the ready. Thus in their devotions here the Chief Workman and his wife honor founders of dynasties, kings with ties to their community, and finally a "local saint," the son of Hapu.

Theban Tomb 284: Pahemnetjer

Our last two examples are located at Dra Abu el-Naga. TT 284, directly below TT 35, was usurped during the Twentieth Dynasty by Pahemnetjer, a Scribe of Offerings of All the Gods.[37] His decorative scheme included statues of a king and queen in procession (Figure 1).[38] Over the shaft in the southwest corner of the transverse hall, Pahemnetjer pictured himself, at the left, worshipping a series of royal personages (Figures 2, 3, 4). At the beginning of the top row, a piece of plaster is missing; after the gap come five queens, clad in sheaths of blue or red. Behind them stands a prince in a short kilt, wearing a sidelock and carrying the crook. He is followed by a man—perhaps a vizier or another high official—wearing a long

Figure 1: TT 284 (5, I) image of queen in procession (courtesy of the Penn Museum, image no. 40116)

Figure 2: Pahemnetjer adores deified royalty (Schott 6682 from the Digital Schott Archive, Egyptological Seminar, University of Trier; PM I^2:1, 366 [2–3, I, 2])

robe, his arms at his sides. This register concludes with six princes and two princesses.

In the lower register, a queen takes the first position; she is followed by three kings who are distinguished by their headdresses—the white crown of Upper Egypt, an indistinct head covering that may be the *ibs*[39] or the "bag-wig" (*ẖꜣ.t*), and the red crown of Lower Egypt. Each of the kings is painted red, wears a short kilt, holds a crook in his right hand, and stands with his right foot advanced. Next come seven queens, again depicted wearing sheaths painted blue or red in turn, each holding a flabellum and outfitted with a blue wig, a modius, and possibly also the vulture diadem. After the queens we find two princes in the same pose and attire as those in the upper row. Seven princesses, also wearing sidelocks and carrying flabella, conclude the series. The total number of individuals may be as high as forty, including at least thirteen queens, three kings, nine princes, nine princesses, and one official. Gabi Hollender has remarked that, although the kings and queens here are shown in traditional clothing, the royal children and the official sport the current (that is, late Ramesside) fashion.[40]

Figure 3: Lower register of royalties in Pahemnetjer's tomb (Schott 6683, from the Digital Schott Archive, Egyptological Seminar, University of Trier; PM I²:1, 366 [2–3, I, 2])

Within the cartouches, paint has faded, and when I visited the tomb in 1988—thanks to the courtesy of Lanny Bell—in no case was I able to make out a name. Redford, who visited the tomb a few years earlier, suggested that the second king might be identified as "(Nebpehtyre)|" (Ahmose I).[41] The queen who leads the second row is most likely Ahmose-Nefertari.

THEBAN TOMB 306: IRDJANEN

In the southern part of the Dra Abu el-Naga cemetery, at the base of the slope, a Door-opener of the Estate of Amun named Irdjanen built himself a tomb, TT 306.[42] Recently Kampp, relying on the owner's titles and the personal names in the tomb, has dated TT 306 to the late Ramesside period, even to the Twenty-First Dynasty.[43]

Figure 4: Continuation of sequence in Pahemnetjer's tomb: queens, royal children, and official (in upper row) (Schott 6685, from the Digital Schott Archive, Egyptological Seminar, University of Trier; PM I²:1, 366 [2-3, I, 2])

Left of the entrance, in the lowest of three registers on the front wall of the transverse hall, Irdjanen was portrayed censing before Ahmose-Nefertari and Amenhotep I (Figure 5). On the right front wall of the transverse hall,[44] the second register has been divided horizontally to accommodate two rows of nine royal figures facing right.[45] As in TT 359, the plaster has badly deteriorated and much detail has been lost. The name of the first figure is illegible; indeed the cartouche seems to have disappeared, although both Porter and Moss[46] and Redford[47] identify her as Ahmose-Nefertari. The king standing behind her, who was depicted wearing the *ḫprš* or the white crown, is identified in Porter and Moss as Seqenenre Tao;[48] following him is "(Djeserkare)|" (Amenhotep I), wearing the *nms*; fourth in line is another king wearing the *nms*, identified as Ahmose;[49] and next is a king who appears to have been depicted in a tall diadem, the white crown or the *ȝtf*. Visible in his cartouche is what appears to be a *nb* sign,[50] so he may be Nebhepetre Mentuhotep II,[51] whose appearance in other tombs of the period[52] and association with Amenhotep I[53] would seem to suggest his presence here. Following Nebhepetre (?), then, are three queens: the first being (Ta[mer][54]...)|; the second, now anonymous; and the third, whose cartouche is damaged, (Nebettawy)|.[55] At the rear of the first row stands a slightly smaller figure, holding the *ḥḳȝ.t*. He seems to lack a diadem; he may be one of the princes who appears in the tombs of Khabekhnet and Anhurkhau: Sapair (the most likely choice), Siamun, or Wadjmose.

Figure 5: TT 306 Irdjanen censes before Ahmose-Nefertari (center) and Amenhotep I (uraeus preserved) (courtesy of the Penn Museum, image no. 34938)

The lower sequence of royalties is less well preserved. The leading figure, which might have been that of a queen, is almost entirely lost; the second figure would appear to be "(Kheperkare)|"[56] (Senwosret I). Behind him stands a queen possibly identified as Sitiah.[57] The figure behind her may be Sitkamose.[58] Fifth in this series is apparently Queen "(Sentseneb)|," mother of Thutmose I, the last whom we can identify with any (slight) degree of confidence. The cartouche belonging to the next personage seems to contain the element *in*; perhaps this was Queen Inhapy. Another queen followed, but her cartouche is lost. Of the figure or figures that originally completed the sequence, almost nothing has survived.

Those kings and queens whom we can identify seem not to have been placed in any particular chronological order. What can be said, then, about Irdjanen's selection of divinized royal figures? He does, to be sure, feature a number of Ahmosid family members,[59] although the presence of Mentuhotep II(?) and Senwosret I demonstrates that Irdjanen wished also to honor royal "founders." The presence here of Seniseneb—if the identification is correct—suggests that Irdjanen may have been aware of a temple relief, perhaps in Hatshepsut's funerary temple, depicting this royal mother. Likewise, in the course of his duties in the estate of Amun, he may have seen a monument that featured Sitiah, the consort of Thutmose

Figure 6: Irdjanen before two rows of deified royalties (courtesy of the Penn Museum, image no. 34949)

III. Irdjanen's series of royalties is not ordered chronologically; maybe he had in mind some imagined topographical constellation of their monuments.[60]

CONCLUDING REMARKS

Irdjanen's painting is the last known representative of its class; indeed, if the late date is correct, then his would have been one of the last tombs decorated in the Theban necropolis.[61] Looking back over the paintings under discussion, we see some similarities: the large number of individuals honored and the arrangement into two rows. But striking differences are also apparent; indeed, this group of paintings breaks down into three subdivisions: the Deir el-Medina examples of Khabekhnet and Anhurkhau, with their enthroned kings in Osirian garb; the later paintings from Dra Abu el-Naga with standing figures; and the more "historical" series of Amenmose.

To begin with, no two of these paintings include the same number of honorees. There are fourteen in Amenmose's tomb, at least twenty-six in Khabekhnet's, twenty-one in Anhurkhau's, around forty in Pahemnetjer's, and eighteen in Irdjanen's. According to Redford, Amenmose might have chosen a group of fourteen to correspond with the number of royal *k3s*; the number also corresponds to the number of royal statues carried in procession during the festival of Min.[62] Pahemnetjer's choice may have been influenced by the number of divine judges in Chapter 125 of the Book of the Dead.

Among the tombs, a standardized orientation for such scenes is not apparent. In Khabekhnet's tomb, the two rows of royalties were placed on the right side wall of his chapel; Anhurkhau's scene—which as we have seen seems to owe its inspiration to Khabekhnet—is placed on the right front wall of the first chamber. Amenmose, however, positioned his assemblage on the left rear wall of the chapel. Pahemnetjer's group occupies the left front wall of the hall and continues on the left side wall. In Irdjanen's tomb, the series of royalties is found on the right front wall of the hall.

In the first three scenes, worship is directed to a series of enthroned individuals (with the exception of the scribe Huy in TT 359); in the last two, the recipients are standing. In the tombs of Khabekhnet and Anhurkhau, the kings and princes are swathed in linen, signifying their Osirification.[63] In all three examples at Dra Abu el-Naga, the kings do not appear in Osirian guise—they wear costumes associated with living kings.[64]

Redford claims that the seated figures are to be understood as statues ("as in the Chamber of Ancestors"); Cherpion and Corteggiani, in their discussion of Anhurkhau's example, state that the royal personages there displayed are probably statues.[65] But the latter authors also point out that the thrones of the upper row rest on a papyrus mat, rather than on socles as statues would—a further indication, along with the white wrappings of the kings, of their Osirian status.[66] In Khabekhnet's tomb, the thrones rest on a ground line; in Amenmose's, they appear to be resting on a mat. The standing figures in the tombs of Pahemnetjer and Irdjanen likewise lack plinths. Inspired by statues or reliefs they may be, but these paintings depict, as Cherpion and Corteggiani assert, an array of divine beings, seated or standing side by side.[67]

In addition to iconographical variations, the selection of individuals to be honored varies. As noted by Redford, Khabekhnet's panel focuses on the Ahmosids, with the exception of Nebhepetre, Prince Wadjmose, and perhaps a few of the individuals whose names are otherwise unknown. Amenmose chose Nebhepetre and then the canonical rulers from the beginning of the Eighteenth Dynasty to his own time, adding Ahmose-Nefertari (perhaps in two manifestations) and possibly another queen. Anhurkhau's group resembles Khabekhnet's so closely that Wadjmose and Sitkamose have been identified in TT 359 on the basis of the corresponding positions in the earlier tomb.[68] The element of personal choice, however, is clearly present in TT 359, for the Chief Workman included Thutmose I, under whom the earliest enclosure wall was built for Deir el-Medina and who therefore was an important figure in the early development of the necropolis community.[69] Ramesses IV, under whom the tomb was decorated, appears in the second row; his popularity among the villagers undoubtedly contributed to his selection.[70] In Irdjanen's group, we find representatives of the Ahmosid clan, dynastic founders (Nebhepetre and Kheperkare), a prince, and possibly two queens of the Thutmosid house (Sitiah and Seniseneb). Finally, Pahemnetjer's selection most likely included Ahmose-Nefertari and Amenhotep I, Nebhepetre, and possibly King Ahmose or Seqenenre.

Amenmose's sequence, then, is an outlier among these paintings, since he does not focus on the Seventeenth and early Eighteenth Dynasties.[71] Exceptionally, he includes only one or two queens. The other four tomb owners have chosen a significant number of queens, princes, and princesses; where names survive, they are for most part Ahmosid. In fact, the tendency is so marked that one wonders if Sitiah and Seniseneb, apparently included in TT 306, belonged to that family.

Perhaps Irdjanen believed that they did! Indeed, the appearance of so many kings' wives, mothers, and daughters in the last four examples reflects the significant political and religious roles played by women in the royal family during the Seventeenth and early Eighteenth Dynasties.[72]

What might have inspired these rare, extensive groupings of deceased royalty in the tombs of private persons? Morkot points to the royal ancestor cult as expressed in the Min processions pictured at the Ramesseum and Medinet Habu: these statues include those of Menes and Nebhepetre as well as Nebpehtyre Ahmose and his canonical successors.[73] Queens and royal children—so prominent in four of the paintings under consideration—are not included, however, in these reliefs. Furthermore, the iconography of the statues in the festival reliefs is standardized, except that the "founders" wear more elaborate kilts than their colleagues in office; in the private paintings, we observe some variation in diadems, and in the tombs of Khabekhnet and Anhurkhau, the kings are presented in their Osirian aspect.

The statues of kings that accompany the barque of Amun in the Twentieth Dynasty tomb of Iymiseba (TT 65) may also be a link to this small subset of private tomb paintings; in TT 65, the iconography of the royal statues is more varied than it is in the Min procession reliefs (see Figure 7). Thus, one possible inspiration for our five tomb owners may have lain in the festivals of Thebes, particularly in the case of Amenmose, whose priestly responsibilities would have familiarized him with the divine images carried in the Beautiful Festival of the Valley. His is also the only one of these paintings in which the selection of kings is canonical, including Nebhepetre, the Ahmosid kings, the Thutmosid house, and the early Ramessides in chronological order.

We may also conjecture that unusual events in the Theban necropolis may have influenced the tomb owners' commissioning of these sequences. In the tomb of the Relief Sculptor Ipuy, a contemporary and relation by marriage of Khabekhnet, a lively and humorous scene depicts craftsmen (possibly under the supervision of Ipuy himself) putting the finishing touches on a "catafalque" and shrine intended for the cult of the deified Amenhotep I; these structures may have been destined for a temple or for a renewal of the king's own burial in the time of Ramesses II.[74] During the Twentieth Dynasty, the High Priest of Amun Ramessesnakht oversaw impressive renovations and remodeling of the courtyard and inner hall of K93.11 at Dra Abu el-Naga, a tomb that could well have been the "Horizon of Eternity" of Amenhotep I.[75] Finally, under Ramesses IX, the tomb robbery scandal and the official enquiry into the status of the late Seventeenth and early Eighteenth Dynasty royal burials would have been known to everybody in Thebes. The impact such circumstances had on the decisions of individual craftsmen or temple personnel will probably be forever unknown, but one cannot entirely dismiss the possibility.

Figure 7: Statues of kings accompany the barque of Amun in TT 65 (Author)

Looking further back into the Eighteenth Dynasty, we recall that Thutmose III, by installing the Chamber of Ancestors at Karnak, celebrated his status as the heir of a long line of rulers.[76] He stressed his link to the Ahmosid line when he constructed the sandstone chapels east of Pylon VI, replacing similar buildings of Amenhotep I; and on their walls the king caused himself and Amenhotep I to be represented in parallel offering scenes.[77] The number of private stelae honoring members of the royal family, originating in or shortly after his reign, suggests Thutmose III's influence on the veneration of royal ancestors by commoners.

Also worthy of note is the fact that all of these tombs also include at least one scene of the veneration of Amenhotep I and Ahmose-Nefertari. The large cultic assemblages, even though they include the divine mother and son, do seem to arise from a different, although related, tradition.

The extensive assemblages may have also have marked status as well as piety. They appear in only a handful of tombs among all the hundreds on the west bank. As Cooney has recently observed, commissioning an unusual, innovative scene for one's tomb in the Nineteenth Dynasty, or one's coffin in the Twentieth or Twenty-First, could have been a means to enhance social prestige, as these accomplishments were displayed to family, neighbors, and colleagues during the funerary ceremonies.[78]

In addition to demonstrating the owner's taste and creativity, a large group of royal family members depicted on a tomb wall emphasized the owner's knowledge of history and, for that matter, of the Seventeenth and early Eighteenth Dynasty royal burials—even if, by the time the work was commissioned, their names and relationships had been confused or forgotten. Like the offering table of Paneb, with its list of thirteen kings plus Ahmose-Nefertari, and Qenherkhopeshef's ostracon and offering table with lists of kings, these five collections could have distinguished the tomb owners as—in the words of the Instruction of Amennakht—men "expert in every kind of work" (*ip m k3.t nb.t*).[79]

The scenes under consideration—with the exception of Amenmose's in TT 19—give special prominence to the late Seventeenth and very early Eighteenth Dynasties: the Ahmosid family, even those who died prematurely, such as Siamun and Sapair. Their association with the reunification of Egypt, the expulsion of the Hyksos, the foundation of the New Kingdom, and the renaissance of Thebes as a capital and religious center provided ample reason for them to live on in the popular memory. Whether there were other reasons—a folk reputation for piety and generosity, perhaps, or extended residence at Thebes itself—we may never know.

The topography of the necropolis itself must also have been significant. Three of our tomb owners were buried at Dra Abu el-Naga, and the other two were members of the necropolis crew, a community with religious links (through their devotion to Ahmose-Nefertari and Amenhotep I) to that part of the Theban necropolis. At Dra Abu el-Naga lay the original tombs of the late Seventeenth and early Eighteenth Dynasty royal family;[80] Carter's discovery, "AN B,"[81] near the summit of Dra Abu el-Naga, remains a candidate for the tomb of Ahmose-Nefertari (or as suggested by Dodson in 2010, a joint tomb of the queen and her husband, Ahmose),[82] while tomb K93.11, recently cleared and studied by Daniel Polz, could from its architectural design, size, location, and orientation have been the tomb of

Amenhotep I—and the neighboring "twin" tomb may have been excavated for Ahmose-Nefertari.[83] Dodson also points out that only Ahmose, among the New Kingdom kings buried in TT 320, was accompanied by family members, and that these account for "something like half of the non-Twenty-First Dynasty material in the tomb," leading him to suggest that they had originally been buried in "close proximity" at Dra Abu el-Naga.[84] Just as all the rock formations extending outward from the Peak of the West partook of its sacred character,[85] so too the Dra Abu el-Naga cemetery shared in the holiness of a royal burial ground—this part of the necropolis itself might have been considered a "Chamber of Ancestors," wherein "Lords of the West" (and their families) rested, surrounded by many thousands of elite and middle-class Thebans. The sequences of kings and their family members on the walls of private tombs underscore the sacred nature of the Theban landscape.

Notes

1. O. Louvre Inv. 698 vso. 14. Jaroslav Cerný and Alan Gardiner, *Hieratic Ostraca* 1 (Oxford: Griffith Institute, 1957), pls. LXXX–LXXXA.
2. William C. Hayes, *Scepter of Egypt: A Background for the Study of the Egyptian Antiquities in the Metropolitan Museum of Art 2. The Hyksos and the New Kingdom (1675–1080 B.C.)* (Cambridge, Mass.: Harvard University Press, 1959), 50–51; Teresa Moore, "The Good God Amenhotep: The Deified King as a Focus of Popular Religion during the Egyptian New Kingdom," (PhD dissertation, University of California Berkeley, 1994), 21–23. For the cult of Senwosret I at Thebes, see Khaled el-Enany, "La veneration post mortem de Sesostris Ier," *Memnonia* 14 (2003), 131–134.
3. Karol Mysliwiec, *Eighteenth Dynasty before the Amarna Period*, Iconography of Religions 16.5 (Leiden: E. J. Brill, 1985): pl. XXIII; Moore, "Good God Amenhotep," 23–24.
4. Jean-Marie Kruchten, "Une stèle signée dédiée à Amenophis Ier et Ahmès Néfertari divinisés," in Sarah Israelit-Groll (ed.), *Studies in Egyptology Presented to Miriam Lichtheim* 2 (Jerusalem: Magnes Press, Hebrew University, 1990), 646–652; Moore, "Good God Amenhotep," 24–25.
5. The stela was found built into the doorway of the Twentieth Dynasty brick building at the northeastern angle of Pylon III at Karnak. PM II^2, 77; Pierre Lacau, *Stèles du Nouvel Empire (Catalogue Général du Musée du Caire, nos. 34001–34064)* (Cairo: Institut français d'archéologie orientale, 1909), 67–68 and pl. XXIII; Karol Mysliwiec, *Le portrait royal dans le bas-relief du Nouvel Empire*, Travaux du Centre d'Archéologie Méditerranéenne de l'Academie Polonaise des Sciences 19 (Warsaw: Éditions Scientifiques de Pologne, 1976), 56, figs. 29 and 95; Moore, "Good God Amenhotep," 26–27.

6 Lacau, *Stèles du Nouvel Empire*, 63–64 and pl. XXII; PM II², 294; Vandersleyen, "L'identite d'Ahmes Sapair," *SÄK* 10 (1983): 311–324; Michel Gitton, *L'Épouse du Dieu Ahmes Néfertary* (Paris: Belles lettres, 1975), 46; Moore, "Good God Amenhotep," 19–21.

7 Lacau, *Stèles du Nouvel Empire*, 10–11 and pl. V; R. van Walsem, "The God Montu and Deir el-Medîna," in R. J. Demarée and Jac. J. Janssen (eds.), *Gleanings from Deir el-Medîna* (Leiden: Nederlands Instituut voor het Nabije Oosten, 1982), 196; Vandersleyen, "L'identite d'Ahmes Sapair," 311, 315, 320; Moore, "Good God Amenhotep," 28–30.

8 PM I²:2, 734. Vandersleyen, "L'identite d'Ahmes Sapair," 320, dates Turin 1455 to the reign of Amenhotep II. Donald B. Redford, *Pharaonic King-lists, Annals and Day-books* (Mississauga: Benben Publications, 1986), 46, assigns Turin 1455 a Ramesside date, but an Atenist erasure is visible on the left side of the upper register; Moore, "Good God Amenhotep," 30–33.

9 E. A. Wallis Budge, *Hieroglyphic Texts from Egyptian Stelae &c. in the British Museum* 6 (London: British Museum, 1922), pl. XXXIII and p. 9, where the provenance is given as "Western Thebes"; PM V, 96; Gitton, *L'Épouse du Dieu*, 45; Lise Manniche, "The Complexion of Queen Ahmose Nefertere," *AcOr* 40 (1979), 11 note 8: "possibly earlier than the reign of Amenophis III." Edward F. Wente, "Genealogy of the Royal Family," in James E. Harris and Edward F. Wente, *An X-ray Atlas of the Royal Mummies* (Chicago: University of Chicago Press, 1980), 125; Franz-Jürgen Schmitz, *Amenophis I.*, Hildesheimer Ägyptologische Beiträge 6 (Hildesheim: Gerstenberg Verlag, 1978), 49–51; Moore, "Good God Amenhotep," 36.

10 Redford, *Pharaonic King-lists*, 47 and 49, dates this stela to the Ramesside Period.

11 Lacau, *Stèles du Nouvel Empire*, 70–72 and pl. XXIV; Redford, *Pharaonic King-lists*, 49 (no. 17); Moore, "Good God Amenhotep," 37–39.

12 TT 181: PM I²:1, 288 (6, I, 1). See also Gabi Hollender, *Amenophis I. und Ahmes Nefertari: Untersuchungen zur Entwicklung ihres posthumen Kultes anhand der Privatgräber der thebanischen Nekropole*, Deutsches Archäologisches Institut Abteilung Kairo, Sonderschrift 23 (Belin: De Gruyter, 2009), 17–19; Moore, "Good God Amenhotep," 46–48. TT 49: PM I²:1, 91–95 (C,a); Norman de Garis Davies, *The Tomb of Neferhotep at Thebes*, Metropolitan Museum of Art Egyptian Expedition 9 (New York: Metropolitan Museum of Art, 1933; reprint, New York: Arno Press, 1973); Hollender, *Amenophis I. und Ahmes Nefertari*, 26–28; Moore, "Good God Amenhotep," 48–53.

13 PM I²:1, 103; Alfred Hermann, *Die Stelen der thebanischen Felsgräber der 18. Dynastie* (Gluckstadt: J.J. Augustin, 1940), 60–63 and pl. 9D. For Queen Ahmose-Inhapi and her possible family relationships, Wente, "Genealogy of the Royal Family," 124; Slawomir Rzepka, "Graffiti of Nubkheperre Intef in Deir el-Bahri," *MDAIK* 60 (2004), 156–157.

14 PM I²:1, 274–275; Lise Manniche, *Lost Tombs: A Study of Certain Eighteenth Dynasty Tombs in the Theban Necropolis* (London: Kegan Paul International, 1988), 177; Lise Manniche, "The Tomb of Nakht, the Gardener, at Thebes (No.

161) as Copied by Robert Hay," *JEA* 72 (1986): 55–78; Baudouin van de Walle, "Identification de trois fragments peints de la tombe du jardinier Nakht," *CdÉ* 40 (1965): 34–45; Stephen Quirke, "The Hieratic Texts in the Tomb of Nakht the Gardener, at Thebes (No. 161) as Copied by Robert Hay," *JEA* 72 (1986): 79–90; Moore, "Good God Amenhotep," 40–46; Hollender, *Amenophis I. und Ahmes Nefertari*, 17–20.

15 See Patricia Spencer, *The Egyptian Temple: A Lexicographical Study* (London: Kegan Paul, 1984), 6–27, for a discussion of this term, which is often translated as "open court" or "forecourt."

16 PM I²:1, 32–34; Georges Foucart, *Le tombeau d'Amonmos (Tombes thébaines. Nécropole de Dirâ Abû'n-Naga)*, MIFAO 57.3 (Cairo: Institut français d'archéologie orientale, 1932) i, v; Hollender, *Amenophis I. und Ahmes Nefertari*, 33–42; Moore, "Good God Amenhotep," 94–107. On the left side wall, in the top register, the cult image of Amenhotep of the Temenos is brought out to see the barque of Amun-Re during the Beautiful Festival of the Valley (PM I²:1, 3, I). In the middle register, a statue of Ahmose-Nefertari is taken out of a temple on a sledge (PM I²:1, 3, II). No text was preserved to indicate which temple this was, or whether the occasion was the Valley Festival. On the rear wall, the top register depicted another festive event: fencing and wrestling bouts at the temple of Thutmose III (PM I²:1, 4, 1, 2). In the upper register on the right side of the rear wall, Amenmose, in his capacity of prophet, presides over an oracular judgment of Amenhotep of the Temenos (PM I²:1, 7, 1). And, on the right side wall, Amenmose, accompanied by his wife, Iuy, and son, Baknay, censes and libates before Re-Harakhty-Atum, Amenhotep I, Hathor, and the Western goddess (PM I²:1, 6, 1).

17 Foucart, *Le tombeau d'Amonmos*, pl. XII; Kenneth A. Kitchen, *Ramesside Inscriptions, Historical and Biographical* III (Oxford: Blackwell, 1980), 392; Kenneth A. Kitchen, *Ramesside Inscriptions, Translated and Annotated: Translations* III (Oxford: Blackwell, 2000), 284.

18 The cult statue in Meniset, the temple of Amun, Ahmose-Nefertari and Amenhotep I near the funerary temple of Sety I, seems to have had exposed skin painted black (or coated with bitumen): Gitton, *L'Épouse du Dieu*, 78; Manniche, "Complexion of Queen Ahmose Nefertere," 19. Amenmose would also have been familiar with other figures of the queen, such as that carried in procession from the temple of Karnak during the Beautiful Feast of the Valley. Ahmose-Nefertari's barque is depicted in reliefs at the mortuary temple of Sety I (PM II², 408) and the Ramesseum (PM II², 439). In Sety's temple, Ramesses II also had himself shown offering to Amun, Ahmose-Nefertari, and Amenhotep I, and running with *ḥs* vases before Amun and the queen (PM II², 420); Ahmose-Nefertari is depicted shaking sistra before Amun (PM II², 421).

19 PM I²:1, 6–9; Bernard Bruyère, *Tombes thébaines de Deir el Médineh à decoration monochrome*, MIFAO 86 (Cairo: Institut français d'archéologie orientale, 1952),

1–65, pl. I–XII; Hollender, *Amenophis I. und Ahmes Nefertari*, 87–101; Moore, "Good God Amenhotep," 247–256.

20 At PM I²:1, 7 (9, I), immediately to the right as one enters the chapel of TT 2, Amenhotep *pꜣ ꜥw* is depicted in procession; next to it at (10, I) was the scene of offering to two rows of seated royalties; at (11,1) Amenhotep, Lord of the Town, appears in procession; on the rear wall at (12, I), Khabekhnet worships Amenhotep I, Ahmose-Nefertari, and Merytamun; in the burial chamber at (24, I) Khabekhnet's brother Khonsu and his wife worship Re, Osiris, and Amenhotep I; at (24, 2), Khabekhnet and his wife adore two manifestations of Amenhotep I and Ahmose-Nefertari. Furthermore, a relief sculpture (17) above the stairway to the burial chamber depicts Hathor emerging from the living rock and protecting a king. On a stela placed in the court at (3), Khabekhnet and his family stand before Amun-Re and Ahmose-Nefertari, and on the lucarne stela (British Museum 555) from Khabekhnet's pyramid, the tomb owner also kneels in adoration before Hathor and a royal statue.

21 Berlin Inv.-No. ÄM 1625. PM I²:1, 10, 1; Kitchen, *Ramesside Inscriptions* III, 806–807; Moore, "Good God Amenhotep," 249–250; Kitchen, *Ramesside Inscriptions, Translated and Annotated: Translations* III, 539–541; Hollender, *Amenophis I. und Ahmes Nefertari*, 92–95.

22 Here spelled *tw-r-s*.

23 Hollender, *Amenophis I. und Ahmes Nefertari*, 94. The name Sekhentyenre is probably a mistake for Senakhtenre, predecessor of Seqenenre. Hollender, *Amenophis I. und Ahmes Nefertari*, 95 n. 381.

24 Redford, *Pharaonic King-lists*, 245.

25 PM I²:1, 421–424; Bernard Bruyère, *Rapport sur les fouilles de Deir el Médineh (1930)*, FIFAO 8.3 (Cairo: Institut français d'archéologie orientale, 1933), 33–70, pl. III–XXIV; Nadine Cherpion and Jean-Pierre Corteggiani, *La tombe d'Inherkhâouy (TT 359) à Deir el-Medina*, MIFAO 128 (Cairo: Institut français d'archéologie orientale, 2010); Moore, "Good God Amenhotep," 231–234; Hollender, *Amenophis I. und Ahmes Nefertari*, 105–108.

26 "F" in the Porter and Moss plan: PM I²:1, 416. A shaft in the courtyard of the tomb gave access to the two subterranean rooms, both of which are vaulted.

27 LD iii, 2 [d]; Bruyère, *Rapport*, 1930, pl. viii–ix; Kenneth A. Kitchen, *Ramesside Inscriptions, Historical and Biographical* VI (Oxford: Blackwell, 1983), 185; Dietrich Wildung, *Imhotep und Amenhotep*, Münchner Ägyptologische Studien 36 (Munich: Deutscher Kunstverlag, 1977), 283–285.

28 Jaroslav Cerný, "Le culte d'Amenophis I chez les ouvriers de la Nécropole thébaine," *BIFAO* 27 (1927), 167–170.

29 Wente, "Genealogy of the Royal Family," 124–127.

30 Wente, "Genealogy of the Royal Family," 125.

31 Cherpion and Corteggiani, *La tombe d'Inherkhâouy* I, 55.

32 Wente, "Genealogy of the Royal Family," 124. Cherpion and Corteggiani, *La tombe d'Inherkhâouy* I, 56; note that Henuttamehu, a daughter of Seqenenre and Inhapy, was a princess, not a queen.

33 Cherpion and Corteggiani, *La tombe d'Inherkhâouy* I, 56.

34 That is, Ahmose Sapair. Vandersleyen, "L'identite d'Ahmes Sapair," passim.

35 Another representation of Amenhotep I? It seems curious that he is identified by nomen rather than by prenomen. Cherpion and Corteggiani, *La tombe d'Inherkhâouy* I, 57, remark that if this King Amenhotep in the lower register is meant to be another manifestation of Amenhotep I, inspired by a different cult statue, one would expect him to be wearing a *ḫprš* rather than the *nms*. A seated statue of Amenhotep I (Turin 1372), however, lacking a secure provenance but believed to have come from Deir el-Medina, does wear the *nms*. Claude Vandersleyen, "La statue d'Amenophis I (Turin 1372)," *OrAnt* 19 (1980), 133–137, makes the case that Turin 1372 is a Ramesside copy of an Eighteenth Dynasty original.

36 Cherpion and Corteggiani, *La tombe d'Inherkhâouy* I, 57–59.

37 PM I:1, 366–367; Hollender, *Amenophis I. und Ahmes Nefertari*, 123–127; Moore, "Good God Amenhotep," 144–146.

38 PM I²:1, 366 (5, I).

39 So Redford, *Pharaonic King-lists*, 54.

40 Hollender, *Amenophis I. und Ahmes Nefertari*, 125.

41 Redford, *Pharaonic King-lists*, 54 n.183.

42 PM I²:1, 384–385 (series of royalties at 5, II); Redford, *Pharaonic King-lists*, 45; Moore, "Good God Amenhotep," 150–155; Hollender, *Amenophis I. und Ahmes Nefertari*, 145–147.

43 Friederike Kampp, *Die thebanische Nekropole: zum Wandel des Grabgedankens von der 18. bis zur 20. Dynastie*, Theben 13 (Mainz: von Zabern, 1996), 571–572.

44 Porter and Moss location 5, II, PM I², 384; Philadelphia photograph 34949. The description of this scene is based upon the photograph. Kampp, *Die thebanische Nekropole*, 571, comments on the poor condition and inaccessibility of TT 306 and its immediate neighbors.

45 Not merely two rows of seven cartouches each, as recorded in PM I²:1, 384, and Redford, *Pharaonic King-lists*, 45. The lower series is so badly damaged that one cannot be absolutely sure whether eight or nine figures are present.

46 PM I²:1, 384.

47 Redford, *Pharaonic King-lists*, 45.

48 PM I²:1, 384. The cartouche is visible but hardly legible.

49 PM I²:1, 384.

50 The apparent *nb* sign occupies the lowest third of the cartouche and the preceding sign is indistinct, so Amenhotep III cannot be ruled out. PM I²:1, 384, even suggested Tutankhamun.

51 As Redford, *Pharaonic King-lists*, 45, suggests.

52 TT 31 (Khonsu), TT 2 (Khabekhnet), TT 277 (Amenemone), TT 19 (Amenmose), TT 359 (Anhurkhau).

53 As on stela BM 690, from Nebhepetre Mentuhotep's Deir el-Bahri temple. PM II², 396.

54 PM I²:1, 384. In Philadelphia photograph 34949, only the article tA is clearly visible.

55 Redford, *Pharaonic King-lists*, 45, gives her name as Ahmose.

56 Redford, *Pharaonic King-lists*, 45.

57 Redford, *Pharaonic King-lists*, 45; PM I²:1, 384. The name does seem to include the *s3* bird.

58 Redford, *Pharaonic King-lists*, 45: "Kamose." In the cartouche the *s3* bird is visible, as pointed out by Hollender, *Amenophis I. und Ahmes Nefertari*, 146 n. 542. The sign or signs below it in the Philadelphia photograph 34949 are illegible.

59 Redford, *Pharaonic King-lists*, 45.

60 Moore, "Good God Amenhotep," 154–155.

61 See discussion by Kathlyn M. Cooney, "Changing Burial Practices at the End of the New Kingdom: Defensive Adaptation in Tomb Commissions, Coffin Commissions, Coffin Decoration, and Mummification," *JARCE* 47 (2011), 5–11. Irdjanen belonged to one of the two communities noted by Cooney as having the ability to commission decorated tombs (or reuse older monuments): the necropolis workmen and those connected with the estate of Amun.

62 Redford, *Pharaonic King-lists*, 52; Epigraphic Survey, *Medinet Habu IV. Festival Scenes of Ramses III*, OIP 51 (Chicago: University of Chicago Press, 1940), pl. 213.

63 Cherpion and Corteggiani, *La tombe d'Inherkhâouy* I, 154.

64 The kings in Irdjanen's series combine the voluminous Ramesside robe with their kilts.

65 Redford, *Pharaonic King-lists*, 45–46; Cherpion and Corteggiani, *La tombe d'Inherkhâouy* I, 52.

66 Cherpion and Corteggiani, *La tombe d'Inherkhâouy* I, 52, n. 168.

67 Cherpion and Corteggiani, *La tombe d'Inherkhâouy* I, 52.

68 Cherpion and Corteggiani, *La tombe d'Inherkhâouy* I, 55, 57.

69 Charles Bonnet and Dominique Valbelle, "Le village du Deir el-Médineh: reprise de l'étude archéologique," *BIFAO* 75 (1975): 429–446.

70 C.A. Keller, "Speculations Concerning Interconnections between the Royal Policy and Reputation of Ramesses IV," in David P. Silverman (ed.), *For His Ka: Essays Offered in Memory of Klaus Baer*, SAOC 55 (Chicago: University of Chicago Press, 1994), 151–154.

71 Amenmose's selection is similar to, although more comprehensive than, that recorded for the lost Qurna tomb (C 7) of Harmose, also a contemporary of Ramesses II; here the owner, an official of the Ramesseum, chose to portray Thutmose I, II, III, and IV, and Amenhotep I and II, along with Horus. PM I²:1, 459.

72 See remarks by Daniel Polz, "New Archaeological Data from Dra' Abu el-Naga and Their Historical Implications," in Marcel Marée (ed.), *The Second Intermediate Period (Thirteenth–Seventeenth Dynasties): Current*

Research, Future Prospects, OLA 192 (Leuven: Peeters, 2010), 351; Daniel Polz, *Der Beginn des Neuen Reiches: zur Vorgeschichte einer Zeitenwende*, Deutsches Archäologisches Institut Abteilung Kairo, Sonderschrift 31 (Berlin: de Gruyter, 2007), 376–377.

73 Robert Morkot, "Nb-maat-Ra-united-with-Ptah," *JNES* 49 (1990), 329 n. 43.

74 PM I:1², 315–317; Norman de Garis Davies, *Two Ramesside Tombs at Thebes*, Robb de Peyster Tytus Memorial Series 5 (New York: Metropolitan Museum of Art, 1927), 64. The discovery of seals bearing the name of the Vizier Paser at K93.11 may support the hypothesis of a renewal of burial for that king at the behest of Ramesses II (Polz, *Der Beginn des Neuen Reiches*, 186–187).

75 Daniel Polz, "The Royal and Private Necropolis of the Seventeenth and Early Eighteenth Dynasties at Dra' Abu el-Naga," in Khaled Daoud, Shafia Bedier, and Sawsan Abd el-Fatah (eds.), *Studies in Honor of Ali Radwan* 2, SASAE 34 (Cairo: Supreme Council of Antiquities, 2005), 240–241.

76 PM II², 111–112. See also remarks by Redford, *Pharaonic King-lists*, 165–177.

77 Gun Bjorkman, *Kings at Karnak*, Boreas 2 (Uppsala: Almqvist & Wiksell, 1971), 77–78; P. Lacau, "Deux magasins à encens du temple de Karnak," *ASAE* 52 (1952), 191. Also see Christian Loeben, "Amon à la place d'Aménophis I: le relief de la porte des magazins nord de Thoutmosis III," *CdK* 8 (1987), 238–239.

78 Cooney, "Changing Burial Practices," 29.

79 Paneb's offering table, sketched by Wilkinson: PM I²:2, 743; Redford, *Pharaonic King-lists*, 44; Morris Bierbrier, "Paneb Rehabilitated?" in R. J. Demarée and A. Egberts (eds.), *Deir el-Medina in the Third Millennium AD: A Tribute to Jac. J. Janssen*, Egyptologische Uitgaven 14 (Leiden: Nederlands Instituut voor het Nabije Oosten, 2000), 52 and pls. IV–V. Qenherkhopeshef's ostracon: Cairo 25646 (Cerný, *Ostraca hiératiques*, 48, 68*, pl. lxiv) and offering table Marseille 204: PM I:2², 753; Redford, *Pharaonic King-lists*, 43–44. See also Andrea McDowell, "Awareness of the Past in Deir el-Medina," in R. J. Demarée and A. Egberts (eds.), *Village Voices* (Leiden: Center of Non-Western Studies, 1992), 95–109. For a recent discussion of the Instruction of Amennakht, see Andreas Dorn, "Die Lehre Amunnachts," *ZÄS* 131 (2004), 38–55.

80 H. E.Winlock, "The Tombs of the Kings of the 17th Dynasty at Thebes," *JEA* 10 (1924), 277; Polz, *Der Beginn des Neuen Reiches*, 115–197.

81 Howard Carter, "Report on the Tomb of Zeser-ka-ra Amenhetep I, Discovered by the Earl of Carnarvon in 1914," *JEA* 3 (1916): 147–154; Elizabeth Thomas, *The Royal Necropoleis of Thebes* (Princeton, 1966), 70–71. For further discussion on the location of the king's tomb, see Schmitz, *Amenophis I.*, 205–232; C.N. Reeves, *Valley of the Kings: The Decline of a Royal Necropolis* (London: Kegan Paul, 1990), 3–9; Polz, "The Royal and Private Necropolis," 238–242.

82 Aidan Dodson, "The Burials of Ahmose I," in Zahi Hawass and Salima Ikram (eds.), *Thebes and Beyond: Studies in Honor of Kent R. Weeks*, SASAE 41 (Cairo: Supreme Council of Antiquities, 2010), 27.

[83] Polz, "The Royal and Private Necropolis," 238–242; Polz, *Der Beginn des Neuen Reiches*, 187–192.

[84] Dodson, "The Burials of Ahmose I," 25.

[85] Bernard Bruyere, *Rapport Deir el-Medineh 1935–40*, I, 12; V.A. Donohue, "The Goddess of the Theban Mountain," *Antiquity* 66 (1992), 871–885.

A Preliminary Report on the Clearance of Theban Tomb 16 in Dra Abu el-Naga at Thebes

Suzanne Onstine, University of Memphis
with Jesus Hererrin and Miguel Sanchez

As part of its ongoing mission, the University of Memphis is excavating Theban Tomb 16. This paper presents some preliminary observations and findings related to its twentieth-century conservation and looting, as well as to artifacts and human remains from intrusive Third Intermediate to Roman Period burials found in the previously unexcavated (but looted) passage of this tomb.

A festschrift dedicated to Richard H. Wilkinson is an appropriate place to publish this preliminary summary of archaeology done in Theban Tomb 16. It was Richard who gave me a love of Egyptology as a real discipline when I was an undergraduate student, and he also gave me my first chance at working in Egypt (in the Valley of the Kings, no less!) in 1995.

In a recent article I outlined the preliminary stages of the epigraphic work done by the University of Memphis in tomb 16 in the Dra Abu el-Naga section of the necropolis at ancient Thebes.[1] While we continue our work in the tomb along many research lines and a full publication is in preparation, it is still useful to present some of the preliminary finds from the clearance of the looted passage leading to what is likely the original burial shaft.[2] Two seasons of clearing the unstratified, looted fill have produced some very interesting material, and, although most of it is quite damaged, we can nevertheless make some general statements here while more thorough analyses are carried out.

The tomb was partially published as part of the Institut français d'archéologie orientale (IFAO) epigraphic mission in the Luxor area in the 1920s.[3] Their publication includes only one of the two decorated rooms, as the second room and the adjoining corridor were apparently blocked up with debris and inaccessible at the time. The plan and description in Porter and Moss similarly indicate the rest beyond the first room was inaccessible.[4] Since that time, at some point between the 1950s and 1980s, the tomb's second decorated room was cleared and both rooms were conserved. Mud with straw temper was used in place of plaster to fill in and stabilize the gaps where the walls had suffered damage. This style of using mud instead of modern plaster is consistent with early conservation practices. Additionally, a cement floor was laid down in the decorated rooms. Records of this work have not been located, but it was most likely carried out by the Egyptian government. A brief reference by Labib Habachi indicates he was connected to work in the tomb, but no publications have been found related to that statement or work at TT 16.[5] His comment, combined with the style of conservation done, leads me to favor a date in the 1960s or early 1970s for the clearance of the second room.

Since previous works, including my own, have focused largely on the epigraphic work in the tomb and on the background on the tomb owners, Panehsy and Tarenu, I will only briefly relate some high points of that material here. Panhesy and Tarenu lived during the reign of Ramesses II. The art style has classic Ramesside features, such as long, pleated garments, slender proportions, and lines indicating neck folds under the chin. In addition, a known steward of Ramesses II named Nebsumenu (buried in TT 183) is depicted in a procession along with Panehsy and his brother.[6] Their relationship to each other is not clear. Panehsy has two titles: overseer of the chanters of the offering table of Amun (*ḥry šmꜥ n pꜣ wḏḥw n ꞽImn*) and priest of Amenhotep of the forecourt (*ḥm nṯr n ꞽImn-ḥtp n pꜣ wbꜣ*).[7] Tarenu bore the title chantress of Amun (*šmꜥyt nt ꞽImn*). There are no children depicted in the tomb, and only Panehsy's brother, Pawah, who is depicted in the procession with Nebsumenu and Panehsy, is named as a relative in the tomb. The decorative program also conforms to general Ramesside decorative standards, as it includes a combination of daily life scenes and those more oriented toward funerary vignettes.[8]

The reliefs are painted plaster, as the geology in this area of the necropolis is largely conglomerate limestone, which is friable and allows no smooth carving surface. In fact, the builders of the tomb had to even out the walls with a very thick mud backing, several centimeters thick in some places, or even mud bricks to fill in larger depressions or irregularities. The mud backing often contains dung, ceramic sherds, and reeds or straw as temper. This layer was then smoothed over with more mud to create an even painting surface.

These techniques are unfortunately very clearly seen in the areas damaged by looters who sawed out six sections of relief (the saw marks are clearly visible, extending into the adjacent scenes), presumably for sale on the international art market[9] (Figure 1). These sections of the tomb reliefs were surely stolen between the 1950s and 1980s, since two of the stolen scenes are in areas blocked by debris and unexcavated prior to the 1950s. Photographs published in the mid-1980s show the damage done, so we have a range of time during which those thefts likely took place.[10] The looters took more generic head and torso pieces of the deceased couple and avoided the well-published scenes of Amenhotep I and the two different temple representations. These would have been more difficult to explain if caught and more risky to sell, since these images had already been published in the 1930s.

The rest of this article will concentrate on the human remains and the material cleared from the sloping passage leading to the burial shaft. The passage had been used for secondary burials from the Third Intermediate Period through the Roman Period. This rough estimate of dates is based on the styles of cartonnage and coffin decoration, as well as the small finds found in the debris. Since many decorative styles are diagnostic of specific periods, it is not difficult to identify the majority of remains as Third Intermediate Period, with Late Period and Graeco-Roman styles also represented. Figures 2 and 3 give a small representation of the types of materials found. This pattern of post-New Kingdom reuse in the Theban necropolis is well known. Many of the tombs in the area of Dra Abu el-Naga have the exact same pattern of secondary burials.[11]

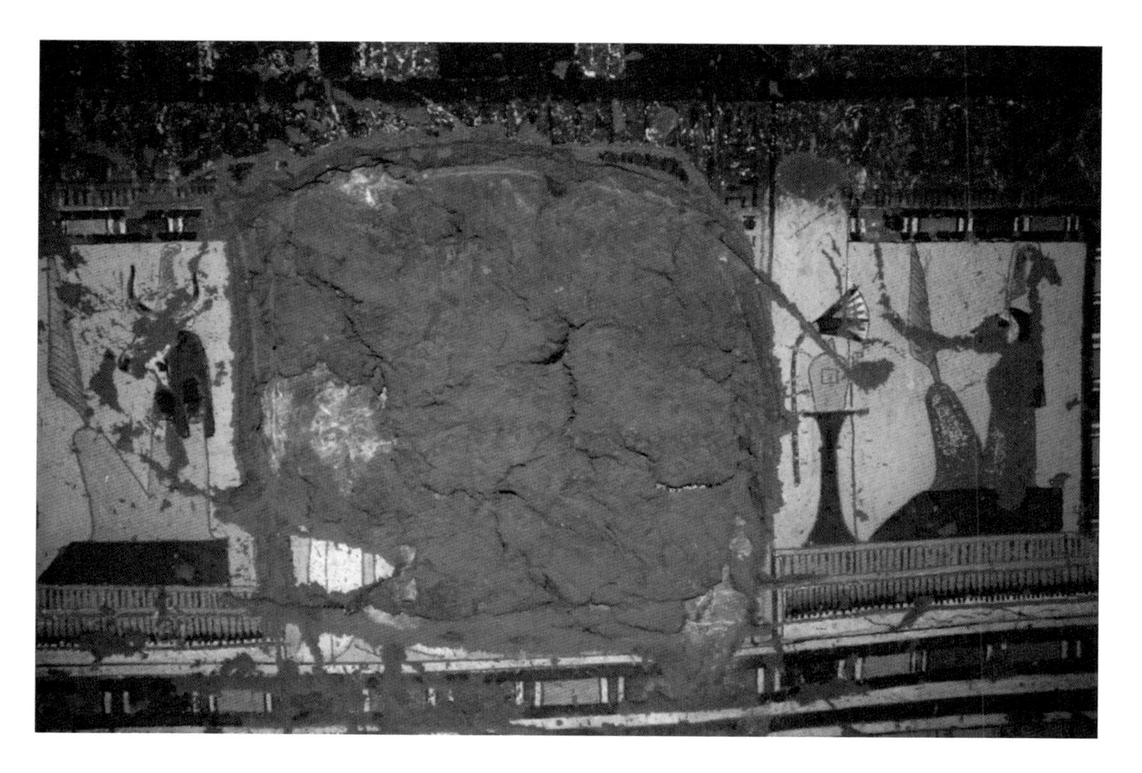

Figure 1: Looter damage in first room, south east wall (Author)

The passage was also thoroughly looted at some point in the twentieth century. Evidence for this lies in the discovery of several modern items mixed in with the loose fill and artifacts at depths of up to 40 cm. Items such as matchboxes, cement bags, plastic sandals, and pumpkin seeds all indicate that the looting occurred at some point in the twentieth century, but perhaps the tomb was revisited over the years up to as recently as the 1980s before a door was installed.[12] Whether the looting of the burials and the thefts of the reliefs occurred at the same time is impossible to know. However, since the tomb was supposedly inaccessible until the clearance of the second room sometime during the 1950s or '60s, this would put the looting of the secondary burials around the same timeframe as the theft of the plaster reliefs.[13] That the looting was modern and intended to fuel the art market can also be shown through the patterns of what was taken and what was left behind.

The artifacts and human remains in the sloping passage all show evidence of rough treatment, mainly the smashing of coffins and cartonnage and the unwrapping and ripping apart of bodies. This behavior is consistent with the search for amulets and precious objects placed on the body. These are the kinds of things that regularly appear on the art market. They are small, portable, and easy to sell, since there is usually no identifying information on them. The burials in question date to the Third Intermediate through Roman Periods. A common practice during the Third Intermediate Period involved the use of cartonnage inner coffins: A papier-mâché-like technique is used to create a molded anthropomorphic form that is sewn up the back around the body. The use of this technique for burials meant that to get at the "goodies" inside, thieves had to smash the cartonnage; they could not be opened as a regular wooden coffin could be. The majority of cartonnage fragments we find are no larger than a few centimeters square, attesting to rough treatment. Similarly, the pattern of things we do not find in the debris is indicative of art-market looting. Cartonnage faces and the wooden panels of outer coffins are the kinds of things that would sell well in the open market. To date, we also have found no funerary stelae or papyri, items that are typically found with burials in the Third Intermediate Period, when the majority of these secondary burials were made. The large numbers of Third Intermediate Period papyri and stelae in museums and private collections worldwide that are not associated with a coffin or mummy speaks directly to this issue.

Artifacts of interest from the coffin assemblages include the wooden hands that would have been attached by dowels to the front of the coffins. Male hands were

Figures 2 and 3: Cartonnage fragments (Author)

painted red and were clenched in a fist that would have additionally held emblems like *ankhs* or *djed* pillars. We did find a couple of fragments of these emblems (Figure 4). Female hands were slender and open or flat against the coffin and yellow in color. There are several cartonnage ears that would have been applied to the interior cartonnage coffin or mask. They were constructed of linen, plaster, and wood, and then gessoed over and painted. The interior details of the ear were well modeled to show the complexity of the ear, and the red lines of paint reinforced the modeling, giving a very convincing recreation of an ear (Figure 5). Pieces of a few wooden faces were recovered, but none is complete.

The most common small finds are Third Intermediate Period shabti figures that are largely fragmentary. This is consistent with the practice of using large numbers of shabtis for an individual burial, complete with overseer figures to manage the regular shabtis in the afterlife. In the 2011 season, we recovered many ceramic shabtis bearing the name of *Ṯnt-šd-ḫnsw* (Figures 6 and 7). The style of these figures—blue-green paint on ceramic, with black details of a wig, fillet, hoes, and seed bag—is typical of the Third Intermediate Period. The name *Ṯnt-šd-ḫnsw* is a common Third Intermediate Period construction of a theophoric name incorporating one of the Theban triad. During the 2013 field season, however, examples representing a different kind of shabti were found; classic blue-green faience with black details and a few new names, including several belonging to *ʿnḫ-n-ḫnsw* (Figure 8). It is from this group that several overseer shabtis were identified. A few of these had the unusual detail of depicting individual toes on the feet of the overseers.

The ceramic corpus is not extraordinary, but much remains to be done to analyze the sherds. A preliminary look at the material reveals a range of dates that are consistent with the post-New Kingdom use of the tomb. No whole vessels have been uncovered, nor are the mendable sherds representative of whole pots in a broken state. The most interesting find related to this is actually a mud stopper, impressed with a seal that says "*irp*" (wine) (Figure 9). The size of the stopper is consistent with a large amphora, several of which must have been in the tomb, as we have many fragments of large amphorae that represent several different vessels.

Regarding the prolific amount of human remains, the University of Memphis mission includes two specialists, Jesus Hererrin (physical anthropologist, Universidad Autónoma de Madrid) and Miguel Sanchez (pathologist, Icahn School of Medicine at Mount Sinai), who are analyzing and interpreting the human remains as we recover them.[14] Thousands of bones have been examined and evaluated. To date we have created more than two hundred individual database records representing at least fifty people. Because the bodies are badly broken up and there are so many pieces of body parts found in a very close area, it will be difficult to reunite limbs and skulls with torsos, impeding a precise accounting of how many individuals are represented in the tomb. The broken pieces of mummies that can be identified as diagnostically significant, however, tell us a great deal about the population that used the tomb. In fact, because the bones have been exposed and unwrapped in many cases, our specialists are able to make many

Figure 4: ***Djed*** **column amulet that would have been held in a hand applied to a coffin (Author)**

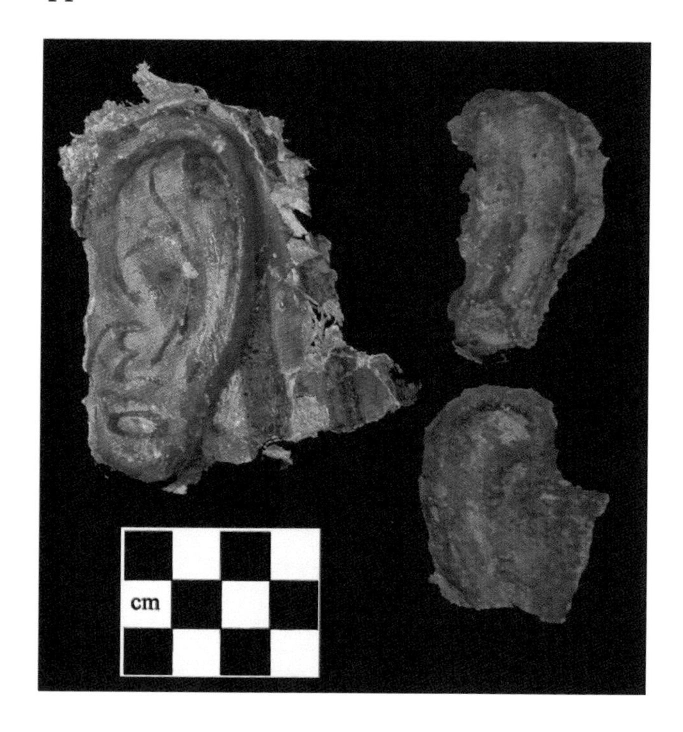

Figure 5: Cartonnage ears (Author)

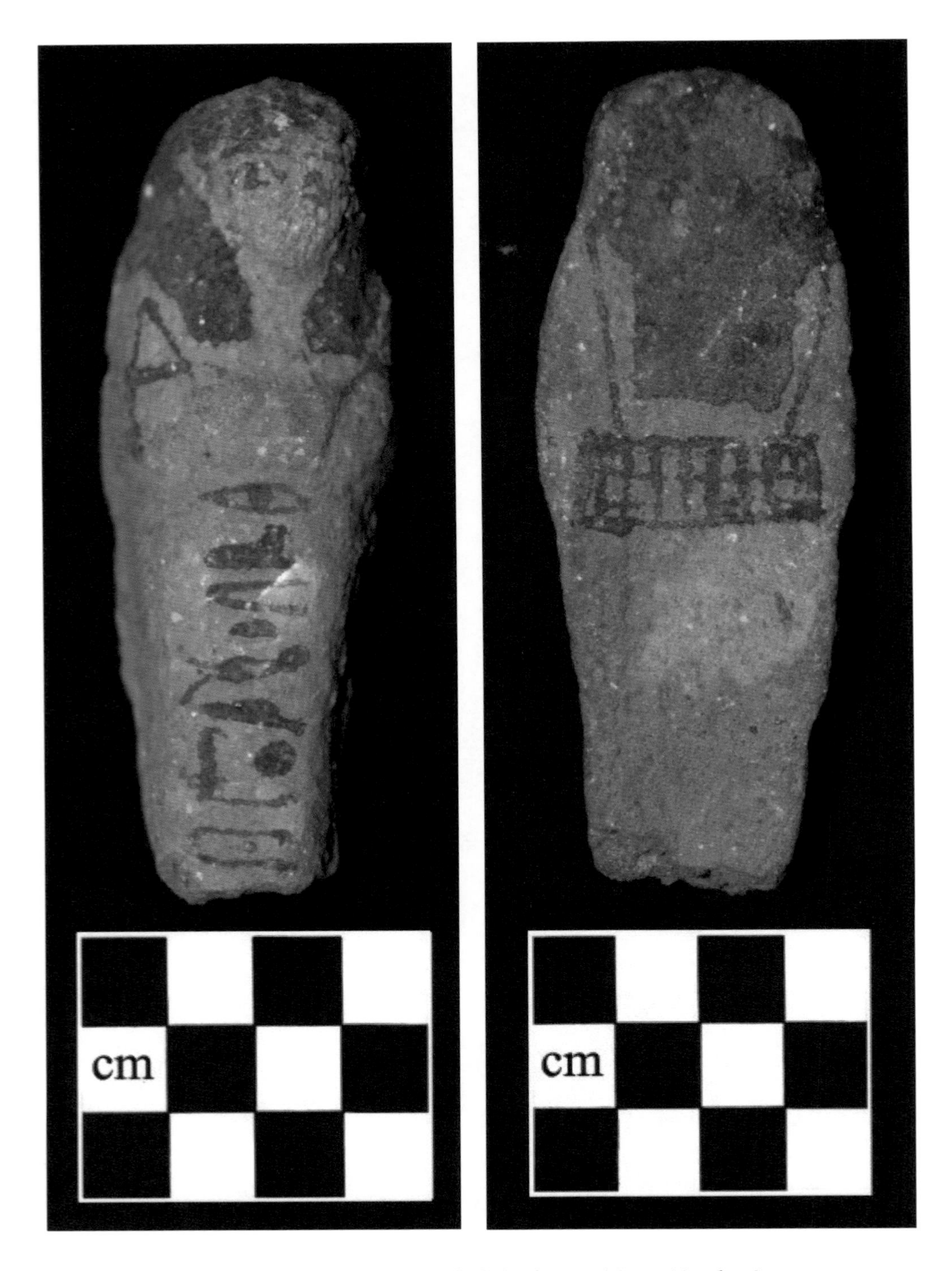

Figures 6 and 7: Shabti of *Ṯnt-šd-ḫnsw* (Author)

Figure 8: Shabti fragments (Author)

observations without the aid of imaging equipment such as X-ray or CT scanning. A few of our initial observations are cited below.

The bodies have been ripped into chunks at the joints or are broken off at weaker areas of the body. The torsos are sometimes connected to arms or legs, but often we find the arms and legs separately. Since the neck is a weak point on the mummy, most skulls are not attached to larger parts of the torsos. Feet and hands are also not often still attached where they should be, although leg and arm bones are often found still wrapped together. The midsections of the bodies have been mostly unwrapped, and in one case it is possible to tell what damage came from the embalmer (the clean incision made in soft tissue to remove organs) and what happened in the looting process (the jagged breaking of brittle skin and bones). This pattern of destruction is again consistent with that of a person looking for the small items placed within the bandages and body of the deceased; rings and bracelets on the hands and wrists, necklaces, and amulets at the neck, amulets inside the wrappings and cavity of the torso—perhaps including a plaque over the embalmer's incision.

Some of the major health concerns that have been noted include an abundance of evidence for arthritis, anemia, and stress injuries. These are conditions we often associate with lower socio-economic classes of people who are doing large amounts of difficult labor or have nutritional deficits, yet these are presumably the individuals who had once-beautiful coffin assemblages and mummification performed on their remains. This calls into question the assumptions people often make about class and economic status in the ancient world; Egypt often seems populated only by very wealthy elites who had burial assemblages such as those we found, or the very poor associated with agricultural labor. Issues such as the existence of a middle class are rarely addressed. Unless we want to imagine a wealthy lady of the house responsible for carrying her own water jug on her head, leading to arthritis in her cervical vertebrae, we may want to reconsider how much a burial assemblage can tell us about wealth and social status. The kinds of activities that lead to stress injuries and arthritis should also suggest that we question our assumptions about the lifestyle an elite person might have enjoyed. Diseases resulting from dietary deficits, such as anemia and possibly rickets, are present in our tomb population and are another indicator that the "wealthy" owners of these coffins may not have been as comfortable as once thought.

Another interesting aspect of our work on the mummies is the identification of at least ten cases in which the embalmer seems to have created what we call "prostheses for the afterlife." The mummies showed signs of having been "perfected" through postmortem manipulation of key areas: the spine, limbs, and skull. These procedures were probably intended to repair or correct defects present in the body. These defects could include scoliosis, which was corrected by shoving a stick through the vertebral column, thereby artificially straightening the spine. Since the spine has a natural S-curve, even when the stick is no longer present (although in a few cases it is still there), it is obvious that the embalmer has made an attempt to manipulate the body to correct the situation, thereby flattening the appearance of the spine. A few limb bundles include sticks to straighten limbs that appear to have been crooked. X-ray analysis in the future will help us interpret those remains that are still wrapped. The most dramatic example of a postmortem repair is the broken pelvis of a young woman that was tied back together in the mummification process (Figure 10). An examination of the pelvis reveals that she may have died in childbirth and that, in the attempt to remove the child from the womb, the woman's pelvis was broken. It was neatly tied together and presumably

Figure 9: Mud jar stopper stamped with the word *irp* (Author)

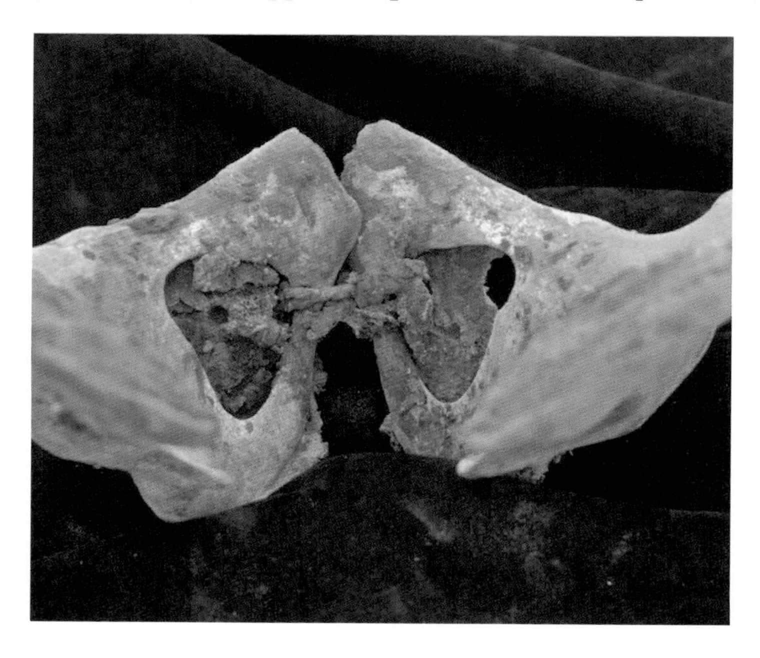

Figure 10: Pelvis of a young woman with postmortem alterations (Author)

replaced in the body. We found it separated from the body but still held together by the ancient string.

Future seasons will likely uncover similar material, judging by what is visible on the surface of the tomb's floor. We still have many seasons of work ahead to complete the clearance and analysis of TT 16.

NOTES

1. Suzanne Onstine, "University of Memphis Mission to Theban Tomb 16: The Life of Panhesy, Chanter and Priest," *JARCE* 47 (2011): 231–236
2. A plan of the tomb and passage, as well as a very brief description of the tomb, is included in Friedericke Kampp, *Die thebanische Nekropole: zum Wandel des Grabgedankens von der XVIII. bis zur XX. Dynastie* (Mainz am Rhein: Von Zabern, 1996), 196–197, fig. 99. The passage is approximately 50 m long, but detailed measurements are not possible until the area is fully cleared of human remains; at present every centimeter of floor surface is littered with broken body parts.
3. M. Baud and E. Drioton, *Le tombeau de Panehsy, in Tombes Thébaines. Nécropole de Dira' Abu'n-Naga*, MIFAO 57.2 (Cairo: Institut français d'archéologie orientale, 1928).
4. PM I²:1, 20, 28–29.
5. A brief comment about finding the funerary cone of a Viceroy of Nubia in TT 16 exists in a footnote in an article he wrote about the viceroys, but no further publication of his involvement with work in TT 16 has been discovered (L. Habachi, "Miscellanea on Viceroys of Kush and Their Assistants Buried in Dra'Abu El-Naga', South," *JARCE* 13 [1976], 113, n. 2).
6. PM I²:1, 289.
7. A manifestation of the deified Amenhotep I.
8. For details about the decorative program, please refer to Onstine, "University of Memphis Mission," and PM I²:1, 28–29.
9. The areas damaged are described briefly in PM I²:1, 28–29, sections 1.I, 4.I, 5.I, 6.I.2 and two others not accessible at the time Porter and Moss compiled the *Bibliography*.
10. Robert Boulanger, *Egyptian Painting and the Ancient East* (New York: Funk and Wagnalls, 1965), 25. Additionally, University of Chicago photographs taken in 1956/1957 show the tomb intact before the SCA conservation and clearing of the second room (University of Chicago Oriental Institute photographs 10296–10305). The photograph published in Lise Manniche, *City of the Dead. Thebes in Egypt* (Chicago: University of Chicago Press, 1987), 75, shows the looter damage done to one of the scenes in the first room and provides a clue regarding the end of the timeframe in which the looting happened. The method used to cut the scenes out is the same in each case, so it is likely they were all stolen at the same time.

11 Cf. Erzsebet Fothi, Zsolt Bernert, Andrea Korosi, with essay by Gabor Schreiber, *Human and Faunal Remains from Theban Tomb 32*, StudAeg 19 (Budapest: Department of Egyptology, Eötvös Loránd University, 2010). Also, I personally saw this in the tombs designated Z-1 and Z-2, being excavated by the SCA in 2011 in the wadi just northwest of TT 16.

12 This information is according to local residents, as well as a general consensus among inspectors, that the 1980s was when security doors were finally installed in many tombs in the area.

13 There are alternative possibilities for the timeline of the looting, but until records from the Ministry of State for Antiquities are located, the state of the passage at the time the second room was cleared is unknown.

14 Specialist studies are in preparation and will appear in paleopathology and anthropology journals, as well as in the final report of the tomb. I thank Sanchez and Herrerin for their help in preparing this summary of the work.

Shooting in KV 55: New Light on Early Photography

Lyla Pinch Brock
Royal Ontario Museum, Toronto

As a result of research and the re-excavation of KV 55 in the Valley of the Kings by the author, ancient and modern material has come to light. This contributes to both the history of photography and the history of this controversial tomb, particularly concerning the tomb's reuse in the last century by photographer Harry Burton.

No one excavating in Egypt today can deny that photography is the greatest ally to recording available.[1] Particularly now, in the digital age, when the problems faced as recently as a decade ago—the spoiling and transport of chemicals, the difficulty of finding an adequate darkroom, the availability and cost of photographic materials—have been virtually eliminated. But for many years after their invention, cameras and photographers were not always readily available, much to the detriment of discoveries. Nowhere is this unfortunate circumstance more evident than in the often contradictory reports of the discovery and excavation of the so-called Amarna cache (subsequently numbered KV 55) in the Valley of the Kings in 1907. The tomb came to involve two photographers, an A. Paul of Cairo and Harry Burton from the Metropolitan Museum of Art. A re-clearance of the tomb by the author from 1993 to 1996[2] has shed some light on puzzling historic events involving both photographers.

Early Photography in Egypt

The invention of the camera provoked much excitement in Egyptian archaeology, and the French were at the forefront. In 1816 Joseph Nicephore Niépce made the first photographic image.[3] In 1839 Louis-Jacques-Mandé Daguerre made a significant advancement with the invention of the daguerreotype,[4] which fixed the image to a plate using a method that prevented the result from fading. The albumin print (using an emulsion made from egg white and silver salts) was introduced by Louis Désiré Blanquart-Evrard in 1850, and the dry-plate negative in 1871. Shortly thereafter, pre-sensitized paper (to produce a calotype) was available commercially.[5] By the 1880s the gelatin glass plate, more sensitive to light and offering better exposure, was in use. "Celluloid plastic" film was invented in the 1890s.[6] The autochrome process for color transparencies was patented in 1904 by Louis Lumière and became available to the public only after 1907.[7]

Probably the first Egyptologist to use the camera in the field was William Matthew Flinders Petrie. Upon hearing about the principle of the invention, Petrie made his own pinhole model, which proved quite adequate for fieldwork.[8] His experiments at Giza from 1881 to 1882 demonstrated that the best place to process photos was in a sealed tomb, a fact Harry Burton, who photographed all the finds from the tomb of Tutankhamun, was later to discover when he put KV 55 to his use.

The *Service des antiquités égyptiennes*, perhaps because of its French connection, was quick to adopt the camera for recording: founder Auguste Mariette included a photographer (Théodule Devéria) in his expeditions in the late 1860s in the Valley of the Kings.[9] The next director of the *Service*, Gaston Maspero, allowed the talented Dutch photographer, banker, and antiquities dealer Jan Herman Insinger to take photographs of the royal mummies discovered in the Deir el-Bahri cache in 1881.[10] Insinger shot them with a Kodak box camera during their unwrapping in the Bulak Museum. Victor Loret, who ran the *Service* from 1897 to 1899, photographed his own explorations in the Valley of the Kings: The eerie candlelit photograph of the mummies found in an antechamber of the tomb of Amenhotep II in 1898[11] is probably his.

American George Reisner[12] worked in Egypt and the Sudan from 1905 onward and considered the camera essential excavation equipment. He was his own site photographer and produced astonishing results. He set down rules for photographing and was adamant about shooting what had to be destroyed in the course of excavating: "If he (the archaeologist) must excavate, it is incumbent on him to make that record. It is his duty conscientiously to deliver such record as he can of the materials he has destroyed." At the same time Reisner admitted that trying to shoot and develop in a hot, dusty country was difficult, if not impossible. He tried to build the perfect darkroom and was ingenious in his developing methods, keeping count of the changes of water by throwing pebbles from a basket into a box.

Early Photography and KV 55

The saga of the discovery and excavation of the mysterious "Amarna cache" in the Valley of the Kings in 1907 unfolded over several decades and came to involve two photographers, A. Paul from a Cairo studio and Harry Burton, employed by the Metropolitan Museum of Art for their Egyptian Expedition.[13]

The story began on January 9, 1907, when archaeologist Edward Ayrton halted his clearing operation across the tourist path from the tomb of Ramesses VI in order to scribble a hasty note to his sponsor, Theodore Davis, and send a workman scurrying to his *dahabiya.* Ayrton had been systematically probing the east side of the wadi in hopes of finding yet another tomb for the lucky Davis, a wealthy American lawyer who had become known as "the man who found a new tomb every year."[14] The day before, Davis had been disappointed with an unfinished tomb,[15] and then suddenly success was in the air: "Ayrton has finally found a real tomb," wrote Davis's cousin and companion, Emma Andrews, in her diary.[16] According to Andrews, Davis went to see Ayrton immediately and was there all day.[17]

According to the sparse reports subsequently published, the entrance to the single-chambered tomb was only partially sealed by a barrier stamped with seals and the contents were damaged by rainwater infiltration. The fragmentary royal burial it proved to contain consisted primarily of a set of canopic jars, a dismantled gilded wood shrine engraved with the name of Queen Tiye, a coffin containing poorly-preserved human remains, and many other small items.

Who actually *was* on hand when the tomb was opened has become the subject of endless speculation. It may have been only Ayrton, Davis, and some workmen. Arthur Weigall, the local inspector, was apparently not present, and Maspero, then Director of the *Service,* did not arrive until January 14,[18] when the tomb was opened officially. Despite claims to the contrary, it appears no photographer was present to photograph[19] the seals on the barrier before it was taken down: Joseph Lindon-Smith, the expedition artist, insists he saw the barrier photographed, but Weigall accused Ayrton of giving the order to remove the barrier before it was photographed.[20] Both Ayrton and Davis later confirmed the seals were those of the priests of the necropolis,[21] and Weigall mentioned seeing a seal of Tutankhamun,[22] but because nothing was photographed, we will never know for certain who sealed the burial. Even the small fragment of cement with a possible stamp I found during a clearance of the tomb in 1993[23] unfortunately adds nothing to our knowledge.

It now appears that Davis's excavation methods were less than optimal, site supervision was lax, and objects went missing. In-fighting among Weigall, Ayrton, and Davis further complicated matters. Davis bullied Ayrton, censored his reports (his records have never been found), and bridled at Weigall's authority. As a result, "it is now extremely doubtful," historian Cyril Aldred concluded, "whether a totally reliable account can be elicited of what was originally discovered in the tomb and the state in which it was found."[24]

If photographic records had been made at the time of discovery, many lingering questions could have been answered. When was the burial made and by whom? Were the objects photographed in their original positions? Had the tomb been robbed, and if so, how many times? But in 1907, despite the advances made by the *Service*, having a camera available at the moment of an archaeological discovery was still not commonplace.

By January 13, according to Andrews, a photographer had finally arrived: "The photographer has worked all day. [Lindon] Smith has finished the Queen. The photographer will monopolise the Tomb Monday and Tuesday."[25] The photographer, A. Paul, had been sent for from Cairo. (A number of photography shops existed in Cairo and Alexandria early in the century, but his name is not mentioned, and I have not been able to find any other record of him.) By the time he arrived, the sections of the shrine found in the corridor had been bridged to provide access to the burial chamber. Paul's first photograph (a calotype)[26] showing that scene was published in Davis's volume *The Tomb of Queen Tiyi,* along with six other photographs.[27] In Paul's photograph of the burial chamber, a small book, perhaps the photographer's own,[28] can be seen on the shelf of the niche, and his camera tripod is visible. Cords suggest electric lighting was in use.

The close-up of the body lying half out of the coffin may not show it as found: Smith says Maspero saw the mummy *inside the coffin* and the lid was cracked but not "caved-in,"[29] as it is in the photograph. The lid also rests oddly atop the cornice piece, as if it had been placed there.

Paul's photographs were, until recently, the only record of the tomb as it purportedly looked upon discovery. But in 1998, during a search through Smith's historical records, I came across one more photograph of the burial chamber, apparently taken before Paul arrived.[30] The photograph answers a number of questions about activity in the tomb shortly after it was discovered. It is a magic lantern slide and lacks the professionalism of Paul's shots; it may even have been taken by Smith himself, since he used magic lantern slides in his public presentations. Other than Smith, the only other person with a camera on the scene at the time was an unknown English visitor who managed to snap Weigall, Ayrton, and Davis posed in front of KV 9.[31]

After all the objects were taken out of the tomb and sent to the museum in Cairo,[32] the tomb was closed until 1923, when Harry Burton took it over for photographing and developing his glass-plate negatives of objects from the tomb of Tutankhamun.

According to Marsha Hill, Burton's biographer,[33] Harry Burton enjoyed a privileged upbringing, highly influenced by the arts. In 1903 he was in Florence and already regarded as "a wonderfully able photographer of art." It was there he met Theodore Davis and joined him in Egypt in 1910 at the age of 29. Davis employed him as an excavator as much as a photographer. He was kept fully occupied clearing around the tomb of Amenhotep III in the Western Valley, the burial chamber of Siptah, and the tomb of Ramesses II until Davis retired. Albert Lythgoe of the Metropolitan Museum of Art was quick to see the possibilities of including Burton in the Metropolitan's Egyptian Expedition and offered him a job at Deir el-Bahri on the west bank, opposite Luxor. Burton took up his new post in 1914, with the specific goal of photographing tombs and temples.

Burton achieved even lighting through a system of mirrors and sometimes used electric light, but he refused to use magnesium flash because of the smoke. He was busy recording the tomb of Sety I when the tomb of Tutankhamun was discovered in 1922 and was seconded to Carter when the latter asked the Metropolitan Museum of Art for help.[34] Carter did not have to be convinced of the value of archaeological photography: "The first and most pressing need was in photography," he said, "... for nothing could be touched until a complete photographic record had been made, a task involving technical skill of the highest order." Burton was clearly up to the task. His photographs, now housed in the Metropolitan Museum of Art and the Griffith Institute, Oxford, stand out as exemplary models of archaeological photography even now, when much more sophisticated materials and equipment are available. His images are sharp and well lit, an extraordinary accomplishment considering the extremely cramped and dusty working conditions he faced. Carter and Burton's relationship was not always amicable, but Burton reluctantly admitted he could learn from Carter: William C. Hayes recalled Burton storming into Metropolitan House, complaining, "That man Carter is quite impossible!" and then reflecting, "but I must admit he showed me how to take a photograph I thought impossible."[35] In the end the two must have resolved their differences, because Burton was one of Carter's executors.

Burton in KV 55: Recent Discoveries

But Burton was not the last person to work in KV 55: on a visit to the tomb in

1989 I observed it still contained some ancient material I thought worth recording and collecting. It appeared that Davis had cleared the tomb, but not thoroughly. I subsequently applied for, and was grateful to receive, permission from the Supreme Council of Antiquities to do a final clearance and study of the tomb.

KV 55 consists of a long corridor ending in a single room with a high ceiling (Figure 1). The square cutting in the wall on the south side of the burial chamber was used as a canopic niche. Mason's marks on the walls suggest the room was planned to be the first pillared hall of a much larger sepulcher.

At first I was puzzled by the patches of black paper glued to the inner and outer sides of the northwest doorjambs at the entrance to this room, but once I realized it was the remains of blackout paper Burton had no doubt tacked over the entrance to the burial chamber to keep out light, further evidence of his presence slowly began to appear.

Since other ancient material was still in the tomb—broken pottery, plaster and mud seals, a fragment of a tomb plan, some blue beads, a bit of door sealing—it seems Burton avoided stirring up dust by simply pushing the debris aside and working in the remaining space. Like Petrie, Burton seems to have discovered that an empty tomb is an ideal place for photographic work. Scattered across the east and south sides of the floor and in the canopic niche were wood shavings—packing material probably for his photographic plates, broken bulbs, and a sheet of literature from Kodak. This was an instruction sheet for "Bromura" photographic print paper.[36] Then shards of his actual photographic plates—probably broken accidentally or rejects—began to turn up in the niche and along the west side of the burial chamber as I began systematically clearing. When reassembled, some shards composed three images:[37] a relief from KV 17 (Figure 2; the tomb of Sety I; Burton also photographed in the conservation laboratory for the objects from the tomb of Tutankhamun, KV 15 [Sety II]), a bow case (Figure 3),[38] and an ivory bracelet belonging to Tutankhamun (Figure 4).[39] Burton used diffused daylight and usually a white background for his exposures, and my plates show how he often used a special semicircular background made of heavy white paper when shooting objects.[40] I showed this material to George B. Johnson and Gerry Allaby, both expedition photographers working in Egypt, and asked for their opinions.

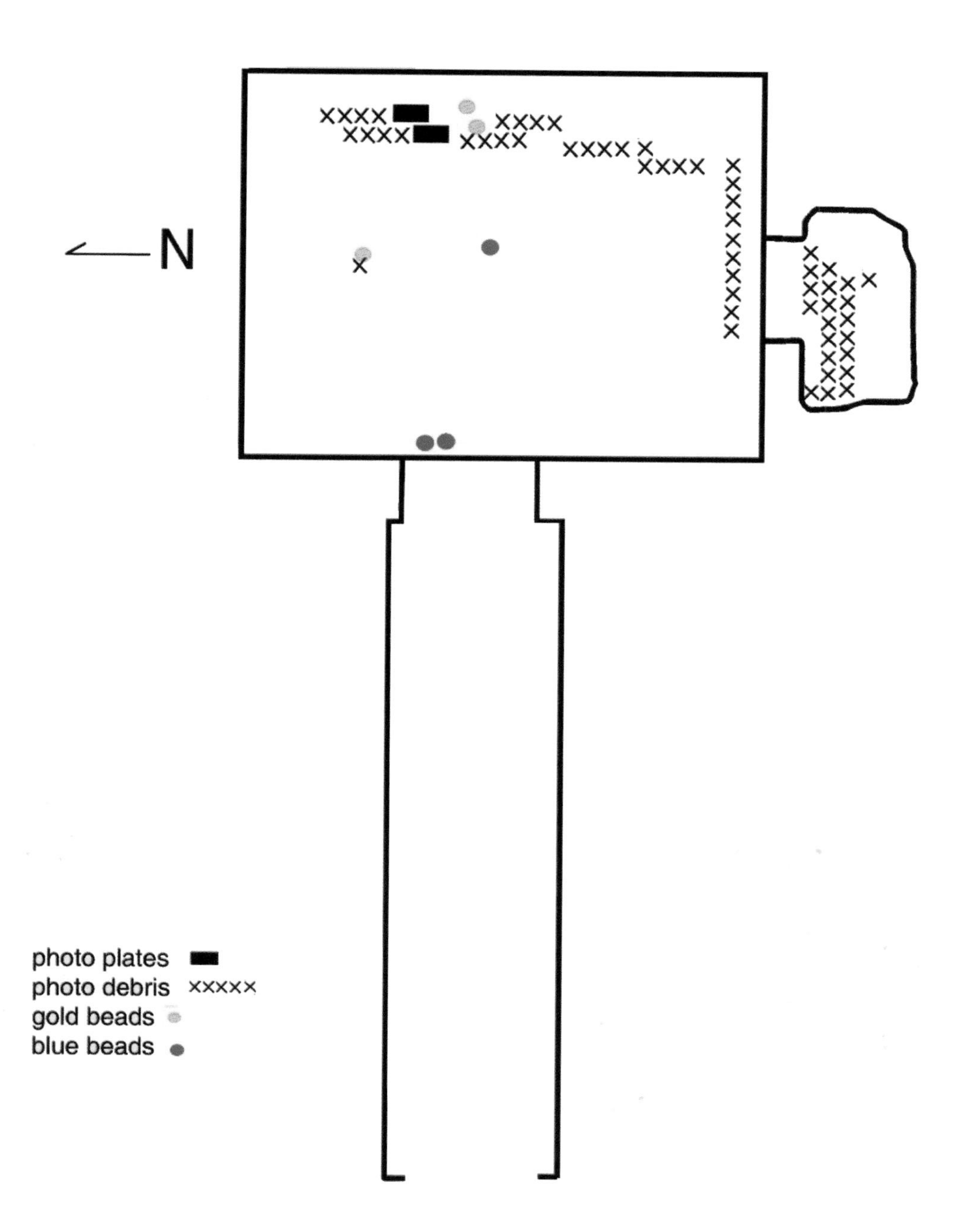

Figure 1: Floor plan of KV 55 showing location of photographic debris and objects found during re-clearance by L.P. Brock (Author)

Figures 2a and 2b: Burton plate from KV 55 (left) showing kneeling goddess from KV 17, the tomb of Sety I (right) (photographs by E. C. Brock)

Figure 3a and 3b: Burton plate from KV 55 (left) showing a bow case from KV 62, the tomb of Tutankhamun, now in the Egyptian Museum, Cairo (right) (E. C. Brock)

Figure 4: Burton plate from KV 55 showing ivory bracelet from KV 62, the tomb of Tutankhamun (E. C. Brock)

Gerry Allaby offered the following comment about the photographic plates:

> The plate emulsion consists of silver-halide crystals suspended in gelatin. Silver bromide, silver chloride, silver iodide were the most common silver-halide crystals used, to which other ingredients were added depending on the type of film needed for a particular usage. The process allowed for manufacture of already sensitised plates in a variety of sizes, the plates boxed and readily available in photographic supply stores.

> Several of these stores were available in Cairo by the 1900s. The large plates used by Burton allowed for easy on-site contact prints from negatives, also developed on site, provided a "darkroom" could be made.

I also found small pieces of red glass, apparently used as a kind of protective filter during the developing process. According to Johnson, the photographic plate would be briefly held up to be viewed with the ruby light behind it to protect it; then brief inspections were made until the negative was developed to the proper density.

Both Allaby and Johnson, after looking at my material, concluded that Burton had been doing color photography. According to Johnson, material to shoot color photos in Luxor was ordered by Burton for presentation slides and publishing. Some of the color photos were published in the London News, but all the plates disappeared, perhaps, as Johnson posited, destroyed in the Blitz. The material from KV 55 is now the only remaining evidence. Johnson added:

> A letter dated 1925, states Agfa color plates were sent to Egypt *"In accordance with instructions received from Mr. Harry Burton."*[41] Agfa color plates have a red, blue and green color screen made of dyed gum arabic. Under magnification these particles appear as polygonal shapes. The fragments found in KV55 are so damaged by exposure and damp that the screens are destroyed, leaving only dye stains that cannot be identified as Autochrome or Agfa.[42]

Photo debris was not the only thing Burton left behind in KV 55: I also retrieved three tiny gold beads that I prised up with a dental pick from cracks in the floor near the east wall (Figure 5). Since these beads do not appear to have any relationship to the jewelry found with the original burial (as far as we know from what remained), I immediately thought of Tutankhamun's jewelry photographed by Burton. The frontispiece of the 1972 edition of Carter's book on the tomb of Tutankhamun shows a photo taken by Burton of two pairs of earrings before they were conserved. When I checked them in the Egyptian Museum, it was obvious that the beads matched.

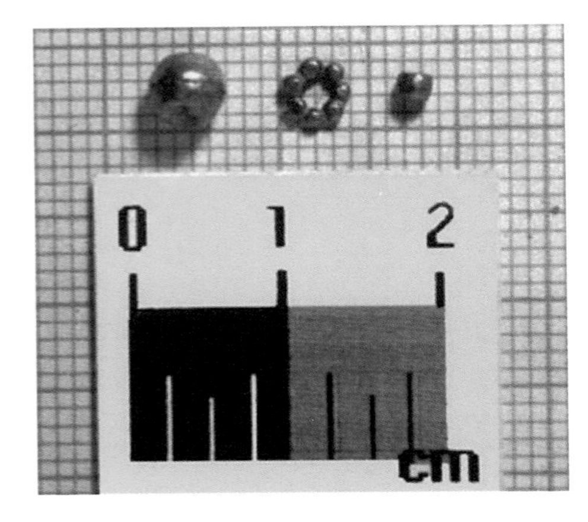

Figure 5: Gold beads found in KV 55 (left); probable source, earring of Tutank-hamun (right), now in the Egyptian Museum, Cairo (E.C. Brock).

NOTES

1 I would like to thank George Johnson, Gerry Allaby, Maarten Raven, and Yarko Kobyleky for providing comments and information relevant to this article.

2 February 19–March 4, 1996, financed by American Research Center in Egypt's Egyptian Antiquities Project under grant No. 263-0000-G-00-3089-00 from the United States Agency for International Development and carried out in collaboration with the Supreme Council of Antiquities, Egypt.

3 Joseph Nicephore Niepce House Museum, "Invention of Photography," http://www.photo-museum.org/pagus/pagus-inv.html.

4 Jack Green, Emily Teeter, and John A. Larson (eds.), *Picturing the Past* (Chicago: Oriental Institute Museum, 2012), 45.

5 Olaf Kaper, "Egypt in the 1880s: Photographs by Jan Herman Insinger: An Exhibition of Original Prints Made in Egypt between 1880 and 1888 on Loan from the Collection of the National Museum of Antiquities in Leiden, 26 September–10 October 1996," Cairo, Netherlands Institute.

6 Gerry Allaby, personal communication, September 25, 1993.

7 Gerry Allaby, personal communication, September 25, 1993.

8 Margaret. S. Drower, *Flinders Petrie, A Life in Archaeology* (London: Victor Gollancz Ltd., 1985), 48.

9 Morris.L. Bierbrier, *Who Was Who in Egyptology* (London: Egypt Exploration Society, 1995), 124.

10 Maarten J. Raven, "In het land der Nijlcataracten (1883)," *MVEOL* 34 (2004). Many of Insinger's photographs are now in the archives of the Leiden Museum.

11 John Romer, *Valley of the Kings* (New York: William Morrow and Company, 1981), 162.

[12] Peter Der Manuelian, "George Andrew Reisner on Archaeological Photography," *JARCE* 29 (1992): 34.

[13] Marsha Hill, "The Life and Work of Harry Burton," in Eric Hornung, *The Tomb of Pharaoh Seti I*, (Zurich and Munich: Artemis, 1991), 27–30. For Burton's photographic techniques, see George B. Johnson, "Painting With Light," *Kmt*, 8.2 (1997): 58–75.

[14] Herbert E. Winlock, *Materials Used at the Embalming of King Tut-Ankh-Amun* (New York: Metropolitan Museum of Art, 1941).

[15] Its probable location was only recently rediscovered: Lyla Pinch-Brock, "The Real Location of KVC?" *JEA* 85 (1999): 223–226.

[16] John A. Wilson, "Mrs. Andrews and the 'Tomb of Queen Tiye,'" in Edward F. Wente and Janet H. Johnson (eds.), *Papers in Honor of George R. Hughes* (Chicago: Oriental Institute, 1976), 273–279.

[17] "Theodore went over to the Valley this morning... and when he got back quite late told us that Ayrton had this time found a whole tomb" (Wilson, "Mrs. Andrews," 274).

[18] Entry of January 14, Wilson, "Mrs. Andrews," 276.

[19] Joseph Lindon Smith, *Tombs, Temples and Ancient Art* (Oklahoma: University of Oklahoma Press, 1956), 66.

[20] Arthur Weigall, "The Mummy of Akhenaten," *JEA* 8 (1922): 193–199. ("Unfortunately Mr. Ayrton destroyed these walls without photographing them.")

[21] Theodore M. Davis, *The Tomb of Siphtah and the Tomb of Queen Tiyi* (London: Constable, 1910), 8.

[22] There may have been both sets of seals on the same doorway, as on the entrance to the tomb of Tutankhamun (Howard Carter, *The Tomb of Tutankhamun* [London: Century, 1933], 88, 90, 92, 94).

[23] Lyla P. Brock, "Theodore Davis and the Mystery of Tomb 55," in Richard H. Wilkinson (ed.), *Valley of the Sun Kings* (Tucson: University of Arizona Egyptian Expedition, 1994): 34–46.

[24] Cyril Aldred, *Akhenaten, King of Egypt* (London: Thames and Hudson, 1988), 196.

[25] Wilson, "Mrs. Andrews," 276.

[26] Martha R. Bell, "An Armchair Excavation of KV55," *JARCE* 27 (1990): 97–137. Here spelled "collotypes."

[27] Davis, *Tomb of Siphtah*, plate XXIV.

[28] Davis, *Tomb of Siphtah*, plate XXVII.

[29] Smith, *Tombs, Temples*, 61: "Maspero peered inside the coffin itself, using his flashlight, and said he could not see much except that the skull was entirely free from the body and there seemed to be a 'flash of gold.' I noticed that everything in the tomb chamber was in the same position that it had occupied on my first visit, except that the lid of the coffin had been removed." Smith, *Tombs, Temples*, 63: "The condition of the mosaic lid was such that the Museum expert had skillfully cradled it in a padded tray before moving it to the floor

where we saw it, split into two pieces because the lid had collapsed inwards on being touched."

30 L. Pinch-Brock, "An Unpublished Photograph of the KV55 Burial Chamber," *GM* 175 (2000): 65–69.

31 Dennis C. Forbes (ed.), *The Tomb of Queen Tiyi* (San Francisco: Kmt Communications, 1990): frontispiece.

32 Except for the shrine parts; these were left in the tomb for a year and as a result may have completely shed their decoration (Weigall, "Mummy," 137). A small part of the "back" of the shrine is on display in the Egyptian Museum in Cairo.

33 Hill, "Life and Work," 27.

34 Carter, *Tomb of Tutankhamun*, 63.

35 T. G. H. James, *Howard Carter, the Path to Tutankhamun* (London and New York: Kegan Paul International, 1992), 240.

36 Kodak Bromure silver-bromide developing out paper, a paper in common usage at the time (per George B. Johnson).

37 Thanks to Ted Brock for photographing these glass plates.

38 According to Johnson, the broken black and white negative plate of Tutankhamen's bow case may be closely dated to 1928: photographs made from similar plates were published in the *Illustrated London News* (October 20, 1928). This suggests Burton was working in KV 55 until at least 1927.

39 The Egyptian Museum *Journal d'Entre* number is JE 62406. The bracelet comes from compartmented box no. 585 (JE 61456), found in the Annex. The inscription giving the names and titulary of Tutankhamun in a band on the side opposite the scene of animals in relief appears on the glass negative fragments.

40 George B. Johnson.

41 Metropolitan Museum of Art Burton archives 12/10/1925.

42 George B. Johnson.

Karabasken and Karakhamun as Precursors of Nespakashuty?

Elena Pischikova
South Asasif Conservation Project

Appointed vizier of Upper Egypt by Psamtik I, Nespakashuty built his tomb in South Asasif, away from that of Psamtik's southern rival, Mentuemhat. The decoration in Nespakashuty's tomb is discussed with that of the neighboring Kushite tombs of Karabsaken and Karakhamun, the apparent sources of inspiration for Nespakashuty's choices of iconography.

I dedicate this article to Richard H. Wilkinson in gratitude for his support of the South Asasif Conservation Project, Luxor (Figure 1).[1] The project is dedicated to the clearing, conservation, and reconstruction of the three Twenty-Fifth–Twenty-Sixth Dynasty tombs of the South Asasif necropolis, Karabasken (TT 391), Karakhamun (TT 223), and Irtieru (TT 390). Today the tombs of South Asasif are known as some of the most beautifully decorated Kushite tombs, and our international team includes hundreds of people working for the project in Egypt and beyond. It was different in 2006 when the project was founded and we started with very few people in badly damaged tombs without a clear understanding of how much of the original material we would be able to find in situ. Richard visited the site in 2007, believed in its potential, and supported it by sending, every year since, a group of his students to volunteer for the project. Over the years, the students of the University of Arizona have been a great asset to the site and made notable contributions to the project.[2]

The title question of the article may sound out of place, but the possible connections among if not these three officials then their funerary monuments seemed quite unusual and worth exploring.

The Nespakashuty in question, Nespakashuty D, the owner of a Theban tomb (TT 312), was the fourth vizier of Upper Egypt known under this name.[3] Nespakashuty D belonged to a prominent Thinite family. The name of his father, Nespamedu, is mentioned on the Rassam cylinder of Ashurbanipal as a ruler of Thinis,[4] the administrative center of the eighth Thinite nome. The necropolis of the Thinite nomarchs was located across the river, in Abydos,[5] and the tomb of Nespamedu (D 57) is the largest and most elaborate in cemetery D. This large family tomb serves as evidence that the family was attached to its native city and had not yet moved to Thebes, though family members could have visited that city on a regular basis to carry out official duties and establish themselves as viziers of Upper Egypt and priests of Theban temples. A considerable number of their statues were found in the Karnak Cachette.[6]

Figure 1: View of the South Asasif necropolis (photograph by K. Blakeney)

Nespakashuty D was probably the first member of the family to move to Thebes. Around the time of his appointment as vizier, his mother, Irtieru, was appointed chief attendant to the divine consort, Nitocris.[7] With two family members holding high Theban offices, a move to Thebes seemed justified. Both of them abandoned their family tradition and built their tombs in Theban necropolises.[8]

There are no extant documents that would reveal the relationship between the families of Mentuemhat and Nespakashuty upon the arrival of the vizier in Thebes, though obviously Mentuemhat, having created the position of "king" of Upper

Egypt for himself, would never have submitted to and would never have shared power with anyone else in Upper Egypt.[9] Probably for that reason Nespamedu had not moved to Thebes. The attempt of Psamtik I to diminish Mentuemhat's power by appointing Nespakashuty vizier of Upper Egypt and his mother chief attendant to his daughter Nitocris could hardly have been successful, though there are no documents to substantiate this. The only consideration is the locations of the tombs of Nespakashuty (TT 312) and his mother (TT 390).[10]

On their arrival in Thebes, two new necropolises were under construction, one in North Asasif, in front of the temple of Hatshepsut, the other 300 m southwest in South Asasif. By the beginning of the reign of Psamtik I, the latter contained tombs of three powerful Kushite officials: Karabasken (TT 391), mayor of Thebes and fourth priest of Amun, from the time of Shabaqo; First *ꜥḳ* priest Karakhamun (TT 223); and Ramose (TT 132), overseer of the treasuries of Taharqo. After these tombs were built in South Asasif, earlier in the Twenty-Fifth Dynasty, Great Steward of the Divine Consort Harwa moved to North Asasif by building his large tomb (TT 37) at the western end of the valley, probably at the time of Taharqo. Harwa could have found South Asasif too confined a place for his ambitious project and, considering prestige and sacredness of the landscape as well, chose the place in front of the temples of Deir el-Bahri. Chief Lector Priest Petamenophis followed Harwa's example, building his huge tomb (TT 33) just northeast of the tomb of Harwa. Great Steward of the Divine Consort Akhamenru, of the time of Tanutamani, built his tomb (TT 404) within the tomb of Harwa, with the entrance on the north side of Harwa's open court.[11]

It was the North Asasif necropolis that Mentuemhat chose for his own ambitious project, which was still under construction when Nespakashuty arrived in Thebes. A number of important, glamorous tombs, including Mentuemhat's, made North Asasif the most prestigious Theban necropolis of the time. Yet, Nespakashuty and his mother obviously decided against building their tombs in Mentuemhat's vicinity. Though he had higher official status, Nespakashuty enjoyed neither more power nor access to vaster resources.[12] Despite the process of consolidation of Saite power and the reunification of Egypt, the newcomers to Thebes had to satisfy themselves with compromises that would keep them at a distance from Mentuemhat and at the same time not damage their dignity.

There was no building activity in South Asasif when Irtieru started construction of her tomb, probably shortly after 656 BCE.[13] About this time, Nespakashuty attempted to reuse the tomb of Karakhamun, the largest in the necropolis and the closest to the tomb of his mother.[14] In most places on the walls and pillars of the first pillared hall, Karakhamun's name and some of his titles were cut out and replaced with plain patches of limestone.[15] Most new name plaques were left uninscribed, which shows that the reuse of the tomb was never completed. The inscribed plaques bear the name of Nespakashuty written in red paint. Not a single carved plaque has been found so far. The limestone bedrock in the tomb of Karakhamun lacks stability. It could have shown signs of weakening while being recarved, and this might have been one of the reasons for abandoning the project. Nespakashuty evidently changed his plans and moved to Deir el-Bahri to create his new tomb on the north cliff. The unfinished state of his tomb at Deir el-Bahri suggests that Nespakashuty died prematurely.

The tomb of Nespakashuty (TT 312, MMA 509a) was carved into the north face of the cliff of Deir el-Bahri (Figure 2).[16] Overlooking the Theban temples of Mentuhotep II (Eleventh Dynasty), Thutmose III (Eighteenth Dynasty), and Hatshepsut (Eighteenth Dynasty), as well as the Asasif valley, it occupies a space within a row of tombs of the highest officials of the Middle Kingdom, between the tomb of the Chief Royal Steward Henenu (TT 313, MMA 510), who held his high position from at least the third decade of Mentuhotep II's reign, and that of First Royal Treasurer Khety (TT 311, MMA 508), who was in office during the latter part of that king's reign. Flanked by the tombs of Henenu to the east and Khety to the west, the tomb of Nespakashuty shares its court with another early Middle Kingdom tomb (MMA 509).

The name of the owner of MMA 509 is unknown, as the tomb is severely damaged and no decoration or inscriptions have survived. J. Allen suggested that this tomb could have belonged to Vizier Bebi, whose name is attested at the end of Mentuhotep II's reign. While his name appears on two occasions that confirm that he held the highest offices, his burial place remains unknown. Given the considerable number of royal stewards, treasurers, and viziers of the Eleventh Dynasty buried on this cliff, it is entirely possible that Bebi's tomb would have been located here. What is certain is that MMA 509, the largest tomb on the cliff, was built for an official of the highest rank.

Possibly Nespakashuty chose this new location for political and religious rather than practical considerations. As he felt uncomfortable about building his tomb in the fashionable necropolis of the time, located in North Asasif, he had to find a "superior" place, and the northern cliff of Deir el-Bahri could definitely have been seen as one of honor and prestige. Located on the high cliff that overlooked major

Figure 2: View of the tomb of Nespakashuty at Deir el Bahri (K. Blakeney)

Figure 3: Entrance gate. Reconstruction. Tomb of Nespakashuty (K. Blakeney)

Figure 4: Seated Nespakashuty. Entrance gate. Outer face (K. Blakeney)

sacred temples and the Asasif valley itself and among viziers of the past, his tomb dominated the sites of new power and wealth.

The sandstone entrance gate to the tomb reconstructed in 2005 features six images of Nespakashuty carved in sunk relief: a seated and a standing figure on either side of the front part and a figure seated at an offering table on each side of the back (Figure 3). Five of the figures are headless (Figure 4). All the images portray Nespakashuty wearing a short kilt, a pelt vest, and a double amulet. The seated figure on the inner east side of the façade has a well-preserved head with delicately carved facial features and a plain shoulder-length wig with a slightly rounded bottom part (Figure 5). The shape of the wig, with a low forehead line, a flat top, a diagonal slope at the back, and a bottom part that is round at the shoulders, is a two-dimensional version of the wigs on two Cairo statues of Nespakashuty. The same kind of wig can be suggested for the other entrance representations of the tomb owner.

Nespakashuty's facial features—elongated, narrow eyes; a long, pointed nose with a depression in the middle; straight, protruding lips; soft flesh under the chin;

Figure 5: Nespakashuty at the offering table. Entrance Gate. Inner face (K. Blakeney)

well-modeled ears; and a long neck—show a clear resemblance to the face of an asymmetrically seated statue of the vizier in the Egyptian Museum, Cairo (JdE 37000). The facial features of both the statue and the reliefs recall the influence of Kushite art. The nasolabial fold on the face and the heavy modeling of the leg muscles are clear evidence of the continuation of the style of the previous dynasty. The question remains: which Kushite source could be the closest reference for this later adaptation?

The stylistic and iconographic history of the Theban necropolis in the Kushite Period is usually traced to the tombs of Harwa, Petamenophis, and Mentuemhat, the largest and most influential tombs of the North Asasif necropolis. Yet Nespakashuty's personal inclinations and taste most probably derived from another group of tombs of the earlier period, located in South Asasif. Nespakashuty's interest in the tomb of Karakhamun influenced his decision to reuse it. At the same time the tomb of Karabasken to the west of Karakahmun and in the nearest proximity could not be unknown to Nespakashuty as well.

As was mentioned before, the Kushite tombs of the South Asasif necropolis were rediscovered by the South Asasif Conservation Project in 2006 in a very damaged condition. Ruined by later occupants and floods, they practically disappeared under the houses of the local village. Seven years of fieldwork revealed vast remains of the architectural and decoration features still in situ and in thousands of collapsed fragments. The vast amount of found material makes them reconstructible. This work has already started and will be continued in future seasons. What we know about the tombs' decoration already today places them among the most beautiful and influential Kushite tombs of the Theban necropolis.

For instance, the entrance to the pillared hall of the tomb of Karabasken, the earliest Kushite tomb built on the Theban west bank, demonstrates in all its simplicity and elegance the arrangement of the structure later employed by Nespakashuty for his main entrance[17] (Figure 6). A limestone ramp leads to a doorway designed with an arched doorframe. The lowest parts of the jambs of the doorframe show two seated figures of the tomb owner that demonstrate the "new" Late Period iconography, which was based on a combination of ancient sources. Karabasken's iconographical choice became extremely popular in later tombs, including that of Mentuemhat, but Nespakashuty's iconography was most probably influenced directly by Karabasken, a tomb more familiar to him than Mentuemhat's for the above-mentioned personal reasons. Karabasken is shown seated on a lion-legged chair with a short back and a papyrus umbel behind (Figure

Figure 6: Entrance to pillared hall. Tomb of Karabasken (K. Blakeney)

Figure 7: Karabasken. Entrance to pillared hall. Tomb of Karabasken (K. Blakeney)

7). He wears a short pleated skirt and a priestly pelt vest supported by a sash tied at the shoulder with a large elaborate knot with long ends. Another addition to his outfit is a broad collar and a double amulet on a string. His head is topped with a shoulder-length, striated wig. The paw placed on the shoulder of the tomb owner is the first example of the new iconographic version of an ancient motif.[18]

The images, which were carved in raised relief in the bedrock and spent many years underground, are not sufficiently preserved to allow analysis of the carving style. The original surface has also been damaged by water that left its mark farther above the figure of Karabasken. If the doorframe was painted, no colors have survived. The original layer of whitewash has eroded and formed brownish clusters on the relief surface; removing them would endanger the top layer. Modeling is lost in many areas due to the extensive emergence of salt on the stone's surface. The face is almost completely deteriorated. In some areas, such as the wig, skirt, or papyrus umbel, where the original layer is relatively well preserved, the delicacy of minute details is visible.

Despite the lack of the top surface layer, the well-preserved outlines of the figure of Karabasken and his attire lead to the notable conclusion that the first decorated Kushite tomb of the Theban necropolis established one of the most popular iconographic images of a seated tomb owner, which influenced the entire Kushite and Saite periods.

The arrangement of Karabasken's entrance doorway, with its reinterpretation of traditional elements, could have been a direct source of inspiration for Nespakashuty. The top part of the doorframe is now extensively damaged, but the remaining elements suggest three layers of superimposed doorframes. The largest outer frame was plain, while three-stem papyrus columns topped with a low lunette form the second frame. The third frame is defined by a torus molding and is topped with a now almost destroyed cavetto cornice designed with the name and titles of Karabasken and his seated figures. Leading to the entrance was a limestone ramp with a traditional graphic design outlining a double staircase. The arrangement of the entrance serves as an introduction of the tomb owner and at the same time replicates the features of a temple façade. Nespakashuty employed the same idea of superimposed doorways but chose simpler forms and a plainer surface over the more complicated profile of Karabasken's doorway, which was popular in the Twenty-Fifth Dynasty and still used in the tomb of Irtieru at the beginning of the Twenty-Sixth Dynasty.

The tomb of Karakhamun was built slightly later than that of Karabasken. Much larger in size and beautifully decorated, it offers a few different iconographic and stylistic versions of the image of a tomb owner. On the east wall of the first pillared hall he is shown with close-cropped hair, wearing a pleated skirt and a broad collar (Figure 8). The overall configuration of the chair resembles that of Karabasken, with the exception of the bovine legs of the chair, which rest on a double pedestal. His facial features—such as soft, full lips, short upturned nose, and long neck—resemble those of Shabitqo.[19]

The face of the seated figure from the entrance to the second pillared hall is much milder and closer to the face of Nespakashuty (Figure 9). Although carved on a limestone block as opposed to Nespakashuty's sandstone, it displays shallow

Figure 8: Karakhamun at the offering table. First Pillared Hall. East wall. Tomb of Karakhamun (K. Blakeney)

carving and less defined features that were partly modeled in now damaged plaster. The quality of limestone in this area, which did not allow crisp lines and precision of carved details, gives the image a sandstone look. The pointed nose with a pronounced depression in the middle, thin protruding lips, and shorter neck are closer to the iconography of the face of Shabaqo.[20]

Figure 9: Fragments of the seated figure of Karakahmun from the second pillared hall. Tomb of Karakahamun (K. Blakeney)

Considering that the overall iconography of the figure of Nespakashuty is much closer to the image of Karabasken than Karakhamun, we could have expected some similarities in the style of the facial features. Unfortunately it is impossible to judge because the faces of the two carved images of Karabasken are badly damaged and the faces of his shabtis are not well defined and display rather generalized Kushite features (Figure 10). Is it possible to suggest that the face of Karakhamun on the second pillared hall entrance was influenced by the image of Karabasken and therefore its similarity to the face of Nespakashuty is evidence of Nespakashuty's image being a direct reference to Karabasken?

Figure 10: Shabti of Karabasken. Tomb of Karabasken. SCA storage, Luxor (K. Blakeney)

At the same time, Nespakashuty imitated another iconographic feature that was not recorded in Karabasken and was probably initiated by Karakhamun. The *ḥ3tt nt ṯḥnw* and *ḥknw* oil jars placed under the chair of the tomb owner became one of the key elements of Late Period private tomb decoration. Before the latest discoveries in the tomb of Karakhamun, the earliest occurrences of this iconography were in the tombs of Mentuemhat and Petamenophis.

Two similar compositions are known from the tomb of Neskapashuty. One, on the north section of the east wall, is relatively well preserved and shows a jar covered with a lotus flower forming a conical lid. It looks as though Nespakashuty had combined the iconography of the figure of Karabasken with an oil jar of Karakhamun.

The circumstantial connection of the tomb of Nespakashuty with the tombs of Karabasken and Karakhamun is just a suggestion. The reality could have differed from the offered reconstruction of events. However, this exercise proves that the Kushite tombs of South Asasif started many iconographic and stylistic trends that survived and developed through the Kushite period to reflect on the Twenty-Sixth Dynasty tombs of the necropolis, starting with Nespakashuty.

NOTES

1 The South Asasif Conservation Project is an American-Egyptian archaeological mission directed by the author. The project currently finished its seventh season and held an international scholarly conference, "Thebes in the First Millennium BC." The members of the project want to express their gratitude to the Ministry of State for Antiquities for its support of the project and the conference.

2 The work done by the South Asasif Conservation Project from 2006 to 2011 will be published this year in the forthcoming volume of collected articles of the team members: Elena Pischikova (ed.), *Tombs of the South Asasif Necropolis: Karakhamun (TT 223), and Karabasken (TT 391) in the Twenty-Fifth Dynasty* (Cairo: American University in Cairo Press, 2013). For the preliminary results, see Elena Pischikova, "Early Kushite Tombs of South Asasif," *BMSAES* 12 (2009): 11–30.

3 Besides his Theban tomb (TT 312), Nespakashuty D is known from two statues in the Cairo Museum (JE 37000 and 36662). See Jack. A. Josephson and Mamduh M. Eldamaty, *Catalogue Général of Egyptian Antiquities in the Cairo Museum: Statues of the XXVth and XXVIth Dynasties* (Cairo: Supreme Council of Antiquities Press, 1999), CG 48634, 79–82. They appear in color in Edna. R. Russmann, *Egyptian Sculpture: Cairo and Luxor* (Austin: University of Texas Press, 1989), 178–179, no. 82, 180–181, no. 83. For the statue in the British Museum (BM 1132/1225), see Edna. R. Russmann, *Eternal Egypt: Masterworks of*

Ancient Art from the British Museum (Berkeley: University of California Press, 2001), 234–237, no. 129. He is also known from his signature on the Brooklyn Oracle Papyrus (no. 47.218.3): R. A. Parker, *A Saite Oracle Papyrus from Thebes in the Brooklyn Museum* (Providence: Brown University Press, 1962), 15.

4 A. Leahy, "Nespamedu, 'King' of Thinis," *GM* 35 (1979): 31–37.

5 For the Kushite burials in Abydos and Cemetery D, see W. M. F. Petrie, *Gizeh and Rifeh* (London: School of Archaeology in Egypt, 1907), 80, pls. 23, 30; A. Leahy, "Kushite Monuments at Abydos," in Christopher Eyre, Anthony Leahy, and Lisa Montagno Leahy (eds.), *The Unbroken Reed: Studies in the Culture and Heritage of Ancient Egypt in Honour of A. F. Shore*, Egypt Exploration Society Occasional Publications 11 (London: Egypt Exploration Society, 1994), 171–192; Anthony Leahy, "Tomb D7 at Abydos: An Onomastic Miscellany," in Christiane Zivie-Coche and Ivan Guermeur (eds.), *Parcourir l'éternité: hommages á Jean Yoyotte* 2 (Turnhout: Brepols, 2012), 741–756.

6 Leahy, "Nespamedu," 33; Günter Vittmann, *Priester und Beamte im Theben der Spätzeit* (Vienna: Institute für Afrikanistik und Ägyptologie, 1978), 154–155.

7 *LD* III, 289, no. 94.

8 In view of the fact that Irtieru became an important member of the court of Nitocris, it does not "defy explanation" (Leahy, "Nespamedu," 39, n. 22) that she was buried in Thebes (TT 390).

9 Mentuemhat claimed to rule the whole of Upper Egypt from Elephantine to Hermopolis; see Jean Leclant, *Montouemhat: quatrième prophète d'Amon, Prince de la ville*, Bibliothèque d'étude 35 (Le Caire: Institut français d'archéologie orientale, 1961), 58–64, doc. 9.

10 Morris L. Bierbrier, "More Light on the Family of Montemhat," in John Ruffle, Gaballa. A. Gaballa, and Kenneth A. Kitchen (eds.), *Orbis Aegyptiorum Speculum: Glimpses of Ancient Egypt: Studies in Honour of H. W. Fairman* (Warminster: Aris & Phillips Ltd., 1979), 116–118.

11 For the development of the Theban necropolis in the Late Period, see Diethelm Eigner, *Die monumentalen Grabbauten der Spätzeit in der thebanischen Nekropole* (Vienna: Verlag der Österreichischen Akademie der Wissenschaften, 1984); David A. Aston, *Burial Assemblages of Dynasty 21–25: Chronology—Typology—Developments*, Contributions to the Chronology of the Eastern Mediterranean 21, Osterreichische Akademie Der Wissenshaften, Denkschriften Der Gesamtakademie 54 (Vienna: Verlag der Österreichischen Akademie der Wissenschaften, 2009).

12 Mentuemhat did not die until year 17 of Psamtik's reign (648 BCE); see Kenneth A. Kitchen, *The Third Intermediate Period in Egypt (1100–650 B.C.)*, second edition with supplement (Warminster: Aris & Phillips Ltd, 1986), 405.

13 Nitocris was installed in office in 656 BCE under the cognomen Shepenwepet III; see Kitchen, *Third Intermediate Period*, 403.

14 There is no information about Karakhamun outside of his tomb. Karakhamun and his family are not mentioned in Kitchen or Vittmann, the most

comprehensive studies of the Third Intermediate Period and Late Period chronology; Kitchen, *Third Intermediate Period;* Günter Vittmann, *Priester und Beamte im Theben der Spätzeit. Genealogische und prosopographische Untersuchungen zum thebanischen Priester- und Beamtentum der 25 und 26. Dynastie,* Veröffentlichungen der Institute für Afrikanistik und Ägyptologie der Universität Wien 3, Beiträge zur Ägyptologie 1 (Vienna: Afro-Pub, 1978). For the chronology of the related period, see Dan'el Kahn, "The Transition from Libyan to Nubian Rule in Egypt: Revisiting the Reign of Tefnakht," in Gerard P. F. Broekman, R. J. Demaree, and O. E. Kaper (eds.), *The Libyan Period in Egypt: Historical and Cultural Studies into the 21st–24th Dynasties: Proceedings of a Conference at Leiden University 25–27 October 2007,* 139–148 (Leiden: Peeters Leuven, 2009), or K. A. Kitchen, "The Third Intermediate Period in Egypt: An Overview of Fact and Fiction," in Gerard P. F. Broekman, Robert J. Demarée, and Olaf E. Kaper (eds.), *The Libyan Period in Egypt. Historical and Cultural Studies into the 21st–24th Dynasties: Proceedings of a Conference at Leiden University 25–27 October 2007,* 161–202 (Leuven: Peeters, 2009). The ongoing discussion on the subject of the chronological framework of the Third Intermediate Period is well outlined in Gerard P. F. Broekman, "The Egyptian Chronology from the Start of the Twenty-second until the End of the Twenty-fifth Dynasty: Facts, Suppositions and Arguments," *JEH* 4 (2011): 40–80.

15 Elena Pischikova, "The Second Tomb of the Vizier Nespakashuty," in *Studies in Honour of Dorothea Arnold* (forthcoming).

16 The tomb was discovered and explored in 1922–1923 by Herbert Winlock of the Metropolitan Museum of Art. It was re-excavated and partially reconstructed in situ in 2001–2005 by the Metropolitan Museum/ARCE expedition directed by the author. The expedition found a large collection of carved limestone fragments of the tomb's decoration and reconstructed the sandstone entrance gate: Elena Pischikova, "Metropolitan Museum/ARCE (AEF Grant) Conservation Project," *BARCE* 187 (2005): 12–16; Elena Pischikova, "Conservation and Reconstruction of the Tomb of Nespakashuty (TT 312) at Deir El Bahri II," *BARCE* 189 (2006): 13–18.

17 Karl Jansen-Winkeln, *Inschriften Der Spatzeit, Teil III: Die 25. Dynastie* (Wiesbaden: Harrassowitz Verlag, 2009), 499; Kitchen, *Third Intermediate Period,* 382, table 14; Herman Kees, *Die Hohenpriester des Amun Von Karnak von Herihor bis zum Ende der Äthiopenzeit,* Probleme der Ägyptologie 4 (Leiden: E. J. Brill, 1964), 276, 283, n. 3.

18 Yvonne Harpur, *Decoration in Egyptian Tombs of the Old Kingdom* (London and New York: KPI, 1987), figs. 34–36.

19 For the face of Karakhamun, see Pischikova, "Early Kushite Tombs"; for the royal parallel, see Karol Mysliwiek, *Royal Portraiture of the Dynasties XXI–XXX* (Mainz am Rhein: Philipp von Zabern, 1988), pl. 34.

20 Mysliwiek, *Royal Portraiture,* pl. 32.

Remarks on Some Toponyms Associated with Tel-er-Rub'a in Light of Recent Excavations*

Donald B. Redford
Pennsylvania State University

Toponymns known from the Great Mendes Stela and related sources have remained unidentified. Excavations at Tel-er-Rub'a are uncovering structures within the Mendean cultic temenos that can now be associated with a number of these place names, including most recently the ỉ3t.

One of the unexpected and exhilarating aspects of the excavations at Tel-er-Rub'a/Mendes is the opportunity, nay, the necessity of "wedding" textual with archaeological evidence. As is well known, Ptolemy II in his Mendes stela has bequeathed to us a "gazetteer" derived from his tour of the city,[1] in which he conveys in detail the buildings inspected; but earlier (and later) worthies of Mendesian origin have contributed in like vein. The result comprises a list of toponyms waiting to be identified and raw evidence for urban planning in a Delta setting. Of these toponyms, some have been identified: the main temple of Ba-neb-djed, variously called *ḥwt-nṯr*,[2] *ỉwnn*,[3] *sḫm*,[4] or *pr-b3*;[5] the hypogeum of the sacred rams, *ḥwt-b3w*,[6] now identified with the large structure containing the ram sarcophagi ca. 200 m west of the main temple;[7] and possibly some of the watery tracts such as the *ʿgn* ("anchorage") or the *š wr*.

Archaeologically the history of the great northwest enclosure, the cultic temenos, is becoming clearer with every season.[8] It was the Nineteenth Dynasty[9] that provided the final façade of the great temple of Ba-neb-djed, adding two pylons and a court on the north side of a mud-brick façade previously contributed by Thutmose III. This structure stood, with minor modifications, until the sixth century BCE. It was Amasis the Saïte who brought the temple and its temenos to the stage known at present. He replaced an earlier (and unknown) installation on the south of the temple by the present naos court[10] and developed the dromos by adding auxiliary buildings. One of the latter, situated ca. 110 m north of the front pylon of the great temple on the west side of the dromos, is a structure that arguably was intended as a mausoleum of the mothers of the rams.[11] Certainly the seventeen scattered basalt coffins,[12] ostensibly for sheep interments, originated in Temple T. foundation deposits retrieved intact identify Amasis as builder.

One of the unidentified toponyms that invite an association with Temple T is conveyed in Late Period contexts by the writing , with or without the canal determinative.[13] In the Mendes stela it is called a *ỉ3t*, i.e., a sacred enclosure devoted to a specific cultic theme, and is the place where the young lamb, newly designated, stays, presumably with his mother, until he is formally inducted.[14] The reading is in doubt. One might render *dn nbḏw*, "decapitating the evil one,"[15] but more likely would be a reading *dn/ds šnỉ*, with reference to "shearing."[16]

It is conceivable that part, at least, of Temple T was given over as a holding place for the young ram designate. This would not preclude the use of part of the structure as a burial place.

Satellite imaging shows a rich profusion of cultic structures complementing the main temple. Undoubtedly many of the names in our "gazetteer" apply to these shrines, and they will be identified in due course. That Amasis should have been the author of this grand layout should come as no surprise, in light of his enormous building program in the Delta.

Notes

* [Although the present manuscript does not cover material within the geographic scope of this book (Valley of the Kings and ancient Thebes), it is included nonetheless as a tribute to Richard H. Wilkinson from a longtime friend and colleague.–Ed.]

1 W. Clarysse, "A Royal Journey in the Delta in 257 B.C. and the Date of the Mendes Stela," *CdÉ* 82 (2007): 201–206.

2 C. Soghar, "Inscriptions from Tell el Rub'a," *JARCE* 6 (1967): 25, 30 fig. 10; P. MacKay and H. de Meulenaere, *Mendes* II (Brooklyn: Brooklyn Museum, 1976), pl. 21 (d), pl. 25 (63).

3 G. Daressy, "Inscriptions historiques mendesiennes," *RT* 35 (1913), 125; *Urk.* II, 49:10.

4 Daressy, "Inscriptions," 125.

5 *Urk.* II, 32:2, 38:5.

6 *Urk.* II, 38:4, 46:9; MacKay and de Meulenaere, *Mendes* II, pl. 23 (58).

7 A. F. and D. B. Redford, "The Cult and Necropolis of the Sacred Ram at Mendes," in S. Ikram (ed.), *Divine Creatures: Animal Mummies in Ancient Egypt* (Cairo: American University in Cairo Press, 2005), 164–198.

8 See the present writer in *City of the Ram-man: The Story of Ancient Mendes* (Princeton: Princeton University Press, 2010), passim; also the various contributions in *Delta Reports* II (forthcoming).

9 D. B. Redford, "The Second Pylon of Ba-neb-djed at Mendes," in S. H. d'Auria (ed.), *Offerings to the Discerning Eye: An Egyptological Medley in Honor of Jack A.*

Josephson (Leiden: Brill, 2010), 271–277; D. B. Redford, "Merenptah at Mendes," in M. Collier and S. Snape (eds.), *Ramesside Studies in Honour of Kenneth Kitchen* (Bolton: Rutherford, 2011), 224–230.

10 D. P. Hausen, "The Excavations at Tell er-Rub'a," *JARCE* 6 (1967), 5–9.

11 For a full report see the present writer, "Temple T at Mendes," in *Delta Reports* II (forthcoming).

12 MacKay and de Meulenaere, *Mendes* II, pl. VI a.

13 H. Gauthier, *Dictionnaire des noms géographiques contenus dans les textes hiéroglyphiques* VI (Cairo: Société royale de géographie d'Égypte, 1929), 98.

14 *Urk.* II, 48:7. The great Edfu nome list (M. de Rochemontiex, *Le temple d'Edfou* I [Paris: Ernest Leroux, 1892]) mentions only the *i3t b3w* for Mendes, as the site of the sacred grove.

15 Cf. C. Leitz,, Dagmar Budde, et al. (eds.), *Lexikon der ägyptische Götter und Göttebez-eichnungen* (Louvain: Peeters, 2002), IV, 199 f.; VII, 548, with possibly Sethian overtones.

16 Cf. P. Montet, *Géographie de l'Egypte ancienne, lère partie, To-mehou, la Basse Egypte* II (Paris: Société royale de géographie d'Égypte, 1957), 148, "*la butte de coupe-toissons*." Other associations are interesting but less helpful in locating the building. It is associated both with Ba-neb-djed and Hat-mehyet, with (curiously) a connection with Heliopolis (Cairo naos 70022; MacKay and de Meulenaere, *Mendes* II, pl. 15 [36], both dating to Nektanebo I); possibly also G. Daressy, "Statues de Mendès," *ASAE* 17 (1917), 22, as well as "the god's-book of Ba-neb-djed" (MacKay and H. de Meulenaere, *Mendes* II, pl. 25 [63]).

An Interment of the Early Ptolemaic Period

Susan Redford
Pennsylvania State University

Countless artifacts have been recovered from the many shafts and burial chambers of the author's tomb concession in the Asasif. Almost all are the rifled remains of funerary assemblages of secondary burials in New Kingdom tombs. The presence of this material reflects the actions of the choachytes of Late Period times. This article focuses on two such items, a sealing giving us the name of the individual and a restored mummy covering that may well be from the same man's interment.

It is a pleasure for me to contribute this article to my colleague and mentor, Prof. Richard Wilkinson, on the occasion of his retirement. I was honored to have Richard as the outside reader of my dissertation and, along with the many others who carry out research in the Theban necropolis, I have benefited greatly from his advice and scholarship

By the third and second centuries BCE, textual sources show that the Theban necropolis was flourishing.[1] Nevertheless, few major tombs were being built, and, while there is the general impression of dilapidation of the monuments there,[2] the crypts of old tombs were being reused. During this time all interments were managed by the office of the *w3ḥ-mw*,[3] rendered in Greek as "choachyte" *(Χωαχυτης)*.[4] Numerous references to the choachytes in Late Period and Ptolemaic archives describe a species of mortuary priest operating in family groups and bound into a guild.[5] Choachytes in general performed the same tasks as the New Kingdom *ḥmw-k3*, "servants of the *ka*," whom they clearly replaced,[6] although there is some overlap.[7] The choachytes, who are already present in the Twenty-Fifth Dynasty when the archives begin,[8] arranged for the embalmment of the deceased (although not doing the same job, they nonetheless worked very closely with embalmers), saw to the burial, and carried on the mortuary service as long as they continued to be paid by the family. Payment was called the "Osiris-ration."[9] Tomb-owners might hand over their tombs to the custodianship of the choachytes, or the latter might take over abandoned tombs and put mummies there. One choachyte could serve as many as twenty-five tombs.[10] Mummies were so numerous that there was sometimes a backlog, and mummies had to be kept in holding areas either in Thebes or in one of the tombs on the west bank (e.g., TT 157 and TT 32[11]).[12] Burial places, each with multiple burials owned or assigned by individual choachytes, could be very numerous: fifteen, twenty-two, and even eighty-eight are attested.[13] Although they did not necessarily own tombs, the choachytes had considerable control over the disposition of tombs, buying, selling, exchanging, and leasing tombs and mortuary property as occasion demanded. The whole business was on a legal basis written up in a "document of cession" (*sšwy*).[14]

Figure 1: Sealing of Pa-di-hor-wer (Author)

Among the innumerable tombs that archaeologically demonstrate the utilization of earlier monuments by the choachytes is a tomb of Ramesside date in the region of the Asasif,[15] which became part of the author's concession as director of the ATP Theban Tomb Survey. The inscribed jamb of the outer doorway identifies the owner of the tomb as: "scribe of the treasury in the Ramesseum, Amenemopet."[16] Amenemopet either bought or was given rights to excavate his tomb, numbered TT 374, into the eastern side of the courtyard bay of TT 188, belonging to Akhenaten's butler, Parennefer. While the destroyed tomb chapel and ransacked burial chambers attest to systematic plundering right up until recent times, evidence of individual and family burials still remained.

The later reuse of one of three chambers in the crypt is established by the presence of at least three separate interments dating from the Late Period to the early Ptolemaic Period. Most notable is that of an individual whose name occurs on a sealing found within this roughly hewn room. The mud-clay sealing itself would have been used to secure the string or binding placed around a papyrus scroll[17] of personal documentation or (more likely) funerary literature. The presence of such a scroll or scrolls is attested by a small number of papyri fragments, unfortunately too minute to permit translation, and also by a second sealing. This latter *bulla* is a wad of dark mud adhering to two linen strips that appear to have been cleanly cut to free the scroll. Two identical, circular impressions have been made on the mud, each adjacent to the other, but unfortunately the symbols or signs of both are unrecognizable. The other, better preserved sealing no longer has the ties it once held together; however, the impression is clear and readable (Figure 1). Three lines of text within a square stamp reveal the owner and his titles:

ḥry-sštꜣ ḫtm·ty-nṯr wd
sš ḥm-nṯrn ḫꜣst Gsi
Pꜣ-di-ḥr-wr-m-nbt

> "Privy to the mysteries and god's sealer,[18] 'embalmer,'[19] scribe, prophet of the 'desert' (necropolis)[20] of Qus, Pa-di-hor-wer-m-nbt[21]"

The owner's distinctive name form of *Pa-di-hor-wer* is attested in the Ptolemaic Period,[22] although names with a "Pa-di-hor" morphology can occur from the Late Period on.[23] While the presence of this sealing in the Theban necropolis does not necessarily prove that our Pa-di-hor-wer had a tomb there,[24] there is, perhaps not so coincidently, mention of the mummy of "a man of Qus" in the archives of the choachytes dated to the early Ptolemaic Period.[25] One wonders if indeed we have the same man's burial here.[26]

Several items of similar date found in close proximity to the sealing point to a possible burial assemblage[27] for this man. These consist of an almost complete set of shabtis, a portion of a cartonnage mummy covering, and remains of a beaded net adorned with *wadjet* eyes and "Sons of Horus" amulets.[28] While all of the objects and fragments recovered from this burial chamber, as is the case within the other chambers, were collected from a context of dirt-laden debris, it can be assumed that all the interments were originally deposited in an orderly fashion and, for the most part, in an environment more or less clean of dirt and other fill.[29] There can be little doubt that the debris clogging the burial chamber is the result of flash flooding, the burrowing of animals, and the activity of robbers both ancient and modern. Nevertheless, items of funerary assemblages temporally and stylistically related can provide a useful basis for assignment to a particular interment. This may be particularly true of mummy cases.

Apart from the thousands of faience beads, the most numerous type of artifact retrieved were fragments of painted cartonnage mummy cases. The deliberate and wanton destruction of the cases and other burial items is indicative of the long-term effects of rampant tomb robbing in the valley that had gone on for over the last two centuries.

From the end of the Thirtieth Dynasty to early Roman times, typically two anthropoid coffins were combined with cartonnage plaques covering the mummy. These coverings generally consisted of a full head mask, a broad collar, a separate piece for the ribcage and abdomen, a long apron, and a foot case.[30] Hundreds of painted cartonnage fragments were collected from the shafts and crypts of TT 188 and TT 374, most of which were on average only a few centimeters long. Nevertheless, restoration was attempted and excellent results achieved.[31] Ten individual collages were assembled, three of which are separate components of a single cover. Several smaller groupings were also assembled possibly each representative of entirely different interments.

What may be Padi-hor-wer's mummy covering is represented by a single plaque (Figure 2). The restored plaque, approximately 85% complete, is a broad collar or *wesekh* 22 cm high (excluding the terminals) and 42 cm wide, and is of almost pristine coloration, being painted in colors of vibrant red, green, blue, yellowish gold, pastel pink, pale green, and powder blue, with some details executed in black. The uppermost part of the collar has a straight edge rendered as a line of rectangles painted in alternating colors of red, pale green, and blue. The flanking terminals of the collar are in the shape of the falcon head with a blue and gold striped cowl and red sun-disk on the crown. The imitation necklace consists of eleven rows of stylized renderings of various shaped beads interspersed with two wide rows of floral design. The pattern in both is of alternating open and closed lotus flowers, although the lotus blossoms of the bottommost row are

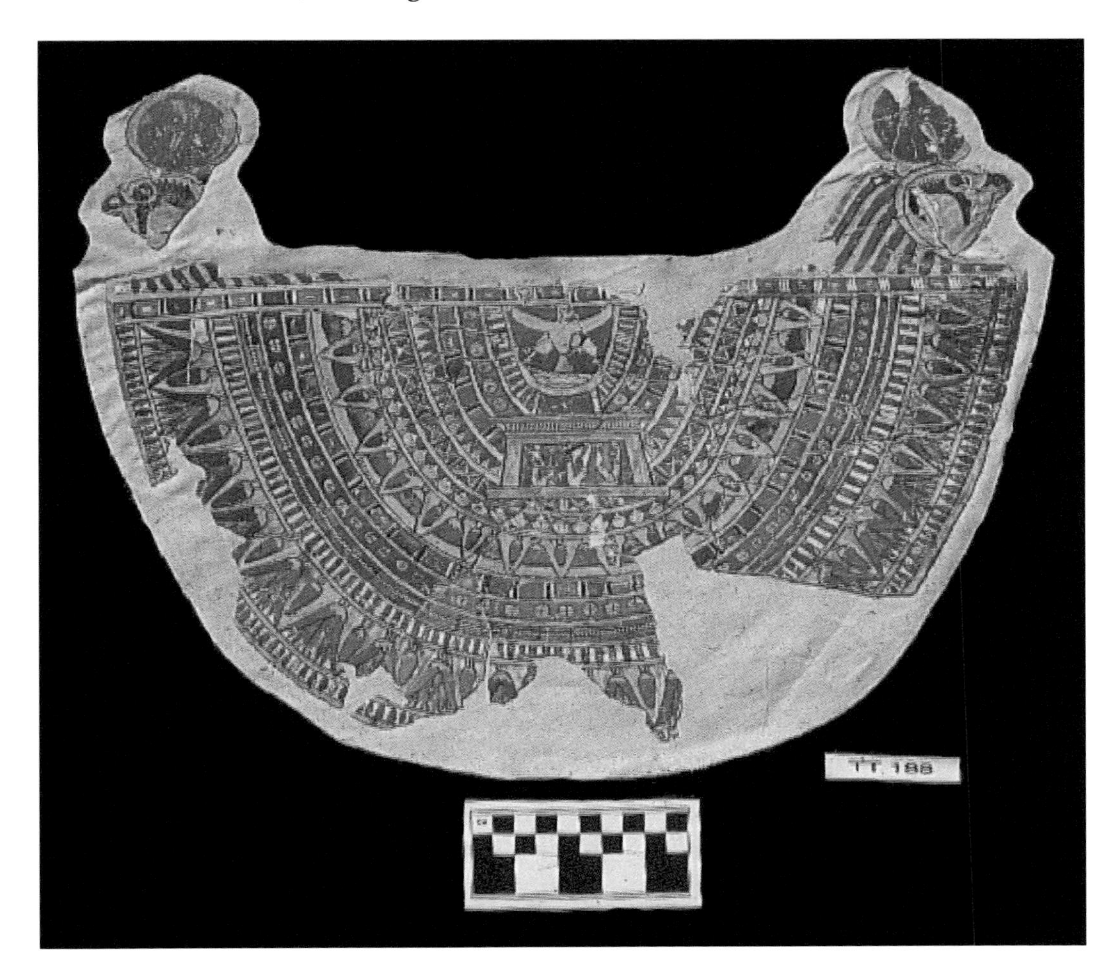

Figure 2: Restored cartonnage plaque (Author)

drawn in much greater detail and color combination. The last row is painted in a teardrop design. Besides the terminals, two religious icons grace the collar: at top center is a painting of a human-headed bird with outstretched wings and legs. The *ba* bird is painted gold on a bright blue-green background. Immediately below is a depiction of a gold pendant overlying the collar in the shape of a corniced shrine.

Within the canopy are three seated deities against a bright red background. Two female deities, possibly representing Nephthys and Isis but with misinterpreted headdresses, face the center deity. Unfortunately, the head of this figure is damaged, but there appear to be traces of pointed ears suggesting Anubis.

The pendant motif, the large falcon-headed terminals, and in fact the overall collar design are peculiar to decoration on Thirtieth Dynasty/early Ptolemaic coffins [32] Similar plaques have been dated as early as the end of the Late Period, although of a much poorer quality.[33] The religious icons as well are rendered in a generic artistic manner distinctive of the Thirtieth Dynasty/early Ptolemaic period. Three additional fragments with a similar color palette are perhaps the remains of the midsection or apron of the same mummy case.

NOTES

1 K.-T. Zauzich, *Die Ägyptische Schreibertradition in Aufbau, Sprache und Schrift Der Demotischen Kaufverträge Aus Ptolemäischer Zeit*, 2 vols., Ägyptologische Abhundlungen 19 (Wiesbaden: Harrassowitz, 1968); Urk. 42.

2 C. Andrews, *Catalogue of Demotic Papyri in the British Museum IV. Ptolemaic Legal Texts from the Theban Area* (London: The British Museum Press, 1990), 73, no. 30, recto 10 ("the place that is destroyed").

3 Although early on in a temple context only, cf. *Wb* I, 257-8-10; C. Insley, "A Bronze Statuette of Unnufer, Choachyte of King Harsiese, in the Fitzwilliam Museum," *JEA* 65 (1979): 167–169; T.E. Peet, *The Great Tomb Robberies of the Twentieth Egyptian Dynasty* (Oxford: Clarendon Press, 1930), pl. v: 4; *Berlin* 8438.

4 Etymology uncertain, cf. J. Vergote, *De Oplossing van een Gewichtig Probleem* (Brussels: Paleis der Academiën, 1960), 35; K. D. van Heel, "The Use and Meaning of the Egyptian term *w3h-mw*," in R.J. Demarée and A. Egberts (eds.), *Village Voices* (Leiden: Center of Non-Western Studies, 1992), 12–19, passim.

5 For what follows, see S. P. Vleeming, "The Office of a Choachyte," in S. P. Vleeming (ed.), *Hundred-Gated Thebes* (Leiden: E. J. Brill, 1995), 241–255; P. W. Pestman, *The Archive of the Theban Choachytes (Second Century B.C.). A Survey of the Demotic and Greek Papyri Contained in the Archive* (Leuven: A. Peeters, 1993), passim.

6 M. Malinine, *Choix de textes juridiques en hiératique anormal et en démotique* (Cairo: Institut français d'archéologie orientale, 1983), 1–5, no. 1; H. De Meulenaere, "Choachyte," *LÄ* I (1973): 957; Insley, "Bronze Statuette," 167–169.

7 Cf. *KRI* VI, 510:7; A. H. Gardiner, *Late Egyptian Stories* (Bruxelles: Fondation égyptologique Reine Elisabeth, 1932), 93:3–4.

8 K. D. van Heel, "Abnormal Hieratic and Early Demotic Texts: Collected by the Choachytes in the Reign of Amasis" (PhD dissertation, Rijksuniversiteit te Leiden, 1996).

9 Andrews, *Demotic Papyri*, 49–50, no. 14, n. 20; Malinine, *Texts Juridiques*, XV, 48.

10 Zauzich, *Ägyptische Schreibertradition I*, 20.

11 L. Kákosy, "The Soter Tomb in Thebes," in S. P. Vleeming (ed.), *Hundred-Gated Thebes* (Leiden: E. J. Brill, 1995), 61–67.

12 Pestmen, *Archive*, 8.

13 Andrews, *Demotic Papyri*, 25, no. 3; 31–33, no. 6; 73, no. 30.

14 Andrews, *Demotic Papyri*, 49, no. 14.

15 According to demotic archives of the Theban area (Van Heel, *Abnormal Hieratic*, passim), the great necropolis on the west of Thebes showed two foci of activity. They were the approach to Deir el-Bahri and the Asasif; (Malinine, *Texts Juridiques*, 17, 50, 114) and the necropolis of Djeme, in the vicinity of Medinet Habu (Andrews, *Demotic Papyri*, passim; once "the upper necropolis of Djeme" is mentioned [no. 2, n. 11, 24]). For "Djeme" see E. Otto, "Djeme," *LÄ* I (1974): 1108–1109.

16 PM I^{2}:1 , 434; F. Kampp, *Die thebanische Nekropole: zum Wandel des Grabgedankens von der XVIII. bis zur XX. Dynastie* (Mainz: Von Zabern, 1996), 597.

17 W. Boochs, *Siegel und Siegeln im Alten Ägypten*, Kölner Forshcungen zu Kunst und Altertum 4 (St. Augustin: H. Richarz, 1982), passim.; R. Parkinson and S. Quirke, *Papyrus* (Austin: University of Texas Press, 1995), 43; S. Shubert, "Seal and Sealings," in D. B. Redford (ed.), *Oxford Encyclopedia of Ancient Egypt* 3 (New York: Oxford University Press, 2001), 252–257.

18 Or "Privy to the mysteries of the divine treasure." On *htm-ty-nṯr*, see D. Jones, *Index of Ancient Egyptian Titles, Epithets and Phrases of the Old Kingdom* (Oxford: Archaeopress, 2000), 767, #2791; for its mortuary function in the New Kingdom and Late Period, see *KRI* II, 370:2, 897:5; C. Traunecker, "Les Graffiti des frères Horsaisis et Horemheb. Une Famille de prêtres sous les derniers Ptolemées," in W. Clarysse, A. Schoors, H. Willems, and J. Quaegebeur (eds.), *Egyptian Religion. The Last Thousand Years* (Louvain: Peeters, 1998), 1205 n. 70; J. Johnson, "Women, Wealth and Work in Egyptian Society," in Clarysse et al., *Egyptian Religion*, 1408.

19 On the writing see P. Wilson, *A Ptolemaic Lexikon* (Louvain: Uitgeverij Peeters en Departement Oosterse Studies, 1997), 271 (writing with *ḏ*). *Wb* I, 379: 9-12; W. Erichsen, *Demotisches Glossar* (Copenhagen: E. Munksgaard, 1954), 693 (with *htm-ty-nṯr*), rendered in Greek as ενταφιαστης.

20 *Wb* III 235:21; H. Gauthier, *Dictionnaire des noms géographiques contenus dans les textes hiéroglyphiques* (Osnabrück: Zeller, 1975), 157; Erichsen, *Demotisches Glossar*, 347–348; the necropolis of Qus on the west bank was of particular importance from early times: H. G. Fischer, *Inscriptions from the Coptite Nome* (Rome: Pontificium Institutum Biblicum, 1964), 4.

21 On the name form cf. *Ḥr-wr-m-ḫnw Gsy*. See C. Leitz, *Lexikon der ägyptischen Götter und Götterbezeichnungen* V (Louvain: Peeters en Departement Oosterse Studies, 2002), 251. For the township of *Nbt* see, Gauthier, *Dictionnaire des noms*, III, 83–84.

[22] For the name see H. Ranke, *Die Ägyptischen Personennamen* (Glückstadt: J.J. Augustin, 1935), 124, no. 21; E. Lüddeckens, (ed.), *Demotisches Namenbuch* (Wiesbaden: L. Reichert, 1988) I, 534; Greek πετεαϱοηϱις: W. Preisigke, *Namenbuch* (Heidelberg: A.M. Hakkert, 1922), 311. The principal deity of the site being Harweris, the present individual is undoubtedly a native.

[23] Preisigke, *Namenbuch*, 311; Ranke, *Ägyptischen Personennamen*, 124, nos. 19 to 125, no. 17; Lüddeckens, *Demotisches Namenbuch*, 534–536.

[24] Originally affixed to a papyrus document, it may indicate nothing more than correspondence between the necropolis administrations of Thebes and Qus.

[25] Andrews, *Catalogue*, 31 (P. BM 10615).

[26] It is ironic that a priest of the cemetery of the town of Qus should be buried at Thebes. (For Qus see W. Helck, *Die altägyptischen Gaue* [Wiesbaden: L. Reichert, 1974], 84; A. H. Gardiner, *Ancient Egyptian Onomastica* [Oxford: Oxford University Press, 1947] 27–28; Gauthier, *Dictionnaire*, 178; F. Gomaà, *Die Besiedlung Ägyptens während des Mittleren Reiches I. Oberaegypten und das Fayyum* [Wiesbaden: L. Reichert, 1986], 161–162; J. Baines, J. Málek, *Atlas of Ancient Egypt* [New York: Facts on File, 1980], 111.)

[27] For a description of similar tomb groups of fifth through third century BCE burials, see D. Aston, "The Theban West Bank from the Twenty-fifth Dynasty to the Ptolemaic Period," in N. Strudwick and J. Taylor (eds.), *The Theban Necropolis: Past, Present and Future* (London: British Museum Press, 2003), 162–163, figs. 15–18.

[28] For dated examples of beaded nets see: J. H. Taylor, *Death and the Afterlife in Ancient Egypt* (Chicago: University of Chicago Press, 2001), 206, fig. 148 (Late Period); H. Schneider, *Life and Death under the Pharaohs: Egyptian Art from the National Museum of Antiquities in Leiden, The Netherlands* (Perth: Western Australian Museum, 2000), 130, #197 (Late Period/Twenty-Sixth Dynasty); S. Aufrère, *Collections Egyptiennes. Collections des Musées départementaux de Seine-Maritime* (Rouen: Musées départementaux de Seine-Maritime, 1987), 44–45, figs. 28–29 (Late Period); O. Berlev and S. Hodjash, *Catalogue of the Monuments of Ancient Egypt from the Museums of the Russian Federation, Ukraine, Bielorussia, Caucasus, Middle Asia and the Baltic States*, Orbis Biblicus et Orientalis 17 (Göttingen: Vandenhoeck und Ruprecht, 1998), XIV.81.82.83, pl. 172 (Late Period); V. Laurent and M. Desti, *Antiquités égyptiennes. Inventaire de collections du Musée des Beauz-Arts de Dijon* (Dijon: Musée des beaux-arts de Dijon, 1997), 160, #205 (Ptolemaic Period).

[29] Undisturbed tombs show that no dirt fill was added after the placement of the body and burial goods. For examples see H. Carter, *The Tomb of Tut-Ankh-Amen* (London: Cassell and Co., 1923–1933), J. E. Quibell, *The Tomb of Yuaa and Thuiu* (Cairo: Institut français d'archéologie orientale, 1908).

[30] This material has been documented in definitive studies by the following: A. Niwiński, *21st Dynasty Coffins from Thebes* (Mainz: Von Zabern, 1988); G. Lapp and A. Niwiński, "Coffins, Sarcophagi and Cartonnages," in D. B. Redford

(ed.), *Oxford Encyclopedia of Ancient Egypt* 3 (New York: Oxford University Press, 2001), 279-287; A. Niwiński, "Sarg NR-SpZt," in *LÄ* 5: 434–468; J. H. Taylor, "The Development of Theban Coffins during the Third Intermediate Period. A Typological Study" (PhD dissertation, University of Birmingham, 1985); D. Aston, "Tombs Groups from the End of the New Kingdom to the Beginning of the Saite Period" (PhD dissertation, University of Birmingham, 1987); C. Riggs, "The Egyptian Funerary Tradition at Thebes in the Roman Period," in N. Strudwick and J. Taylor (eds.), *The Theban Necropolis: Past, Present and Future* (London: British Museum Press, 2003), 189–201.

31 I am indebted to the Theban Tomb Survey's staff artist, Rupert Nesbitt of Newport, Rhode Island, for this painstaking feat of restoration.

32 J. H. Taylor, *Egyptian Coffins* (Aylesbury: Shire Egyptology, 1989), 61; S. Ikram and A. Dodson, *The Mummy in Ancient Egypt: Equipping the Dead for Eternity* (London: Thames and Hudson, 1998), 241, figs. 324, 326.

33 Cf. Aufrère, *Collections Egyptiennes*, figs. 17–18.

Love Letters from Luxor: Arthur Weigall and the Tomb of Yuya and Tjuyu[1]

Nicholas Reeves
Department of Egyptian Art, The Metropolitan Museum of Art, New York

The Metropolitan Museum of Art preserves extensive archives relevant to the history of Egyptology. Among its holdings are letters written by Arthur Weigall to his fiancée, Hortense Schleiter, during the time the Theban tomb of Yuya and Tjuyu was being excavated. These letters, transcribed here, reveal elements of Weigall's character as well as events at the tomb.

Although The Metropolitan Museum of Art is justly famed for the quality and diversity of its Egyptian collections, less well known is that the institution's extensive archives preserve a mass of evocative writings which the pursuit of Egyptology has over the years managed to generate or inspire. Perhaps the most

Figure 1: Shabti figures and shabti boxes from the tomb of Yuya and Tjuyu Metropolitan Museum of Art 30.8.60a–b, .59a–b, .58, .56, .57. Theodore M. Davis Collection, Bequest of Theodore M. Davis, 1915 (image © The Metropolitan Museum of Art)

captivating of these is the manuscript first volume of Howard Carter and Arthur C. Mace's fairy-tale-like trilogy, *The Tomb of Tut.ankh.Amen*—the first-hand account (in Mace's handwriting) of Egypt's greatest ever archaeological find.[2] But *Tut.ankh.Amen* represents merely the tip of an iceberg—of documentation relevant not only to a range of important excavations in which the Metropolitan Museum has played a key role but also to several individual artworks which chance to have found their way to New York either by gift or purchase.

Particularly notable among the Egyptian Department's object-accessions is a small group of materials—shabti-figures,[3] -boxes,[4] and -implements,[5] storage jars,[6] sandals,[7] and linen[8]—from the Valley of the Kings' *second* greatest discovery: the burial of Yuya and Tjuyu.[9] This grouping, the most significant parts of which arrived in New York with the Theodore M. Davis[10] Bequest in 1915 (Figure 1), may now happily be augmented—by extracts from a recently acquired archive:[11] six

Figure 2: Gaston Maspero, Howard Carter, and James E. Quibell: sketches by Arthur Weigall (left undated, centre and right from a letter to Hortense Schleiter, February 3, 1905). Metropolitan Museum of Art, Department of Egyptian Art, Weigall Archive (images © The Metropolitan Museum of Art)

letters that span the twenty-three days in February and March 1905 during which Yuya and Tjuyu's tomb was found and cleared. To this major archaeological event the new Metropolitan Museum correspondence provides a unique, highly personal backdrop—a fascinating snapshot of Egyptological politics, excavation life, and (as the title of this paper intimates) unyielding affection at a moment when much was afoot in the world of archaeology on the Nile. The great Gaston Maspero[12] (Figure

Figure 3: Arthur E. P. B. Weigall and Hortense Schleiter. Metropolitan Museum of Art, Department of Egyptian Art, Weigall Archive (images © The Metropolitan Museum of Art)

2, left) was well into his second spell as Director of the Antiquities Service and Museum; Howard Carter[13] (Figure 2 center) in some considerable difficulty after permitting his Egyptian guards to defend themselves against a party of drunken French tourists ("the Saqqara affair");[14] and the Luxor Inspectorate in a state of limbo pending the formal confirmation of its new Chief Inspector of Antiquities for Upper Egypt.[15]

The writer of these letters, and the principal focus of the archive from which they are drawn, was that same Inspector-designate: a twenty-four-year-old Englishman by the name of Arthur Weigall[16] (Figure 3, left), successor to the archaeologist James E. Quibell[17] (Figure 2, right), who had himself taken over the Luxor post but a matter of months before on Carter's transfer to Saqqara in the north. The recipient of Weigall's heated correspondence was a captivating

American—Hortense Schleiter (Figure 3, right), of Pittsburgh and Chicago, to whom the young Egyptologist was engaged and whom he clearly adored to complete and utter distraction.[18]

This very human glimpse behind the scenes of one of Egyptian archaeology's most important discoveries is offered in honor of my esteemed colleague and sometime collaborator, Richard H. Wilkinson. As an archaeologist, Richard is one of the few Egyptologists today to have known, with Weigall, the excitement of digging in that extraordinary royal cemetery where Yuya and Tjuyu lay undisturbed for more than three thousand years; and, as an accomplished writer, he will surely relish these tentative beginnings of what, for Arthur Weigall, would soon blossom into a full and successful literary career. Indeed, the young Weigall's correspondence strikes many chords. It offers a reminder not only of the high stakes for which all who dig in the Valley of the Kings inevitably play but also of that work's timeless routine—the inexpressible delights of the Egyptian countryside, the highs (and occasional lows) of professional companionship, and those hard-felt absences from the ones who are precious to us.

Our young Inspector-designate was inevitably a creature of time and place: mildly bigoted, somewhat patronizing towards women, something of a snob, and public-school confident to the point of exasperation—a characteristic product of Great Britain's colonial Empire at its height. But dig a little deeper and one finds a man truly to like and admire. Weigall was rapidly to establish himself as one of the most competent and far-sighted archaeologists of his generation, and, in the same way that his achievements continue still to inform and inspire,[19] the passions of this young man in love reach out to touch us all.

LETTER I: FRIDAY-SATURDAY, FEBRUARY 10-11, 1905[20]

> [In pencil:]
> *Medinet Habu*
> *Luxor*
> *Friday*
>
> *Sweetheart, I wish I could describe to you some of the wonders of this place.*[21] *Now as I sit on the verandah of this house it all seems so delicious that I can't help writing to you about it. It is an acknowledged fact in my mind now that anything really delicious at once reminds me of you & makes me long for you with extraordinary intensity. Imagine, then, this large*

verandah in the deep blue shade, & immediately outside imagine the burning sun & the bluest sky. In our new house the verandah will be even nicer & from it we shall be able to look over the garden (1) & over the river (2) & the green fields & villages (3) to the yellow towering cliffs (4). The numbers are rather pedantic, but are necessary as I can't draw.

Figure 4: "[...] we shall be able to look over the garden (1) & over the river (2) & the green fields & villages (3) to the yellow towering cliffs." Letter I (image © The Metropolitan Museum of Art)

Here I look out over a rather barren garden with a few trees, & a pigeon house where the pigeons are cooing; then behind it I get a glimpse of the cliffs & at their foot a ruined temple.[22] *The sparrows are all singing, & there is a feeling of summer in the air, just like those summer days at Feldafing.*[23]

All the morning (it is now 12 o'c) I have been scrambling over the hills, getting some idea of the tombs there. The hillside is honeycombed with tombs, & I am trying to make an estimate of the cost of putting on iron doors in order to preserve the paintings in them. This has been done in about 20 of them but there are hundreds still to clean up & put under lock and key.[24]

I have come home now feeling deliciously hot, for up on the hillside the sun is very strong; & here in the shade, with a lemon squash by my side, & the various noises of summer blowing up on the cool wind, I am at peace with the world—except that I want you *so much & can't have you.*

In the garden, & now blinking foolishly at me, is a great shaggy yellow dog, a bob-tailed sheep-dog I'd call it in England—just the sort of dog that Miss Elsie Carter (or whatever her name was) thought to be a bear, you know. Everyone warned me against him, & said he was so fierce & that he bit everybody. However he took a fancy to me, & now we are good friends. He will even let me chain or unchain him, & take him for a walk. He originally belonged to Carter,[25] *& was handed over to Quibell.*[26] *Now he comes to me I suppose, but everybody said I ought to have him shot. But I think not; & at any rate I will await your orders, madam; as he is also your property now, being part of my worldly goods (O isn't it* gorgeous *to think that everything about me belongs to you!). He is an awful fool, fights every dog, attacks every Arab, & bites every visitor. He also has some very embarrassing habits. But as he has very plainly told me he likes me very much indeed, thank you, I don't think it would be* quite *kind to blow his brains out. He seems to have a great reputation in this neighbourhood. As I ride or walk about, nobody salutes me, for they do not know who I am yet; but when they see Bobby (that is his name) they spring to attention, knowing that he is the terrible Carter's dog.*

I must say I do wish Quibell would go—in other words I wish my nomination would come. He is so slack*, & I see many things going wrong which at present I cannot alter for fear of hurting his feelings, he being still nominal inspector. In Carter's time everything was spick & span, but already I can see laziness showing itself in the form of—let me say—orange peel left about by a visitor in some temple, & not picked up by the guards; or a guard leaving his post for half an hour without fear of punishment, apparently. I see that there is so much to be done that one will have to have a proper programme each day. Quibell does little bits of many things, but never seems to get anything accomplished.*

Saturday*. I don't seem to have much time for writing. Yesterday I had to break off because some people came to lunch, & in the afternoon an* *ambassador came to tea. Today I have been racing about inventing a route for the Duke of Connaught*[27] *to visit the tombs. Quibell has gone off to Edfu to meet them, but I have asked leave to stay here till they come (tomorrow night) & not go to Edfu. This afternoon I have to go over to the Tombs of the Kings—& here is a great excitement. Our excavations there (over which I shall have to superintend, each winter) have just resulted in the finding of the door of a King's tomb & we shall be in in a few days.*[28] *As soon as we get in it will be very exciting unless the place has been anciently robbed & cleaned out. Quibell & I will take turns up there day & night guarding the place with policemen & guards, for actually one must expect a raid from the Arabs if there is much stuff inside. You see the price of antiquities is so high & the market so great that a tomb can easily have say £20,000 worth of stuff in it. They are hoping that the Duke may just be in time to be present at the opening; but I am going this afternoon with the firm intention of dropping an avalanch* [sic] *of stones over the mouth of the tomb from the hillside above, so as to delay it.*[29] *You can imagine that when one enters a tomb one wants a good week's quiet work inside recording the positions of things before they are touched; & it won't do to have Princesses & people fooling round, will it? It is just the same as in the case of a house sealed up by the police when a crime has been committed there. One doesn't want a crowd tumbling around it till the most thorough examination is made.*

How you will love this place darlingest! I believe that this month is the crisis of the season, & we are not to judge of the place by the present conditions. There won't always be this host of people. Unfortunately, however, our new house is on the high road to Karnak & we shall have crowds to tea each day during the season. Do you mind, dearest love?

O Hortense I want you so. The longer I am away the more I seem to love you; & now I am consumed with fear lest you should grow to forget me—or rather to cease to love me with all that dear intensity with which I love you.

No, of course I don't mean that; but you can understand, I expect, how afraid I am always, & how I rebel against this separation.

I have spoken to Maspero about getting leave & he seems to think I could only take a month & that in Sept. The Carter affair,[30] *however, may change matters. If he has to go, as I rather expect, poor old chap, then we shall be all new men here & in order not to all go away together next year one of us must take leave this year. So if he goes I shall at once apply for my 3½ months leave this year commencing June 15th. However I fear that it is a rather wild hope & it is based on an event which I trust will not occur, for we can't afford to lose so good a man as Carter.*

I don't see how your father can refuse to let you come out at once, darlingest. I am rather vague as to how we shall manage here & where we shall stay; for at present I shall be in the hotel (I go there this afternoon) & the Quibells won't turn out of their house till my nomination comes & the new house is not ready. However, don't bother about that: I will arrange something. As regards clothes you will want summer things, but something warm for the nights which are still cold.

I am so anxious about your throat. I do hope you will telegraph to me so that I shall know it is all right. I shan't be content till I see you, though. God bless you my darling wife. O when shall I feel your darling arms around me again—O Hortense I love you so!

Your most passionately loving husband
Arthur

Best love to Aunt Carrie.[31] *I will write to her as soon as I have a moment*

Letter II: Tuesday-Thursday, February 14–16, 1905[32]

[Hotel stationery:] PAGNON'S HOTELS / LUXOR & ASSOUAN
LUXOR HOTEL – LU[XOR]

Thursday evening

Darling love—you will find enclosed a description of what I have been doing. As I haven't any time at all for writing just now you must be content with this scrappy account & you must send it on to Mother, for I haven't written to her at all!

There is so much I want to answer in your dear letter, & I have in my heart such a vast store of love for you which cannot be expressed. I am so relieved that you now are happy about the new appointment.

Carter seems likely to take his departure & in that case I shall probably have no difficulty in getting leave this year from June to September. But I don't like to think much about it yet in case of disappointment. I am so anxious about your throat, & I want to know so much where you are at present. Hortense I love you most desperately much. I wish I could get you out of my thoughts sometimes, but the aching want keeps me reminded of you. You will be very bored, in the following account, with the talk about the visitors to our tomb; but Mother is deeply interested in the people I meet & likes to hear about these Princes & people. So you mustn't mind, darling love. I am very anxious about your coming visit—if you don't come I'll never speak to your Father again!

O Hortense I want you so—!
God bless you, Heart of my heart,

Your own madly loving husband
Arthur

This part of my letter I want you to send on to Mother. It is to be an account of my wild adventures during the last two days, & as I haven't time to write it twice this is the only thing for me to do.

First of all I want to tell you that among the great desert hills on the west of the river there is a valley called The Valley of the Tombs of the Kings (Wady Biban El-Malûk) & here among the rocks all the kings of the XVIIIth & XIXth Dynasties were buried—kings who reigned, that is, about B.C. 1600–1200.[33] *The tombs are usually made in the form of a great tunnel cut into the mountain side & sloping down for about 100 feet until the burial chamber is reached. About 20 of them are now open to the public that is to say they have iron doors to them which are opened by a guard, & there is electric light inside worked by a little engine nearby.*[34] *The Valley is some five miles from Luxor, & except from 9 to 1 o'c each morning when the light is working & the tourists come, it is a silent, impressive, aloof kind of place, hemmed in by the huge cliffs & tumbled-looking rock hills, & inhabited only by the guards, jackals, & owls. All of the tombs have been open for ages & have been completely plundered, & are now practically empty.*

Davis,[35] an American millionaire, some time ago offered to pay all expenses if the Govt. would excavate round the valley for the purpose of finding new tombs, & it has been the duty of the inspector to run these excavations. The year before last Davis uncovered the tomb of a rather famous King,[36] which, however, was much plundered & damaged. Then last year he got the tomb of a still more famous Queen.[37] This year he has been digging steadily, & a few days ago the men struck the mouth of a tomb—a plain flight of stairs leading down to a door which was blocked with stones & rubbish—the whole thing being covered with rubbish thrown out from other tombs, & quite hidden.[38]

This is where I come into the story. Quibell & I were ordered up to Edfu to take the Duke of Connaught round the temple there; but as it seemed likely that we should soon get into this tomb I asked to stay & see to it.[39] So (on Sunday [February 12]) I spent most of the day up in the valley & in the evening the stones at the door were removed & we could see through a small hole into the tomb. Davis was with me & we crawled in together, into the slanting passage which appeared to lead down right into the mountain.[40] As soon as we got in we found lying on the floor a lovely staff with an enamel top, & some other antiquities.[41] We followed the passage down some distance, down another flight of steps, & then we came to a doorway bricked up and sealed with a seal which we at once recognized as that of the Priests of Amen of the XVIIIth dynasty. There was a small hole in one corner of this brick wall; & it was evident that a man had been into the tomb & had robbed it, & had thrown aside the staff etc in his hurry to escape. The fact that the mouth of the tomb was covered with XIXth dynasty rubbish undisturbed showed plainly that the thief had been in about B.C. 1300[42] & that after that date nobody had entered the place.[43]

The tomb thus being open, somebody had to guard it during the night; so as I was in charge (& Quibell in Edfu) I offered to sleep there.[44] In our party there was a man called Eldon [sic] *Smith[45] who promptly offered to sleep with me too;[46] & at about 8 o'c he arrived with his wife[47]—an energetic New Yorker. I was rather startled to find a woman on the scene, for I was going to sleep in the open on the ground. However, she seemed an old stager, & rather enjoyed the possibility of an attack by the Arabs (who were of course very excited about the tomb & were inclined to raid the place and steal the things). We had a funny scrappy sort of dinner, & then shoulder to shoulder we all three lay down on the ground at the mouth of the tomb, with a blanket each for covering. My guards slept around us, so there was no danger of course, as they all had their guns. It was a moonlight* [sic] *night & absolutely heavenly from a scenic point of view. None of us slept much, but we rather enjoyed ourselves & went for some scrambles over the rocks at different times in the night. At sunrise we had breakfast & then waited for Davis and Maspero to arrive for the formal opening of the tomb.*[48]

As they were rather late I crawled into the tomb again myself & had a good look through the plunderer's hole into the inner chambers, & I could just see by the light of my candle that there were several antiquities inside; & of course I was pretty frantic to get in.[49] *At last Davis arrived (with all his party) & Maspero came too; & we three pulled down the first wall & entered. Then we slipped & slid down the long, steep passage to the blocked door, & with some difficulty we crawled into the inner chamber.*[50] *For some moments we couldn't see anything much, but as our eyes got used to the candle light we saw a sight which I can safely say no other living man has ever seen. The chamber was pretty large—a rough hewn cavern of a place. In the middle of the room were two enormous sarcophagi of wood inlaid with gold. The lids had been wrenched off by the plunderer & the coffins inside had been tumbled about so that the two mummies were exposed. The plunderers had evidently very hurriedly searched the bodies for the jewels but had not touched anything else. All round the sarcophagi—piled almost to the roof—were chairs, tables, beds, vases, & so on—all in perfect condition. You know the Egyptians buried this sort of furniture with the dead for their use in the next world; but a tomb has never been found before with the things in such perfect preservation or in anything like such large numbers. In one corner a chariot—quite perfect—as clean as a London hansom—lay; & by it a huge bedstead of inlaid wood something like Chipendale* [sic]. *Here there was a group of lovely painted vases—here a pile of gold & silver figures. In one corner were some jars of wine, the lids tied on with string; & among them was one huge alabaster <u>jug full of honey still liquid</u>.*[51] *When I saw this I <u>really</u> nearly fainted. The extraordinary sensation of finding oneself looking at a pot of honey as liquid & sticky as the honey one eats at breakfast and yet <u>three thousand five hundred years old</u>, was so dumbfounding that one felt as though one was mad or dreaming. The room looked just as a drawing room would look in a London house shut up while the people were away, for the* *summer. But with this terrifying difference—that everything was in the fashion of 34 centuries ago—in the fashion of a period hundreds of years before Moses & the Exodus. There were lovely gold & wood arm chairs with cane bottoms. There were cushions stuffed with feathers & down—as soft as though they were only made yesterday.*

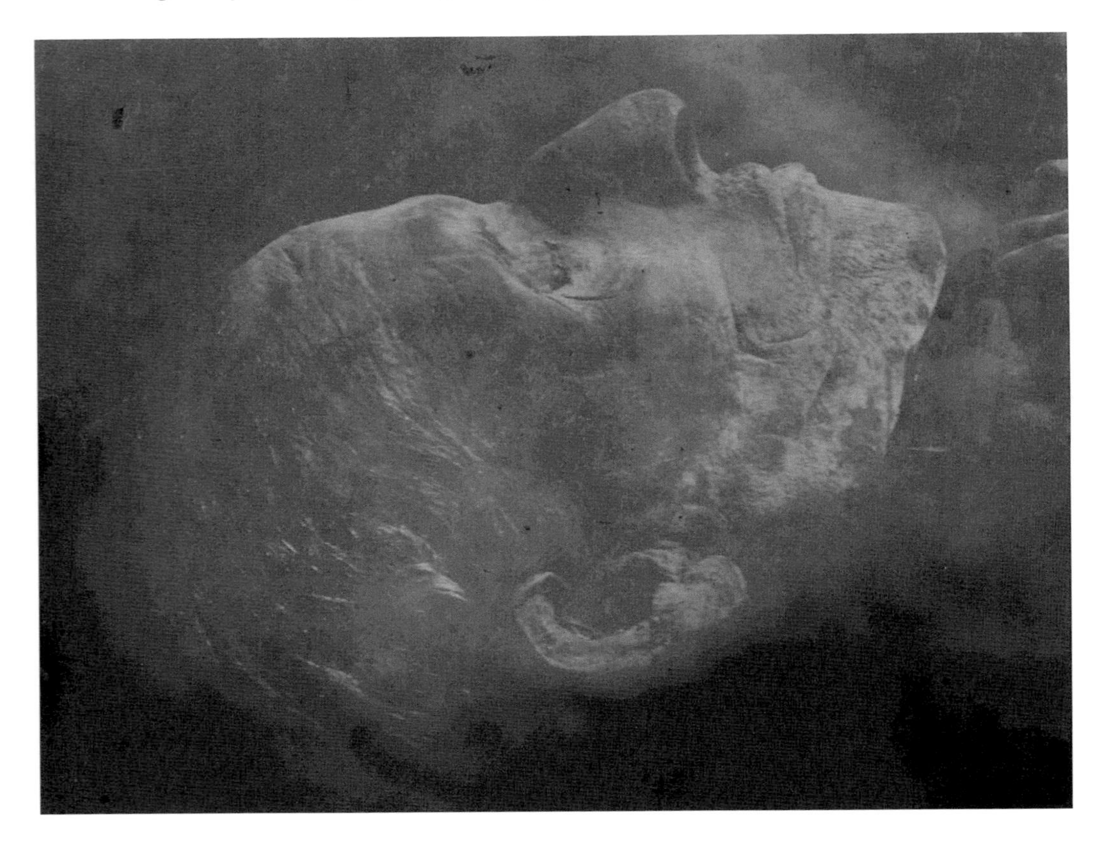

Figure 5: The mummy of Yuya, at the time of discovery: photograph by Arthur Weigall, 1905. Metropolitan Museum of Art, Department of Egyptian Art, Weigall Archive (image © The Metropolitan Museum of Art).

Maspero, Davis, & I stood there gaping & almost trembling for a time—& I think we all felt that we were face to face with something which seemed to upset all human ideas of time & distance. Then we dashed for the inscribed objects, & read out the names of Prince Auai[52] *& his wife Thuai*[53]*—the* *famous mother & father of Queen Thy.*[54] *They had been known so well & discussed so often that they seemed old friends. For they are well known historical persons. But nobody had ever expected to see them; & as we looked at the mummies—Princess Thuai with her hair still plaited & elaborately dressed, and Prince Auai with his eyes peacefully closed & his mouth a little open* [Figure 5][55]*—an awful feeling came over me. All three of us very soon crawled out of the tomb & into the sunlight—one step from the seventeenth century before Christ*[56] *to the twentieth century after him.*[57] *At the mouth of the tomb the others were waiting, & Maspero gave me permission to take Mr. and Mrs. Eldon* [sic] *Smith in, which I did. To show you how impressive the sight was I must tell you that Mrs. Smith burst into a torrent of tears & cried so much that we had to pull her out into the sunlight again. Then after this, while Smith & I were down there fixing on some electric lamps which we had connected up by wires with the engine house,*[58] *Davis came in again. But he had hardly looked for more than a minute when he cried "O my God!" & pitched forward in a bad faint. Smith & I fanned him & were pretty badly scared, as he is an old man. And when he fainted a second time we shouted for help & all carried him to the surface, where he soon recovered.*[59]

*I am afraid you will think us all very hysterical, but you have not experienced the blank, utter amazement of finding oneself carried back & dumped into the 17*th *century B.C.* [sic]*! And in all seriousness, I can say that nobody but ourselves has ever seen such a sight.*

After this Davis went home, & I remained making a register of the antiquities before moving them. I was hard at work & filthy dirty & hot when Maspero came to the door of the tomb and called me. I hurried up, & brushed myself clean on the way, & when I got to the surface Maspero said "The Duke of Connaught" & I found myself being led up to a large party of people, & presently I was shaking hands with the Duke. Of course they wanted to see the tomb, so I took the whole party down one by one, but didn't let them go farther than the entrance of the burial chamber as the place was so littered with objects. They were all very impressed & interested but of course not so much as we had been who had been actually inside the room. After this I had to take them to see the other tombs. The Duke was awfully nice & quite informal—begged me to keep my hat on & all that sort of thing; & we had quite a long conversation about my new appointment etc. He was pleased with my guards, who saluted him & stood at attention in the best possible manner! The Princesses (his daughters) were very nice too.

I had tea with them all in pic nic [sic] *fashion;*[60] *and after they had gone I hurried back to the tomb where I found several people had arrived—the news of the discovery having spread like lighting. A gruff, rude old man began to talk very fast to me & I soon discovered that he was the Duke of Devonshire;*[61] *then came Sir John Evans*[62] *who had to be taken down to see the tomb. Then came some Egyptologists & a mixed crowd of foolish English and French Dukes, Marquises, etc. for Luxor at present teems with them. A little dark man asked me to take him down but I got out of it. He proved to be the Crown Prince of Norway*[63] *afterwards.*

By this time it was dark; & as I felt it necessary to sleep again over the tomb, I galloped back to Luxor & had dinner & a bath & then galloped over to the valley again by moonlight. I was soon joined by Quibell, who had returned from Edfu;[64] *& we slept again just flat on the ground. That was last night, & this morning we started early to work in the tomb, & Smith & Ayrton*[65] *soon joined us (Ayrton had been excavating a few miles away).*[66] *All the morning we slaved in the hot room moving & sorting the furniture. Then came a pic-nic lunch brought by Davis. By this time, with two such exciting days & two bed-less nights in the open, & the Turkish-bath like temperature of the tomb, I was pretty tired. People kept coming to see the place (with special invitations from the Director or somebody) & just after lunch the Empress Eugenie*[67] *arrived. Quibell & I hurriedly tidied ourselves & we showed her round—a very cross, hot, old lady she was too.*[68] *With her was a very delightful Count-somebody or other who showed enormous interest in it all. After the old lady had gone he sneaked back & asked if he might stay with us. He was A.d.c to the Empress but she didn't seem to want him just then. So he stripped & set to with us & worked like a n***** till dusk. Then I rode back to Luxor with him, & tonight I am staying at the hotel, but tomorrow I shall sleep over at the tomb, & so on alternately Quibell & I will take charge till all the antiquities are removed to our office, where we can start the catalogue. This may be about a week or ten days if we can work steadily; but we may not be able to get out of going round everywhere with the Duke; but I hope I at any rate shall be allowed to stay at the tomb. Then so many visitors keep coming that we are much disturbed.*[69]

We have now got policemen guarding the tomb so everything is quite safe. Of course all else—work, play—everything has to stand over. For instance tomorrow at 9 a.m. I go off to the tomb & shall stay there till the day after tomorrow evening working hard. But it is still extremely exciting.

Wednesday afternoon, 4 o'c. All day long we have been working at the tomb & now the others have gone & I am up at the valley for the night.[70] *Tonight there is an Italian Count Malvoletsi de Medici*[71] *I think his name is, coming to sleep up here too. I met him the other day & he offered to come up. He seems a very nice sort of fellow. The peerages of the world seem to be concentrated at Luxor just now! This afternoon we had all sorts of well-known people up, but we refused them all admittance except Lord & Lady Dalhousie,*[72] *who appeared to be rather vulgar & silly but who brought a letter from the Govr.*[73] *& therefore had to be considered. The Empress's a.d.c. also came again, & the Duchess of Devonshire*[74] *who was very awful. Then Prof. Sayce*[75] *came up with a luncheon party with whom I fed. Just at present I am getting my meals in a very scrappy way, & as for camping things I haven't anything with me. I just sleep as I am, on the ground, & if possible I get over to Luxor for half an hour for a bath. But it is a long ride over.*

I don't know how long it will be before the antiquities are packed off & we can resume our natural duties. I am now regarded as inspector, & do my share of the work; but my nomination I understand will probably still take some weeks—but that doesn't much matter. At present all our thoughts are on the tomb.

Figure 6: "One piece was a little chest made entirely of inlaid wood [...]. It looked as though it had been made yesterday." Letter II (image © The Metropolitan Museum of Art)

In the tomb we have today found some exquisite bits of furniture. One piece was a little chest [Figure 6] *made entirely of inlaid wood, the inlay being jasper, blue porcelain, & gold, in beautiful patterns. It had a charming lid, & inside were some jewels. It looked as though it had been made yesterday. The lady Thuai has a fine face, & we have been hunting about her body & have found some jolly scarabs & amulets. Her head is bound up in white linen, & all the features of the face are perfect. She must have been an old woman.*

Poor soul how she must have hated having an electric lamp blazing in her eyes after 34 centuries of darkness! We have not yet examined her husband closely, but he stares solemnly at us all the time, as we work & whistle & swear about the tomb. It is getting dark now so I must stop writing.

Thursday night. I have just returned here very tired after the two days of heavy work & no proper night's rest between. Today the tomb progressed well, & we have now nearly cleared the chamber. The things are more and more wonderful. Today we have carried out into the daylight a large trunk made of wicker work, with trays inside for clothes—all as perfect as a modern thing. We have also got another nice gold & ivory bedstead, & another jewel case.[76] *I awoke this morning about 7 o'c, having slept all through the night in spite of the hard ground. I was cleaning myself up about 8 o'c when the Duke of Connaught arrived & said he wanted to see the tomb again. So I took him down with his a.d.c. & a Sir Somebody MacKenzie.*[77] *The Duke was most delightful & was enormously interested in the tomb. He is a very good looking man, & I could not help thinking how really "royal" he looked when he stood in the tomb just in his shirt and trousers. (It is so hot that we have to take off most of our clothes down there.) He was very jovial & quite informal, & I thoroughly enjoyed talking to him for the hour he was with us.*

When at last we got to the surface we found the Duke of Devonshire had come again, with a Mr. & Mrs. Macquire[78]*—South African millionaires I think. His Grace looked very old & groggy, & his clothes didn't pretend to fit him. I got pretty angry with him, as he would tread so carelessly & nearly broke some of our antiquities. The Duke of Connaught seemed to be very respectful to him, & was very nice in the way he helped him down the stairs of the tomb.*

After these people had gone came Mr. Thorneycroft[79]*—the battleship builder—a nice old man, who has the sense to see that our time was being*

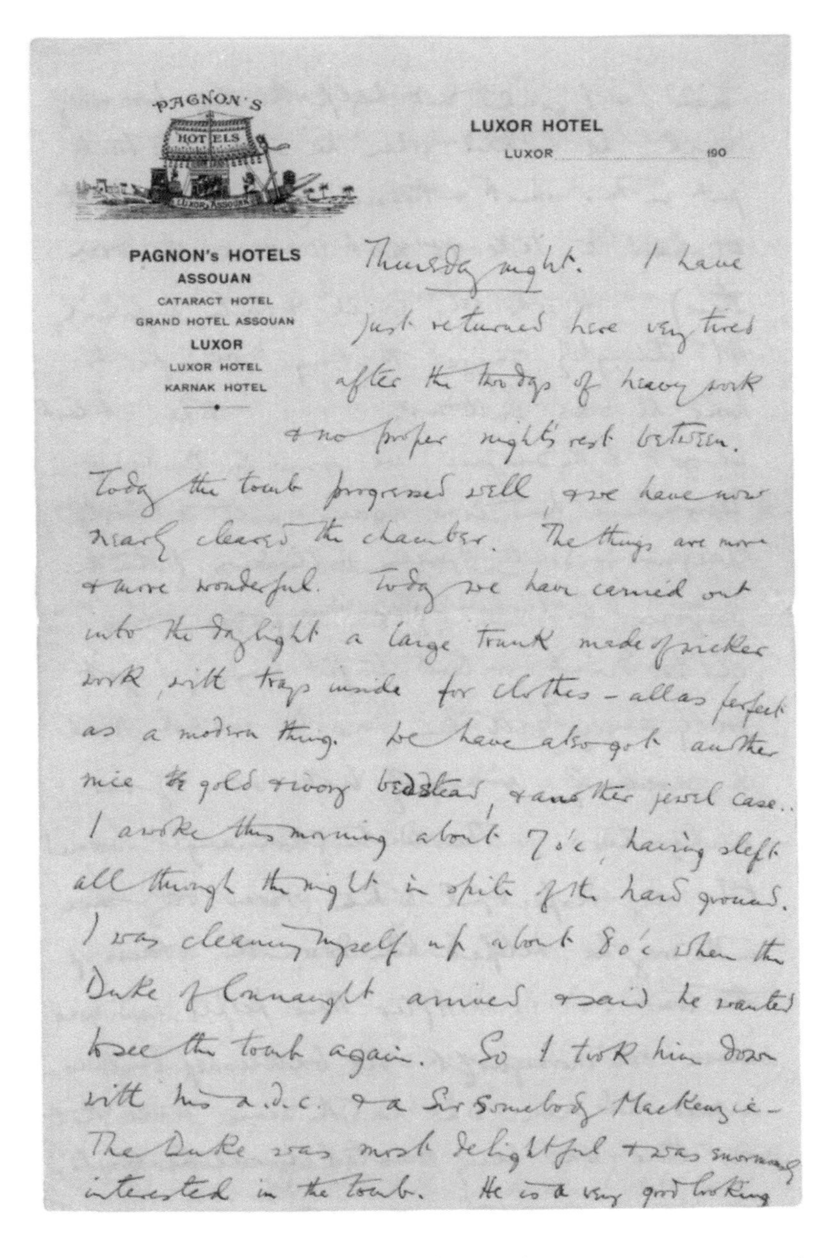

PAGNON'S HOTELS

LUXOR HOTEL
LUXOR 190

PAGNON's HOTELS
ASSOUAN
CATARACT HOTEL
GRAND HOTEL ASSOUAN
LUXOR
LUXOR HOTEL
KARNAK HOTEL

Thursday night. I have just returned here very tired after the two days of heavy work & no proper night's rest between. Today the tomb progressed well, & we have now nearly cleared the chamber. The things are more & more wonderful. Today we have carried out into the daylight a large trunk made of wicker work, with trays inside for clothes – all as perfect as a modern thing. We have also got another nice gold & ivory bedstead, & another jewel case.. I awoke this morning about 7 o'c, having slept all through the night in spite of the hard ground. I was cleaning myself up about 8 o'c when the Duke of Connaught arrived & said he wanted to see the tomb again. So I took him down with his a.d.c. & a Sir Somebody Mackenzie – The Duke was most delightful & was enormously interested in the tomb. He is a very good looking

Figure 7: Extract, Letter II: Thursday, February 16, 1905, Arthur Weigall to Hortense Schleiter. Metropolitan Museum of Art, Department of Egyptian Art, Weigall Archive (image and content © The Metropolitan Museum of Art)

wasted by all these visits. He said he wasn't going to interfere in a matter of such international importance as this discovery, & he refused to stay more than a moment, which was very nice of him.

However, we had hardly got to work again when the Crown Prince of Sweden and Norway arrived; & this time I let him in, & he proved to be very nice.

After we had got rid of him we worked pretty steadily until sunset & then I rode back here. Tomorrow I shall work up there & sleep the night. I am afraid there is not much chance of my being able to write letters properly for some time as I shall be up there all day every day, and shall only return here every other night just for the evening & night.

As I write now I am pretty dead tired, as you can imagine.

The Arabs believe that we have found £20,000 worth of gold & an attack is possible; but we now have masses of police & guards. As a matter of fact the market value of the stuff in the tomb is at least £50,000!

Letter III: Monday, February 20, 1905[80]

[Hotel stationery:] PAGNON'S HOTELS / LUXOR & ASSOUAN
LUXOR HOTEL, LUXOR

[In ink:]
Monday 20th 1905[81]

Little girl, I can't yet write you a proper letter for this old tomb still goes on, & I am up there all day long, only coming back to the hotel every other night just to sleep. I am getting really very tired of it, & need a rest badly. It may go on for another week or ten days I expect. At present we are busily packing the things,[82] *but many of them have to be photographed & patched up before they can be sent off. Luckily it is full moon just now, & we therefore have rather lovely nights, though they are still cold. I do so wish we had been married, because you could have slept up there with me, darling; and then we could have been a real Bint and Ibu*[83] *among our prehistoric cliffs & mountains.*

The social side of things is still going strong, but we have now got rid of all the Princes & such like, I am glad to say.

I was really awfully glad that you talked about the education of our children in your last letter, for it was such a relief, & afforded such a change of thought after the constant mental discussions about the tomb.

I feel bitterly unhappy about not having you here with me now, my precious love: you could have been so much to me. You know Quibell is married, but his wife[84] *has been away all this week. Consequently our camp has been pretty rough; but today she returned & promptly everything became nice, meals were served properly, beds arrived as though by magic (for we have been sleeping on the ground up till now) & everything became suddenly temam,*[85] *as the Arabs say. Women are marvelous creatures!*

By the way, I wonder how you will like looking after the servants & all that sort of thing, darlingest. But if you don't like it, it won't matter, because I can do it fairly well now; & I know all about marketing—at least I know how to direct my servant to do it fairly properly.

I am eagerly waiting for news from you about your visit to Egypt. We shall then be able to talk about everything of the kind. My nomination, I hear, will probably come very shortly now; as people are all rather dissatisfied with Quibell & his sleepy old methods. This tomb business has pushed me forward, I fear rather at his expense, poor old chap; & people are all saying "If only Weigall had been in charge—" not because they know anything about me, but simply because they feel that anybody else would have got things on faster. The feeling among the guards is that I am going to be very severe, & they realize that their two months of go-as-you-please-but-don't-worry-me under Quibell is coming to an end. This is due simply to the fact that they can see my irritation at Quibell's easy methods.

As regards Carter, I have heard nothing very definite; but his resignation or dismissal seems probable I am sorry to say. Playing for such high stakes as he did, he was bound to win hands down or kill himself. Personally I thought he would win.

I am raging to get to work properly on the district. I am going to propose a huge new scheme, but I don't think it will be accepted. I want to dismiss every one of our 300 guards (or whatever their number is) & put in their place only old soldiers. At present the guards are ordinary natives in native dress; & I want to be barbarous enough to have them all in uniform, to drill them, put them through regular gymnastic exercises & keep them in hand as a regular little army. But I must talk about this with you when you come.

O but darling you must come soon. I want you so frightfully badly; and at this critical time in our lives it is so necessary that you should be here to understand all the plans & to advise me & arrange everything properly. O, only to touch you again, to feel you kiss me!—O God!—how I need you Hortense. It is so hateful having to write these horrid little notes when I have so much to say, & when there is so much to answer in your darling letters.

God bless you, my wonder love, my wife. I am always, and every moment, your worshipping husband—Arthur.

Much love to Aunt Carrie

LETTER IV: FRIDAY, FEBRUARY 24, 1905[86]

[In pencil:]
The Valley of the Tombs
Friday 25th [sic]

How I wish you could be up here with me this evening my dearest darling. I am sitting at the mouth of an empty tomb next door to our new one.[87] *All around me the cliffs rise in a stately circle, dark against the latest colours of the sunset. The stars are just showing; & things down here are almost as quiet as they—except for the scrappy conversation of the policemen & guards who are sitting over their fire near the tomb; with just one unfortunate man standing sentry—a rather lonely looking figure, half leaning on his rifle with its fixed bayonet—fixed goodness knows why, for I hope all danger of a raid is over. There is now something of a camp up here that is to say there is a bed, a chair, a table, a lamp, a kitchen, & a cook with all that pertains to his office. But if only you were here, sweetest, we could sleep so snugly in each other's arms under the stars all night. It is now fairly warm—that is to say one hardly realizes that one is outside. The night noises are so delicious, too. Sometimes it is the cry of a jackal, sometimes the hooting of an owl, or the jarring noises of some night bird.*

Since writing the above I have been round making a tour of inspection. The guards proper of the valley live in a little house some 200 yards off,[88] *and as I pass they all come trotting out & form up in a line & salute—I haven't got used to it yet, & this evening I felt quite shy! It is now quite dark, & the circle of cliffs is pitch black against the deepest blue of the star-covered sky. It is simply wonderful. But O my heart is hungry for you, my sweet wonder love.*

We have now done most of the packing & shall not be here more than another three or four days. By that time I am hoping that my nomination will have come & that I can get to work properly on the district. There is such a lot that ought to be done.

I am so anxious about your throat, too, darlingest. I do trust it will not give you any pain, & will not pull you down at all. What was the silly thing that you did which made you ill? You mention it in your darling letter which I got last night; but you don't give me much of a clue—& I especially want to know!

I am altogether most worried about our plans. I believe that things have been squared up with regard to Carter by them sending him to live at Tanta,[89] *a town about an hour's train journey from Cairo on the way to Alexandria. He keeps his district except for Sakkâra which is to be managed by Quibell who will be living there as you know. Carter may regard this as insulting his dignity (& at any rate it is a calamity for us all that the Lower Egyptian inspectorate should not include Sakkâra, & should not have had its head quarters at Cairo). And therefore he may resign. In that case, as I have said, I could probably get my 3½ months leave this summer & then we might be married without difficulty wherever you suggest—perhaps in London at St George's, Hanover Square, or some such regulation marriage church (this to avoid the possibility of St Saviour's). If Carter doesn't go I think I could obtain six weeks marriage leave in September, if you would like me to come home to be married. But it would be almost as easy for you to come out here & £60 less expensive! But I shall know more definitely in a few weeks time. At any rate you see the absolute necessity of your coming out here next month, don't you sweetheart? As to our being married then I don't know what to say—my heart & my mind have such different views about it. I don't see how we are going to wait, & yet I feel that to be married at once would be most impolitic. In the first place we should be thought so eccentric that it would be sure to be discussed. Nobody has ever before got married just at the beginning of the summer you see! You could not stay out after May–June, very well. I fear that the Powers would say "This man Weigall must be a bit of a wrong 'un. He hasn't the decency to wait till the proper time to be married; & anyway what about his work?" You see, sweetheart, I feel more & more that as we are going to take up our position as respectable members of an English-speaking community, with a certain amount of social formalities, we ought to be married in a conventional sort of way (& by Gad!—won't we make up for it when we are by ourselves!). I think Ibu & Bint should have the conventional frock coat & white satin or whatever it is!—it's hateful, & remember it is in no way necessary if you object; but I feel that we ought to conform to the rules of society for this once—(hang it all!). This can be avoided by us being married in Cairo; but in this case we must be strictly correct as to the time of year & such things. We must not be discussed as curiosities!*

O love come soon to me—you know you can't well stay beyond the middle of April, & even then it can be unbearably hot & nasty. Have you received no reply from your father yet, I wonder? You will find Luxor not full in March & we can all have a very jolly time at the hotel; and we can charge the new house too. I have just bought a lot of furniture from the Quibells—chests of drawers, wash-stands, etc. etc; a nice set of dining room chairs made of carved wood in Egyptian style; & three divans, with cushions. As regards colouring the rooms, I think very pale green or pale yellow will do for the wash, don't you? Of course there are no wall papers. But all this you ought to be here to decide, you know darling.

When you come up you should certainly take an Austrian Lloyd from Trieste to Alexandria & should then take train to Cairo. Nothing could be simpler, & all you need do is to wire me the name of the boat & date of arrival & I will have you met. Only come soon beloved!

[In ink:]

I am in awful fear in case this letter is too late for the mail. O love forgive me if it is. I do so hate to seem so horrid about writing letters, but I know you will understand. I do so wish your throat was all right & am anxious about it.

God bless you my sweet wife. Come soon—very soon to your most unspeakably loving husband

Arthur

(   ) At last I am able to send a kiss to you again.

Best love to Aunt Carrie

LETTER V: TUESDAY, FEBRUARY 28, 1905[90]

LUXOR HOTEL, LUXOR

[In ink:]
Feby 27th [sic] *Tuesday*

Dear heart, I can only write you a short note again. It is too bad; but as soon as this tomb is finished I shall have more time. But even then my nomination & consequent business will be arriving! Your darling letter of the 17th-19th arrived this morning. I wonder why you have suddenly taken to addressing me as Weigall without any other names. I am hugely tickled by it, sweetheart: I suppose I must have said "address me as Weigall—Inspector in chief etc"; but of course I didn't mean that the rest of my name was to be dropped. You are a gorgeous darling!—& I should like to hug you for being so funny.

I have, by the by, been having rather an amusing time about my name lately. You know my father's cousin—one Henry Weigall[91] *married a certain Lady Rose Vane, daughter of the Marquis of Westmoreland, who was a relative of his by some earlier connection. Lady Rose Weigall is now an old woman, but she has the most amazing number of friends; and as they are rather rich, she & Henry Weigall have become kind of high-cockalorums of Kent where they live. Personally as my father died so early,*[92] *& as I was entirely brought up by my mother's people, I hardly know these cousins of mine, & the only real connection I have with them is that all the sons were at Wellington.*[93] *Constantly when people hear my name, they effect an introduction by saying that they know my dear mother, or aunt, or cousin, Lady Rose. (They always presume that she is some relation). She must be extraordinarily popular. Then her son—commonly called Gerry Weigall—is a rather well-known sportsman & in this way also people are always claiming relationship; & I get pretty sick of it. But yesterday the climax was reached. I was showing some people round a famous tomb near our new one, when suddenly two old gentlemen passed me, & one whispered something to his guide, who immediately told him who I was, & then shouted out "Hullo Weigall". I didn't know him from Adam; but he said he kind of knew me &*

then started on the Lady Rose business. He was evidently rather a snob, & startled my sensibilities by saying "My name is Parker[94]*—my nephew is Lord Macclesfield—I am member for Oxford—don't you know." All this was leading up to his request to see our new tomb, & as I had nothing else to do I took him there afterwards. He & his friend, an old General, at once became absurdly familiar—& treated me as an old friend! "My dear old Weigall" was the usual way of addressing me! Then he said "By the way I was just telling your dear cousin Lord Londesburg*[95]*—so & so." I said "My cousin??" He said "Why, yes, didn't you see them—they were here a few days ago—they are your cousins you know." I said I didn't know it; but he proved it to me right enough. After that he named various other people—& talked about the "dear old Duke"—also my cousin! Yesterday evening I dined at their table at this hotel, where they are staying, & they gave me very good champagne (which I enjoyed) & I received wild invitations to stay with Parker at his place—something Castle. I should really like to know who I am. Can you tell me, dearest love? I suppose the Londesburgs are some sort of cousins by marriage & I suppose it was pretty rude of me not to take any notice of them when they were here the other day. But as for the rest of the peerage that he mentioned—that's what comes of neglecting to know one's relatives, for as you know I don't care a damn about them. But it is awkward to have strangers giving one information. I must really consult a directory & see who I am!!!*

[In pencil:]

The Valley. No chance of finishing this letter I fear, darlingest. It must go off at once to the post & I must go to my packing. O love I love you madly. I do hope your throat is all right. How I dread that operation. I do wish it were over. The weather is already pretty hot—it seems pretty mad to come out here just as everybody has left (& the place is already emptying) but you MUST come, beloved, to your wildly loving husband Arthur

Letter VI: Saturday, March 4, 1905[96]

[In pencil on a page torn from a notebook:]
Saturday 4th

Sweetheart, I seem to be writing to you from all sorts of odd places. This time it is from the railway station,[97] & the hour is the hottest of the day—1-30 o'c. I am just seeing the boxes of antiquities from the tomb loaded into the train, to be carried to Cairo, & in two hours we shall have said goodbye to the old tomb for good & all.[98]

Your letter of the 24th I found at the hotel today. It was full of a complaint at my not having written. O love, I did try so hard to keep you well posted during that terribly busy time; but I expect the fact of addressing to Hamburg delayed the letters somewhat. I got by the same post a complaint from Mother saying that you hadn't forwarded to her the letter I mentioned to her which gave an account of my adventures. But apparently you hadn't received it yourself. Darlingest, I am so sorry to have appeared so remiss, but you understood, didn't you?

I am so worried about your operation, & also about your coming to Egypt. There has surely been time by now for your father to answer our letters. I am only sorry you didn't hurry on the operation at once, so as to get it over & to be ready to start. However, I suppose the fact of your having been ill delayed it unavoidably. But when I feel the weather getting hotter & hotter & still no sign from you either that you are ready to start or that you have got leave to, I feel pretty wild!! I find that people are already beginning to leave Luxor, & unless you get here by the 20th of the month it will practically be impossible for you to come at all. At least Luxor is empty by the end of March, & the thermometer about 98" or so. O I am so worried, & my nature—which is all for doing things promptly—simply rebels at this delay. I don't know what I shall do if you don't come at all. I don't know how I am going to get through six months & more of absolute isolation & intolerable heat, without the sight of you to start me off comfortably, my precious, precious darling. I am so thoroughly angry with your father about it all.

O I love you so Hortense. I must see you soon. I feel so impotent here—so unable to act. Do O do act for me so that you can come out very soon. God bless you my blessed darling

Your most devotedly loving husband
Arthur

I must dash off now to my boxes

*

How does the story end? Well, Weigall's "boxes" made it safely to the Egyptian Museum in Cairo, where their contents were unpacked and installed under Maspero's supervision, initially in Room T on the upper floor.[99] Here they would be studied by Quibell, under whose name a detailed publication appeared in the *Catalogue général* series in 1908, to complement the volumes *de luxes* Theodore Davis himself put out in 1907 and 1908.[100] In the two principal of these books, the Inspector-designate's efforts received but passing mention,[101] though this would be amply compensated for in the several accounts Weigall penned himself in the years to follow. And of course the young man's confirmation in post eventually did arrive, and it was a job that proved to fit him like a glove.

Soon after his Tanta exile Carter indeed resigned from the Antiquities Service, to eke out a parlous living buying and selling antiquities and painting watercolors,[102] until eventually, in January 1909,[103] Egyptology's *enfant terrible* was taken on by the fifth Earl of Carnarvon to direct his work at Dra Abu'l-Naga. When Davis's concession finally lapsed at the end of 1914, Carter and his sponsor could at last move on to the Valley of the Kings; here, on November 4, 1922, the pair would stumble upon the tomb of Tutankhamun—a find destined to change the face of Egyptology for good and all.

As for Hortense, she and her mother, Carrie, did eventually travel to Luxor—in mid-April, staying in Egypt for six weeks before returning to London to prepare for the wedding. This took place in Cairo after all, on October 11, 1905, and would be followed by a leisurely honeymoon on the Nile, the couple's *dahabiya* venturing as far south as Abu Simbel. These would be happy days, Hortense delighting in her new husband and her exotic surroundings; and though the relationship would ultimately end in tears,[104] Weigall's own breathless adoration held firm for a further twenty years—the consuming passion of a passion-filled life.

Notes

1. Thanks to Elizabeth Fleming, Julie Hankey, Sarah Ketchley, Diana Craig Patch, Catharine H. Roehrig, and Liana Weindling. All Weigall archive quotations and illustrations © The Metropolitan Museum of Art, New York, 2013.
2. MMA 1995.534. Gift of Margaret Orr, 1995.
3. MMA 30.8.56–.58. Theodore M. Davis Collection, Bequest of Theodore M. Davis, 1915.
4. MMA 30.8.59a–b–.60a–b. Theodore M. Davis Collection, Bequest of Theodore M. Davis, 1915.
5. MMA 30.8.6–.64. Theodore M. Davis Collection, Bequest of Theodore M. Davis, 1915.
6. MMA 11.155.7, .9. Gift of Theodore M. Davis, 1911.
7. MMA 10.184.1a–b. Gift of Theodore M. Davis, 1910.
8. MMA 07.316.2–.3. Gift of Mrs. Emma B. Andrews, 1907.
9. Theodore M. Davis, *The Tomb of Iouiya and Touiyou* (London: Archibald Constable & Co., Ltd., 1907); Edouard Naville, *The Funerary Papyrus of Iouiya* (London: Archibald Constable & Co., Ltd., 1908); James Edward Quibell, *The Tomb of Yuaa and Thuiu* (Cairo: Service des antiquités de l'Égypte, 1908)—the most informative contemporary description of the find in situ, with a detailed drawing of the layout. For an archaeological discussion of the deposit, see Nicholas Reeves, *Valley of the Kings: The Decline of a Royal Necropolis* (London: KPI, 1990), 148–153, 160–165; Nicholas Reeves and Richard H. Wilkinson, *The Complete Valley of the Kings* (London: Thames and Hudson, 1996), 174–178.
10. Theodore Montgomery Davis (1838–1915): Morris L. Bierbrier (ed.), *Who Was Who in Egyptology*, fourth revised edition (London: Egypt Exploration Society, 2012), 145–146. See further Daniel Gordon, *The Robber Baron Archaeologist: An Essay about the Life of Theodore M. Davis* (Baltimore: Johns Hopkins University, 2007); John M. Adams, "'Generous Benefactor' or 'Arrogant Ignoramus'? Theodore M. Davis and his Excavators 1900–1914," *Kmt* 22.2 (2011): 54–65; Adams, *The Millionaire and the Mummies* (New York: St Martin's Press, 2013).
11. Held in the Department of Egyptian Art, The Metropolitan Museum of Art.
12. Gaston Camille Charles Maspero (1846–1916): Bierbrier, *Who Was Who*, 359–361. See Elisabeth David, *Gaston Maspero 1846–1916: Le gentleman égyptologue* (Paris: Pygmalion, 1999); David (ed.), *Lettres d'Égypte: correspondance avec Louise Maspero, 1883–1914* (Paris: Seuil, 2003) (not seen).
13. Howard Carter (1874–1939): Bierbrier, *Who Was Who*, 105–106. Thomas Garnet Henry James, *Howard Carter: The Path to Tutankhamun* (London: Kegan Paul International, 1992); H. Victor F. Winstone, *Howard Carter and the Discovery of*

the Tomb of Tutankhamun, revised edition (Manchester: Barzan, 2006); Nicholas Reeves and John H. Taylor, *Howard Carter Before Tutankhamun* (London: British Museum Press, 1992).

14 See James, *Howard Carter*, 97–120; Reeves and Taylor, *Howard Carter*, 80–84; Julie Hankey, *A Passion for Egypt: Arthur Weigall, Tutankhamun and the "Curse of the Pharaohs"* (London: I.B. Tauris, 2001), 51–52 and passim. Carter's own detailed file on the incident is preserved in the Griffith Institute, Oxford: Carter MSS, v. 107–148.

15 It is a period well covered from various angles in a range of sources: see in particular Emma B. Andrews' "A Journal on the *Bedawin* 1889–1912: The Diary Kept on Board the Dahabiyeh of Theodore M. Davis During Seventeen [*sic*] Trips up the Nile" (typescript "by E. P. B.," 1918; copies in the Department of Egyptian Art, The Metropolitan Museum of Art, and the Library of the American Philosophical Society, Philadelphia [Mss. 916.2.An2]); Hankey, *Passion for Egypt*; James, *Howard Carter*, 97–120; Joseph Lindon Smith, *Tombs, Temples, and Ancient Art* (Norman: University of Oklahoma Press, 1956), 26–42.

16 Arthur Edward Pearse Brome Weigall (1880–1934): Bierbrier, *Who Was Who*, 570; Julie Hankey, "Arthur Weigall and the Tomb of Yuya and Thuyu: A Letter from Luxor, 1905," *Kmt* 9.2 (1998): 41–45; Hankey, *Passion for Egypt*, which draws upon and quotes from the letters I here publish in full. The Metropolitan Museum Weigall archive includes greater or lesser coverage of the following topics: Petrie Abydos excavations, 1901; the so-called "Saqqara Incident," which resulted in Howard Carter's resignation from the *Service des Antiquités* in 1905; monuments of Lower Nubia; the excavations of Theodore M. Davis in the Valley of the Kings from 1905 on (including the discovery of Yuya and Tjuyu [KV 46], Tomb 55, the Gold Tomb [KV 56], Horemhab [KV 57], and other finds); the early work of Lord Carnarvon at Thebes; Weigall's efforts towards the preservation and administration of the private tombs at Thebes (in collaboration with Alan Gardiner, for their *Topographical Catalogue of the Private Tombs of Thebes* [London: Bernard Quaritch, 1913]); Weigall's investigations in the Eastern Desert; Antiquities Department and general Egyptological politics during the period 1901–1914; the social aspects of life as Chief Inspector of Antiquities in Luxor between 1905–1914; events surrounding the discovery of the tomb of Tutankhamun, 1923. The archive includes many letters covering the periods 1901–1914 and 1923–1924 and later, many from Weigall to his wife but others from professional correspondents including: Edward R. Ayrton; Wilhelm von Bissing; James Henry Breasted; the fifth Earl of Carnarvon; Howard Carter; Norman de Garis Davies; Theodore M. Davis; Cecil Firth; Alan H. Gardiner; Francis Llewellyn Griffith; Henry Reginald Hall; Georges Legrain; Albert M. Lythgoe; Arthur C. Mace; David Randall-MacIver; Gaston Maspero; Sir Robert Mond; Flinders Petrie; James E. Quibell; Günther Roeder; Archibald Henry Sayce; Grafton Elliot Smith; Herbert E. Winlock;

and Leonard Woolley. There are also a number of pencil or ink sketches of various Egyptologists, either stand-alone or within the text of letters, three of which are reproduced here as Figure 2.

17 James Edward Quibell (1867–1935): Bierbrier, *Who Was Who,* 450–451.

18 Hankey, *Passion for Egypt,* passim.

19 To mention just one: Weigall's perceptive analysis of "Tomb 55" in the Valley of the Kings, which remains one of the sanest treatments of that controversial burial: Arthur Weigall, "The Mummy of Akhenaten," *JEA* 8 (1922): 193–200.

20 Numbered in ink: "82." Plain envelope. Addressed to "Miss Hortense Schleiter / Pension Herter / Kramgasse 5. / Berne Switzerland," and postmarked "Louxor 11 I *[sic]* 05." The reverse is annotated in Hortense's hand: "Written Luxor Medinet Habu, LUXOR, / Friday Noon February 10th / & Saturday February 11th 1905. / Received Berne Friday Evening / February 17th / Answered Friday February 17th & Saturday 18th."

21 Weigall is evidently sitting in the Antiquities Service house, described in a letter Carter wrote home to his mother on August 24, 1900, illustrated with photographs, when he first took up the post: see Reeves and Taylor, *Howard Carter Before Tutankhamun,* 57–58. The veranda is seen in the photograph on page 57.

22 See the Carter photographs in Reeves and Taylor, *Howard Carter Before Tutankhamun,* 57 and 58, bottom left and right.

23 A municipality in Starnberg district, Bavaria, on the western shore of Lake Starnberg, southwest of Munich, where Arthur and Hortense had evidently spent time together.

24 The safeguarding of the Theban private tombs would be a priority and notable achievement of Weigall's time as Inspector, engendering the *Topographical Catalogue of the Private Tombs of Thebes* (London: Quaritch, 1913), prepared in collaboration with Alan H. Gardiner. For the background to Weigall's efforts in that enterprise and the somewhat fraught matter of publication, see Hankey, *Passion for Egypt,* passim.

25 See above, note 13.

26 See above, note 17.

27 Prince Arthur, Duke of Connaught and Strathearn (1850–1942), the seventh child and third son of Queen Victoria and Prince Albert of Saxe-Coburg and Gotha.

28 The work of this season began on December 17, 1904 (Quibell, *Yuaa and Thuiu,* i) and the tomb's "top step" was uncovered "in the late afternoon of February 5, 1905" (Smith, *Tombs, Temples,* 27). Davis seems to have been alerted only the next day: see Andrews, "Journal," entry for Monday, February 6—"A very windy day—Theo and the girls in spite of it, went over to the Valley, where when Theodore appeared the workmen greeted him with a cheer, and he knew it meant some sign of promise—and the men had found the lintel of a door to a tomb. They said they might clear it to the entrance in a few days. Very encouraging." Shortly after the "second and third steps were found, …

the rubbish above came down in an avalanche, making further progress difficult" (Smith, *Tombs, Temples*, 27).

29 Clearly a second "avalanche": see the previous note. The intention clearly came to naught. Joseph Lindon Smith records the sight that met the excavators' eyes on February 11 (*Tombs, Temples*, 27): "On February 11, the top of the doorway was uncovered." He continues: "It had originally been walled up, but the seals had been broken, therefore the tomb below was not an 'untouched' one. The workmen were dismissed and they scrambled over the *gebel* to their Qurna homes, to spread the news. Weigall kept with him only the *reis* [foreman] of the diggers and his small son, who was 'captain' of the basket carriers."

30 See above, note 14.

31 Caroline Schleiter, née Hazlett, mother of Hortense. Her husband, Hortense's father, was Oscar, a financier: see Hankey, *Passion for Egypt*, 38–39.

32 Numbered in ink: "83." Luxor Hotel envelope (PAGNON'S HOTELS. [etc.]/ LUXOR & ASSOUAN). Addressed to "Miss Hortense Schleiter. / c/o Herrn Kapitän Hermann Volborth. / Osterstrasse 143 / Eimsbüttel / Hamburg. Germany" and postmarked "Louxor 17 II 05." The letter was then forwarded to "[...] Pension Herter / 5 Kramgasse / Bern Schweitz[?]." The reverse is annotated in Hortense's hand: "Written Luxor—Tues 14th, Wed 15th & Thursday Evening 16th / Re[ceive]d Berne—Saturday afternoon / Feb. 25th / Answered Thursday / March 2nd." There is too in the archive a copy of the principal, descriptive section of this letter, evidently in Hortense's hand for circulation to Weigall's mother, as he had requested.

33 A modern dating, to include the Twentieth Dynasty, would be 1502–1086 BCE.

34 See below, note 58.

35 See above, note 10.

36 Thutmose IV (KV 43): Theodore M. Davis et al., *The Tomb of Thoutmôsis IV* (Westminster: Archibald Constable & Co., 1904). Archaeological discussion: Reeves, *Valley of the Kings*, 34–38 and 50–53; Reeves and Wilkinson, *Complete Valley of the Kings*, 105–108.

37 (Thutmose I and) Hatshepsut (KV 20): Davis, *The Tomb of Hâtshopsîtû* (London: Archibald Constable & Co., Ltd., 1906). Archaeological discussion: Reeves, *Valley of the Kings*, 13–17 and 27–29; Reeves and Wilkinson, *Complete Valley of the Kings*, 91–94.

38 Cf. Henry Copley Greene, "A Great Discovery in Egypt. The Tomb of the Parents of Tii," *The Century Magazine* 71.1 (November 1905): 60–75, with a plan and cross-section of the tomb and stratigraphical section over the entrance on page 75. The upper layer of debris is there labeled as "Rubbish of Ramses III," the lower as "Rounded pebble and gravel deposit Ramses III and Ramses XII [scil. XI]." These data had been prepared by Joseph Lindon Smith (*Tombs, Temples*, 39), clearly the source too for the photographs and much of the detail.

[39] A Weigall photograph of the tomb entrance at the time of the discovery is reproduced in Arthur E. P. Weigall, "Excavating in Egypt, Where Rich Treasures Sometimes Reward the Digger," *Putnam's Magazine* 6 (April–September 1909): 402.

[40] Smith (*Tombs, Temples*, 27) provides colourful detail: "Davis arrived posthaste from his *dahabieh*. A course of the walled-up doorway was taken down, the ... turban [of the *reis*'s young son—see above, note 29] was unwound and tied under [the child's] arms, and his father lowered him through the opening much against the boy's will, as he kept crying out that he was afraid of *afreet* (evil spirits) in the dark. Weigall's purpose was to have the boy discover whether the passageway was empty of rubbish and if there were inscriptions on the walls ... The heart-rending cries of the thoroughly scared little boy ended his ordeal. After he had said that there were no inscriptions or reliefs on the wall and the entrance passage was clear, he was hauled out by his father."

[41] As Smith suggests (*Tomb, Temples*, 27), these were actually recovered by the *reis*'s son.

[42] For the robbery of the tomb and its dating, see Reeves, *Valley of the Kings*, and Reeves and Wilkinson, *Complete Valley of the Kings*, as in note 9, above.

[43] Mrs. Andrews' journal completes the tale on "6th Sunday after Epiphany—Feb. 12:" "... Theo and Weigall rode over to the Valley of the Kings this afternoon—when Theo got home he brought with him two or three queer parcels—and he had an air of great elation. He first unwrapped a yoke of a chariot, finely decorated in gold and colour—in perfect condition, then a long baton, or wand of office—also finely decorated—then produced a large beautiful green, hard stone scarab, with gilded bands, beautifully inscribed even to the wings. He said that the workmen had reached the door of the tomb chamber, and they went down into it. A small aperture had been broken in this door, large enough to admit a man. This door was of stone, plastered with mud—with many seals on it—and the tomb had been broken into in ages gone by—for the things Theo found in the corridor and brought home, had no doubt been dropped by the thieves. Weigall remained behind, to sleep with the guards at the tomb, and Mr. and Mrs. Smith [see next note] also went over to stay with him. Theo wrote a note to M. Maspero and Mr. Sayce [see note 75] who arrived on the [*dahabiya*] Istar yesterday, to come and see the things. They all came over in the evening. Mrs. Sheldon Amos, who is staying with Mr. Sayce, also came."

[44] This is not quite the way that Smith, *Tombs, Temples*, 28, remembers it: "At that moment Weigall arrived [at Davis's boat], and Maspero, turning to him, asked: 'Who is guarding the tomb through the night?' Weigall explained that there were planks across the entrance and the door was walled up and sealed, and that in the valley were twelve *ghaffir* (tomb guards), all picked men who had fought under Kitchener at Khartoum, and who took turns on duty, six by day

and six by night. Maspero said emphatically that this was not enough in the way of protection. 'I have already heard in Luxor this afternoon that a tomb has been found in the valley filled with gold ... You must yourself spend the night near the tomb.'"

45 In fact Joseph Lindon Smith (1863–1950): Bierbrier, *Who Was Who*, 516. His papers, including a diary for the period in question, are preserved in the Archives of American Art, Smithsonian Institution, Washington.

46 Smith, *Tombs, Temples*, 29, indicates that the nervous "Weigall accepted the offer eagerly."

47 Corinna Putnam (Lindon) Smith, who edited Joseph Lindon Smith's posthumous memoir *Tombs, Temples, and Ancient Art* (note 15, above) for publication after his death. Her papers are preserved in the Schlesinger Library, Radcliffe Institute for Advanced Study, Harvard, though apparently contain nothing of immediate note.

48 Quibell, *Yuaa and Thuiu*, i. The events of the day are described in Mrs. Andrews' journal, entry for Monday, February 13, 1905: "We all made an early start for the Valley this morning. Alice [Emma Andrews' niece] had not been feeling very well for a few days—and was so melancholy at the idea of being left behind on the opening day of the tomb, that I persuaded Theodore to send for one of the Victorias [French horse-drawn carriages] that occasionally take people over—and she and I rode over most comfortably. We had to go on our donkeys across the wide sand waste—and then take the carriage and we had to get out for the ascent and descent of the high canal embankment. But the moment we entered the valley, the going was very good. We found Weigall and the Smiths, the native Inspector, and Maspero and his Secretary soon arrived. The inner door was ordered down—and while it was being done, Theo and M. Maspero made a long and hot climb to look at a certain site the latter thought favourable—and the rest of us sat on the rocks, or in the carriage from which the horses had been taken. Mrs. Smith who was wildly enthusiastic about the whole thing, said that the night had been one of the most beautiful she had ever spent. They felt the cold very much, and got up twice to make tea—and again very early and climbed to one of the highest points to see the sun rise."

49 Mrs. Andrews' journal, entry for Monday, February 13, provides a little more detail: "In half an hour the native Inspector came out of the tomb and said to Weigall 'the entrance is free.' He and Mr. Smith went down, and in a short time Weigall came up pale and breathless. I thought he had been affected by bad air—but it was only excitement—for he ejaculated 'wonderful' 'extraordinary' etc. Mr. Smith said, 'there is everything there but a grand piano,—the place is crowded with furniture and coffins ...'"

50 Mrs. Andrews again, Monday, February 13, 1905: "We waited until M. Maspero and Theodore were back, when they at once went down and stayed a long time. The tomb was so accessible, opening by its first flight of steps on a level with the pathway—from which a short descending corridor leads to

another short stairway, which gives immediate access to the tomb chamber. It lies just between No's 3 and 4—the former an unfinished tomb intended for Ramses III—4 also unfinished—the tomb of Ramses XII [scil. XI]. Neither M. Maspero or Quibell thought this site worth working, but Theo in his thorough way said he should go on clearing up both sides of that side valley—and it was just by this method that he found the tomb of Thothmes IV and Hatshepsut. It is remarkable that this tomb, crowded in between 3 and 4 could have escaped complete spoilation [*sic*] ..."

51 Alfred Lucas's analysis later revealed these still-viscous remains to be castor oil: Quibell, *Yuaa and Thuiu*, 75–76.

52 In current spelling Yuya.

53 In current spelling Tjuyu.

54 Current spelling Tiye, the wife of pharaoh Amenhotep III.

55 The Weigall archive includes a sepia photograph of the face of Yuya's mummy taken by Weigall shortly after the discovery: see Figure 5. The sole previous publication of this image appears to have been Weigall, *Putnam's Magazine* 6 (1909), 406.

56 The dates again require correction. Yuya and Tjuyu lived during the fifteenth–fourteenth centuries BCE.

57 Mrs. Andrews' version of events, Monday, February 13: "When these men [Davis, Maspero, and Quibell] at last appeared they told us wondrous tales, and allowed us one by one to go down—by the light of candles I could see a dim glitter of gold everywhere and a confusion of coffins and mummies."

58 Mrs. Andrews' journal, the same day: "Arrangements were made at once for bringing electric wires into the tomb, as the Duke of Connaught was expected in the afternoon and M. Maspero was very pleased to be able to give him such a sight." The "engine room," in which the Valley of the Kings' electric generator had been installed by Carter in early 1903 (Howard Carter, "Report on General Work Done in the Southern Inspectorate," *ASAE* 4 (1903): 43), was tomb KV 18 (the tomb of Ramesses X); photographs of the apparatus, which is still in place, may be found in Hanna Jenni, *Das Grab Ramses' X (KV18)* (Basel: Schwabe & Co. AG, 2000), 17–19.

59 Mrs. Andrews, February 13: " ... we all went up to the Thothmes IV plateau, where Jones (the butler) had lunch for us. Too soon after this M. Maspero and Theo started for the tomb again in the hot sun—and we followed. They went immediately into it—and when in about 20 minutes I saw one rushing up and demanding water and brandy, I knew that Theo must have fainted as he did a few years ago, under exactly the same circumstances. When I reached the first flight of steps, I saw that two people were supporting him at the bottom step, bathing his head and hands. He called up to me however that he was about over it—and was soon able to be helped up—and took refuge in the carriage—and soon seemed none the worse for it."

60 Mrs. Andrews, "Journal," Monday, February 13: "... About 4 o'clock, the Duke and his party arrived with a military escort—and went down into the tomb.

We had withdrawn to a respectful distance and were sitting on the rocks—when the Duke, a fine soldierly looking fellow and M. Maspero emerged. The Duke strode over the rocks to where Theodore was, and heartily congratulated him, and begged to present him to the Duchess ..."

61 Spencer Compton Cavendish, eighth Duke of Devonshire (1833–1908). Maspero was at that moment showing the tomb to Corinna Smith, and an amusing commentary of what occurred next may be found in Smith, *Tombs, Temples*, 33: "[Maspero:] 'Doubtless you are the first woman that's been in this tomb chamber alive—there's a dead one over there,' and he pointed out the coffin containing the body of [Tjuyu]"—at which point the Duke of Devonshire, ignoring Weigall's warning of the tomb's lack of air, entered the burial chamber. "He glared at [Corinna Smith] and she heard him mutter angrily, 'So it's a d— American woman using up the air!'"

62 Sir John Evans, KCB, FRS (1823–1908), English archaeologist and geologist, author of *The Ancient Stone Implements, Weapons and Ornaments, of Great Britain* (second edition, London: Longmans, Green, and Co., 1897).

63 Oscar Gustaf Adolf, the future King Gustav V of Sweden (1858–1950).

64 Emma B. Andrews, "Journal," February 13: "... After they [the Duke and Duchess of Connaught] left, Mr. Quibell came very much disgruntled, to find the tomb had been opened in his absence ..."

65 Edward Russell Ayrton (1882–1914): Bierbrier, *Who Was Who*, 29.

66 At Deir el-Bahri, where he was working at the Eleventh Dynasty temple of Nebhepetre Mentuhotep with H.R. Hall and the Egypt Exploration Fund.

67 Doña Maria Eugenia Ignacia Augustina de Palafox-Portocarrero de Guzmán y Kirkpatrick, sixteenth Countess of Teba and fifteenth Marquise of Ardales (1826–1920)—the wife of Napoleon III and Empress Consort of France, 1853–1871.

68 Weigall makes no mention of the now-infamous Eugénie incident later recounted by Joseph Lindon Smith, *Tombs, Temples*, 41–42: "Without knowing who she was, Quibell said, 'I am sorry your Highness has come at so late a date that nothing remains of the treasures that were found in the tomb when we opened it.' The woman replied, 'Do tell me something of the discovery of the tomb.' Quibell said, 'With pleasure, but I regret I cannot offer you a chair.' Quickly came her answer: 'Why, there is a chair which will do for me nicely.' And before our horrified eyes she stepped down onto the floor of the chamber and seated herself in a chair which had not been sat in for over three thousand years! But the anticipated catastrophe did not take place." If the incident ever occurred, Smith may simply have adapted the chronology for dramatic effect.

69 Mrs. Andrews' journal, Tuesday, February 14: "Another day with all the family again to the Valley. Again I had the carriage and took Mme. Maspero with me. Mr. Sayce and Mrs. Sheldon Amos also went over—and we had an open lunch table at the Thothmes plateau—all of these, with the Abbe Théadent, Weigall, Smith and Ayrton ... The tomb was visited today by the Ex-Empress Eugénie, and also by Prince Gustave Adolphe of Sweden. He and

Theo seem to have struck up quite a friendship. Theo was much pleased with him—a sensible, intelligent young fellow. He was very enthusiastic about what he saw, and said 'Moi, Je suis aussi explorer—je fouille dans mon pays—si ca m'arrivera de venir ici pour fuiller comme vous!' One of his aide-de-camps after sent Mr. Davis a note thanking him again and again. Also the Duke and Duchess of Devonshire saw it."

70 Emma B. Andrews, "Journal," Wednesday February 15: "Theo and Mr. Sayce went over to the tomb and spent the day—we stayed at home ..."

71 Count Malvezzi de' Medici. He "informed us volubly about being a Coptic scholar, and that Bernard Berenson [the Renaissance art historian] said about him that he'd been 'brought up by too many maiden aunts'" (Smith, *Tombs, Temples*, 30).

72 Arthur George Maule Ramsay, fourteenth Earl of Dalhousie (1878–1928).

73 Presumably Evelyn Baring (1841–1917), first Earl of Cromer, British Consul-General of Egypt.

74 Louisa Frederica Augusta Cavendish, Duchess of Devonshire, formerly Louisa Montagu, Duchess of Manchester, née Luise Fredericke Auguste Countess von Alten (1832–1911).

75 Revd. Archibald Henry Sayce (1845–1933): Bierbrier, *Who Was Who*, 489–490. See his *Reminiscences* (London: Macmillan and Co., 1923), 323.

76 Mrs. Andrews' journal, Thursday, February 16: "A warm, calm day—over to the Valley again, but I in my donkey chair. I saw the different things found in the tomb well today for the first time—as they had been brought out of the tomb and placed in that of Ramses XII [scil. XI]. The most wonderful and varied collection of beautiful things in perfect condition. The 2 mummies of Yuaa and Tuaa, well preserved and very impressive, despite the fact that Tuaa's eyes are wide open. They had double coffins of the finest workmanship literally overlaid with gold—chairs, boxes, 3 funeral couches, vases, scarabs, a great roll of papyrus, etc. etc. extraordinarily rich—a wonderful find ..."

77 Unknown.

78 Unknown.

79 John Isaac Thornycroft (1843–1928), founder of the Thornycroft shipbuilding company, Church Wharf, Chiswick.

80 Letter no. [84]. No envelope.

81 For Saturday, February 18, Mrs. Andrews' journal records: "Theo and the girls [Mrs. Andrews' nieces] went to the Valley again—Weigall came back with them and had tea. He still sleeps at the tomb." The next day the Davis party sailed for Aswan ("I don't know for what unless to give Theodore a rest"), leaving the archaeologists to continue with their work.

82 Tellingly, Smith mentions that *he* had been charged by Quibell to be his assistant in this; perhaps Weigall was no longer in such good odour with the colleague he had found so much fault with!

83 Mrs. and Mr.

84 Annie Abernethie Quibell (née Pirie) (1862–1927), an Egyptologist in her own right: Bierbrier, *Who Was Who*, 450.

85 Fine.

86 Numbered in ink: "85." Plain envelope. Addressed to "Miss Hortense Schleiter. / c/o Herrn Kapitän H. Volborth. / Osterstrasse 143 / Eimsbüttel / Hamburg Germany" and postmarked "Louxor 26 II 05." The letter was then forwarded to "[...] Pension Herter / 5 Kramgasse / Bern Schweitz[?]." The reverse is annotated in Hortense's hand: "Written Valley of Tombs of the Kings / Friday Feb. 24th 1905 / Re[ceive]d Wednesday Noon March 8th / Answered Wednesday Evening March 8th."

87 Weigall may be referring to KV 3 (tomb of an unidentified son of Ramesses III), which Smith, *Tombs, Temples*, records was being used as a workshop during the clearance of KV 46. Alternatively, KV 4, on the opposite side of the Yuya-Tjuyu tomb, commonly known as "the lunching tomb," may have been equipped with a table and chairs.

88 Cf. the photograph in Howard Carter and Arthur C. Mace, *The Tomb of Tut.ankh.Amen* I (London: Cassell and Company Limited, 1923), pl. XI.

89 See James, *Howard Carter*, esp. 122–140.

90 Numbered in ink: "86." Plain envelope. Addressed to "Miss Hortense Schleiter / Pension Herter / Kramgasse 5. / Berne. Switzerland.," and postmarked "Louxor 1 III 05." Weigall has written on the back of the envelope: "Forgive the address written with a piece of wood. I suppose you are now definitely at Berne I can address to the pension again." The reverse is further annotated in Hortense's hand: "Written Luxor Tuesday Feb. 28th 1905 / Re[ceive]d Berne Tuesday Evening March 7th / Answered Wednesday Evening March 8th."

91 For these various family relationships see Hankey, *Passion for Egypt*, 5–16.

92 Weigall's father, Captain Arthur Archibald Denne Weigall, died on active service in the Afghan Expedition at Kandahar. He had been Paymaster to the 11th (North Devon) Regiment. See Hankey, *A Passion for Egypt*, 5.

93 Wellington College at Crowthorne in Berkshire, the British public (i.e. private) school where Weigall was educated.

94 Presumably the Hon. Francis Parker (1851–?), who served as Conservative Member of Parliament for South Oxford, 1886–1895.

95 Presumably Charles John Brinsley Butler, seventh Earl of Lanesborough (1865–1929).

96 Numbered in ink: "87." Luxor Hotel envelope (PAGNON'S HOTELS / LUXOR & ASSOUAN). Addressed to Miss Hortense Schleiter, Pension Herter, Kramgasse 5, Berne, Switzerland, and postmarked "Louxor 5 III 05." The letter was then forwarded to "Guisisana, Theresien Strasse 82, München, Germany." The reverse is annotated in Hortense's hand: "Written Railway Station Luxor Saturday Afternoon March 4th 05 / Received Munich, Tuesday evening March 14th / Answered Thursday Afternoon March 16th."

97 Luxor.

[98] Smith, *Tombs, Temples*, 40: "After nearly three weeks the 'working' of the tomb was finished, and a large number of heavy cases were ready for camel transport to the river. Over one hundred men were assembled for the difficult job which began at dawn. Unfortunately, the day was unusually hot. Quibell slept on the river bank that night, to be on hand for putting the cases on the train under a police guard." (Greene, "Great Discovery," 66, shows a photograph of the baggage train duly loaded on donkeys(?) and about to depart the Valley of the Kings; Weigall, "Excavating in Egypt," 404 shows a Quibell photograph of Yuya's gigantic wooden outer coffin standing upright outside the tomb, a series of wooden planks presumably for the construction of its crate lying on the ground behind; on page 405 is a Weigall photograph of one of the beds sitting upon its wooden crate ["No. 28"].) The "most valuable objects" were to make the trip to Cairo on board Davis's *dahabiya* (Smith, *Tombs, Temples*, 38).

[99] Gaston Maspero, *Guide to the Cairo Museum*, translated by J. E. and A. A. Quibell, third edition (Cairo: Service des Antiquités, 1906), 431–440.

[100] See above, note 9.

[101] Davis, *Iouiya and Touiyou*, xxvi–xxviii; Quibell *Yuaa and Thuiu*, ii. Weigall would, however, produce an article in 1909 in which he included an account of the Yuya-Tjuyu find: Weigall, "Excavating in Egypt," 397–411. The discovery is discussed on pages 403–407. This would later form the basis of chapter seven of Arthur E. P. B. Weigall, *The Treasury of Ancient Egypt* (Chicago and New York: Rand McNally and Company, 1912), 165–184, and of the same author's revised *The Glory of the Pharaohs* (New York: G.P. Putnam's Sons, 1923), 127–130.

[102] Including the colour illustrations for Davis, *Iouiya and Touiyou*, pls. I, XIII, XVIII–XXVII–XXIX, XXXII, XXXV, XXXVII–XXXIX, XLIII, and the ink sketches on pp. 36, 38–40, 43.

[103] See T. G. H. James, "Howard Carter and Mrs Kingsmill Marrs," in Peter Der Manuelian (ed.), *Studies in Honor of William Kelly Simpson* I (Boston: Museum of Fine Arts, 1996), 420, note 11.

[104] See Hankey, *Passion for Egypt*, 288–291.

The Temple of Millions of Years of Amenhotep II at Thebes: New Discoveries

Angelo Sesana
Centre for Egyptology Francesco Ballerini

This brief report describes recent excavations of tombs of Middle Kingdom and Third Intermediate Period date found during excavations of the Temple of Millions of Years of Amenhotep II at Thebes. Among the finds were remains of burials, including that of an infant. Regarding the temple itself, preparations are being made to remove the dekka, and restoration of the temple ramp is underway.

> *To Richard H. Wilkinson,* in recognition of his extraordinary contribution to Egyptology and his outstanding commitment to the archaeological world.

In 1997, when I looked at the piles of dirt and debris located north of the Ramesseum, I wondered what could still remain of Amenhotep II's "temple of millions of years,"[1] which dates back to the middle of the Eighteenth Dynasty. The famous British archaeologist W. M. Flinders Petrie, during his hasty excavations in the late 1800s,[2] had already identified the monument as belonging to the famous "pharaoh athlete."

Encouraged by the French Egyptologist Christian Leblanc (under whom I worked for several years), I decided that maybe it would be worthwhile to free the temple area from the layers of debris, to reveal the few ruins that still remained of Amenhotep's monument. The Egyptian authorities of the Supreme Council of Antiquities granted permission to excavate and restore the archaeological remains, and then the Centre for Egyptology Francesco Ballerini (Como, Italy), of which I am director, proceeded with the difficult job.

During the fifteen archaeological expeditions that have since followed without interruption, it did not take long to obtain good results.[3] Thanks to the plans that were gradually drawn up, we can now imagine the grandeur of the monument and speculate on the reason for its rapid transformation and destruction (Figure 1).

During the archaeological excavations, my collaborators and I have been able to identify, and investigate thoroughly, twenty-four funerary shafts dating to the Third Intermediate Period and Ptolemaic Period. Most had been pillaged, both in ancient times and more recently. Here, we present the latest discoveries that have allowed us to determine the occupation of the area, which was used as a necropolis long before the construction of Amenhotep II's temple.

Figure 1: The area of the temple of Amenhotep II in 2012 (photograph © T. Quirino, CEFB)

The shaft of L13, dug into the conglomerate and filled with scattered human and animal bones and pottery dating to different periods (Ptolemaic, Roman, and Coptic), leads to two chambers, one of which had already been excavated. This year the excavation was therefore concentrated on the second and larger chamber, B, measuring about 3 x 3.5 m. Inside, the remains of at least four coffins in a poor state of preservation were brought to light; only scattered traces of painted stucco (red or blue lines on a white background) have been preserved. However, one of the fragments still showed a rather large stretch of figurative decoration on the bottom. Alongside the coffins, two boxes containing mud shabtis with a blue wash (in imitation of faience) were also found.

Figure 2: Canopic jars discovered in Third Intermediate Period tomb R11 (photograph © T. Quirino, CEFB)

R11 is the last of the twenty-four funerary shafts of the Third Intermediate Period identified and excavated in the area of the Temple of Amenhotep II. In the filling of the shaft we found many earlier materials, including two amphorae almost completely reconstructed from fragments mixed with animal bones. At the bottom of the shaft, which reaches the depth of ±4 m, we found two chambers: one toward the west (B) and the other toward the east (A). For the time being, we are working in chamber B. Inside we found four canopic jars, certainly part of the funerary equipment (Figure 2), and, in a coffin that was virtually destroyed, we found a skeleton showing evidence of mummification. Next to the coffin we found about 400 shabtis in raw clay, still showing a light blue colour; these were probably once contained in a wooden box, which has now totally vanished. Along with the four canopic jars we found a roughly made and still unfinished dummy canopic jar.

In the cleaning of the area around the burial located in F23 (excavated during the last archaeological expedition) we found another burial, excavated in a niche between the conglomerate and a layer of compacted sand, certainly belonging to the Middle Kingdom (late Twelfth–early Thirteenth Dynasty): the sepulchre of a baby.[5] The sarcophagus in which the infant was buried is made out of terracotta. Along with the poorly preserved remains of the small skeleton, inside the sarcophagus itself we found three small vases, two small supports for vases, and four small bowls (Figure 3). The sarcophagus was closed by a thick cover also made out of terracotta. We have been able to restore the sarcophagus, which, while being in good condition, showed a crack in one corner of the main body. The cover was in bad condition, as it was broken. The restoration allowed us to reconstruct most of the item, but part of the cover is still missing.

Figure 3: The terracotta sarcophagus under excavation (photograph © T. Quirino, CEFB)

The excavation of tomb D21, which dates to the Middle Kingdom–Second Intermediate Period, started in 2007 but was interrupted due to safety concerns. This very large tomb, partially excavated in the conglomerate and in the solid sand, is still under study. The structure consists of a corridor and at least two chambers excavated in the conglomerate level. It is completely lacking in decoration, and the ceiling has partly collapsed. The tomb is nevertheless full of pottery and human remains, the study of which will be of great interest. The materials excavated during this mission, including hemispherical bowls, beer jars, and a stone kohl pot, confirm the chronology estimated for this burial. The very bad state of the conglomerate compelled us to stop the excavation again. In order to protect the tomb itself and to create safe conditions to continue our work, we have begun to secure the ceiling by constructing some vaults along the corridor leading to the inner rooms. We hope to continue this work during the next expedition.

Figure 4: The ramp leading to the columned courtyard after consolidation work (photograph © T. Quirino, CEFB)

During the last mission, we have also taken up the cleaning of the small chambers delimited by thin walls in sectors A11-13/B-C10, in order to remove the *dekka* (flooring of different periods). The investigation will allow us to reach the foundation level of the constructions in this area, next to the innermost part of the temple. During the cleaning we found, as in the past, fragments of blue kohl tubes inscribed with the name of Amenhotep III and scattered fragments of New Kingdom pottery. At the northwest corner of the room in C10 we unearthed a limestone structure partly brought to light in previous excavations. It consists of a quadrangular basin (64 x 66 cm) with a spout. It is slightly sloping toward the spout, under which we found a big jar partly covered by clay. Inside the big jar we found fruit (dates and figs) and broken vessels, partly or totally reconstructible (bowls and beer jars).

A very important task, which is still in progress, consists of restoring the ramp leading to the columned courtyard. The ramp of this temple is the only surviving example of this kind of construction in a temple of millions of years dating to the Eighteenth Dynasty. The structure consists of a central staircase of shallow steps, about 3.5 m wide, flanked by two slides of 1.5 m each and by two parapets set approximately at the outermost part of the slides (Figure 4).

Much work still has to be done: we have to investigate, at the southern part of the temple area, a quantity of intricate small mud-brick structures that could help us to understand better what happened soon after the reign of Amenhotep II. Work remains in progress.

NOTES

1. See the chapter by Danielle Phelps and Pearce Paul Creasman in this volume for extrapolation regarding the temples of millions of years.
2. W. M. F. Petrie, *Six Temples at Thebes, 1896* (London: B. Quaritch, 1897), 4–6.
3. A. Sesana, "Le temple d'Amenhotep II à Thèbes-Ouest: du passé au présent," in C. Leblanc and G. Zaki (eds.), *Les temples de millions d'années et le pouvoir royal à Thèbes au Nouvel Empire. Sciences et nouvelles technologies appliquées à l'archéologie, International Symposium (Luxor, 3–5 January 2010)*, Cahier Supplémentaire des Memnonia 2 (Le Caire: Dar El-Kutub, 2010), 73–79. Also: Sesana, "Preliminary Report of the Seventh Italian Archaeological Mission—Temple of Amenophis II at Western Thebes," *Memnonia* 16 (2005): 219–226; Sesana, "Preliminary Report of the Eighth Italian Archaeological Mission—Temple of Amenophis II at Western Thebes, Egypt—Winter 2005/2006," *ASAE* 82 (2008): 261–28; Sesana, "Preliminary Report of the Ninth Italian Archaeological Expedition—Temple of Amenhotep II, Western Thebes, Egypt—Winter, 2006/2007," *ASAE* 83 (2009): 393–416.
4. This is the reference number of the square where the entrance of the tomb was discovered.

[5] Another Middle Kingdom tomb, A17, has been fully excavated: A. Consonni and A. Sesana, "The Pottery from a Middle Kingdom Tomb at the Temple of Millions of Years of Amenhotep II, Thebes," in B. Bader, C. M. Knoblauch, and E. C. Köhler (eds.), *Vienna 2—Ancient Egyptian Ceramics in the 21st Century, Proceedings of the International Conference held at the University of Vienna 14th-18th of May, 2012* (Leuven: Peeters, forthcoming).

Ancient Robbery in Theban Tombs

Nigel Strudwick
University of Memphis/University of Cambridge

Tomb robberies in the Theban cemeteries during ancient times are examined in light of textual and archaeological sources, which differ considerably between the New Kingdom and Third Intermediate Period.

When the modern excavator enters a Theban tomb, a shocking scene of chaos usually meets his or her eyes; the contrast with the (rare) undisturbed and serene view that greeted Ernesto Schiaparelli when he entered the tomb of Kha at Deir el-Medina in 1906 could not be stronger. In honor of Richard H. Wilkinson, I present here a number of preliminary thoughts and pieces of evidence that point to how and when these chaotic conditions might have arisen, in the hope of provoking and encouraging further discussion.

This is the second part of a study dealing with robbery in Theban tombs from the New Kingdom onward.[1] The first part looked briefly at the ways in which tombs were robbed in modern times and considered what modern tomb robbers sought and why. This study looks at the aims and methods of the ancient robber using evidence from the New Kingdom and the first millennium BCE and considers the motivations of the robbers of those periods. Although no new material is presented here, it is hoped that the presentation of this data will be new and interesting to Richard Wilkinson and to our colleagues.[2]

Before reviewing the evidence, it is worth reminding the reader very briefly of the considerable difference between an elite Theban burial in the New Kingdom and one of the Third Intermediate Period, as together they form the bulk of examples that have been discovered.

Well-equipped tombs for the upper echelons of society seem to have been the norm in the Eighteenth and earlier Nineteenth Dynasties, but in the course of the New Kingdom the stress shifted away from goods that might be characterized now as having more immediately realizable material value toward those whose worth was primarily in the religious sphere. Thus in the Third Intermediate Period, items such as metal vessels, valuable oils, and elaborate jewelry mostly disappeared in favor of coffins, shabtis, amulets, stelae, and Ptah-Sokar-Osiris figures.[3] The argument has been made that this could have been as a result of changes in religious or cultural practice,[4] or as a defensive reaction to tomb robbery.[5]

Sources for Ancient Robbery

A mix of textual and archaeological sources inform us about ancient robbery. Unfortunately, for us to be able to discern the physical effects of an ancient robbery, it is necessary for the tomb to have survived largely undisturbed since the time of that robbery, without the evidence being obscured by modern depredations. It must also have been well excavated. The number of such Theban tombs is minimal.

Textual Sources

New Kingdom

The late New Kingdom abounds in textual sources for robbery and related issues, and it is necessary to obtain an overview of these to see how, where, and why the perpetrators were stealing.[6] The principal source is the loose group of texts known as the Tomb Robbery Papyri. These texts provide evidence for the actual mechanics of robbery and what was stolen from individual tombs and temples. In addition, there are a number of miscellaneous written references in text groups, widely separated by context and date. A selective and summary presentation of some of the main sources is given in Tables 1–4. Table 1 is a collection of texts that relate to tomb robbery; Table 2 is an illustrative sample of references to thefts from temples; Table 3 presents two examples of text that list items of unspecified origin found in the possession of robbers or other persons on the Theban west bank; and Table 4 gives the main miscellaneous references to robbery from outside the robbery papyri dating from the end of the Eighteenth Dynasty to the very end of the Twentieth.

Many of the examples in these tables will be referred to in this paper without further specification.

Text	Date	Lines	Content	Publication
Papyrus Leopold-Amherst	Year 16 of Ramesses IX, referring to a robbery in year 13	2, 5–19	Description of break-in to the tomb of King Sebekemzaf, robbery of burials, removal of gold, silver and copper, and burning of coffins	J. Capart, A. H. Gardiner and B. van der Walle, "New Light on the Ramesside Tomb-Robberies," *JEA* 22 (1936), 171–172.
		3.5–7	Continuity of robbery, and how everyone is involved	
Papyrus BM EA 10052	Year 1 of *wḥm mswt*	1, 18–19	Theft and breaking up of a coffin and mummy board[7] of gold and silver from tomb of Queen Hebrezet[8]	T. E. Peet, *The Great Tomb-Robberies of the Twentieth Egyptian Dynasty* (Oxford: Oxford Clarendon Press, 1930), 143–156.
		3, 5–6	Robbery and breaking up of a mummy board of gold and silver	
		3, 26–28	Robbery of tomb of scribe Pen… theft and breaking up of a mummy board of gold and silver	
		5, 7–10	Removal of gold and silver from a tomb	
		5, 13	Robbery and breaking up of a mummy board of silver	
		8, 5	Robbery in the tombs of Iumiteru (*near Gebelein*)	
		10, 5–8	Reference to a (stolen) coffin in the Island of Amenopet	
		15, 4	Reference to the wife of the goldworker Ramose who used to melt down gold and silver for (the robbers)	
Papyrus BM EA 10053	Recto, year 17 of Ramesses IX	Recto	Depositions of eight robbers as to whom they passed on the proceeds of their thefts in the Valley of the Queens. I sum the proceeds to 983 *deben* of copper, one silver *deben* and 15 *qedet* of gold	Peet, *Great Tomb-Robberies*, 104–109.

Table 1, Part 1: A selection of the most relevant tomb robbery texts from the Tomb Robbery Papyri

Text	Date	Lines	Content	Publication
Papyrus BM EA 10054	Tomb robbery texts date to years 16–18 of Ramesses IX	Verso I, 8–9	Reference to breaking into tombs, bringing out coffins, and stripping off their gold and silver	Peet, *Great Tomb-Robberies*, 60–62.
		Recto I, 3–10	Robbery of the tomb of Tjanefer (TT 158). The coffins were taken to the Island of Amenopet, where fire was set to them and the gold stolen. Robbery in a tomb in the quarter of Nefer…; gold stripped off with a chisel and coffin set on fire, and bronze vessels removed	
		Recto 2, 10–11	Breaking up of coffins bearing gold and setting fire to them in the tomb	
		Recto 2, 14–16	Robbery of the tomb of Amenkhau. Opening of a sandstone sarcophagus; the mummy was left in the tomb but the coffin and mummy board were removed and stripped	
		Verso I, 8–9; Recto 2, 8–12; Recto III, 4–5	Unspecific references to tomb robbery, referring to entering tombs on the west of Thebes and removing gold and silver, and also destroying coffins	
Papyrus Mayer A	Year 1 of *wḥm mswt*	4.1–4.8	Robberies of the tombs of queens Nesmut (identity unsure) and Bakwerel (wife of Sety I), and an unnamed person, presumably in the Valley of the Queens. Among items stolen were 3 *deben* of silver and 150 *deben* copper in the form of vessels and a large quantity of linen	Peet, *The Mayer Papyri A & B: Nos. M. 11162 and M. 11186 of the Free Public Museums, Liverpool* (London: Egypt Exploration Society, 1929),12–13.
Papyrus Mayer B	Perhaps Ramesses IX[9]	9–14	Robbery of the tomb of Ramesses VI, theft of 500 *deben* of copper and two chests of linen	Peet, *Mayer Papyri*, 20.
Papyrus BM EA 10221 (P. Abbott)	Year 16 of Ramesses IX	2, 12–17	Partially bored-into state of the tombs of Nubkheperre Inyotef and Sekhemrewepmaat Inyotef	Peet, *Great Tomb-Robberies*, 38–39.
		3, 17–18	The tombs of the Divine Adoratrices: intact 2, robbed 2, total 4	
		4, 14	Comment that all the tombs of citizens had been ransacked	

Table 1, Part 2: A selection of the most relevant tomb robbery texts from the Tomb Robbery Papyri

Text	Date	Lines	Content	Publication
BM EA 10053	Year 9, either of Ramesses XI or *wḥm mswt*	Verso	A range of materials, including gold, silver, and wood, are noted as having been stolen from the Ramesseum	Peet, *Great Tomb-Robberies,* 117–120.
BM EA 10054	This section, year 18 of Ramesses IX	Recto 3, 7–17	Gold is removed from statues in a monument of Ramesses II	Peet, *Great Tomb-Robberies,* 62–63, 54–55, 58.
Papyrus Mayer A	Year 1 of *wḥm mswt*	1.1–3.5	Robberies from shrines of Sety I and Ramesses II; it is mentioned that one family used copper from the robbery for "trading and spending"	Peet, *Mayer Papyri,* 10–11.
BM EA 10383	Year 2 of *wḥm mswt*	2	Enumerates no fewer than 2,672 copper *deben* stolen from doors of various palaces and administrative and funerary buildings	Peet, *Great Tomb-Robberies,* 125.
Rochester MAG 51.346.1	Probably year 1 of *wḥm mswt*	All	Inspection of damage to and thefts of metal by Djehutyhotep in the temple of Amun-Re at Karnak	O. Goelet, Jr, "A New 'Robbery' Papyrus: Rochester MAG 51.346.1," *JEA* 82 (1996): 107–127; J. F. Quack, "Eine Revision im Tempel von Karnak (Neuanalyse von Papyrus Rochester MAG 51.346.1)," *SAK* 28 (2000): 219–232.

Table 2: Illustrative sample of references to temple thefts in the Tomb Robbery Papyri

Text	Date	Lines	Content	Publication
BM EA 10053	Year 9, either of Ramesses XI or *wḥm mswt*	Verso	A range of materials, including gold, silver, and wood, are noted as having been stolen from the Ramesseum	Peet, *Great Tomb-Robberies,* 116.
BM EA 10054	This section, year 18 of Ramesses IX	Recto 3, 7–17	Gold is removed from statues in a monument of Ramesses II	Peet, *Great Tomb-Robberies,* 62–63, 54–55, 58.

Table 3: Illustrative sample of references to stolen goods (from unspecified locations) found in the possession of individuals in the Tomb Robbery Papyri

Text	Date	Lines	Content	Publication
Tomb of Thutmose IV	Year 8 of Horemheb	South wall, chamber I	Restoration graffito of Maya	H. Carter and P. E. Newberry, *The Tomb of Thoutmôsis IV* (Westminster: A. Constable and Co., 1904), xxxiii fig. 7; C.N. Reeves, *Valley of the Kings. The Decline of a Royal Necropolis* (London: K. Paul International, 1990), 36–37.
BM EA 10055 (P. Salt 124)	Later Nineteenth Dynasty	Recto 2,7; verso 1,11	Tomb robbery is one of the many accusations laid against the foreman Paneb	J. Černý, "Papyrus Salt 124 (Brit. Mus. 10055)," *JEA* 15 (1929): 243–258.
Turin 1880 (Turin Strike Papyrus)	Year 29 of Ramesses III	Recto 4, 5–6	Two workmen are referred to as removing stones from above the tomb of Ramesses II	A. H. Gardiner, *Ramesside Administrative Documents* (London: P. Lund, Humphries and Co. 1940), 57, 10–12; W. F. Edgerton, "The Strikes in Ramses III's Twenty-Ninth Year," *JNES* 10 (1951), 141; P. J. Frandsen, "Editing Reality: The Turin Strike Papyrus," in S. I. Groll (ed.), *Studies in Egyptology: Presented to Miriam Lichtheim* I (Jerusalem: Magnes Press, 1990), 193–194.
		Recto 2,8–10	The workman Mose seems to be threatening tomb robbery in one of the walk-outs: "Today I shall go to sleep only after having made preparations for robbing a tomb"[10]	Gardiner, *Ramesside Administrative Documents,* 54,15–55,2; Frandsen, "Editing Reality," 186. Compare Edgerton, "Strikes," 140.
		Recto 3,18a	A completely decontextualized reference to a man named Userhat robbing in the Valley of the Queens: "Weserhat made plans for robbing his tomb and implemented them in the Valley of the Queens"	Gardiner, *Ramesside Administrative Documents,* 58,11–12; Frandsen, "Editing Reality," 197. Compare Edgerton, "Strikes," 142.
BM EA 10375	Ramesses XI	Verso 10–11	Seemingly the only written evidence for the state-sanctioned robbing of royal tombs: "Uncover a tomb among the foremost tombs and preserve its seal until (I) return"	J. Černý, *Late Ramesside Letters* (Bruxelles: Édition de la Fondation égyptologique Reine Élisabeth, 1939), 47, 12–13; E. F. Wente, *Late Ramesside Letters*, SAOC 33 (Chicago: University of Chicago Press, 1967), 61.

Table 4: Principal other textual references to robbery in New Kingdom sources

First Millennium BCE

No textual sources are known to me that may be used to throw light on robberies in the Third Intermediate Period or later.

ARCHAEOLOGICAL SOURCES

New Kingdom

The archaeological evidence for ancient robbery in Theban tombs has been examined in most detail for the Valley of the Kings. As an example, when Davis found the tomb of Yuya and Tjuyu in 1905, the coffins were open, the mummies rifled, and all items of metal, all oils, and items of comparable value were gone, the result of several robberies that happened from shortly after the burial to the end of the Twentieth Dynasty.[11] A similar picture arises from the tomb of Maherpra;[12] in the case of the tomb of Tutankhamun, there were at least two ancient robberies, and the robbers showed interest in metal objects, glass vessels, valuable oils, and linen, although the mummy remained untouched.[13] There appear to have been no attempts in any of these robberies to detach gold leaf from the coffins or to remove the gold masks. The conclusion must be that the items removed from these burials were quickly stolen, highly portable, and relatively easy to conceal.[14]

The Valley of the Kings additionally presents us with the phenomenon of state-sponsored dismantling of royal burials, as proposed originally by Reeves and Taylor.[15] While this is not "conventional" robbery, being officially sanctioned by the high priests of Amun and on a scale unparalleled elsewhere (to our knowledge), the same types of valuable materials were without doubt the principal targets for reuse and recycling, and the gold and other valuables from these tombs must have made a major contribution to state funds in a manner similar to but on a larger scale than that in which more conventional robbery helped the private economy.

Outside the Valley of the Kings, the preponderance of source material for tombs that survived substantially intact until modern times is also largely limited to burials of the Eighteenth Dynasty, the subject of a study by Smith.[16] To my knowledge, there is only a single burial of the Ramesside Period that remained substantially intact, that of Sennedjem and his family in TT 1; although the available information about this burial leaves something to be desired, there is no obvious evidence of earlier violations from Toda's account.[17] Cooney points out how much modification this burial might have undergone in ancient times.[18]

Totally untouched tombs, such as that of Kha (TT 8) and that of Ramose and Hatnefer, are very rare (see part I of this study). Several of the substantially intact tombs seem to exhibit some trace of robbery or re-opening, although we are dependent on the accuracy of the excavators' reports. Possible ancient robberies may be detected, using the data of Smith, outside the Valley of the Kings in the tomb of Hatiay,[19] Deir el-Medina tombs 1352[20] and 1159,[21] and Carter/Carnarvon tomb 37.[22]

The contrast between the intact and the rifled tombs is nowhere clearer than in the variable survival of metal and stone vessels; the metal vessels would certainly have had an immediately marketable value, while it is likely that the stone vessels, as well as having value in themselves, may have contained precious oils that would have had some immediate resale value in the world of the living and the industry of burying the dead. This is brought out in Table 13 of Smith's analysis:[23] the burial of Yuya and Tjuyu, which must have contained such items, was devoid of them, while the comparable items of Kha were definitely present (along with vessels of glass, presumably also a rather exotic and valuable category of object).

The ancient robbery of items in such tombs is, however, not to be attributed to forced entry alone; the use of a funerary monument as a family tomb by its nature[24] meant that the burial place would need to be accessed from time to time by those with the right to do so.[25] During such re-openings, as well as the inevitable rearrangement of the contents, it cannot be excluded that some unofficial rifling of the existing contents took place.[26] In some cases it is quite possible that robberies may even have taken place during the original interments themselves, for example in the tomb of Ramose and Hatnefer, which does not seem to have been closed more than once.[27] It is very likely that those who removed elements from some of the Twenty-First Dynasty coffins found in the Deir el-Bahri cache were members of the (re)burial parties.[28] No doubt New Kingdom burials were also robbed by those seeking space for new interments after the end of the New Kingdom; a case in point is the burial of Minmose uncovered by the Metropolitan Museum near the temple of Hatshepsut.[29] A further combination is seen in the Twenty-First Dynasty cache of burials close to the aforesaid interment of Minmose: some of the damage to the coffins may have been caused by the nefarious activities of the original burial party and some by those who effected further burials.[30]

We are almost never likely to know the identities of those who carried out the actual burials in the tomb. However, given the cramped nature of most private burial chambers, it is surely more likely (for elite burials, at least) that members of the family of the deceased would have remained outside the actual burial apartments and instead employed workmen or undertakers to make the actual interments. Such persons were perhaps more likely than family members to make a quick opportunistic grab for valuables as the tomb was about to be closed. Winlock's reconstruction of the insertion of the Twenty-First Dynasty burial into the tomb of Merytamun may not be that far from the truth.[31]

There is as yet little clear archaeological evidence relating to the robberies of the late New Kingdom. Nonetheless, excavations in TT 233 have uncovered evidence of burnt funerary equipment, including fragments of gold leaf, in Ramesside levels in the courtyard, conforming with the methods for removal of gold described in the Tomb Robbery Papyri.[32] Something probably very similar was found by Mond and Emery in the complex contents of the main shaft of TT 97: I interpret their comment "the original burial of Amenemhāt had been plundered and burnt out"[33] as meaning that fires were set as a result of the robbers' activities, no doubt to remove gold; one burial probably from the original interment does seem to have had the gilding on the face removed manually, unless the limited fire damage described as being on the coffin was the result of application of the burning technique.[34] Robbery during the New Kingdom may have given the opportunity for new burials in a tomb: excavations suggest that TT 148 may have been used for further burials over and above those of the tomb owner following the ransacking of other family tombs, particularly TT 158 (Papyrus BM EA 10054).[35]

First Millennium BCE

A different approach has to be taken for the first millennium BCE, primarily the Third Intermediate Period. The source material is very different, in that vastly more material from this epoch has survived from Thebes than from the earlier period—witness the preponderance of coffins and cartonnage cases of this date in museum collections. However, only a tiny proportion of this material has been excavated in such a fashion as to shed light on the state of an intact tomb or to give clear evidence of ancient robbery. There are no syntheses available to parallel those of Reeves and Smith noted above for the New Kingdom, although Aston's extensive survey of tomb groups from the period is an essential resource which includes well-excavated material alongside material whose original disposition is unknown.[36] Here I select a sample of the better-documented tomb groups and examine what information is available.[37]

Several intact burials were found in the Berlin excavations led by Möller in 1911 and 1913, at several sites in a large area roughly between Deir el-Medina and the Ramesseum.[38] At least two tombs of the eighth to seventh centuries BCE were found intact (Grab 23 and 29),[39] while Grab 28 and Grab G1 were robbed in ancient times, according to the excavator.[40] Unfortunately, the evidence on which these opinions were based and the disposition of the intact tombs are not given.

The mixture of burials found in the burial shaft of TT 97 seems to have been largely misdated by the excavators, although some burials are clearly of the Third Intermediate Period.[41] Mond and Emery make the occasional reference to tombs being robbed in ancient times, although again the evidence is not readily available; it was perhaps an assumption on their part.[42]

Perhaps the best evidence comes from the Austrian excavations led by Manfred Bietak in the Asasif in 1969–1977.[43] The lower parts of Grab VII, discovered in 1971,[44] consisted of two principal chambers (Grabkammer 2 and 3) in which were found the robbed but nonetheless relatively well-preserved burials of Kheriru and Iru of the Twenty-Fifth–Twenty-Sixth Dynasties. In the burial of Kheriru, the mummy was removed by robbers; in the other chamber it is less clear what was taken, but the upper coffins were open and damaged, although the room seems to have been left in a relatively unransacked condition.[45] It is not easy to differentiate between entry to the tomb chambers by the tomb-owning family for further burials and entry for robbery.[46] The date and purpose of the robbery, although ancient, must remain unclear.

Sources for the later first millennium are much sparser. There is a general problem identifying the burials of this period,[47] and very few interments of this period have survived to be found by modern archaeology.[48] A general lack of available comparanda prompts me to omit this period from the present study.[49]

Discussion and Conclusions

Although we are fortunate to have both archaeological and textual sources to consult in the search for answers, the time periods of these sources are widely separated, and there are significant gaps. The earlier New Kingdom robberies have largely to be learned about from archaeology, while, in contrast, the textual sources date almost exclusively from the reign of Ramesses IX and later, up to 400 years later than the burials whose robberies are described. Evidence from the Third Intermediate Period is at present entirely archaeological. One clutches at straws to find evidence to fill these gaps and gain a fairer balance between the two types of material in the New Kingdom. Only occasionally do the two source types relate to each other, such as the Horemheb text referring to robberies in the later Eighteenth Dynasty, or the marks of burning found in tombs, seemingly referred to in the tomb robbery papyri with mentions of fires set by the robbers.

HOW DID ANCIENT ROBBERS OPERATE?

The archaeological sources suggest that the bulk of earlier robberies were above all opportunistic, either by those charged with guarding the tombs themselves, perhaps entering with the excuse of a security check, or by robbers in a lightning attack while the attention of guards might be elsewhere—a hack through the tomb sealing, a quick glance around the chambers, opening likely looking chests in the dim light from a taper, and removing obvious and highly portable valuables that could be concealed without too much trouble. Many or most robberies known from archaeology, in general, occurred not long after the burial, when knowledge of the contents and their locations was still relatively fresh. But would we be able to distinguish complete ancient destruction from its modern version?

The majority of textual sources describe a different type of tomb robbery. They suggest that the robbery of a Theban tomb at the end of the New Kingdom was a well-organized and quite violent affair. The Leopold-Amherst Papyrus is the only one to describe passing through the various passages of the burial chambers in the progress to the interment, but this and several other texts describe the removal of valuable items in the form of gold and other metals. To modern eyes the most dramatic references are to the burning of the coffins, but this of course is not an act of deliberate defilement but rather would have been the quickest method of removing the gold leaf present on the coffins of the most wealthy, and above all, of the kings. Mostly this stripping was done in the tomb itself, but there is a reference in BM EA 10054 10, 5 to the removal of coffins to the island of Amenopet,[50] where the same fate awaited them; in BM EA 10052 Recto 1, 6, a different coffin is already on the same island, suggesting that this was not simply an isolated occurrence.

The violence and damage caused in the robberies related in the Tomb Robbery Papyri contrasts strongly with the archaeological picture from admittedly a different era, with their opportunistic stress on the removal of portable material. Clearly the unsettled context of the late New Kingdom seems to have encouraged more serious attempts at robbery, culminating in the systematic dismantling of burials. Even allowing for the possible erratic survival of documents, there does seem to be copious evidence for private and lesser royal tombs being robbed in the relative chaos of the end of the Ramesside period.

What Were the Robbers Seeking?

Both texts and archaeology show that items made of or bearing metals (gold, silver, and copper/bronze) were without doubt the most important commodity to the New Kingdom robbers. Further evidence of the amount of valuables taken by the thieves can be gained from an examination of the lists of material confiscated from robbers (see Tables 2 and 3 above). While it cannot be certain that these pertain to material just from tombs, as it has been seen above that there is also considerable evidence of robbery from temples, it is highly likely that these lists at least indicate convincingly what the thieves were seeking above all else.[51]

One other item of evident value that makes its appearance in the Tomb Robbery Papyri is linen, mentioned, for example, in the robbery of the queens' tombs and in the break-in of the tomb of Ramesses VI (Mayer B). Large quantities of non-mummy linen were found in the tomb of Kha[52] and in that of Ramose and Hatnefer,[53] both in the tiny group of completely undisturbed tombs. While none was obviously located in the intact tomb of Neferkhuit,[54] it is almost certain that the lack of this material in the high-status burials of Yuya and Tjuyu[55] and Maherpra[56] is due to robbery; likewise there is evidence that linen was stolen in the relatively minor robberies in the tomb of Tutankhamun.[57] Metals and linens (unless inscribed) aptly fit the description "goods of an untraceable nature."[58]

The typical robber of the New Kingdom was evidently looking primarily not only for objects that were relatively portable and of high value but also those that could be relatively easily disposed of or recycled without drawing too much attention from the authorities. Presumably these high-value contents were also the principal target of the state-sanctioned dismantling of the royal tombs at the very end of the New Kingdom. A rare example of gilded objects that somehow escaped the latter activity is a small group of dummy vessels bearing the name of Ramesses II.[59]

There is limited evidence that some of the remaining items of funerary equipment were in demand. The presence of glass vessels in the burial of Kha and the lack thereof elsewhere has been noted above, as has the absence of oils in the burials of Tutankhamun and Yuya and Tjuyu; in the former cases it appears that some, at least, of the oils may have been emptied out of their containers, whereas in the latter the containers themselves appear to have been taken.[60] As before, these items fall into the category of portable and easily reused materials.

But what happened to the tomb equipment that did not have intrinsic high value—the ritual items, furniture, and the like—or that could not be easily reused once stripped of valuables? Research has so far noted very few other items from burials that have found an identifiable further use in any context; for example, Aston published a shabti of Ramesses II which had been turned into a Twenty-First Dynasty Osiride figure, perhaps for the restoration of the king's burial.[61]

The most likely scenario from the tomb robberies in the papyri is that the other objects were mostly left behind, as they were (relatively speaking) of little value. There is definite evidence for this in the Valley of the Kings: in addition to the obvious examples of the surviving stone sarcophagi, several of the tombs that remained hidden from the first millennium BCE until recent times still contained quantities of funerary goods that I have not included above as "valuable" at the end of the New Kingdom (non-gilded figures, shabtis, faience objects, broken pieces of furniture, and the like).[62] Such "missing" objects would have principally consisted of coffins and large pieces of funerary furniture, which presumably were removed to locations where they could more easily be stripped of their gilding and semi-precious stones.[63] The principal survivals of this process are some of the coffins intended for reuse in the reburials of their original owners or other royalty; several of these from the Deir el-Bahri cache show clear evidence of the removal of the gilding with an adze.[64]

None of the textual evidence regarding robbery of the private tombs suggests that large items such as coffins were taken with reuse in mind; rather, the papyri suggest that they were regularly smashed up and burned in the quest to extract metal overlaid on them. However, evidence from coffins themselves suggests that body containers were also being recycled in the later New Kingdom, a suggestion first made by Niwiński.[65] Cooney now estimates that in the Twentieth as well as the Twenty-First Dynasties, the percentage of coffins that seem to have been reused from earlier examples was as high as 61.5%.[66] Cooney assumes that these types of reuse might have happened "legally," from an accepted practice of reusing the body containers of those deceased for whom there was no longer anyone to practice rituals.[67] These coffins cannot have come from the robberies described in the papyri; unless there was another type of robbery of which no written evidence has survived, it must be assumed that Cooney's "legal" or customary approach existed alongside its violent cousin. The acquisition of coffins for reuse was clearly a separate development or perhaps even reflects a practice that had been ongoing, about which we are only now starting to learn. The (admittedly limited) tomb inventories from this period might hint at this sort of event.[68]

It would appear, however, that coffin reuse was not so significant after the Twenty-First Dynasty.[69] Indeed, it is much harder to envisage what those who robbed tombs in the first millennium BCE stood to gain by their efforts. The clearest item removed from the burial of Kheriru in Asasif Grab VII Grabkammer 2 was the mummy—the only conceivable use of a mummy to robbers of that period would have been the extraction of the presumed amulets,[70] but then the average amulet of the period would not appear to have been a particularly valuable commodity. Two shabti boxes found in the same burial between them contained 377 (uninscribed) shabtis,[71] so clearly these were not regarded as worthy of theft. It is less clear what was removed from the Iru burial in Asasif Grab VII Grabkammer 3; does the lack of shabti boxes mean these were removed or that they were not present? The simple uninscribed shabtis of the period could at least have been reused in other burials, although one cannot imagine that they were a costly commodity.

This limited documentation of anciently robbed Twenty-Fifth and Twenty-Sixth Dynasty burials thus shows no indication that coffins or parts thereof were particularly targeted by the thieves. This contrasts with the (admittedly more elaborate) coffins of the Twenty-First Dynasty, where Cooney observes that much of the gilding was subsequently removed[72] and, as noted earlier, coffins themselves were recycled. Precious metals and other intrinsically valuable items were almost non-existent in most Third Intermediate Period burials, and, unless the tomb equipment was simply to be recycled, for which there is little evidence after the Twenty-First Dynasty, one can only make the rather improbable suggestion that either the robbers were ill-informed as to what would await them or they were not expecting great returns for their efforts. This contrasts strongly with the New Kingdom, when the incentive to rob burials for quick gain was much higher.

Robbery clearly went through several different phases in the period 1400–600 BCE, with the targets of the robbers changing dramatically. The final (future) part of this study will review the condition of the Theban necropolis at certain points in its history since the New Kingdom, will contrast ancient and modern theft, and will offer some thoughts on how and whether one can distinguish between them.

NOTES

1. I thank Helen Strudwick for reading, commenting on, and discussing several drafts of this article, and for looking at some of the sources. John H. Taylor and Kathryn Cooney have also provided very helpful information and discussions, and I thank them both; Cooney has also generously shared unpublished manuscripts. The first part of the study, entitled "Modern Robbery in Theban Tombs," will appear in another *Festschrift* in 2013.
2. The term "ancient" is used in relation to activity which can probably be dated before the end of the Roman Period, while "modern" refers to activity from roughly the twelfth century CE on.
3. D. A. Aston, *Burial Assemblages of Dynasty 21–25: Chronology —Typology — Developments*, DÖAWW 54 (Wien: Verlag der Osterreichischen Akademie der Wissenschaften, 2009), 393–396, lists sample contents for Theban burials of the Third Intermediate Period; compare the sketches of such groups in D. A. Aston, "The Theban West Bank from the Twenty-Fifth Dynasty to the Ptolemaic Period," in N. Strudwick and J. H. Taylor (eds.), *The Theban Necropolis: Past, Present and Future* (London: British Museum Press, 2003), 138–166.
4. J. H. Taylor, "Changes in the Afterlife," in W. Wendrich (ed.), *Egyptian Archaeology* (Oxford: Wiley-Blackwell, 2010), 233–237; particularly interesting is the argument made by M. A. Leahy ("The Libyan Period in Egypt: An Essay in Interpretation," *Libyan Studies* 16 [1985], 51–65) that the cultural shift of Libyan rulers may also have simplified some earlier features. See also related articles by R. Ritner ("Fragmentation and Re-integration in the Third Intermediate Period," in G. P. F Broekman, R. J. Demarée, and O. E. Kaper (eds.), *The Libyan Period in Egypt: Historical and Cultural Studies into the 21st–24th Dynasties. Proceedings of a Conference at Leiden University, 25-27 October 2007* [Leiden: Nederlands Instituut voor het Nabije Oosten, 2007], 327–340) and G. P. F. Broeckman ("Libyan Rule over Egypt: The Influence of the Tribal Background of the Ruling Class on Political Structures and Developments during the Libyan Period in Egypt," *SAK* 39 [2010]: 85–99).
5. K. M. Cooney has argued that the shift in burial contents in the later Ramesside Period that led to the more restricted contents typical of the Twenty-First Dynasty may have been driven as much by practical constraints and the desire to minimize robbery as by changes in funerary ideology ("Changing Burial Practices at the End of the New Kingdom: Defensive Adaptations in Tomb Commissions, Coffin Commissions, Coffin Decoration, and Mummification," *JARCE* 47 [2011]: 17–20).
6. Cooney also lists some examples in "Changing Burial Practices," 12, and in her forthcoming paper, "Private Sector Tomb Robbery and Funerary Arts Reuse according to West Theban Documentation," in J. Toivari-Viitala (ed.), *Deir el Medina Studies: Helsinki, Finland 24th–26th of June 2010* (Helsinki: Helsinki University, forthcoming).

7 K. M. Cooney, *The Cost of Death: The Social and Economic Value of Ancient Egyptian Funerary Art in the Ramesside Period*, Egyptologische uitgaven 22 (Leiden: Nederlands Instituut voor het Nabije Oosten, 2007), 17–31. This word, *swḥt*, is constantly translated by Peet as "shroud."

8 See Peet, *Great Tomb-Robberies*, 139; this woman might be the mother of Isis, mother of Ramesses VI (Valley of the Queens tomb QV 51, PM I²:2, 756)—but it could also refer to someone else.

9 C. Aldred, "More Light on the Ramesside Tomb Robberies," in J. Ruffle, G. A. Gaballa and K. A. Kitchen (eds.), *Glimpses of Ancient Egypt: Studies in Honour of H. W. Fairman* (Warminster: Aris & Phillips, 1979), 92; not challenged in C.N. Reeves, *Valley of the Kings. The Decline of a Royal Necropolis* (London: Kegan Paul International, 1990), 119, although E. Thomas (*The Royal Necropoleis of Thebes* [Princeton: n.p., 1966], 268) quotes Wente as suggesting the reign of Ramesses XI.

10 See K. Baer, "Ein Grab verfluchen?" *Orientalia* 34 (1965), 428–438 for the expression *wꜥꜣ ist* used in this and the next text.

11 Reeves, *Valley of the Kings*, 148–153.

12 Reeves, *Valley of the Kings*, 147.

13 Reeves, *Valley of the Kings*, 68.

14 Summary, Reeves, *Valley of the Kings*, 275.

15 Reeves, *Valley of the Kings*, 276–278; J. H. Taylor, "Aspects of the History of the Valley of the Kings in the Third Intermediate Period," in C. N. Reeves (ed.), *After Tut'ankhamūn: Research and Excavation in the Royal Necropolis at Thebes* (London: Kegan Paul, 1992), 187–190. See also K. Jansen-Winkeln, "Die Plünderung der Königsgräber des Neuen Reiches," *ZÄS* 122 (1995): 62–78 and E. Graefe, "Über die Goldmenge des Alten Ägypten und die Beraubung der thebanischen Königsgräber," *ZÄS* 126 (1999): 27–34.

16 S. T. Smith, "Intact Tombs of the Seventeenth and Eighteenth Dynasties from Thebes and the New Kingdom Burial System," *MDAIK* 48 (1992): Appendix, 225–231 (this includes some of the aforementioned Valley of the Kings burials).

17 E. Toda, "Son Notém en Tebas: inventario y textos de un sepulcro egipcio de la XX dinastía," *Boletín de la Real Academia de la Historia* 10 (1887): 91–148, part translated in G. Daressy, "La découverte et l'inventaire du tombeau de Sennezem," *ASAE* 20 (1920): 145–160.

18 Cooney, "Changing Burial Practices," 15.

19 G. Daressy, "Rapport sur la trouvaille de ," *ASAE* 2 (1901): 1–13; Smith, "Intact Tombs," 229.

20 B. Bruyère, *Rapport sur les fouilles de Deir el Médineh (1933–1934)*, FIFAO 14 (Le Caire: Institut français d'archéologie orientale, 1937), 95–109; this was not available during the writing of this article, so the reader is referred to Smith, "Intact Tombs," 229.

21 B. Bruyère, *Rapport sur les fouilles de Deir el Médineh (1928)*, FIFAO 6 (Le Caire: Institut français d'archéologie orientale, 1929), 45–47; Smith, "Intact Tombs," 229.

22 The Earl of Carnarvon and H. Carter, *Five Years' Explorations at Thebes. A Record of Work Done 1907–1911* (Oxford: Oxford University Press, 1912), 64–88; Smith, "Intact Tombs," 231.

23 Smith, "Intact Tombs," 210.

24 My article "Use and Re-use of Tombs in the Theban Necropolis: Patterns and Explanations," *CRIPEL* 28 (2009–2010), 239–261, stresses how Eighteenth Dynasty tombs almost certainly had a strong family identity and were not always just the burial places of the noble by whose name we now know them. Cooney's comment on TT 1 just noted shows how much this was also the case in the Ramesside Period ("Changing Burial Practices," 15).

25 See also the discussion of reuse and robbery of burials by C. Näser, "Jenseits von Theben—Objektsammlung, Inszenierung und Fragmentierung in ägyptischen Bestattungen des Neuen Reiches," in C. Kümmel, B. Schweitzer, and U. Veit (eds.), *Körperinszenierung—Objektsammlung—Monumentalisierung: Totenritual und Grabkult in frühen Gesellschaften; archäologische Quellen in Kulturwissenschaftlicher Perspektive* (Münster: Waxmann, 2008), 435–455; a revised version of this article in English which came to my attention only at proof stage is C. Naeser, "Equipping and Stripping the Dead: A Case-Study on the Procurement, Compilation, Arrangement, and Fragmentation of Grave Inventories in New Kingdom Thebes," in S. Tarlow and L. N. Stutz (eds.), *The Oxford Handbook of the Archaeology of Death and Burial* (Oxford: Oxford University Press, 2013), 643–664. Cooney suggests that an amalgam of Nineteenth and Twentieth Dynasty burials was found in TT 1 ("Changing Burial Practices," 15).

26 Compare the similar situation suggested for the tomb of Djehutynakht at el-Bersha (S. D'Auria, P. Lacovara, and C. Roehrig [eds.], *Mummies and Magic* [Boston: Museum of Fine Arts, 1988], 109), or indeed that in the cemeteries of Riqqa (R. Engelbach, *Riqqeh and Memphis VI* [London: School of Archaeology in Egypt, 1915], 21–22).

27 A. Lansing and W. C. Hayes, "The Museum's Excavations at Thebes," *BMMA* 32 part II (1937): 28–30.

28 Reeves, *Valley of the Kings*, 189, 218 n. 57. Winlock speculated that something similar happened during the Twenty-First Dynasty interment in the tomb of Merytamun (H. E. Winlock, *The Tomb of Queen Meryet-Amun*, PMMA 6 [New York: Metropolitan Museum of Art, 1932], 55).

29 H. E. Winlock, "The Museum's Excavations at Thebes," *BMMA* 19 part II (1924), 22.

30 Winlock, "Museum's Excavations at Thebes" (1924), 28. Also note the unrelated but relevant restoration text on a Twenty-First Dynasty mummy board (BM EA 15659, W. Spiegelberg, "Varia," *RT* 17 (1895), 96–98).

31 Winlock, *Tomb of Queen Mereyt-Amun*, 54–56.

32 B. G. Ockinga, "Use, Reuse, and Abuse of 'Sacred Space': Observations from Dra Abu al-Naga'," in P. F. Dorman and B. M. Bryan (eds.), *Sacred Space and Sacred Function in Ancient Thebes*, SAOC 61 (Chicago: Oriental Institute, 2007), 146–147.

33 R. Mond and W. B. Emery, "The Burial Shaft of the Tomb of Amenemhāt," *Annals of Archaeology and Anthropology* 16 (1929), 50.

34 Mond and Emery, "Burial Shaft," 56.

35 Ockinga, "Use, Reuse, and Abuse," 144–146.

36 Aston, *Burial Assemblages*, 157–268 (Theban material only).

37 Another example of robbery described by the excavator came to my attention in a paper presented by Ute Rummel at the First Vatican Coffin Conference in June 1913, referring to a number of Twenty-Second Dynasty coffins robbed in the forecourt of K93.12 in Dra Abu el-Naga. This project is described in Deutsches Archäologisches Institut, "The Tomb Complexes K93.11/93.12 in Dra' Abu el-Naga/Western Thebes (Luxor)," http://www.dainst.org/en/node/24162 (accessed 17 July 2013).

38 R. Anthes,"Die Deutschen Grabungen auf der Westseite von Theben in den Jahren 1911 und 1913," *MDAIK* 12 (1943): 1–68. The tomb groups from these excavations are summarised in Aston, *Burial Assemblages*, 248–251.

39 Anthes, "Deutschen Grabungen," 30–33, 37–40.

40 Anthes, "Deutschen Grabungen," 34–36, 43–44.

41 Aston, *Burial Assemblages*, 235.

42 Mond and Emery, "Burial Shaft," 51, 64.

43 M. Bietak, *Theben-West (Luqsor). Vorbericht über die ersten vier Grabungskampagnen (1969–1971)* (Wien: H. Boehlaus, 1974); M. Bietak and E. Reiser-Haslauer, *Das Grab des 'Anch-Hor, Obersthofmeister der Gottesgemahlin Nitokris*, 2 vols., DÖAWW 6–7 (Wien: Osterreichische Akademie der Wissenschaften, 1978–1982); J. Budka, *Bestattungsbrauchtum und Friedhofsstruktur im Asasif: eine Untersuchung der spätzeitlichen Befunde anhand der Ergebnisse der österreichischen Ausgrabungen in den Jahren 1969–1977*, DÖAWW 59 (Wien: Osterreichische Akademie der Wissenschaften, 2010).

44 Bietak, *Theben-West (Luqsor)*, 39–35; now Budka, *Bestattungsbrauchtum*, 111–134.

45 Bietak, *Theben-West (Luqsor)*, Taf. XXIII.

46 Compare the data in Budka, *Bestattungsbrauchtum*, 126–127 (Tabelle 13–14).

47 D. A. Aston, "Dynasty 26, Dynasty 30, or Dynasty 27? In Search of the Funerary Archaeology of the Persian Period," in A. Leahy and J. Tait (eds.), *Studies on Ancient Egypt in Honour of H. S. Smith* (London: Egypt Exploration Society, 1999), 17–22.

48 A rare example is the Thirtieth Dynasty burial of Wahibre in complex 10 of TT 414 (Bietak and Reiser-Haslauer, *Anch-Hor* II, 183–220).

49 Aston, "Theban West Bank," 162–163. For post-Thirtieth Dynasty material, see G. Schreiber, "Early and Middle Ptolemaic Funerary Art at Thebes (ca. 306–88 BC)," in Z. Hawass, T. A. Bács and G. Schreiber (eds.), *Proceeding of the Colloquium on Theban Archaeology at the Supreme Council of Antiquities November*

5, 2009 (Cairo: Supreme Council of Antiquities, 2012), 105–139.

50 See Capart et al., "New Light," 181–182 for comments on this location.

51 Putting relative values on these materials is not easy and beyond the aims of this paper. See Graefe, "Über die Goldmenge," 19–27 for the problem of the value of a gold versus a copper *deben*. As well as issues with the relative weight of the *deben*, there is considerable fluctuation of the relative value of the metals gold, silver, and copper themselves; see, for example, J. R. Harris, *Lexicographical Studies in Ancient Egyptian Minerals* (Berlin: Akademie Verlag, 1961), 42, and Graefe, "Über die Goldmenge," 25, both based on the relative values proposed in 1954 by J. Černy ("Prices and Wages in Egypt in the Ramesside Period," *Cahiers d'histoire mondiale* 4 [1954], 906).

52 E. Schiaparelli, *Relazione sui lavori della Missione Archeologica Italiana in Egitto (anni 1903-1920) II: La tomba intatta dell'architetto "Cha" nella necropoli di Tebe* (Torino: Museo di Antichitá, 1927), 90–100, fig. 64–67. The amount of linen is not specified in detail but is referred to as *"magnifico saggio."* I thank John Taylor for checking this reference.

53 Three chests, Lansing and Hayes, "Museum's Excavations at Thebes," 24–26.

54 W. C. Hayes, "The Tomb of Nefer-Khēwet and His Family," *BMMA* 30 part II (1935):17–36.

55 Reeves, *Valley of the Kings*, 149; N. Reeves and R. H. Wilkinson, *The Complete Valley of the King: Tombs and Treasures of Egypt's Greatest Pharaohs* (London: Thames and Hudson, 1996), 177.

56 Reeves and Wilkinson, *Complete Valley of the Kings*, 181.

57 Reeves and Wilkinson, *Complete Valley of the Kings*, 125; N. Reeves, *The Complete Tutankhamun: The King, the Tomb, the Royal Treasure* (London: Thames and Hudson, 1990), 156.

58 Reeves and Wilkinson, *Complete Valley of the Kings*, 192.

59 BM EA 35273–5: J. H. Taylor, *Death and the Afterlife in Ancient Egypt* (London: British Museum Press, 2001), 192, fig. 135.

60 Reeves, *Valley of the Kings*, 68, 149.

61 BM EA 69672: D. A. Aston, "Two Osiris Figures of the Third Intermediate Period," *JEA* 77 (1991): 95–99.

62 For example, those of Thutmose III, Amenhotep II and Thutmose IV (G. Daressy, *Catalogue général des antiquitiés égyptiennes du musée du Caire: Fouilles de la Vallée des Rois [1898–1899]* [Le Caire: Institut français d'archéologie orientale, 1902]; H. Carter and P. E. Newberry, *Catalogue général des antiquitiés égyptiennes du musée du Caire: The Tomb of Thoutmôsis IV* (Westminster: A. Constable and Co., 1904). Summaries of the equipment found in each royal tomb will be found in Reeves and Wilkinson, *Complete Valley of the Kings*.

63 Reeves, *Valley of the Kings*, 121–123 considers the evidence for the stripping of royal valuables in the tomb of Ramesses XI.

64 For example, those of Thutmose III and Ahmose Sapair (G. Daressy, *Catalogue général des antiquitiés égyptiennes du musée du Caire: Cercueils des cachettes royales*

(Le Caire: Institut français d'archéologie orientale, 1909), pl. XIV and X [CG 61014/JE 26203; CG 61007/JE 26221]).

65 A. Niwiński, *21st Dynasty Coffins from Thebes: Chronological and Typological Studies*. Theben 5 (Mainz: P. von Zabern, 1988), 13 n. 43. See also Cooney, "Changing Burial Practices," 31–36; K. M. Cooney, "Objectifying the Body: The Increased Value of the Ancient Egyptian Mummy during the Socioeconomic Crisis of Dynasty 21," in J. K. Papadopoulos and G. Urton (eds.), *The Construction of Value in the Ancient World* (Los Angeles: Cotsen Institute of Archaeology Press, 2012), 143. Although Cooney's research is at an early stage, the initial examples quoted suggest that the original coffins which were reused were of the Nineteenth Dynasty.

66 Cooney, "Changing Burial Practices," 31.

67 Cooney, "Changing Burial Practices," 32.

68 K. M. Cooney, "Private Sector Tomb Robbery."

69 John H. Taylor (personal communication) has indicated to me that he has seen little evidence of reuse later in the Third Intermediate Period—some of this may of course be attributed to the use of cartonnage mummy-cases in that period, which lend themselves less well to reuse, but he has not seen reuse in the wooden coffins in which they were placed (compare comment by Cooney, "Objectifying the Body," 158).

70 Aston, *Burial Assemblages*, 374–376.

71 Budka, *Bestattungsbrauchtum*, 618–620; the shabtis appear not to be illustrated.

72 Cooney, "Changing Burial Practices," 28; Cooney, "Objectifying the Body," 146. Cooney suggests that this may have discouraged the use of gilding.

List of Contributors

Hussein Bassir, *The Grand Egyptian Museum (Giza, Egypt)*

Teresa Bedman, *Institute of Studies of Ancient Egypt (Madrid, Spain)*

Mansour Boraik, *Ministry of State for Antiquities (Luxor, Egypt)*

Edwin C. Brock, *Royal Ontario Museum (Toronto, Canada)*

Pearce Paul Creasman, *University of Arizona (Tucson, Arizona)*

Noreen Doyle, *University of Arizona Egyptian Expedition (Tucson, Arizona)*

Richard S. Harwood, *University of Arizona Egyptian Expedition (Luxor, Egypt)*

Nozomu Kawai, *Waseda University (Tokyo, Japan)*

Karin R. Kroenke, *University of California (Berkeley, California)*

Nanno Marinatos, *University of Illinois at Chicago (Chicago, Illinois)*

Francisco J. Martín Valentín, *Institute of Studies of Ancient Egypt (Madrid, Spain)*

Teresa Moore, *University of California (Berkeley, California)*

Suzanne Onstine, *University of Memphis (Memphis, Tennessee)*

Danielle Phelps, *University of Arizona (Tucson, Arizona)*

Elena Pischikova, *South Asasif Conservation Project (Asasif, Egypt)*

Lyla Pinch Brock, *Royal Ontario Museum (Toronto, Canada)*

Donald B. Redford, *Pennsylvania State University (State College, Pennsylvania)*

Susan Redford, *Pennsylvania State University (State College, Pennsylvania)*

Nicholas Reeves, *The Metropolitan Museum of Art (New York, New York)*

Angelo Sesana, *Centre for Egyptology Francesco Ballerini (Como, Italy)*

David Soren, *University of Arizona, (Tucson, Arizona)*

Nigel Strudwick, *University of Memphis (Memphis, Tennessee) & University of Cambridge (Cambridge, England)*

Kent R. Weeks, *The American University in Cairo (New Cairo, Egypt)*

Index

B

C

D

E

F

G

H

I

J

K

L

M

T

U

V

W

Y

Z

4478927R20212

Made in the USA
San Bernardino, CA
22 September 2013